Acknowledgements

Generous funding from Canada's Department of National Defence, the Department of History and Faculty of Graduate Studies at the University of Victoria, and the Social Sciences and Humanities Research Council of Canada made research and travel for this book possible. Material is used with permission from the keeper of the Churchill College Archives Centre, the trustees of the Liddell Hart Centre for Military Archives, and the Montgomery committee at the Imperial War Museum. The author extends his special thanks to Dr. David Zimmerman, Dr. Perry Biddiscombe, Dr. Michael Hadley, Dr. Holger Herwig, Dr. Mariel Grant, Dr. Patricia Roy, Lieutenant-Commander Doug McLean, Dr. Roger Sarty, Lieutenant-Commander Bill Glover, Dr. Bill McAndrew, Dr. Carl Christie, Dr. Terry Copp, Bill Kenny, Commander Bill Fenrick, Timothy Mulligan, Kathleen Lloyd, Jim and Gail McCaul, Peter Wilson, and Dr. Hugh and Patricia Johnston. Robert Easton and his staff at Frank Cass improved the final product considerably. Michael Stone was the copy editor. Finally, the author must acknowledge the patience, hard work, and support of his wife Siân. She started him on the academic track many years ago.

Acknowledgements

Series Editor's Preface

This book examines the validity of the commonly accepted argument that the British in general and the Royal Navy in particular were so engrossed in 1945 in the coming of the Cold War that they dragged their heels on German disarmament in order to harness Germany to their crusade against Stalinism. Chris Madsen has re-examined this hypothesis, having conducted multinational archival research in Britain, Canada, Germany and the United States.

On the basis of his impressive international research, Madsen first examines British wartime planning for German disarmament; then traces the Royal Navy's efforts at disarming German shore facilities and floating assets, and the level of German cooperation in this undertaking; next he details the degree of cooperation between British and Soviet occupying forces; and closes with a succinct summary of his findings and their impact on the established historiography. Especially in the chapters dealing with the scientists, archives and admirals (7) and with the war crimes trials (8) he shows a balance and maturity remarkable in such a young scholar. Madsen's sensational treatment of the Royal Navy's support for *Kriegsmarine* courts martial for alleged 'deserters and shirkers' – well after 'the first soldier of the Reich', Adolf Hitler, had deserted via suicide on the last day of April 1945 – is sure to elicit much debate.

In short, this book is highly revisionist in the best sense of the word; it challenges well-established and widely accepted generalizations on the basis of solid research and cogent argumentation.

Holger H. Herwig
Series Editor

Introduction

In June 1919 in a final act of defiance, German sailors scuttled the interned warships of the German High Seas Fleet in the British naval anchorage at Scapa Flow. The Treaty of Versailles appeared to end forever the German threat to the Royal Navy's control of the sea lines of communications to the British Isles. The Allied powers banned Germany from ever possessing the dreaded U-boats, reduced the German surface fleet to a coastal defence force of obsolete battleships, light cruisers, and destroyers, and limited the number of naval personnel to 15,000. Less than twenty years later, the Royal Navy once again found itself in a life or death struggle with a resurgent German navy in the Second World War.

Even before the Allies stemmed the tide in 1943, the Royal Navy began to plan for the final elimination of German naval power. Mindful of the failure in 1919, the Admiralty was determined that it would not repeat the same mistakes with the *Kriegsmarine*. During the final three years of the war, the Royal Navy planned carefully for the dismantlement of every aspect of German naval power. Everything, from the warships and submarines which proved such deadly foes to the shipyards that built and maintained them and the shore establishments which trained and administered their crews, was designated for disposal. In the first two years of the immediate post-war period, implementation of the plans for German naval disarmament was a top priority for the Royal Navy. Despite the great importance placed on this programme by the Admiralty, an account of the planning and carrying out of the Royal Navy's scheme for terminating German naval power has never been told. This study, based on available archival material, is the first examination of the extraordinary project.

A preoccupation with Great Britain's role in the origins of the Cold War has inhibited critical assessments of Germany's disarmament and occupation in the immediate post-war period. Revisionist historians argue, in various degrees, that British political and military leaders recognized the Soviet Union as a potential enemy before the end of the war against Germany, and sought out Allies in Europe and across the Atlantic to meet the new threat.[1] They also suggest that British planners considered an economically and militarily strong western Germany as a possible addition to a future alliance of Western nations. The presumed ascendancy of the belligerently minded Chiefs of Staff over the more moderate Foreign Office in the field of post-war planning underscores the argument.[2]

Apart from the obvious problem of hindsight, the approach misconstrues overall British priorities within the government and the Admiralty at the time. At least until mid-1944 most work performed on various planning bodies dealt with armistice and occupation matters rather than with post-war strategic planning. The Admiralty lacked conviction in attempting to predict future strategic contingencies or situations. Instead, post-hostilities planning bodies were predominantly used to develop and formulate the Royal Navy's ideas for German naval disarmament. In this supposed period of radical strategic reorientation, the complete elimination of German naval power remained a central goal. For the Royal Navy, German naval disarmament was certain and tangible, whereas a possible naval conflict with the Soviet Union was distant and less than probable. Adoption of hard-line attitudes towards the Soviet Union eventually took place, but at a much later date and not on British terms. Irreconcilable differences between the Western powers and the Soviet Union caused the final breakdown of relations. At least until mid-1947 many officials in the Admiralty and the Foreign Office tried to pursue collaboration and cooperation with the Soviets. As long as defeated Germany remained the perceived enemy, the Soviets and British could potentially work together.

Although among the victor nations, Great Britain emerged from the war in a weakened position, particularly in terms of its relative economic, military, and naval power. World War II was perhaps the Royal Navy's last claim to greatness. British fleets would never again be as large or as far-reaching in their operations. The eclipse of British sea power was inseparable from Great Britain's decline as a Great Power.[3] The Royal Navy experienced a difficult period of adjustment. Overshadowed by the emergence of the United States and the Soviet Union as the pre-eminent superpowers in the world, Great Britain attempted to maintain status and a crumbling empire in a state of near bankruptcy. The Admiralty struggled with too many commitments and too few resources.

The Royal Navy confronted many challenges in the immediate post-war period: rapid technological change; crippling personnel shortages; limited operating and procurement funds; lacklustre alliances or associations; continued maintenance of ships and bases around the world; and a gradually changing strategic environment. Economy and consolidation underscored its activities after 1945.[4] The Admiralty faced several hard choices in terms of function and organization, compounded by an intense struggle within the British armed forces over scarce resources. The Royal Navy still saw sea power as an instrument to sustain Great Britain's world role and to restore former greatness.[5] This study examines one aspect of the Royal Navy's activities in this crucial period of transition.

The formulation of naval policy involved many different factors and people. The almost exclusive concentration of British naval writing on the war at sea has so far overlooked the important contribution of knowledgeable opinion, good organization, and sound staff work.[6] This administrative process involved extensive interaction between naval officers and civil servants in London. The Admiralty's practice of circulating files for staff opinion is a great aid in understanding how naval policy on particular subjects developed. Diaries and papers of those involved in German naval disarmament also indicate that much work was done on an informal basis during lunch at Claridges, after social functions, and through personal contacts.[7] Debates and decisions took place at both an official and unofficial level.

Writing on the *Kriegsmarine* has also predominantly focused on operational and technical aspects, but for different reasons. Memoirs by former senior *Kriegsmarine* officers intentionally avoided difficult questions concerning the navy's involvement in the National Socialist state.[8] Self-interest was a strong motivation. After Nuremberg, the German naval community rallied around the image of the honourable, apolitical sailor. Yet, German naval officers played a far larger part in the Nazi regime than they have previously admitted.[9] The realization extends beyond the realm of academic debate into matters of tradition and institutional identity. The fact that a large number of former officers later found employment under the West German flag raises a number of serious moral and ethical questions, which subsequent generations of German naval officers must confront.

Indeed, the Royal Navy's intentions regarding German naval disarmament reopens the entire issue of continuity between the *Kriegsmarine* and the later *Bundesmarine*. Even historians critical of the relationship attribute some conscious part to the Royal Navy in the perpetuation of German naval power.[10] Such an argument, however, misrepresents actual British intentions in the early post-war period. Naval formations were kept intact for specific tasks of a temporary nature. The Admiralty never believed that the German navy needed nurturing and protection. On the contrary, British authorities did everything in their power to accelerate final disbandment of the remaining parts. British support for creation of the *Bundesmarine* in 1956 resulted from later negotiations and the activities of interest groups within the context of the North Atlantic Treaty Organization, the Korean War, and relations with the Soviet Union.[11] These events properly belong to a different time period.

As this study will show, the Royal Navy played a significant and prominent part in the demilitarization of Germany after World War II. For various historical, institutional, and strategic reasons, German naval disarmament became an important commitment for many Royal Navy officers. Based upon extensive planning and preparation, British naval authorities arrived with a remarkably clear idea of what they wanted to achieve in Germany. They worked towards complete elimination of German naval power in a comprehensive and thorough manner. The aspiration was almost an obsession. Although practical considerations placed limits on what could be done and how quickly the desired goal was realized, British policy towards German naval disarmament was consistent, focused, and pragmatic.

NOTES

1. Arthur L. Smith Jr., *Churchill's German Army: Wartime Strategy and Cold War Politics, 1943–47*, (Beverly Hills, CA: Sage, 1977). Victor Rothwell, *Britain and the Cold War 1941–1947*, (London: Jonathan Cape, 1982). John Baylis, *The Diplomacy of Pragmatism: Britain and the Formation of NATO, 1942–49*, (London: Macmillan, 1993). Anne Deighton, *The Impossible Peace: Britain, the Division of Germany and the Origins of the Cold War*, (Oxford: Clarendon Press, 1990). Julian Lewis, *Changing Direction: British Military Planning for Post-War Strategic Defence, 1942–47*, (London: Sherwood Press, 1988).
2. Martin Kitchen, *British Policy Towards the Soviet Union During the Second World War*, (London: Macmillan, 1986), pp.196–206. Elisabeth Barker, *The British Between the Superpowers, 1945–50*, (London: Macmillan, 1983), pp.6–8. Graham Ross, 'Foreign Office Attitudes to the Soviet Union 1941–45', *Journal of Contemporary History* 16 (1981), pp. 528–31.
3. Paul M. Kennedy, *The Rise and Fall of British Naval Mastery*, (London: Macmillan, 1983), pp. 321–3.
4. Eric Grove, *Vanguard to Trident: British Naval Policy Since World War II*, (Annapolis: Naval Institute Press, 1987).
5. John B. Hattendorf, R.J.B. Knight, A.W.H. Pearsall, N.A.M. Rodger, and Geoffrey Till, eds., *British Naval Documents 1204–1960*, (Aldershot: Scholar Press, Naval Records Society, 1993), pp. 787–92.
6. Stephen Roskill, *The War at Sea 1939–45*, 3 Volumes, (London: Her Majesty's Stationery Office, 1954–61). Stephen Roskill, *Churchill and the Admirals*, (London: Collins, 1977). Correlli Barnett, *Engage the Enemy More Closely: The Royal Navy in the Second World War*, (London: Hodder & Stoughton, 1991).
7. British Library, Department of Manuscripts (hereafter BL), Admiral of the Fleet Andrew Browne Cunningham, Add. Ms. 52577/8. Robert W. Love, Jr. and John Major, eds., *The Year of D-Day: The 1944 Diary of Admiral Sir Bertram Home Ramsay*, (Hull: University of Hull Press, 1994). National Maritime Museum (hereafter NMM), Admiral Sir Geoffrey Blake, RN, BLE/10, Letter from Henry V.

Markham to Vice-Admiral Geoffrey Blake, 30 Oct. 1945. Churchill College Archives Centre (hereafter CCAC), Albert Victor Alexander, AVA 5/9 and 10. National Archives (hereafter NA), RG 313, COMNAVEU, Series II, File 172, Admiral Harold R. Stark Diary, 1942–44.

8. Erich Raeder, *My Life*, (Annapolis: United States Naval Institute Press, 1960). Karl Dönitz, *Memoirs: Ten Years and Twenty Days*, (London: Weidenfeld & Nicolson, 1959). Friedrich Ruge, *In Vier Marinen*, (München: Bernard und Graefe, 1979).

9. Charles S. Thomas, *The German Navy in the Nazi Era*, (London: Unwin Hyman, 1990).

10. Michael Salewski, *Die deutsche Seekriegsleitung 1935–45*, Vol. 2, (München: Bernard und Graefe, 1975), pp.562–77.

11. Saki Dockrill, *Britain's Policy for West German Rearmament 1950–55*, (Cambridge: Cambridge University Press, 1991).

Abbreviations

ACNS(H)	Assistant Chief of the Naval Staff (Home)
ADM	Admiralty
AdK	Admiral der Kleinkampfverbände
	Flag Officer, Small Battle Units
Adm Qu	Admiralquartiermeister
	Quartermaster Admiral
AGWAR	Adjutant General, War Office
ANCXF	Allied Naval Commander Expeditionary Force
BAD	British Admiralty Delegation
BA/MA	Bundesarchiv-Militärarchiv (Freiburg)
	Federal Military Archives (Germany)
BAOR	British Army of the Rhine
BdU	Befehlshaber der Unterseeboote
	Commander of Submarines
BL	British Library
BNCinCG	British Naval Commander-in-Chief, Germany
CAB	Cabinet
CCAC	Churchill College Archives Centre (Cambridge)
CCG(BE)	Control Commission for Germany (British Element)
CCS	Combined Chiefs of Staff
CinC	Commander in Chief
CNMO	Canadian Naval Mission Overseas
CNO	Chief of Naval Operations
COMINCH	Commander in Chief United States Fleet
COMNAVEU	United States Commander Naval Forces Europe
COS	Chiefs of Staff
COSSAC	Chief of Staff, Supreme Allied Commander
DCNS	Deputy Chief of the Naval Staff
DCOS	Deputy Chiefs of Staff
DEFE	Ministry of Defence
DF	Direction Finding

DHist	Directorate of History, Department of National Defence Headquarters (Ottawa)
DNB	Dictionary of National Biography
DNI	Director of Naval Intelligence
DofP	Director of Plans
DTD	Director of Trade Division
DTM	Director of Torpedoes and Mining
EAC	European Advisory Commission
FdS	Führer der Schnellboote Leader of Motor Torpedo Boats
FdZ	Führer der Zerstörer Leader of Destroyers
FlU	Forward Interrogation Unit
FO	Foreign Office or Flag Officer
FOCBNFG	Flag Officer Commanding British Naval Forces, Germany
GM/SA	German Minesweeping Administration
GRT	Gross Registered Tonnage
HMCS	His Majesty's Canadian Ship
HMDS	His Majesty's Danish Ship
HMNS	His Majesty's Norwegian Ship
HMS	His Majesty's Ship
HQ	Headquarters
IMT	International Military Tribunal
IWM	Imperial War Museum (Lambeth)
JAG	Judge Advocate General
JCS	Joint Chiefs of Staff
JIC	Joint Intelligence Sub-Committee
JIS	Joint Intelligence Staff
JPS	Joint Planning Staff
KCB	Knight Commander of the Bath
KFK	Kriegsfischkutter Armed Trawler
KTB	Kriegstagebuch War Diary
LC	Library of Congress (Washington)
LCT	Landing Craft, Tank
LST	Landing Ship, Tank
M-Boot	Minensuchboot M-Class Minesweeper
MDG	Marinedienstgruppen Naval Labour Formations

MOK	Marineoberkommando
	Naval Area Command
Mrst	Marinerüstung
	Naval Construction and Supply Department
MSC	Military Sub-Committee
MTB	Motor Torpedo Boat
Mwehr	Marinewehramt
	Naval Personnel Department
MWT	Ministry of War Transport
NA	National Archives (Washington)
NAC	National Archives of Canada (Ottawa)
NAM	National Army Museum (Chelsea)
NATO	North Atlantic Treaty Organisation
NDL	US Navy Department Library
NHB	Naval Historical Branch (Whitehall)
NHC	National Historical Center (Washington)
NID	Naval Intelligence Division
NMM	National Maritime Museum (Greenwich)
NOIC	Naval Officer-in-Charge
ObdM	Oberbefehlshaber der Marine
	Naval Commander in Chief
OHRO	Oral History Research Office, Columbia University (New York)
OKM	Oberkommando der Marine
	Naval High Command
OKW	Oberkommando der Wehrmacht
	High Command of the Armed Forces
PHPC	Post-Hostilities Planning Committee
PHPSC	Post-Hostilities Planning Sub-Committee
PRO	Public Record Office (Kew)
QuA	Quartiermeisteramt der Seekriegsleitung
	Admiralty Quartermaster's Department
RA	Royal Artillery
R-Boot	Minenräumboot
	R-Class Minesweeper
RCN	Royal Canadian Navy
RCNVR	Royal Canadian Naval Volunteer Reserve
RCNR	Royal Canadian Naval Reserve
RDN	Royal Danish Navy
RM	Royal Marines
RN	Royal Navy
RNN	Royal Netherlands (or Royal Norwegian) Navy
RNR	Royal Naval Reserve

RNVR	Royal Naval Volunteer Reserve
RNZNR	Royal New Zealand Naval Reserve
SAC	Supreme Allied Commander
SAS	Special Air Service
SBNO	Senior British Naval Officer
SD	Sicherheitsdienst
	German Security Service
SEP	Surrendered Enemy Personnel
SHAEF	Supreme Headquarters Allied Expeditionary Force
SKL	Seekriegsleitung
	Naval War Staff
SO	Staff Officer
SS	Schutzstaffeln
TS	Treasury Solicitor
TVA	Torpedoversuchsanstalt
	Torpedo Experimental Establishment
USMC	United States Marine Corps
USN	United States Navy
USNR	United States Naval Reserve
UVic	University of Victoria Archives (Canada)
VACBNFG	Vice-Admiral Commanding British Naval Forces, Germany
WFSt	Wehrmachtführungstab
	Armed Forces Command Staff
WO	War Office
WRNS	Women's Royal Naval Service
30 AU	30th Assault Unit

1

Post-Hostilities Planning

The Royal Navy's preoccupation with German naval disarmament arose from a peculiar interaction between past experience and future concerns. German sea offensives brought Great Britain dangerously close to disaster in two world wars. The Royal Navy only defeated the U-boat menace at an extremely high cost in lives and material and with considerable Allied support. As the Royal Navy's participation through various governmental and interallied planning bodies demonstrates, British authorities saw the prospective work in Germany as preventative. The Royal Navy wished to eliminate Germany's capability to wage another aggressive sea campaign against Great Britain. Such feeling was particularly strong among senior British officers, many of whom had as juniors first fought the Germans in World War I. In naval planning, Germany persisted as the traditional and principal maritime enemy. The rapid rise of German naval power in the interwar period showed the potential for resurgence. Despite conflicting priorities, the Admiralty considered control and disarmament of the *Kriegsmarine* as important and vitally necessary.

The origins of the Royal Navy's planning for German naval disarmament began before the Allies won major victories against the German armed forces in the Soviet Union, North Africa, and the Atlantic. On 1 June 1942 the War Cabinet approved the establishment of a Military Sub-Committee to work with the Ministerial Committee on Reconstruction Problems. It was nominally under the Chiefs of Staff Committee's general direction through the Directors of Plans.[1] The purpose of the Military Sub-Committee – composed of three members from the War Office, Air Ministry, and the Admiralty – was to consider armistice and post-hostilities problems affecting the British services.

The Admiralty appointed Rear-Admiral Roger Mowbray Bellairs, RN, to represent the Royal Navy on the Military Sub-Committee. The selection was both convenient and logical. His senior rank guaranteed the chairmanship of the sub-committee. Bellairs made sure no important or controversial decisions were taken without the Admiralty's consent.[2] Although accepting the need for post-hostilities planning, the First Sea Lord, Admiral of the Fleet Sir Dudley Pound, RN, was anxious that these activities should not interfere with current operational planning. Events changed too quickly and unexpectedly to warrant more than the formulation of general principles. Bellairs, a retired flag officer whom Pound had called back at the beginning of the war to study the German surface raider problem, seemed uniquely qualified for the task.[3] He was an intelligent naval officer familiar with committee work and the complex foreign policy issues affecting navies. Bellairs had been director of the Admiralty's Plans Division between 1928 and 1930, adviser at several interwar naval disarmament conferences, and a representative on the League of Nations Permanent Advisory Commission. In 1942 he was the Director of Naval Intelligence's deputy for the appreciation of German intentions on the Joint Intelligence Committee.[4] The Military Sub-Committee position continued parallel to these other duties. The Admiralty assigned Paymaster Captain Cecil Kingsley Lloyd, RN, an officer who had previously worked with Bellairs, to assist the Military Sub-Committee.[5] The backgrounds of the appointees indicated that the Royal Navy took post-hostilities planning for German naval disarmament seriously from an early date.

In keeping with the Admiralty's desire to refrain from specifics until later, the Military Sub-Committee's work was predominantly exploratory and educational. A directive from the Chiefs of Staff emphasized the importance of historical example:

> The Sub-Committee will first undertake a study of the military aspects of lessons that may be drawn from previous attempts to secure lasting peace. Previous armistice conventions, policies and methods of disarmament and peace treaties are to be studied to this end.[6]

The peace settlement after World War I was the most obvious precedent, but the various interwar disarmament conferences and the French armistice in 1940 were also considered pertinent. The Military Sub-Committee studied past experience in a systematic and extended fashion. As contemporaries of the events themselves, Bellairs and his colleagues sincerely believed that mistakes in the past could be identified and corrected.[7] The Royal Navy expected to learn from history.

Following extensive study of the historical lessons, the Military Sub-Committee turned towards general armistice and disarmament problems associated with a proposed Allied occupation. Draft surrender terms were discussed with a parallel Foreign Office committee.[8] For the sake of clarity, the services' representatives favoured a detailed surrender document. In early 1943 the Military Sub-Committee, as the first British planning body to consider future occupation zones, recommended that British forces should occupy the north-west region of Germany.[9] Bellairs, in particular, noted the Royal Navy's interest in the coastline and the major ports. Nonetheless, the careful and methodical pace of the Military Sub-Committee's work seemed too slow in some quarters.[10] The supposed effects of Allied strategic bombing, the German capitulation in Tunisia, and dramatic Soviet advances in the east made a looming German collapse appear plausible.

At the instigation of the Foreign Office, a Post-Hostilities Planning Sub-Committee replaced the Military Sub-Committee. The Admiralty received, with some suspicion, arguments for a new mandate and a wider membership.[11] The Military Sub-Committee was sufficient for the Royal Navy's needs, and Admiralty officials privately believed that the reorganization was an attempt by the Foreign Office to control post-hostilities planning. Nonetheless, the Chiefs of Staff approved formation of the Post-Hostilities Planning Sub-Committee in mid-1943.[12] The Military Sub-Committee's original three members remained, but Gladwyn Jebb, head of the Foreign Office's Economic and Reconstruction Department, replaced Bellairs as chairperson. Jebb's ostensible role was to ensure effective coordination between civil and military post-hostilities planning. At the same time, additional services representatives augmented the new planning body.

The enlarged Post-Hostilities Planning Sub-Committee compelled the Admiralty to devote more staff to post-hostilities planning. Claud Humphrey Meredith Waldock, head of the Military Branch I, the section within the Admiralty which handled international law questions, and later a principal assistant secretary, joined Bellairs as an official member.[13] The choice was ideal for several reasons. Waldock, the author of numerous fleet orders earlier in the war, had formulated and interpreted many aspects of British naval policy. Within the Admiralty, he had gained the reputation of being a clever thinker. Furthermore, Waldock's position brought him into frequent contact with other service and civil departments within the government. Lloyd, who continued as an assistant, represented the Post-Hostilities Planning Sub-Committee for a short time in Washington.[14] As the number of topics and resulting workload increased, the Admiralty devoted more staff to post-hostilities planning. A captain, two lieutenant-commanders, and WRNS secretarial staff joined the sub-committee.[15] This assignment of qualified personnel and resources was indicative of the fact that the Admiralty took a growing interest in armistice and post-hostilities work.

Placed under direct control of the Chiefs of Staff Committee, the Post-Hostilities Planning Sub-Committee acquired more power to make

3

detailed plans for the post-war period than the Military Sub-Committee. Since Italy was soon out of the war and Japan was principally an American concern, the sub-committee focused on Germany's occupation and control. Planners felt that the physical presence of Allied occupation forces was needed to bring home the reality of defeat to the German people. With the experience after World War I in mind, the British intended to send two naval squadrons, consisting of battleships, cruisers, destroyers, and smaller craft, to the main naval bases at Wilhelmshaven and Kiel.[16] Once established in Germany, the Royal Navy was to control all major ports, with the exception of Rostock and Stettin which were earmarked for the Soviets, and institute regular patrols on the River Rhine and Kiel Canal. Bellairs also acquainted the sub-committee with the Admiralty's proposals for a central Allied organization to supervise mine clearance operations in European waters.[17] The Royal Navy expected to make full use of German minesweepers under the armistice terms. The planned naval occupation, which envisaged complete control and disarmament through four distinct stages, was 'to demonstrate the failure of the German navy and of the U-boat campaign'.[18] The Royal Navy approached the post-hostilities planning with a clear idea of what it wanted to achieve in Germany.

The assumption that the British should occupy a north-west zone in a three-way division of Germany underscored the Post-Hostilities Planning Sub-Committee's work. In early December 1943 the American Joint Chiefs of Staff, at the insistence of President Franklin D. Roosevelt, proposed American occupation of north-west Germany under 'Rankin Case C', an operational plan for an Allied return to the continent in the event of a sudden German collapse or armistice.[19] The large German ports, the Americans argued, were required for logistical supply and evacuation of US armies. Of course, the proposal went against British post-hostilities plans. In response to the suggestion that the Americans might want to occupy a north-west zone, Waldock stressed the Royal Navy's proprietorial stake in German naval disarmament:

> The events of the last thirty years have made the naval disarmament of Germany a matter of such peculiar interest to us that we have an obvious and strong claim to seeing that it is carried out with the utmost thoroughness and efficiency. The same experience has left us better equipped than any other Power to ensure that this disarmament is carried through. The occupying naval forces are in any case likely to be British because the American naval forces over here will not be adequate for the purpose.[20]

Naval arguments alone made a British-occupied north-west zone imperative. The intention of US officials to withdraw American occupation forces from Germany at the earliest opportunity certainly did not inspire trust in the Americans to do the job properly. During a meeting of the Combined Chiefs of Staff, Admiral Sir Percy Noble, RN, head of the British Admiralty Delegation and the First Sea Lord's representative in Washington, asserted that 'owing to her geographical position, the rapid and effective disarmament of the German naval bases from Kiel to the Baltic was obviously of vital importance to Great Britain'.[21] The Royal Navy viewed the elimination of German naval power as its special preserve. When Roosevelt sent a renewed appeal for an American north-west occupation zone, the Prime Minister, Winston Churchill, again evoked the argument for German naval disarmament to justify a British presence in north-west Germany.[22] Although the issue of occupation zones was not finally resolved until the Quebec Conference in September 1944, the British presented definite proposals for Germany's control and disarmament.

Drawing upon the work of the Post-Hostilities Planning Sub-Committee, the British took the lead in interallied post-war planning. At the Moscow Conference of Foreign Ministers in November 1943, the United States, Great Britain and the Soviet Union agreed to establish an interallied body, subsequently named the European Advisory Commission, to work out armistice terms and problems associated with the surrender.[23] From the beginning, the British were the prime movers behind the organization, and the European Advisory Commission met in London. On 15 January 1944 Sir William Strang, the British representative, tabled three Cabinet-approved Post-Hostilities Planning Sub-Committee memoranda, which set out at length the British approach to the surrender and occupation.[24] They favoured a long and detailed armistice document, Germany's total occupation and disarmament, interallied control machinery, and three national zones with the British in the north-west. The earlier planning meant that the British were much better prepared to consider specific proposals than the Americans and the Soviets.[25] While work on surrender terms was finished by late February, differences in opinion over the occupation, points of authority, and periods of implementation prolonged discussion on other topics. The European Advisory Commission's slow progress in general policy and principles influenced naval planning.

For naval-related subjects, the European Advisory Commission drew upon the expertise of naval advisers at a sub-committee level. Admiral Harold Raynsford Stark, USN, the Commander United States Naval Forces in Europe (COMNAVEU), accepted a request from Washington to assist the American ambassador.[26] Stark, who took a sincere interest in these matters, was well-informed about the Admiralty's control and disarmament plans through his liaison officer, Vice-Admiral Sir Geoffrey

Blake, RN. Pro-British and Eurocentric, Stark favoured a similar US naval commitment to Germany's occupation. When not attending meetings himself, Stark delegated Lieutenant-Commander Willis H. Sargent, USNR, a prominent Democratic attorney from Syracuse, New York, to handle the often highly legalistic work.[27] On the British side, Bellairs and his staff advised Strang. For this purpose, two additional representatives from the Admiralty joined the Post-Hostilities Planning Sub-Committee.[28] Rear-Admiral H.N. Kharlamov, head of the Soviet Naval Mission in London, assisted the Soviet ambassador. The small Soviet mission, however, remained primarily interested in acquisition of Allied technical information.[29] Thus, the attention of Soviet officers was mostly focused elsewhere.

The Royal Navy held the advantage of a clearer sense of purpose. The first informal meeting of the European Advisory Commission's naval advisers took place at the American embassy on 2 February 1944.[30] They discussed the Admiralty's plans for Germany's surrender and occupation. Although welcoming offers of assistance, the British felt that German naval disarmament was primarily a responsibility for the Royal Navy. Apart from obvious strategic interests, Great Britain was the only country in the European theatre with sufficient forces to oversee the work effectively.

In contrast, a lack of guidance from Washington restricted Stark and Sargent. In late 1943 Admiral Harry Ervin Yarnell, USN, head of a special planning section which considered post-war matters for the US Navy, resolved that 'the immediate post-war European problems of boundaries and disarmament [were] to be settled by Great Britain and Russia'.[31] Domestic politics and America's vital strategic interests in the Western Hemisphere precluded a commitment to prolonged occupation in Germany. Indeed, Fleet Admiral Ernest Joseph King, USN, Commander-in-Chief of US Naval Forces and Chief of Naval Operations, wished to disengage American naval forces from Europe as quickly as possible for redeployment in the Pacific. A prolonged presence in Germany was a virtual non-issue within the Navy Department. Stark formed a post-hostilities committee in London to ponder possible American participation, but he recognized 'that in general, the British would exercise control here as opposed to our interest and control in the Pacific'.[32] No commitments were possible until firm decisions were made at higher levels. Two visitors from Washington, Captain G.H. Bahm, USN, and Colonel D.R. Nimmer, USMC, stated that they 'knew something was being done but did not believe it was given a very important place among the numerous tasks being undertaken by planning groups of the Navy Department or Joint Chiefs of Staff'.[33] In naval matters, the European Advisory Commission proved little more than a sounding board for British plans with the Americans and Soviets.

Related developments took place outside the European Advisory Commission. In late 1943 the Soviets requested a share of the surrendered Italian fleet.[34] The British and Americans agreed that the claim – ostensibly compensation for heavy Soviet losses in the east – was justified and difficult to refuse on political grounds. But, the Admiralty feared that withdrawal of Italian ships might adversely affect naval operations in the Mediterranean and the cooperative attitude of Marshal Pietro Badoglio's Italian government. After some persuasion, the Soviets agreed to substitute British and American warships until the end of the war, pending the promised final division of the Italian fleet.[35] Vice-Admiral Gordei Ivanovich Levchenko, a deputy commissar of the Red Navy, arrived in Britain with Soviet crews to take possession of loaned British warships. The Admiralty found exasperating Levchenko's undiplomatic style and firm insistence on extensive sea trials and repairs for the worn-out ships, which the British tried to give the Soviets.[36] The deal with regard to the Italian vessels, a precedent for the German fleet's division, showed that the Soviets were interested in restitution from the Axis navies, and drove a hard bargain in negotiations at the naval level. The experience was important because the Royal Navy later encountered Levchenko in a similar capacity during allocation of surrendered German warships.

Arrangements were also made for a naval sub-commission within the proposed control machinery for Germany. In November 1943 the Post-Hostilities Planning Sub-Committee recommended the creation of a nucleus of air, naval, and military sections within the British element of the Control Commission for Germany.[37] Although Allied consensus on the control machinery's actual framework was still unsettled, the British decided to assign staff officers for preparatory organization and planning. For the naval section, the Admiralty designated Captain Bryan Fullerton Adams, RN, a naval officer with previous experience on the League of Nations' Permanent Advisory Committee.[38] Working closely with the Post-Hostilities Planning Sub-Committee, Adams was responsible, through the Director of Plans, to the Assistant Chief of the Naval Staff (Home) for consideration of German armistice terms and naval disarmament matters. Adams was the first officer to form a nucleus of a naval section within the Control Commission.

The British papers before the European Advisory Commission provided a sufficient basis to begin work on a general framework for a naval sub-commission. In early February 1944 Adams submitted a provisional organizational diagram for control of the *Kriegsmarine*.[39] The outline, which proposed parallel Allied and German naval commands, put British flag officers in Kiel, Berlin, and the liberated countries. Bellairs commented on the arrangement:

> The most efficient method of obtaining control of the German Naval machine, and of exercising strict supervision over naval disarmament and demobilization, will be by making the most possible use of this machine and superimposing United Nations Commanders wherever necessary throughout the German chain of command.[40]

For efficiency and economy, the Royal Navy expected to use the existing naval command structure. As a statement of intent, the diagram was a good start, but much detailed planning still remained to be done.

To undertake this work, the naval section needed to grow in size. The number of papers from various planning bodies, the Control Commission, and Admiralty departments threatened to overwhelm Adams; the workload simply became too much for a single person. After consulting with Bellairs and the Director of Plans, the Admiralty decided to increase the naval section's complement.[41] Officers from the Post-Hostilities Planning Sub-Committee were transferred to the Control Commission. Paymaster Captain Arthur Dyce Duckworth, RN, an officer with some legal knowledge, also joined the naval section to handle questions concerning German demobilization and administration.[42] At the end of May a Post-Hostilities Planning Staff, which adopted a wider focus on strategic issues, replaced the Post-Hostilities Planning Sub-Committee. With this reorganization, Bellairs left to become head of the naval section.[43] The Control Commission was the direct repository of the Royal Navy's accumulated talent pool in post-hostilities planning. Individuals rather than the various planning bodies themselves provided continuity.

The Royal Navy also undertook post-hostilities planning at the operational level. In October 1943 Lieutenant-General Frederick Morgan, chief of staff to the vacant Supreme Allied Commander post, directed military and naval authorities to begin work on 'Rankin Case C', a contingency plan for a sudden German collapse or armistice.[44] The British believed that strategic bombing would cause an eventual disintegration or breakdown in German morale. Churchill, in particular, felt that 'Rankin Case C' might take place before a full-fledged Anglo-American invasion.[45] Consequently, the Chiefs of Staff directed planners to prepare for the possibility. The 1st Canadian and 2nd British Armies were designated for occupation duties.[46] The Royal Navy assumed responsibility for sea transport of these ground troops from Great Britain to the Continent. In late November Admiral Sir John Cronin Tovey, RN, the Commander-in-Chief Nore, helped draft a joint services plan for the occupation of a British sphere within Germany under 'Rankin Case C'.[47] The Royal Navy undertook to sweep channels through minefields and land Allied troops at selected ports. To ensure the Germans furnished minefield information and pilots for navigation, Tovey intended to establish control over German naval forces through a British flag officer at the Hoek van Holland.

'Rankin Case C' focused attention on the necessity for further detailed post-hostilities planning on the naval side. Shortly after submission of the British joint plan, Tovey asked the Admiralty for guidance in regard to the prospective surrender and disarmament of the *Kriegsmarine*.[48] Before definite plans could be made, naval authorities required a clear statement of general policy. Tovey assumed that the task fell beyond the naval forces currently allocated to 'Rankin Case C'. Based upon a meeting between Bellairs, Waldock, and interested department heads, Rear-Admiral Sir Neville Syfret, RN, the Vice Chief of the Naval Staff, submitted a paper to the First Sea Lord.[49] The group reached specific conclusions in regard to surrender and disarmament. The Admiralty intended to issue a clear directive to German naval authorities, to sail surviving German warships to British ports, and to occupy major German naval bases and establishments.[50] As appropriate naval commands commenced planning on this basis, the Admiralty submitted the proposals for higher approval.

The Chiefs of Staff Committee considered the Royal Navy's recommendations in late February 1944. Pound's successor as First Sea Lord, Admiral Andrew Cunningham, presented a memorandum, which outlined the Admiralty's intentions towards surrender of the German fleet.[51] The response was favourable, but the suggestion that the policy should also apply after successful conclusion of the Allied invasion required consultation with the Americans. The British Chiefs of Staff forwarded the Admiralty's memorandum to the Combined Chiefs of Staff.

The British proposals for surrender of the German fleet under 'Rankin Case C' received a mixed reception in Washington. Admiral Noble introduced the topic for discussion towards the end of March.[52] While acknowledging the necessity for such arrangements, the US Joint Chiefs of Staff asserted that the European Advisory Commission was a more appropriate forum to discuss policy for the German naval surrender, and refused to make binding commitments without the Soviets. The Americans were not so much concerned with 'the actual distribution of ships or places of surrender, but in avoiding action to which the Russians might, with some reason, take exception, thus unduly complicating current negotiations'.[53] The Soviets would most likely disagree with the proposed sailing of warships to British ports.

9

Slow progress on the European Advisory Commission guaranteed that arrangements for the German fleet were not discussed between the three countries in the near future.

In the absence of Allied agreement, the Admiralty delegated responsibility for post-hostilities planning at the operational level. Planning under 'Rankin Case C' represented a hodgepodge of overlapping authorities. The Admiralty chose Tovey to oversee coastal traffic, minesweeping, and immediate surrender measures. On the other hand, Admiral Sir Bertram Home Ramsay, RN, the Allied Naval Commander Expeditionary Force (ANCXF) since October 1943, prepared surrender and disarmament plans within the framework of the Supreme Headquarters Allied Expeditionary Force (SHAEF). Although staff planning under 'Rankin Case C' was suspended in favour of 'Overlord' in early March 1944, General Dwight D. Eisenhower, the Supreme Allied Commander, directed Ramsay to continue examining naval-related post-hostilities problems.[54] In due course, Ramsay made specific recommendations to the First Sea Lord. In his opinion, co-ordination of planning needed 'a superior naval authority outside the Admiralty ... if the Navy is not to be left behind when the requirements of the post-hostilities period are being discussed'.[55] The Admiralty was still to provide general guidance in matters of policy, but actual supervision of planning would be devolved to a chosen authority with a delegated staff.

As candidate for the job, Ramsay recommended Tovey. Nonetheless, in a meeting at the Admiralty on 22 March, the First Sea Lord asked Ramsay to assume the responsibility.[56] The latter's position at SHAEF provided certain advantages in terms of resources and contacts. To the surprise of everyone present, Ramsay accepted the extra duty without protest.[57] Post-hostilities planning became consolidated under ANCXF.

At this stage of planning, the project for German naval disarmament was fortunate to acquire a leader of Ramsay's ability and experience. Ramsay, whose organizational and management skills were recognized as exceptional, was among the Royal Navy's most intelligent and capable officers.[58] In 1936 he had been forced to retire over a disagreement with Admiral Sir Roger Backhouse, RN, the Commander-in-Chief Home Fleet, concerning the proper use of staff officers. Returning to active service at the outbreak of the war, Ramsay executed Operation 'Dynamo', the evacuation of British troops from the beaches of Dunkirk.[59] He subsequently planned Allied amphibious landings in North Africa, Italy, and finally Normandy. Having never commanded a fleet, Ramsay was a staff admiral. As the earlier treatment attested, his brains and efficiency evoked mistrust within the Admiralty. The ANCXF position was due primarily to Churchill's political intervention.[60] SHAEF

10

provided Ramsay with the autonomy and independence in which he excelled. The British admiral, an avid golfer, maintained a friendly and close relationship with the Supreme Allied Commander. Although in close touch with the Admiralty, Ramsay was responsible to Eisenhower, who in turn was solely answerable to the Combined Chiefs of Staff.[61] In terms of naval planning, Ramsay was given a free hand within SHAEF.

Since planning for 'Overlord' was in full swing, Ramsay accepted responsibility for post-hostilities planning only on the condition that an additional officer be appointed to his staff for the purpose. Ramsay requested a recently retired commander to work under Captain R.N. Walker, his assistant chief of staff, as a member of SHAEF's Combined Planning Staff, 'with the view to his ultimately being appointed on the staff of the Naval Section of the Control Commission'.[62] In response, the Admiralty made clear that Ramsay, not the Control Commission, was the coordinating naval authority for post-hostilities matters until the dissolution of SHAEF. Since the Normandy landings were still the priority, the Admiralty was 'under no misapprehension concerning the extent to which you will be able to give your personal attention to post-hostilities matters in the coming months'.[63] Commander H.O. Owen, RN, reported to Ramsay for post-hostilities work. Owen began to familiarize himself with the overwhelming amount of paper generated by the SHAEF bureaucratic machine and to coordinate with other departments and divisions.

Owen established a close relationship with the Control Commission's naval section. Bellairs emphasized the importance 'from the naval aspect to the establishment as soon as possible of naval sub-commissions at the principal German ports, especially at Kiel and Wilhelmshaven'.[64] To this end, the naval section's small staff began work on draft directives and handbooks to govern control and disarmament activities. Considerable overlap existed between post-hostilities planning in the Control Commission and ANCXF.[65] At a meeting with Owen, Bellairs decided that the naval section should also draft an outline plan for the entry into Germany.[66] There was a need for uniformity because Ramsay was responsible for implementing surrender terms until establishment of the Control Commission. With Treasury approval, the Admiralty appointed Admiral Sir Francis Tottenham, RN, an officer who had served on the Inter-Allied Armistice Commission after World War I, to assist the naval section.[67] He imparted first-hand knowledge on German naval disarmament. Introduction of a new occupation scheme provided a sharper focus for the work.

In July 1944 SHAEF replaced 'Rankin Case C' with a new plan for the occupation of Germany called 'Talisman'. The success of the Allied invasion made much of the previous post-hostilities planning obsolete.

11

The Western Allies no longer faced a sudden return to the Continent, but instead advanced across France towards German frontiers. Owen submitted to SHAEF planners a draft paper dealing with the proposed naval organization under 'Talisman'.[68] The recommendations reflected the interaction between Owen and Bellairs. Under ANCXF guidance, designated naval control parties were to exercise authority through the German naval command structure after the surrender, pending hand-over to the Control Commission. Nonetheless, after Ramsay described the arrangements for 'Talisman' during a meeting at the Admiralty on 1 August, Cunningham gave a strong warning 'against plans being made on the assumption that large numbers of naval personnel could be made available'.[69] Given the manpower shortages affecting the Royal Navy, economy was important. The First Sea Lord turned down a request from Ramsay for a flag officer to oversee post-hostilities planning at ANCXF.

Practical considerations, however, forced the Admiralty to fulfil Ramsay's demand. Owen was a capable and hard-working officer, but his inferior rank proved a disadvantage at SHAEF in rooms full of American generals and colonels.[70] In some cases, Owen was not even invited to meetings. In order to receive a fair hearing, the Royal Navy required seniority. After considering the problem, Waldock agreed that a flag officer was justified.[71] Since Bellairs and Tottenham were busy on the Control Commission, the Admiralty appointed Rear-Admiral William Edward Parry, RN, to become Ramsay's chief of staff for post-hostilities planning. Parry, an officer with extensive staff and operational experience, began working with a small planning staff at SHAEF's headquarters in Bushy Park, Middlesex.[72] When Ramsay moved ANCXF's main headquarters to the Continent in early September, Parry stayed behind in Great Britain to coordinate post-hostilities planning at SHAEF's rear headquarters.

While ANCXF remained responsible for overall implementation of surrender terms and disarmament, the Admiralty delegated post-hostilities planning duties to individual operational commands. On 1 July 1944 the Admiralty had issued directives to the Commanders-in-Chief Nore, Home Fleet, and Western Approaches to prepare independent plans for entry of naval forces into Kiel through the Skagerrak and Kattegat, reception of the German surface fleet, and surrender of U-boats.[73] Relations between Tovey and Ramsay were not easy. When the draft 'Talisman' naval plan assigned the opening of certain ports to Nore, Tovey bluntly told Ramsay that provision of naval parties was now ANCXF's responsibility.[74] The Admiralty subsequently ruled in Nore's favour.

Transfer of German warships to British ports was less contentious. The Commander-in-Chief Home Fleet, Admiral Sir Henry Ruthven

12

Moore, RN, outlined his intention to sail major units in the German surface fleet to the Royal Navy's main anchorage at Scapa Flow.[75] The idea may seem fantastic in hindsight, but Moore fully appreciated the location's historical significance. To prevent a repeat of the scuttling in 1919, the Home Fleet planned to reduce German crews, to site covering guns on shore, and to remove all lifeboats.[76] As a safeguard, Moore even suggested grounding the largest warships, such as the battleship *Tirpitz*, in shallow water by flooding selected compartments. The Admiralty selected the code-word 'Wardance' for the German surface fleet's surrender.[77] Submarines were handled separately. The Commander-in-Chief Western Approaches, Admiral Sir Max Kennedy Horton, RN, proposed collecting an estimated 238 surrendered U-boats at selected northern Irish ports, under an operation named 'Pledge'.[78] The Royal Navy intended to land German crews and group submarines for ease of security. Minimal maintenance was required because the Admiralty sought Allied approval for wholesale scrapping of German submarines at an early date.[79] Specific British plans for surrender of the German surface and underwater fleets were ready.

In the meantime, Parry and the ANCXF post-hostilities staff hurriedly performed general surrender, control, and disarmament planning. The Combined Intelligence Committee concluded in August that German resistance was 'unlikely to continue beyond 1 December 1944 and that it may end even sooner'.[80] Although the Allied setback at Arnhem soon showed that the assessment was optimistic, German armies retreated in the west and the east. Since early activation of 'Talisman' now appeared likely, Ramsay met on 1 September with Rear-Admiral Edward Desmond Bewley McCarthy, RN, the new Assistant Chief of the Naval Staff (Home), and Cunningham to discuss immediate appointments of British flag and naval officers-in-charge for Germany and the liberated countries.[81] In conjunction with Parry, these officers were to undertake detailed planning and preparations for port and control parties. Ramsay told SHAEF that 'the main task of the post-hostilities section of my staff is, at present, to make the naval arrangements necessary to implement the 'Talisman' plan and I consider its retention in the United Kingdom essential'.[82] The ANCXF post-hostilities staff moved from Bushy Park to Bryanston Square in London to facilitate closer liaison with the Control Commission and the Admiralty. Planners began work on various post-hostilities memoranda for the information and guidance of the naval parties.[83] Preparation of special orders for issue to the German naval high command at the time of the surrender received special attention.

The Admiralty regarded detailed special orders as the most effective means to establish British control over German naval forces. Since deliberations on the European Advisory Commission were slow, Waldock recommended that the Admiralty should draft its own special naval orders for operational use.[84] The orders were to set out specific duties and responsibilities for German naval authorities during the surrender. The ANCXF post-hostilities staff duly prepared draft orders 'with the idea of having something ready in case of need'.[85] Yet, planners expressed some concern about implementation. During a meeting with Bellairs, Parry questioned the assumptions behind the special orders:

> What shall we find in the ports? Aren't we likely to find them completely wrecked, the warships scuttled in the worst possible positions and the seamen all away looking for their bombed out families? I am sure we should prepare for utter chaos and be ready to deal with it. But this is certainly not the official view at present.[86]

The Admiralty gambled on a functional German naval hierarchy to obey Allied orders in a strict and prompt manner. As Parry pointed out, such a situation might not exist at the time of the surrender.

Notwithstanding, the Royal Navy sought approval for the special naval orders from the American and Soviet navies. Bypassing the European Advisory Commission altogether, the Admiralty acted through service channels. As Waldock candidly remarked: 'This may set a precedent of some importance.'[87] Fortunately, the Royal Navy maintained a relatively good relationship with the People's Commissariat for Naval Affairs in Moscow. In contrast to a virtual quarantine on most members of the British Military Mission, Rear-Admiral Ernest Russell Archer, RN, and his predecessors enjoyed regular and easy access to Admiral of the Fleet Nikolai Gerasimovich Kuznetsov, the People's Commissar of the Red Navy, and the Soviet naval staff.[88] British naval representatives always had more to offer than the Soviets could give in return, particularly in regard to technical information and tactical experience. As the British Admiralty delegation approached King in Washington, the Admiralty forwarded the draft special orders to Archer, instructing him not to take any action until receiving a reply from the Americans.[89] Tripartite agreement was important.

The response was positive. According to Noble, King approved the proposed orders and directed Rear-Admiral Clarence Edward Olsen, USN, senior member of the US Naval Mission in Moscow, to help the British approach the Soviet naval staff.[90] In conjunction with Olsen, Archer submitted the draft special orders to the Red Navy. After a meeting with Admiral I.S. Isakov, chief of the naval staff and a deputy commissar of the Red Navy, Archer reported:

> The Soviet Naval Staff concurred in basic orders with the reservation that they be subject to such changes as may be necessitated by final agreements reached between the three governments on armistice terms ... Chief of Naval Staff, while stress[ing the] fact that their agreement was on a naval level only, stated orders were considered comprehensive and that consequently any alterations would be merely of a minor technical nature.[91]

By approaching the Red Navy directly, the Admiralty achieved agreement in principle on special orders for the surrender of the *Kriegsmarine*. A week later, the British used the Soviet naval staff's endorsement to gain preliminary agreement at the technical level of the European Advisory Commission.[92] Naval contacts allowed the Admiralty to perform a successful end-run on the formal interallied planning process.

Differences over complements for the naval parties were less easily solved. The Second Sea Lord, Vice-Admiral Sir Algernon Usborne Willis, RN, acknowledged the need for sufficient personnel to implement control and disarmament in Germany.[93] Before full assembly of naval parties could take place, naval authorities needed to know exact numbers. ANCXF's revised 'Talisman' naval plan stated a minimum figure of 585 officers and 1,159 other ranks.[94] As Owen pointed out, the numbers were modest in comparison to larger air force and army estimates. The scale of prospective work was recognizably large. The Control Commission naval plan, which called for 706 officers and 1,247 other ranks, stated clearly the Royal Navy's ambitious goal:

> We this time intend that no vestige of the German Navy either in respect of its personnel, its material, its dockyards, its manufacturing, its establishments, its schools, its depots, its barracks, or anything which might assist in keeping alive any form of German naval *esprit de corp* (such as it is), or permit of a revival of a German Navy, shall remain.[95]

Provision of too few British personnel could delay or impede the attainment of complete German naval disarmament. The First Sea Lord, however, told Bellairs to cut the proposed complement in half. Ramsay, who believed that the numbers should be higher, lamented 'the impediments in the Admiralty, in particular A.B.C. [Cunningham] who wants to do it on the cheap'.[96] To be effective, disarmament required enough personnel for implementation. American intentions necessarily influenced British plans.

Stark wanted the US Navy to participate fully in German naval disarmament. COMNAVEU increasingly felt left behind as the British began detailed plans for the surrender of the *Kriegsmarine*.[97] American officers were familiar with British post-hostilities planning through contacts at the Admiralty and involvement on the combined ANCXF staff. In a memorandum to Stark, Vice-Admiral Bernard H. Bieri, USN, Ramsay's chief representative on SHAEF's Combined Planning Staff, asked several searching questions about the US Navy's intentions towards the occupation of Germany.[98] As Bieri knew, Stark did not have the answers, but he had settled views. A letter to King recommended a large American commitment to control and demilitarization activities.[99]

Thereafter, the American naval headquarters in London grasped at any sign indicating a change in the unofficial policy of disengagement. After a trip to Washington, Captain T.J. Doyle, USN, reported that 'there was great interest in the Navy Department in Post-Hostilities and this interest is still growing'.[100] The arrival of Vice-Admiral William Glassford, USN, to head the naval segment of the newly formed US Control Council encouraged optimism. The Admiralty was surprised to learn that COMNAVEU planning budgeted 5,000 American naval personnel for Germany's occupation, a number larger than the projected British complement. During a meeting with Parry, Glassford submitted a proposal from Stark for a parallel control organization with British and American flag officers in each major German port.[101] Although American personnel provided a possible solution to the Admiralty's manpower problems, policy-makers in Washington decided differently.

The US Navy adopted a smaller role in the occupation of Germany than Stark expected. At the Quebec Conference on 14 September 1944 Roosevelt accepted a southern occupation zone in return for Churchill's signature on the Morgenthau Plan. During a Combined Chiefs of Staff meeting the next day, King and Cunningham agreed to US control over Bremen and Bremerhaven.[102] The American enclave in north-west Germany put an end to a parallel port organization. The US Navy assumed complete responsibility for control and disarmament in just two German ports. When Stark tendered a letter from King calling for a drastic reduction in American naval officers on ANCXF's existing staff, Ramsay became 'livid with rage & told him just what I thought of the Washington attitude to myself as ANCXF since the inception of Overlord.'[103] King made clear that no additional American personnel would be sent to the European theatre for German naval disarmament.

American command arrangements posed further difficulties. Without consulting Ramsay, Eisenhower asked King to designate Vice-Admiral Alan Goodrich Kirk, USN, the Commander US Naval Forces in France, 'as my senior U.S. Naval man for operational purposes, to act as such anywhere within the area that the Combined Chiefs of Staff want me to carry on the campaign.'[104] Since extension of Kirk's command into Germany contradicted ANCXF's intention to establish separate geographical naval authorities, Ramsay worked out a compromise. Kirk became responsible for all US naval forces on the Continent until the end of active operations.[105] In the meantime, Vice-Admiral Robert L. Ghormley, USN, the designated American flag officer for Germany, remained in London to undertake post-hostilities planning with Bellairs and Parry. Despite his own personal misgivings, Ramsay named Kirk as deputy ANCXF to reinforce the American admiral's operational role.[106] Although the extent of American participation was finally settled, the Admiralty's stinginess undermined plans for the control and disarmament of the *Kriegsmarine*.

Decisions at the Quebec Conference overburdened the Royal Navy. In accord with the previous post-hostilities planning, the British attained formal responsibility for the German coast and most major German ports. Bellairs, therefore, made only minor changes to port parties in a second version of the Control Commission's naval plan.[107] Supporters of German naval disarmament within the Admiralty felt that the proposed staffs were reasonable. The Director of Plans, the Second Sea Lord, and other divisions stressed 'the high importance of finding the necessary personnel to ensure the total abolition of the German Naval potential.'[108] Willis stated that experienced and qualified personnel were available, but they needed to be assigned quickly. American acceptance of a British fleet in the Pacific, the First Sea Lord's favourite project, imposed an enormous drain on manpower.[109] Formation of the fleet brought even more stringent calls for economy. Appalled at the suggested size of his port staff, Commodore Hugh Turnour England, RN, the Commodore-in-Charge Hamburg designate, 'did not think the Admiralty fully realised the extent of the problem.'[110] The Royal Navy simply did not have enough personnel for a large commitment to the Pacific as well as German naval disarmament. Yet, the Admiralty still tried to do both. Waldock informed Parry that 'Their Lordships do not approve the provision of personnel on the full scales proposed.'[111] Instead, Syfret arbitrarily imposed a ceiling of 290 officers and 802 other ranks. The ridiculously low numbers bore no relation to existing post-hostilities plans.

Ramsay relentlessly tried to convince the Admiralty to provide requisite naval personnel for post-hostilities duties and German naval disarmament. In early November 1944 SHAEF replaced 'Talisman' with the code-word 'Eclipse' after the Germans captured compromising post-hostilities documents.[112] The change focused attention on deficiencies in the existing arrangements. Under a revised 'Eclipse' plan issued by ANCXF, the army undertook to perform certain naval commitments, which included guarding ships and naval establishments.[113] The

Admiralty pointed to this arrangement to justify lower naval complements on the assumption that the army would simply do the work. When Field Marshal Bernard Montgomery, Commander-in-Chief of 21st Army Group, advised that military forces were unavailable for these duties, Ramsay requested three battalions of Royal Marines, totalling 3,176 officers and other ranks.[114] The General Officer Commanding Royal Marines implored the Admiralty to persuade Montgomery, through the War Office's Adjutant General, to fulfil the commitment in Germany because the Royal Marines were needed in the Far East. The Director of Plans, however, felt that the Admiralty should increase proposed naval personnel estimates to 3,000.[115] If the army refused to perform the commitment, the Royal Navy certainly required more personnel than currently allocated for surrender of the *Kriegsmarine* and German naval disarmament.

This limited success encouraged Ramsay to become more ambitious. On 30 November ANCXF requested 732 officers and 4,026 other ranks, excluding those required for the Control Commission in Berlin, for the naval parties:

> When the full implication of the task before these parties is considered and its importance to the future safety of our country is appreciated, it becomes apparent that sufficient personnel to ensure success must be provided. Lack of efficient control in Germany after the last war was one of the mistakes which nearly caused our annihilation in 1940 and it is surely a paramount necessity to avoid a similar mistake now.[116]

Despite the compelling argument, the Admiralty was unyielding. The personnel were simply not available. At a meeting on 6 December Syfret warned Ramsay 'that it would be impossible to find officers now, on the scale proposed by him.'[117] Manpower constraints and commitments in the Far East taxed the Royal Navy's resources. In a private letter to Montgomery, Ramsay wrote: 'It is annoying that what is the best and only solution cannot be made and that it seems we shall always have to accept an unsatisfactory compromise.'[118] The Admiralty's parsimonious stance raised the possibility of an entry into Germany with understaffed naval parties. Ramsay, who cared too much about the work to allow this to happen, prepared for a fight. A final showdown with the Admiralty over the importance of German naval disarmament was only averted by a personal tragedy.

For some time, Ramsay had asked for the appointment of a flag officer to head the naval control mission in Germany. He did not wish to assume the position for personal reasons.[119] In a compromise worked out with Syfret and Cunningham, the ANCXF post-hostilities staff and

18

the naval section of the Control Commission amalgamated, whereby Parry, who replaced Bellairs, was designated Ramsay's eventual representative in Berlin.[120] Syfret promised to appoint another flag officer at the earliest opportunity after SHAEF's eventual dissolution. Personal correspondence between Cunningham and Ramsay gave the impression that the command problem was resolved.[121] As SHAEF brought the surprise German offensive in the Ardennes under control, ANCXF planned combined operations with 1st Canadian Army along the northern coast.

Ramsay did not live to see Germany's surrender. On 2 January 1945 his plane crashed shortly after takeoff from Toussus airfield near Paris, killing all on board.[122] In a cruel twist of fate, the Royal Navy lost an articulate and fervent champion of German naval disarmament. Nonetheless, the Royal Navy's post-hostilities plans and organizational arrangements for control and disarmament of the *Kriegsmarine* were far enough advanced to permit formation of naval port parties under a new Allied Naval Commander Expeditionary Force.

NOTES

1. F.S.V. Donnison, *Civil Affairs and Military Government: Central Organization and Planning*, (London: Her Majesty's Stationery Office, 1966), pp. 82–3.
2. Public Record Office (hereafter PRO), ADM 1/12072, Staff Minute by Rear-Admiral Roger Bellairs, 10 Aug. 1942.
3. BL, Cunningham, Add. Ms. 52560, Letter from Admiral Dudley Pound to Admiral Andrew Cunningham, 1940. In early 1941 Bellairs and Rear-Admiral Victor H. Danckwerts, RN, represented the Admiralty in secret staff talks with the Americans in Washington. Richard Hough, *The Greatest Crusade: Roosevelt, Churchill, and the Naval Wars*, (New York: William Morrow & Co., 1986), p. 179. Sally Lister Parker, *Attendant Lords: A Study of the British Joint Staff Mission in Washington, 1941–1945*, Ph.D dissertation, (College Park: University of Maryland, 1984), p. 42.
4. Imperial War Museum (hereafter IWM), 74/96/1, Admiral John H. Godfrey, RN, 'The Naval Memoirs of Admiral J.H. Godfrey', Vol. 5, pp. 156–8. Patrick Beesly, *Very Special Admiral: The Life of Admiral J.H. Godfrey, CB*, (London: Hamish Hamilton, 1980), pp. 220–1. After the war, Bellairs became director of the Admiralty's naval historical branch. Naval Historical Branch, Ministry of Defence, Rear-Admiral Roger Mowbray Bellairs, RN, Box B.4.
5. PRO, ADM 116/5067, Letter from C.A. Cooper, C.E. Branch I, Admiralty to H.J. Oram, Treasury, 4 Sept. 1942. The Admiralty required the Treasury's approval for appointment of officers above the rank of commander to headquarters' posts.
6. PRO, CAB 80/37, Directive from Chiefs of Staff Committee to Military Sub-Committee, 21 Aug. 1942.
7. Donald Cameron Watt, 'Every War Must End: War-time Planning for Post-War Security, in Britain and America in the Wars of 1914–18 and 1939–45. The Roles of Historical Example and of Professional Historians', *Royal Historical Society Transactions* 28(1978), p. 164.
8. PRO, ADM 1/12795, Letter from Frederick Boveschen to Henry Markham, 25 Nov. 1942.

9.   Tony Sharp, *The Wartime Alliance and the Zonal Division of Germany*, (Oxford: Clarendon Press, 1975), p. 36.

10. PRO, ADM 1/12853, Chiefs of Staff Committee, COS(43)199, 'Military Problems Arising on the Cessation of Hostilities', 25 July 1943.

11. PRO, ADM 1/12853, Letter from A.V. Alexander to Sir Edward Bridges, 29 July 1943.

12. PRO, CAB 79/27, Minutes of 117th Meeting Chiefs of Staff Committee, 22 July 1943. Anthony Gorst, 'British Military Planning for Postwar Defence, 1943-45', Ann Deighton, ed., *Britain and the First Cold War*, (Basingstoke, Hampshire: Macmillan, 1990), p. 993.

13. PRO, CAB 81/40, Minutes of 1st Meeting Post-Hostilities Planning Sub-Committee, 9 Aug. 1943. Waldock was one of the many capable civil servants which the Admiralty employed during the war. Trained as a barrister, he interrupted an academic career at Brasenose College, Oxford. Waldock served on various international commissions and bodies in the years after the war, and eventually became president of the International Court of Justice at the Hague in 1979. *Dictionary of National Biography* (hereafter *DNB*) *1981–85*, p. 403.

14. PRO, CAB 81/40, Minutes of 20th Meeting Post-Hostilities Planning Sub-Committee, 23 Oct. 1943.

15. PRO, ADM 116/5067, Staff Minute by Cly Cardo for Head of Military Branch I, 15 June 1944.

16. PRO, CAB 81/41, PHP(43)7 (Final), 'Military Occupation of Germany after Her Defeat', 6 Sept. 1943.

17. PRO, CAB 81/41, PHP(43)10, Note by Rear-Admiral Roger Bellairs, 7 Sept. 1943. In May 1943 the Admiralty established a committee, with Vice-Admiral Edward L.S. King, RN, as chairman and Cly G.H. Cardo as secretary, to consider problems associated with post-war mine clearance. PRO, ADM 167/124, B.400 'Admiralty Committees on Post-War Problems', 30 Jan. 1945.

18. PRO, CAB 81/41, PHP(43)43 (Final), 'The Military Occupation of Germany', 24 Nov. 1943.

19. Combined Chiefs of Staff (hereafter CCS), *Wartime Conferences of the Combined Chiefs of Staff, 1941–45*, (Wilmington, DE: Scholarly Resources Inc., 1983), Reel 2, Frame 478, Minutes of 134th Meeting Combined Chiefs of Staff, 4 Dec. 1943. Paul Y. Hammond, 'Directives for the Occupation of Germany: The Washington Controversy', Harold Stein, ed., *American Civil-Military Relations*, (Birmingham: University of Alabama Press, 1963), pp. 322–3.

20. PRO, ADM 116/5132, Letter from C.H.M. Waldock to Lieutenant-Commander D. Marshall, 22 Dec. 1943.

21. Paul Kesaris, ed., *Records of the Joint Chiefs of Staff, Part 1: 1942–45 Meetings*, (hereafter *JCS*), (Frederick, MD: University Publications of America, 1981), Reel 4, Minutes of 143rd Meeting Combined Chiefs of Staff, 28 Jan. 1944. Noble simply reiterated the First Sea Lord's views. Sharp, p. 59.

22. Francis L. Loewenheim, Harold D. Langley, and Manfred Jonas, eds., *Roosevelt and Churchill: Their Secret Wartime Correspondence*, (New York: E.P. Dutton & Co. 1975), p. 432. United States *Foreign Relations of the United States: Diplomatic Papers 1944* (hereafter *FRUS*), Vol. 1, (Washington: Government Printing Office, 1966), p. 181.

23. Edward John Francis Thomas, *The European Advisory Commission and Allied Planning for a Defeated Germany, 1943–45*, Ph.D dissertation, (Washington: American University, 1981), p. 11.

24. United States *FRUS*, 1944, Vol. 1, pp. 112–59. Strang was Assistant Under-Secretary of State in the Foreign Office and a member of Deputy Prime Minister Clement Attlee's Armistice and Post-War Committee. The American and Soviet ambassadors in London, John G. Winant and Feodor T. Gousev, represented their respective countries.

25. PRO, ADM 199/443, Letter from J.M. Knight to C.H.M. Waldock, 'Draft German

Armistice', 1 Dec. 1943.
26. NA, RG 313, COMNAVEU, Series II, File 58, 'Activities of Political Warfare Section, Week ending 22 Jan. 1944'. Stark was a long-time friend of the Royal Navy. As Chief of Naval Operations between 1939 and 1941, he had guided the US Navy towards Britain's side during the period of official American neutrality. Shameful incrimination and inter-service backstabbing after Pearl Harbor brought the tarnished admiral to London. Affectionately called 'England's oldest American resident', Stark had previously served in London during World War I on the staff of Admiral William S. Sims, USN. CCAC, Alexander, AVAR 5/10/37, Memorandum from US Fleet, US Naval Forces in Europe to Captain Merrington, RN, 7 Aug. 1945.
27. B. Mitchell Simpson III, *Admiral Harold R. Stark: Architect of Victory, 1939–1945*, (Columbia, SC: University of South Carolina Press, 1989), pp. 237–8.
28. PRO, CAB 81/40, Minutes of 4th Meeting Post-Hostilities Planning Sub-Committee, 27 Jan. 1944.
29. Great Britain. Foreign Office, *British Foreign Office: Russian Correspondence 1941-1945* (hereafter FO/SU), (Wilmington, DE: Scholarly Resources Inc., 1976–82), 1943, Reel 11, Frames 193–6, Memorandum by Rear-Admiral E.G.N. Rushbrooke, DNI, 'Composition and Activities of the Soviet Naval Mission London', 1 May 1943.
30. NA, RG 313, COMNAVEU, Series II, File 58, 'Activities of Political Warfare Intelligence Section, Period from 31 Jan. to 12 Feb. 1944'.
31. Operational Archives Branch/Naval Historical Center (hereafter OAB/NHC), Admiral Harry Ervin Yarnell, USN, Series II, Box 7, File 3, Memorandum by Admiral H.E. Yarnell, Special Planning Section to Vice Chief of Naval Operations, 'Fundamentals of Post-War Treaty', 6 Oct. 1943.
32. NA, RG 313, COMNAVEU, Series II, File 59, 'Minutes of Conference of COMNAVEU Post-Hostilities Committee 29 March 1944', 3 April 1944.
33. NA, RG 313, COMNAVEU, Series II, File 59, Minutes of 9th Meeting COMNAVEU Post-Hostilities Committee, 17 May 1944. Library of Congress (hereafter LC), Admiral Frederick Joseph Horne, USN, Box 3, File 'Speech File Congressional Statements 1943-45', 'Statement of Vice-Admiral Horne Before Select Committee of Congress on Post-War Policies', 10 May 1944.
34. Woodward, Ernest Llewellyn, *British Foreign Policy in the Second World War*, Vol. 2, (London: Her Majesty's Stationery Office, 1970–76), pp. 586–7.
35. David Dilks, ed., *The Diaries of Sir Alexander Cadogan, 1938–1945*, (London: Cassell, 1971), p. 602. The British and Americans loaned the Soviets the battleship HMS *Royal Sovereign*, the cruiser USS *Milwaukee*, nine old Lend-Lease destroyers, and four Royal Navy submarines. Jürg Meister, *Soviet Warships of the Second World War*, (London: Macdonald and Jane's, 1977), p. 24. Kemp Tolley, *Caviar and Commissars: The Experiences of a US Naval Officer in Stalin's Russia*, (Annapolis: Naval Institute Press, 1983), p. 205.
36. PRO, ADM 205/40, Minutes of Meeting between Admiral Sir Charles E. Kennedy Purvis, Deputy First Sea Lord and Vice-Admiral Gordei Levchenko, 20 May 1944. The First Lord considered asking Moscow to recall the obstinate admiral, but a Foreign Office official, present at the formal transfer ceremony, observed that Levchenko: 'was as unpleasant to the Soviet Ambassador and the other Russians as he was to our people, and at dinner he and M. Gousev sat in stony silence and said as little as possible to each other. ... I am certain that the Russians found him far from easy, that he is a very unpleasant man in any circumstances and that he has not necessarily put on this act for our benefit.' FO/SU, 1944, Reel 2, Vol. 43276, Frame 26, Staff Minute by George Wilson, 'Loan of British Warships to Russia', 21 June 1944.
37. Donnison, p. 96.
38. PRO, ADM 116/5393, Staff Minute by A. Madden, Assistant to Second Sea Lord, 30 Nov. 1943.

39. PRO, ADM 1/16180, 'Skeleton Organization of the Naval Control Sub-Commission for the Naval Control of Germany Through German Naval Commands', 10 Feb. 1944.

40. PRO, ADM 116/5393, Letter from Rear-Admiral Roger Bellairs, 'United Nations Naval Control in Germany on Cessation of Hostilities', 10 Feb. 1944.

41. PRO, ADM 116/5393, Memorandum from Director of Plans to Vice Chief of Naval Staff, 'Post-Hostilities Planning – Position of CCMS', 13 April 1944.

42. Arthur Dyce Duckworth, *An Introduction to Naval Court Martial Procedure*, (Devonport: Hiorns & Miller, 1943). Lieutenant-Commander R.S. Armitage, RNVR, assisted Adams with disarmament matters, while Lieutenant-Commander D. Marshall, RNVR, concentrated on bases and fortifications.

43. PRO, ADM 116/5067, Staff Minute by Cly Cardo for Head of Military Branch I, 15 June 1944. PRO, FO 1032/15, 'Minutes of First CCMS Weekly Conference held on Friday, 16 June 1944'.

44. OAB/NHC, World War II Command Files, Box 581, War Department, Adjutant General's Office, 'History of COSSAC, Chief of Staff to SHAEF 1943–44', p. 25. PRO, WO 205/5A, COSSAC(43)60, 'Operation Rankin Case C', 30 Oct. 1943. IWM, 86/47/1, General Sir Leslie Hollis, 'Random Reminiscences', p. 89. L.F. Ellis, *Victory in the West*, Vol. 1, (London: Her Majesty's Stationery Office, 1962), p. 39.

45. Roger Parkinson, *A Day's March Nearer Home: The War History from Alamein to VE Day based on the War Cabinet Papers of 1942 to 1945*, (London: Hart-Davis, MacGibbon, 1974), p. 209.

46. PRO, WO 205/1B, 'Executive Planning Meeting No. 1 held at 1800 hours on 4th Nov. 1943', 5 Nov. 1943. Directorate of History, Department of National Defence Headquarters, Ottawa (hereafter DHist), File 312.009 (D26), 'Notes of Commander-in-Chief's Conference of Army and Corps Commanders on 18 Nov 43 at HQ 21 Army Group', 19 Nov. 1943.

47. National Archives of Canada (hereafter NAC), RG 24, Vol. 10,440, File 212.C1.(D88), Admiral Sir John Cronin Tovey, General Sir Bernard Paget, and Air Marshal D'Albiac, 'Operation "Rankin" Case "C"', 23 Nov. 1943. Since the Royal Navy also undertook to transport American troops, Admiral Sir Charles Little, RN, the Commander-in-Chief Portsmouth, drafted a similar naval plan for the US sphere. OAB/NHC, Admiral Alan Goodrich Kirk, USN, Series III, Box 16, File 'Task Force 122: Staff Organization 3 Dec. 1943', Memorandum from Captain H.J. Wright to Vice-Admiral Alan Kirk, 'Rankin Case C – Notes on Discussion held at Portsmouth Combined HQ.', 15 Nov. 1943. NA, RG 331, SHAEF, General Staff, G-4 Division, Executive Section, File 381/3, 'Operation Rankin Case C Outline Naval Plan – United States Sphere', 30 Nov. 1944.

48. PRO, ADM 1/16180, Letter from Admiral John Tovey to Secretary of Admiralty, 28 November 1943.

49. PRO, ADM 205/40, 'Aide-Mémoire for Meeting with First Sea Lord (Implementation of German Armistice)', 26 Jan. 1944.

50. PRO, ADM 116/5029, Memorandum from C.H.M. Waldock to ANCXF; Commanders-in-Chief Nore, Portsmouth, Plymouth, Dover, Home Fleet, 30 Jan. 1944.

51. PRO, ADM 116/5123, Memorandum COS(44) 201(0) 'Policy for Surrender of German Fleet', 25 Feb. 1944.

52. JCS, Part 1 1942–45: European Theatre, Reel 9, Frames 154–7, 'Policy for the Surrender of the German Fleet under Rankin Case C Conditions', 30 March 1944.

53. JCS, Part 1 1942–45: European Theatre, Reel 9, Frames 169–72, Memorandum by Joint Chiefs of Staff, 'Policy for the Surrender of the German Fleet under Rankin Case C', 2 May 1943.

54. PRO, ADM 1/16180, Letter from Lieutenant-General Frederick Morgan to Admiral Bertram Ramsay, 6 March 1944.

55. PRO, ADM 205/40, Memorandum from Admiral Bertram Ramsay to Admiral Andrew Cunningham, 17 March 1944.

56. PRO, ADM 1/5123, 'Naval Action upon the Surrender of Germany', 31 March 1944. Love and John, pp. 46–7.
57. PRO, ADM 116/5123, Staff Minute by C.H.M. Waldock, 25 April 1944.
58. Kenneth Edwards, *Seven Sailors*, (London: Collins, 1945), p. 20. David Woodward, *Ramsay at War: The Fighting Life of Admiral Sir Bertram Ramsay KCB, KBE, MVO*, (London: William Kimber, 1957).
59. William S. Chalmers, *Full Cycle: The Biography of Admiral Sir Bertram Home Ramsay*, (London: Hodder & Stoughton, 1959), p. 59. *DNB 1941–1950*, p. 707.
60. The Admiralty wanted to appoint Admiral Little, the ANCXF designate before Ramsay's arrival from the Mediterranean. Roskill, *Churchill and the Admirals*, p. 235.
61. Forrest C. Pogue, *The Supreme Command*, (Washington DC: Office of the Chief of Military History, Department of the Army, 1954), p. 53.
62. PRO, ADM 116/5123, Letter from Admiral Bertram Ramsay to Secretary of Admiralty, 13 April 1944. The Admiralty mistook Ramsay's statement as an attempt 'to wriggle out of the responsibility he accepted at the meeting with the First Sea Lord.' PRO, ADM 116/5123, Staff Minute by C.H.M. Waldock, 25 April 1944.
63. PRO, ADM 1/5123, Letter from C.H.M Waldock to Admiral Bertram Ramsay, 27 April 1944.
64. PRO, FO 1032/15, Rear-Admiral Roger Bellairs to Major-General C.A. West, 'Note on Naval Control Organisation for Germany', 22 June 1944.
65. PRO, ADM 116/5393, Staff Minute by Cly Cardo for Head of Military Branch I, 30 June 1944. PRO, ADM 116/5067, Office Memorandum No. 218, 'The Control Commission (Military Sections)', 5 July 1945.
66. PRO, FO 1038/122, Minutes of Control Commission Military Sections (Naval) Meeting, 11 July 1944.
67. Tottenham served in the rank of rear-admiral under Bellairs. PRO, ADM 116/5393, Staff Minute by Rear-Admiral Roger Bellairs, 15 July 1944.
68. NA, RG 331, SHAEF, General Staff, G-4 Division, Plans Branch, File SHAEF/241/2/GDP-2, First Draft Paper from Commander H.O. Owen, ANCXF (SHAEF) to Lieutenant-Colonel G.A. Eden, 'Naval Organization in North-West and South Germany during Middle Period', 26 July 1944. Love and Major, p. 111.
69. PRO, ADM 1/16349, Minutes of Meeting, 'Entry of Naval Forces into German Ports', 1 Aug. 1944. Love and Major, p. 115. In his diary afterwards, the First Sea Lord wrote: 'I blew some of the grandiose ideas about personnel to the winds. A very useful meeting which cleared the air a lot.' BL, Cunningham, Add. Ms. 52577, Diary, 1 Aug. 1944.
70. PRO, ADM 1/16349, Memorandum from Admiral Bertram Ramsay to Secretary of Admiralty, 'Naval Plans for Surrender of Germany', 16 Aug. 1944.
71. PRO, ADM 1/16349, Staff Minute by C.H.M. Waldock, 18 Aug. 1944.
72. IWM, 71/19, Admiral William Edward Parry, RN, Box 6, 'Post-Hostilities Planning 1944', 31 Aug. 1944. PRO, ADM 199/628, Admiral Blake War Diary, Serial No. 305, 9 Sept. 1944.
73. PRO, ADM 116/5202, Instructions from Admiralty to Commanders-in-Chief Nore, Home Fleet, and Western Approaches, 1 July 1944.
74. NA, RG 331, SHAEF, ANCXF War Diary, 18 Aug. 1944.
75. PRO, ADM 1/16180, Letter from Admiral Henry Moore to Secretary of Admiralty, 13 Aug. 1944. Moore's predecessor, Admiral Bruce Fraser, RN, had asked the Admiralty to forward a copy of previous orders for surrender of the German High Seas Fleet at the end of World War I. PRO, ADM 116/5029, Memorandum from Admiral Bruce Fraser to Secretary of Admiralty, 'Requirements for German Naval Disarmament', 8 Feb. 1944.
76. IWM, 66/13/2, Vice-Admiral Sir Peveril William-Powlett, RN, Meeting Agenda from Commander-in-Chief Home Fleet, 'Orders for Surrender of German Fleet', 11 Sept. 1944. PRO, ADM 1/16076, Memorandum from Admiral Henry Moore to Secretary of Admiralty, 'Surrender of German Fleet', 20 Sept. 1944.

77. PRO, ADM 116/5512, Note from C.H.M. Waldock to Admiral Henry Moore, 12 Sept. 1944.
78. PRO, ADM 116/5202, Memorandum from Admiral Max Horton to Secretary· of Admiralty, 'Surrender of U-boat Fleet', 5 Aug. 1944. Lisahally and Loch Ryan were the designated reception ports.
79. PRO, ADM 116/5202, Letter from Admiralty to Admiral Max Horton, 21 September 1944.
80. DHist, File 193.009 (D35), CCS/660 'Prospects of a German Collapse or Surrender (As of 25 Aug. 1944)', 27 Aug. 1944.
81. Love and Major, p. 129. BL, Cunningham, Add. Ms. 52577, Diary, 1 Sept. 1944. Ramsay described the meeting as 'very uphill work'. CCAC, Admiral Sir Bertram Home Ramsay, RN, RMSY 8/27B, Letter from Admiral Bertram Ramsay to Wife, 3 Sept. 1945.
82. NA, RG 331, SHAEF, Office of the Chief of Staff, Secretary of General Staff, File 381 Eclipse (Case No. 1) Misc. Correspondence, Memorandum from Admiral Bertram Ramsay to Lieutenant-General Walter Bedell-Smith, 'Post-Hostilities Planning Staff', 22 Sept. 1944.
83. PRO, ADM 116/5300, Memorandum by Rear-Admiral W.E. Parry, 'Allied Expeditionary Force Post-Hostilities Planning Memoranda', 8 Oct. 1944.
84. PRO, ADM 1/18187, Staff Minute by C.H.M. Waldock, 'Special Orders to German Command upon Surrender or Cessation of Hostilities', 7 Aug. 1944.
85. PRO, ADM 1/18187, Staff Minute by C.H.M Waldock, 5 Sept. 1944. The Admiralty expressed general agreement with these orders. PRO, ADM 1/16099, Memorandum from C.H.M. Waldock to Rear-Admiral W.E. Parry, 7 Sept. 1944.
86. IWM, Parry, Box 6, 'Post-Hostilities Planning 1944', 28 Sept. 1944. Parry's comments echoed general SHAEF concerns about the possibility of a German descent into chaos. NA, RG 165, CAD 014 Germany, SCAF 68 from SHAEF to AGWAR for Combined Chiefs of Staff, 23 Aug. 1944.
87. PRO, ADM 1/18187, Letter from C.H.M. Waldock to Sir William Strang, 10 Sept. 1944.
88. FO/SU, 1943, Reel 11, Vol. 36970, Frame 169, Message from Rear-Admiral Douglas Fisher, RN, to Director of Naval Intelligence, 26 1115C October 1943. R.C.S. Garwood, 'The Russians as Naval Allies 1941–45', M.G. Saunders, ed., The Soviet Navy, (New York: Frederick A. Praeger, 1958), p. 76. N.K. Kuznetsov, 'The War Years', International Affairs 12(1968), p. 102. The Royal Navy's support proved useful in the unending political battles within the Soviet government, the Communist Party, and the armed forces. On one occasion, Kuznetsov warmly congratulated Rear-Admiral Sir Geoffrey John Audley Miles, RN, 'on a victory over our common enemy – the Soviet People's Commissariat for Foreign Affairs.' Anthony Courtney, Sailor in a Russian Frame, (London: Johnson, 1968), p. 46.
89. PRO, ADM 1/18187, Letter from C.H.M Waldock to Rear-Admiral Ernest Archer, 10 Sept. 1944.
90. PRO, ADM 1/18187, Message from British Admiralty Delegation Washington to Admiralty, 27 1411 Sept. 1944. OAB/NHC, Rear-Admiral Clarence Edward Olsen, USN, File 2, Address by Rear-Admiral C.E. Olsen at the Men's Presbyterian Club, 'Some Things Inside Russia', 18 Jan. 1952.
91. PRO, ADM 1/18187, Message from Rear-Admiral Ernest Archer to Admiralty, 24 1511A Oct. 1944.
92. PRO, ADM 1/18187, Letter from C.H.M Waldock to Sir William Strang, 2 Nov. 1944.
93. PRO, FO 1038/122, Minutes of Control Commission Military Sections (Naval) Meeting, 26 July 1944. As Second Sea Lord, Willis was also chief of naval personnel. IWM, P186, Admiral of the Fleet Sir Algernon Usborne Willis, RN, 'War Memoirs of Admiral of the Fleet Sir Algernon Willis 1939–45', p. 80.
94. PRO, ADM 1/16076, SHAEF Draft Plan, 'The Enforcement of the Naval Terms of the Instrument of Surrender of Germany, and the Complete Disarmament of Germany, Outline Plan', 28 Aug. 1944. PRO, ADM 1/16099, Memorandum from Rear-Admiral

W.E. Parry to Secretary of Admiralty, 'Operation Talisman', 11 Sept. 1944.

95. PRO, ADM 1/15711, Rear-Admiral Roger Bellairs, CCG(BE)(N), NFD (44)1, 'Outline Plan for the Control, Disarmament and Disbandment of the German Navy', 28 Aug. 1944.

96. Love and Major, p. 133. To be fair to Cunningham, lack of manpower was a major problem facing the Royal Navy in late 1944. Michael Simpson, 'Admiral Viscount Cunningham of Hyndhope (1943–46)', Malcom H. Murfett, ed., *The First Sea Lords: From Fisher to Mountbatten*, (Westport, CT: Praeger, 1995), p. 203.

97. NA, RG 313, COMNAVEU, Series II, File 59/1, Memorandum from COMNAVEU to COMINCH, 'Role of US Navy in Occupation and Post-Hostilities Activities in Europe', 15 May 1944.

98. NA, RG 313, COMNAVEU, Series II, File 59/1, Memorandum from Vice-Admiral Bernard Bieri to Admiral Harold Stark, 'Notes on Post Surrender Planning', 7 June 1944. Vincent Davis, *Postwar Defense Policy and the U.S. Navy, 1943–1946*, (Chapel Hill: University of North Carolina Press, 1966), p. 77. Despite British qualms, King had sent Bieri to provide proportional American representation at ANCXF during the invasion period. Alfred D. Chandler and Stephen E. Ambrose, eds., *The Papers of Dwight David Eisenhower: The War Years*, Vol. 3, (Baltimore and London: Johns Hopkins Press, 1970), pp. 1830–1, 1855–6. BL, Cunningham, Add. Ms. 52577, Diary, 17 May 1944. Love and Major, p. 71.

99. NA, RG 313, COMNAVEU, Series II, File 59/1, Letter from COMNAVEU to COMINCH, 'Role of US Navy in Occupational and Post-Hostilities Actions in Europe', 8 June 1944.

100. NA, RG 313, COMNAVEU, Series II, File 59/2, Minutes of 33rd Meeting COMNAVEU Post-Hostilities Committee on 27 July 1944, 29 July 1944.

101. IWM, Parry, Box 6, 'Post-Hostilities Planning 1944', 9 Sept. 1944.

102. CCS, Reel 3, Frames 232–3, Minutes of 176th Meeting Combined Chiefs of Staff, 16 Sept. 1944.

103. Love and Major, pp. 139–40. Pressure from Eisenhower and Stark eventually made King reverse this order. Chandler and Ambrose, Vol. 4, pp. 2178, 2197.

104. Chandler and Ambrose, Vol. 4, pp. 2255–6. Love and Major, p. 165. NA, RG 313, COMNAVEU, Series II, File 170, Memorandum from Commodore H.A. Flanigan, USN, to Admiral Harold Stark, 'Report of Semi-Monthly Visit to Continent 27 to 30 Oct., inclusive', 1 Nov. 1944.

105. OAB/NHC, Kirk, Series IV, Box 31, File 'Cragg, R.T. Lt., Flag Sec. 1944–45: Correspondence, Misc.', Message from COMINCH/CNO to COMNAVEU, 05 1613Z Nov. 1944.

106. PRO, ADM 228/86, Staff Minute by Captain L.A. Thackrey, USN, 1 Nov. 1944. Love and Major, p. 145. Relations between the two admirals were cool. During the Normandy landings, Kirk had violated the chain of command by going over Ramsay directly to Eisenhower. Oral History Research Office, Butler Library, Columbia University (hereafter OHRO/Columbia), Transcript of Interviews with Admiral Alan Kirk, 1962, p. 224.

107. PRO, ADM 1/16186, Outline Plan from Rear-Admiral Roger Bellairs, 'Initial Parties for the Naval Occupation and Control of Germany', 25 Sept. 1944.

108. PRO, ADM 1/16186, Staff Minute from C.H.M. Waldock to Vice-Admiral Neville Syfret, 29 Sept. 1944.

109. BL, Cunningham, Add. Ms. 52577, Diary, 14 Sept. 1944. Richard Ollard, *Fisher and Cunningham: A Study in the Personalities of the Churchill Era*, (London: Constable, 1991), pp. 149–50. Merrill Bartlett and Robert William Love, Jr., 'Anglo-American Naval Diplomacy and the British Pacific Fleet, 1942–45', *American Neptune* 42(1982), pp. 213–15.

110. PRO, FO 1038/122, Minutes of Control Commission Military Sections (Naval) Meeting, 3 October 1944. PRO, ADM 1/16211, Memorandum from Rear-Admiral G.C. Muirhead-Gould, 'Appointments at Hamburg and Wilhelmshaven', 13 Oct. 1944.

111. PRO, ADM 1/16186, Letter from C.H.M. Waldock to Rear-Admiral W.E. Parry, 18 Oct. 1944. At the same time, the Admiralty accepted 30 Nov. 1944 as a permissible planning date for implementation of 'Talisman'. PRO, ADM 116/5073, Memorandum from C.H.M. Waldock to Vice-Admiral Neville Syfret, 'Directive to Deputy Commissioners of British Element of Control Commission COS(44)195', 9 Oct. 1944.

112. PRO, WO 205/253, Message from GST 2nd Army to 21st Army Group, 29 2335 October 1944. NA, RG 331, SHAEF, Office of the Chief of Staff, Secretary of General Staff, Telegram from SHAEF Main signed Eisenhower to AGWAR for Combined Chiefs of Staff, S-6638611, 11 Nov. 1944. PRO, ADM 116/5050, Lieutenant-General W.B. Bedell-Smith, 'Operation Eclipse – Appreciation and Outline Plan', 24 Nov. 1944.

113. PRO, WO 205/253, Memorandum from Admiral Bertram Ramsay, 'Operation ECLIPSE (TALISMAN) – Revised Naval Plan', 14 Nov. 1944. Military authorities accepted this specific responsibility at a previous meeting with ANCXF. PRO, FO 1038/127, Brigadier C. Richardson, 21st Army Group to ANCXF, 'Minutes of Meetings Held at Main HQ 21 Army Group with ANCXF (Post-Hostilities Planners) on 28 and 29 October 1944', 30 Oct. 1944.

114. PRO, ADM 1/17198, Letter from Admiral Bertram Ramsay to Secretary of Admiralty, 13 Nov. 1944.

115. PRO, ADM 1/17198, Staff Minute by Cly Cardo for Head of Military Branch I, 28 Nov. 1944.

116. PRO, ADM 1/16186, Memorandum from ANCXF to Secretary of Admiralty, 30 Nov. 1944.

117. PRO, ADM 1/16186, Staff Minute by C.H.M. Waldock, 11 Dec. 1944. Cunningham insinuated that Ramsay could be replaced as ANCXF if he did not accept the Admiralty's arrangements. Love and Major, p. 187.

118. IWM, Field Marshal Bernard Law Montgomery, Reel 9, BLM 97/69, Letter from Admiral Bertram Ramsay to Field Marshal Bernard Montgomery, 11 Dec. 1944.

119. CCAC, Ramsay, RMSY 8/27B, Letter from Admiral Bertram Ramsay to Lady Ramsay, 10 Dec. 1944.

120. Love and Major, pp. 187–8. NA, RG 331, SHAEF, ANCXF War Diary, 15 Dec. 1944. The Admiralty received permission from the Treasury to keep Bellairs on the planning staff in London until establishment of control in Germany. PRO, ADM 116/5393, Memorandum from Head of Civil Establishment Branch to Director of Establishments, 9 Jan. 1945.

121. BL, Cunningham, Add. Ms. 52571, Letter from Admiral Bertram Ramsay to Admiral Andrew Cunningham, 1 Jan. 1945.

122. PRO, ADM 205/44, Letter from Rear-Admiral E.G.N. Rushbrooke to First Sea Lord, 6 Jan. 1945. IWM, Montgomery, Reel 8, BLM 91/2, Tribute by Field Marshal Bernard Montgomery, 'Admiral Sir Bertram Ramsay and Air Chief Marshal Sir Trafford Leigh-Mallory', 3 Jan. 1945. 'Admiral Sir Bertram H. Ramsay, KCB, KBE, MVO: Two Personal Tributes', *Naval Review* 33(1945), pp. 2–4. 'D-Day Ramsay Killed', *Daily Express* (3 Jan. 1945), p. 1.

2

Preparations and Operations

The last five months of the war were hectic for the Royal Navy and ANCXF's staffs. On short notice, a new British admiral assumed responsibility over naval activities within the SHAEF operational area. The British and Americans, fearful of a renewed U-boat offensive, expanded bombing and air attacks against German ports and naval bases with marginal success. The *Kriegsmarine* meanwhile bolstered defences along the German coast, and evacuated civilians and soldiers from the besieged eastern territories. In spite of procrastination at the Admiralty, ANCXF eventually formed naval port and control parties, in accord with the 'Eclipse' plan. Post-hostilities planning increasingly merged with general operations as the Allied armies penetrated German frontiers. Royal Navy intelligence teams and port parties entered Germany with British and Canadian military forces.

The Admiralty quickly found a suitable replacement at SHAEF. Ramsay's unexpected death created an awkward situation. Kirk, who had been made deputy ANCXF on the condition that he would never fill the higher position, was now acting ANCXF.[1] The temperamental and chauvinistic American admiral commanded mostly British naval forces in an area of particular British interest. Whatever the theory behind the combined command, the Admiralty considered Kirk's promotion as purely temporary.[2] The need for a British flag officer in the important post was unquestioned. With the concurrence of Eisenhower and King, Vice-Admiral Sir Harold Martin Burrough, RN, became ANCXF in the acting rank of admiral.[3]

In background and temperament, Burrough was almost Ramsay's opposite. As an officer with extensive sea experience in destroyers, he had served primarily in the Mediterranean in command of a naval force during the North African landings and then as the flag officer at Gibraltar.[4] On friendly terms with Cunningham and Eisenhower, Burrough was aggressive in nature, and inclined towards action. He fitted closely the British ideal of a 'fighting' admiral.[5] Burrough was a natural choice to oversee naval operations in support of the advancing Allied armies. During a press conference, he told reporters: 'The coasts of Germany and the remainder of Western Europe still occupied by the enemy offer opportunities for the use of Sea Power.'[6] The Royal Navy conducted amphibious landings and offensive naval operations, protected sea lanes of communication, opened liberated ports for reinforcement and supply of the advancing armies, and organized naval forces for duties in Germany and the liberated countries.

Burrough's arrival brought minimal change in the existing ANCXF administrative and planning structure. In due course, Commodore Hugh Webb Faulkner, RN, replaced Commodore Maurice James Mansergh, RN, as chief of staff at ANCXF's main headquarters in France.[7] Substitutions were generally selective because Burrough realized the value of continuity. Captain Robert Otway-Ruthven, RN, Ramsay's naval representative on the planning staff at SHAEF's forward headquarters, continued to work on 'Eclipse' planning, while the ANCXF post-hostilities staff in London was left virtually untouched. Parry remained Burrough's chief of staff for post-hostilities planning and his rear link with the Admiralty.[8] Despite the increased emphasis on operational matters, Burrough proved a staunch supporter of German naval disarmament.

To a large extent, Burrough simply picked up from where Ramsay had abruptly left off. The Admiralty still faced difficult decisions about allocation of personnel and resources. Shortly after Burrough's appointment, a meeting between the Second Sea Lord, Waldock, and the Assistant Director of Plans determined that no material changes could be made to ANCXF's earlier estimates without seriously undermining the goal of complete German naval disarmament.[9] The Director of Manpower and the Director of Plans agreed with this conclusion. A suggestion was put forward to cease temporarily the manning of warships in order to furnish personnel.[10] The choice was clear. The Royal Navy had either to award necessary priority for the work in Germany or to lower its expectations for occupation and disarmament. During January the Western Allies defeated the German attack in the Ardennes and the Red Army opened a great offensive on the Vistula.[11] Release of personnel for training and organization into naval parties was critical because the end of the war in Europe now seemed only a matter of time.

Estimates on Germany's capacity to continue resistance varied widely. SHAEF planners predicted an early German collapse. Spectacular victories by the Red Army suggested that German armies were at the point of disintegration in the east. In spite of impressive Allied advances on land fronts, the impending introduction of new U-boats – the Type XXI and Type XXIII – showed that the *Kriegsmarine* was far from beaten.[12] Consequently, the Admiralty adopted a more sceptical view. The First Sea Lord forecasted renewed submarine offensives some time during mid-February or early March in the Atlantic and the in-shore waters around Great Britain.[13] This expectation inevitably influenced planning calculations. Sensitive to maritime threats, the Admiralty adopted 30 June as the earliest and 1 November 1945 as the latest likely dates for an end to the war with Germany.[14] During this period, British planners certainly believed that the *Kriegsmarine* could sustain opposition. Even with the defeat of Germany proper, Norway and Denmark provided possible operating bases for the *Kriegsmarine* to continue the U-boat war.[15] This fear was the Admiralty's version of the 'Alpine Redoubt', the prospective mountain fortress which so worried the Americans in southern Germany. At the Yalta Conference, the Combined Chiefs of Staff formally accepted, for planning purposes, 1 July as the earliest and 31 December 1945 as the latest date for the surrender of Germany.[16] Although somewhat wide guesses, the estimates necessarily guided Admiralty policy towards formation of naval parties for the occupation.

The Yalta Conference also considered several important issues touching on the naval sphere and the assault on Germany. During tripartite military discussions, Kuznetsov candidly asked Cunningham if the Royal Navy planned any amphibious operations on the German coast or Denmark.[17] The First Sea Lord responded that the possibility had been studied, but was considered unlikely. In reality, Eisenhower and SHAEF dismissed seaborne assaults against Norway and Denmark as impractical since 'the diversion of shipping and military forces necessary to ensure success would militate seriously against the main effort across the Rhine.'[18] The Admiralty instead advocated increased air operations against naval targets as a partial solution to the U-boat threat. At Yalta, Cunningham asked the Combined Chiefs of Staff to intensify bombing on shipbuilding and U-boat assembly yards in Germany.[19] Although the Americans expressed some interest, Air Marshal Charles Portal and the Royal Air Force resisted diversion of planes from the strategic bombing of oil targets, the current priority. Consequently, the existing marginal bomber effort was maintained. When the weather was poor over other targets on the priority list, naval installations received precedence.[20] Although Cunningham was unable to gain higher priority for naval targets within the overall strategic bombing campaign, the combined efforts of the Allied air forces still hampered the *Kriegsmarine* in the last months of the war.

Offensive minelaying was perhaps the most sustained and productive air activity. British aircraft had dropped sea mines in German territorial waters almost continuously since April 1940.[21] These mines caused direct losses to German shipping through sinkings, and forced the *Kriegsmarine* to maintain considerable minesweeping forces in the Baltic and the North Sea. In early 1942 the Royal Air Force concentrated all minelaying efforts under Bomber Command, devoting approximately ten per cent of that command's total capacity.[22] Bomber Command embraced the role because aerial sea mining complemented the larger concept of strategic bombing. The British air staff regularly used minelaying sorties as diversions for dispersal of German fighter defences during main bombing raids on cities and industrial centres.[23] The practice led to lower loss rates among bomber crews. Furthermore, planes could be employed almost interchangeably between bombing raids and mining sorties with little or no physical alterations. As long as the Royal Air Force maintained control over the timing and strengths of sorties, Bomber Command enthusiastically supported sea mining.

For the *Kriegsmarine*, the effects of British aerial minelaying were cumulative. Between August 1944 and March 1945 Stirling, Halifax, Lancaster, Wellington, and modified Mosquito bombers deposited some 10,000 sea mines – over half from 15 January – in a planned programme of 27,000 in waters around and inside Germany.[24] The British would have dropped more, but increased production of sea mines – approaching almost 5,000 per month – exceeded the Royal Air Force's existing capacity. Air-laid mines interfered with U-boat training areas in the eastern Baltic, hampered movements of warships, and restricted the flow of shipping with occupied and neutral countries.[25] There were also important political repercussions. In early 1945 Sweden used the extreme mine threat in the Baltic as a convenient pretext to close all seaborne trade with Germany.[26] The German minesweeping organization attempted to keep pace with the increasing number of mines. Bomber Command's intensified minelaying campaign, however, eventually overwhelmed German capabilities.[27] In this situation, the existence of mines posed a threat to the expected entry of Allied naval forces into German ports. Burrough requested that the sterilisation period for aerial-laid mines be fixed at twenty-seven (later reduced to eighteen) days.[28] After this time, mines became inactive. Bomber Command's mining operations proved an enormous nuisance for the *Kriegsmarine*.

German minesweepers, auxiliaries, warships, submarines, and merchant ships also faced the danger of Allied air attacks. From October 1944 onwards Coastal Command conducted extensive air patrols in the Baltic and off the Norwegian coast.[29] Employing the new air-to-surface vessel Mark VII radar, strike wings of Beaufighters and Mosquitoes hunted and attacked German shipping with rockets and cannon fire during the night. Results generally came at a high cost. Between January and early May Coastal Command sank an estimated 81 merchant and escort ships, in return for the loss of 103 aircraft to German fighters and anti-aircraft defences.[30] As British pilots discovered, German ships were not passive targets, but instead represented formidable gun platforms with the ability to mount concentrated and deadly arcs of fire.

As Allied air attacks expanded into daytime hours, the Germans became more determined to stand and fight aircraft. In March Typhoon fighter-bombers from 2nd Tactical Air Force joined the air assault on shipping from forward airfields behind the advancing Allied land armies.[31] Normally employed in an anti-armour role, these aircraft proved surprisingly effective against ships, which presented larger targets than tanks to hit with 3-inch rockets.[32] As well, Soviet torpedo bombers, Yak-9 fighters, and Lend-Lease Liberators appeared in large numbers over the Baltic as the Red Army advanced westwards. Between January and May aircraft from the Red Banner Baltic Fleet flew 11,744 sorties against German shipping and ports.[33] As the *Luftwaffe*'s limited defensive powers dwindled, active ship air defence assumed more importance in performing essential activities, such as minesweeping, reinforcement and supply of German troops, and U-boat training. German naval authorities grouped vessels for self-defence, increased anti-aircraft armaments, and sailed heavily armed auxiliary ships called *Sperrbrecher* with most convoys.[34] The *Kriegsmarine* coped in adversity, and accepted the higher risk of air attack. Attacks from Allied aircraft were disruptive rather than overwhelmingly destructive.

Strategic bombing of ports, naval installations, and U-boat assembly yards demonstrated the limitations of Allied air power. Earlier bombing raids in France had proved ineffective against reinforced concrete submarine pens.[35] Once completed, these structures were almost impervious to most Allied gravity bombs, even the 12,000-pound 'Tallboy'. The Germans increased the thickness of protective roofs and built burster beams and deflection screens to minimize penetration.[36] With these improvements, bombing just became wasted effort. When Churchill and the Admiralty suggested attacks against U-boat shelters at Trondheim and Bergen in late 1944, Bomber Command and the US 8th Air Force were less than enthusiastic.[37] In terms of actual destruction, strategic bombing of cities and industries brought better results.

Nonetheless, the urgent need to delay the anticipated introduction of new U-boats grudgingly brought some priority, somewhere near sixth on the overall strategic bombing list. Concentrated attacks began on U-boat shelters and main building yards at Hamburg, Bremen, Wilhelmshaven, Kiel, and Danzig.[38] For small warships and submarines safely ensconced in protective bunkers, bombing raids met only minimal success. Unfinished shelters and prefabricated U-boats in various stages of assembly on exposed slipways, however, proved more vulnerable. Besides the direct effects of blast and explosions, strategic bombing interrupted work schedules, and caused numerous minor delays in the delivery of completed submarines.[39] The Germans tried to disperse assembly work to different locations as much as possible, but the use of shipbuilding and repair facilities in the main ports remained essential for fitting out warships and submarines. Combined with the systematic devastation of transportation networks and petroleum industries, strategic bombing against naval targets caused dislocation.

The strategic air forces scored some spectacular successes against larger warships. In Operation 'Catechism' on 12 November 1944 Lancasters of Bomber Command's 617th Squadron capsized the battleship *Tirpitz* in Tromsö Fjord, Norway, with several direct hits from 12,000-pound bombs.[40] The *Tirpitz*'s destruction removed a major threat to the Arctic convoys, and allowed release of larger British warships for service in the Pacific. Soon after, the German naval staff transferred the remaining surface vessels from Norwegian waters to the Baltic to support encircled land armies and evacuate refugees.

Often immobile in ports for lack of fuel and ammunition, these warships became prime targets for Allied strategic bombing raids in the final weeks of the war. The *Kriegsmarine* lost its major warships in quick succession: the ruined battle-cruiser *Gneisenau* was scuttled as a block-ship in Gdynia harbour; the Royal Air Force capsized the pocket battleship *Admiral Scheer* in dry dock, severely damaged the light cruiser *Emden*, and reduced the heavy cruiser *Admiral Hipper* to a smouldering wreck in Kiel; American bombers sank the light cruiser *Köln* at dock in Wilhelmshaven; and Soviet aircraft ravaged the old battleship *Schlesien* and the unfinished heavy cruiser *Lützow* at Swinemünde.[41] Compared to discouraging attacks on concrete submarine pens, heavy bombs proved remarkably effective against large, stationary warships, particularly when depleted anti-aircraft defences allowed accurate bomb runs. The abandoned and poorly defended surface ships were easy prey for Allied bombs.

Destruction of so many major warships created optimism within the Admiralty. The First Sea Lord had feared that the *Kriegsmarine*'s surface fleet, when faced with certain defeat, might attempt a last desperate sortie through the Straits of Dover to attack Allied shipping, similar to Admiral Reinhard Scheer's foiled death ride in 1918.[42] The idea may appear far-fetched in retrospect, but the Admiralty took the threat seriously. Arrangements were made to counter a possible breakout by German warships under the code-name 'Broomstick'.[43] The successes of Allied bombing against the *Kriegsmarine*'s major surface ships now appeared to remove the threat.

The First Sea Lord even doubted whether any German warships would remain at the time of the surrender. Since the Admiralty's intention was to scrap the entire fleet, vessels lost to air attacks were simply less to worry about later.[44] The sinkings, however, must be kept in perspective. Removal of crews for service in U-boats or naval infantry brigades indicated that naval authorities had already given up on the large warships. Possessing neither resources nor time to repair worn-out and damaged surface vessels, the *Kriegsmarine* concentrated on keeping surviving destroyers, motor torpedo boats, minesweepers, armed trawlers, and U-boats operational. Smaller warships enjoyed the protection of concrete shelters, were easily dispersed or camouflaged, and used manoeuvrability or the ability to submerge to escape air attacks. Whatever Cunningham's private views, air attacks were no substitute for the final defeat and disarmament of the *Kriegsmarine*.

Besides continuing the war at sea, the *Kriegsmarine* assumed a major part in the defence of Germany proper during the last months of the war. The German Supreme Command, the *Oberkommando der Wehrmacht* (OKW), became concerned about possible Allied landings on the Dutch, German, and Danish coasts.[45] Accordingly, naval authorities strengthened coastal defences and flotillas of strike craft. Fast motor torpedo boats and small battle units operated against Allied sea communications from bases in Holland and north-west Germany.[46] Steady advances by Allied armies, however, threatened to cut off these locations from the front-lines. To meet this contingency, Brunsbüttel, Cuxhaven, Wesermünde, Wilhelmshaven, Emden, Delfizjl, as well as the islands of Sylt, Helgoland, Wangerooge, Norderney, and Borkum were declared naval fortresses.[47] Taking over general defensive measures, German authorities formed improvised naval infantry brigades to meet Canadian and British troops. Adolf Hitler ordered that command positions in the western area 'should be filled mainly by naval officers, since many fortresses have been given up, but no ships were ever lost without fighting to the last man.'[48] Defiant garrisons in surrounded ports and the Channel Islands provided examples for further resistance. On 8 March a naval force under Vizeadmiral Friedrich Hüffmeier conducted a raid from Guernsey against the French port of Granville, destroying harbour facilities, freeing German prisoners of war, and carrying off ships in prize.[49] Even in hopeless situations, the *Kriegsmarine* attempted the seemingly impossible.

The *Kriegsmarine*'s evacuation of soldiers and refugees from the eastern Baltic was little short of miraculous. Soviet offensives left German forces in a series of isolated pockets along the coast. The sea became the only means of reinforcement, supply, and ultimately escape. Konteradmiral Conrad Engelhardt, the chief of sea transport, took charge of naval rescue operations in the Baltic.[50] All available war and merchant ships were pressed into service. The heavy cruiser *Prinz Eugen* and other surface vessels bombarded shore targets in support of the army.[51] As a result, the *Kriegsmarine* saved several million soldiers and civilians from the Soviet assault on East Prussia. A few ships were lost. The Soviet submarine S-13 sank the overloaded liners *Wilhelm Gustloff* and *General von Steuben*, killing or drowning almost 10,000.[52] Since the alternative was Soviet captivity and retribution, many Germans accepted the risk of death in sea or air attacks. Humanitarian efforts in the Baltic allowed the *Kriegsmarine* to finish the war with the enduring gratitude of the German people.

The evacuation was just one of many signs that the war for Nazi Germany was irretrievably lost. Bit by bit, German government agencies, service channels, and administrative arrangements broke down under the cumulative weight of strategic bombing and the advances of Allied land armies. Stepping into the void, the naval staff took over coal transportation, care and storage of petroleum products, operation of ports, and reinforcement of land fronts.[53] The *Kriegsmarine*'s command structure remained intact. General orders exhorted officers and sailors to continue performing their duties for the good of the German nation.[54] Although a pretence to final victory remained, even the most stalwart defenders realized that defeat was near. Based upon an assessment of British and American port clearance efforts, the naval staff recommended use of sea mines and block-ships rather than demolitions to deny harbour facilities to the Allies.[55] The *Kriegsmarine*, which had systematically wrecked French and Italian ports before surrender, was less enthusiastic about destroying German installations. In order to preserve the ports for future use, naval authorities ignored Hitler's general destruction orders.[56] The change ensured that port facilities in north-west Germany and the occupied countries survived for the Royal Navy's control parties.

The question of personnel for the 'Eclipse' naval parties finally achieved some resolution. In discussions about accommodation, staff officers from the Commander-in-Chief Nore and the ANCXF post-hostilities staff stressed the need for 'complete parties being in "formation" establishments for a period before they are required to move to their embarkation point.'[57] Only the naval party for Hamburg approached such a state because the Admiralty still had not decided on final numbers. Military planners, dissatisfied with the Admiralty's blatant attempt to pass the burden on to the army, forced the issue. The 21st Army Group's detailed 'Eclipse' plan, distributed at the end of January, provided assistance to naval forces within the limits of military resources and after consideration of other commitments.[58] In effect, 21st

Army Group formally opted out of previous understandings. The plan made the Royal Navy directly responsible for guarding warships, merchant ships, and Allied naval establishments.[59] Since more personnel meant vastly enlarged naval parties, the Admiralty naturally took the news badly. Even worse, ANCXF openly supported 21st Army Group.[60] The Admiralty appeared to be shirking its duties in the control and disarmament of the *Kriegsmarine* in favour of other operational priorities.

After considerable posturing and heated debate, the Admiralty reluctantly consented to use the 116th and 117th Royal Marine Brigades – currently under 21st Army Group's operational control – on the condition that later redeployment to the Far East was not postponed.[61] The compromise, which closely resembled Ramsay's earlier request, reflected the perseverance of the ANCXF post-hostilities staff, supporters inside the Admiralty, and 21st Army Group. Provision of personnel for German naval disarmament was never given, but represented a protracted struggle over scarce resources within the Royal Navy.

The British lagged behind the Americans in actual formation of the main naval parties. Ghormley and his staff submitted naval occupation plans in January and early February.[62] Stark immediately released American personnel from existing complements in Great Britain and on the Continent to fill US naval parties for Bremen and Bremerhaven, designated collectively as Task Force 126. Officers and other ranks began language courses, attended lectures on German history and military government, and undertook speciality training at the US naval base in Rosneath, Scotland.[63] Intensive instruction over many months provided American naval personnel with rudimentary background knowledge for occupation tasks in Germany. The ANCXF post-hostilities staff intended to integrate the movement of American and British naval parties from Great Britain to the Continent.[64] Nevertheless, the Admiralty's reluctance in releasing personnel delayed proper organization and training of British naval parties.

ANCXF became anxious about timely provision of British naval personnel for surrender, control, and disarmament duties. The Admiralty finally agreed to 4,480 officers and other ranks for the main port parties and the Control Commission in Berlin, a number close to ANCXF's previous minimum estimates.[65] Since this allocation was only in principle, actual personnel were not forthcoming. Parry, who requested immediate establishment of advance reconnaissance parties, suggested that 'some acceleration in the tempo of preparations is now advisable.'[66] Yet, the Admiralty cited manpower stringency to refuse release of personnel. Although selected naval officers attended classes at Army and Royal Air Force occupation schools, the vast majority of sailors remained in depots without assigned billets.[67] The Admiralty held on to personnel until the last possible moment, on the slim chance that they might not be needed in Germany.

The strategic situation eventually forced the Admiralty into action. When Eisenhower ordered American naval parties to proceed to the Continent in early March, the British naval parties were not even formed.[68] As resistance slowly disintegrated, the British and American armies prepared to cross the Rhine River into Germany. Asking SHAEF for a probable date for the start of 'Eclipse', ANCXF stated that 'an error on the early side would at least have the advantage of jolting those who are a bit slow in the uptake'.[69] The comment was obviously directed towards certain persons in the Admiralty. In response, SHAEF told the Royal Navy to be ready at one week's notice after 15 April.

The projection accentuated the Admiralty's utter lack of arrangements. Burrough responded that 22 May was the earliest date possible for arrival in Germany 'and if parties were urgently required earlier than this date they could only be provided at the expense of their training and satisfactory equipment.'[70] As SHAEF quickly pointed out, everything depended on the Germans, who seemed almost on the verge of collapse. Syfret approved release of personnel for north-west ports on 29 March, followed a few days later by personnel for Baltic ports.[71] Cunningham finally conceded that personnel had to be made available for the work in Germany. British naval parties formed just as the Americans left for the Continent.[72]

The ANCXF post-hostilities staff hastily threw together port and control parties. As personnel collected in camps in the south-east of England, it became evident that the Admiralty had taken the opportunity to send the oldest sailors from the naval barracks. Rear-Admiral Harold Tom Baillie-Grohman, RN, the Flag Officer Kiel designate, commented on the personnel chosen for his party:

> It was very unusual at this period of the war to find even a half dozen two-badge men serving in a ship the size of a cruiser, so the spectacle of these splendid types fallen in at assembly camps, all with badges to their credit, was a rare and refreshing one.[73]

Although it was probably not the intention, these mature sailors were in fact well-suited to the prospective work. Besides, their background and experience alleviated some deficiencies in training; many were specialists or were familiar with what the navy expected. Older married men were much more likely to follow SHAEF's strict non-fraternization policy than their younger counterparts. The assignment in Germany was simply another berth in lengthy careers with the Royal Navy.[74] Given the delay in formation, the Royal Navy could do little better.

The Royal Navy's intention was to send the naval parties by land in the vanguard of 21st Army Group. The danger from mines and other obstacles in sea approaches to ports and a shortage of air lift capacity precluded alternative conveyance.[75] As land forces steadily advanced towards German ports, the Royal Navy's absence became disconcerting for military authorities. Planners at 21st Army Group decided that 'the Naval parties should try to be ready by 7 April.'[76] The Admiralty's belated formation of naval parties, however, made the suggestion quite unrealistic. Commodore England's Hamburg contingent was the sole British naval party sufficiently organized for transport.[77] The others required more training and preparation. A revised 'Eclipse' naval plan, issued on 10 April, set out the objectives and responsibilities of the respective naval commands.[78] Sufficient progress was made to allow ANCXF to adjust its earlier estimates. Burrough informed SHAEF that the 'majority of British naval parties could in [an] emergency, be at one week's notice from 20 April.'[79] In the meantime, selected naval officers left for liaison duties with Canadian and British armies.

The Admiralty and ANCXF assumed that German ports and naval bases along the North Sea would be captured first. Therefore, Rear-Admiral Gerard Charles Muirhead-Gould, RN, the Flag Officer Wilhelmshaven designate, became naval liaison officer at 21st Army Group's main headquarters, serving as Burrough's representative 'in all matters concerning the occupation of German ports and the disarmament of German naval forces.'[80] His job was to ensure effective coordination between the Royal Navy and military forces and to call forward naval parties at appropriate times. Naval officers assigned to perform similar functions were attached to the 1st Canadian and 2nd British Armies.[81]

Military forces continued offensive operations into Germany. On 22 April Montgomery issued an operational directive to 21st Army Group for the 'capture of Emden, Bremen, Hamburg, and Lübeck, and to clean up all German territory north of this general line.'[82] German ports were expected to be in Allied hands within the next fortnight. Military planners anticipated that Emden would most likely capitulate first to 2nd Canadian Corps.

ANCXF decided to move the North Sea port parties across the Channel immediately. Eisenhower informed Burrough that the 'Eclipse' plan, 'as appropriate to current operations, will be put into effect without delay.'[83] The post-hostilities planning was now formally activated. Fortunately, the Admiral Superintendent at Chatham had sent stores and equipment for the naval parties to Antwerp aboard the merchant ship *Empire Snowdrop* earlier in the month.[84] After receiving khaki battledress with Royal Navy flashes, webbing, and rations, officers and naval ratings departed from Tilbury Docks for Ostend on 21 April in sea transports and landing craft. The naval parties then waited in former cavalry stables, converted into a naval concentration area under the authority of Captain Percival James, RN, at Bourg Léopold near Brussels until called forward by naval liaison officers or military authorities.[85] The time allowed further training, checking of stores, and maintenance on Royal Navy-allocated motor transport.

The Royal Navy also deployed a special naval commando formation to seize ports and naval installations of particular intelligence value before destruction by the Germans. The so-called 30th Assault Unit was the brainchild of Commander Ian Fleming, RNVR, stockbroker in civil life, personal assistant to the Director of Naval Intelligence, and later writer of the popular James Bond spy novels.[86] Intelligence work appealed to his lively imagination. Although dismissing most of Fleming's ideas as outrageous or impractical, Godfrey and his successor, Rear-Admiral Edmund Rushbrooke, RN, supported formation of a small naval commando unit to accompany Allied military forces into captured ports. Inspired by the chance finally to prove his ideas, Fleming recruited a motley collection of Arctic explorers, adventurers, linguists, Royal Marines, and technical experts.[87] These men underwent specialized training in the finer arts of explosives and intelligence in Canada, the United States, and Great Britain. Fleming even hired a professional criminal to teach lock-picking and safe-cracking. As part of combined service intelligence organizations known as 'T' forces, Fleming's private army obtained valuable items and information for the Royal Navy in North Africa, Italy, and Normandy.[88] After the success of 'Overlord', the 30th Assault Unit withdrew to re-equip and train in Great Britain for the final offensive against Germany.

The 30th Assault Unit worked in conjunction with other formations devoted to discovery and accumulation of naval intelligence. In early 1945 the US Navy established a naval technical mission, comprising naval officers and civilian technical specialists under the authority of Commodore H.A. Schade, USN, to exploit naval, industrial, and scientific establishments after capture.[89] Mindful of the war against Japan, the Americans were particularly interested in equipment and information of immediate operational value. Both the Royal Navy and US Navy also employed forward interrogation units to question German prisoners of war. A naval intelligence sub-section within the G-2 Division at SHAEF's main headquarters coordinated the activities of the various naval intelligence bodies.[90] The 30th Assault Unit fell under this naval intelligence umbrella organization.

Accordingly, the 30th Assault Unit enjoyed considerable autonomy for the work in Germany. Returning to the Continent in early February, an advanced party established a headquarters at Baisy-Thy near Brussels.[91] No longer part of any 'T' force, the 30th Assault Unit was directly responsible to ANCXF and the Admiralty. In other words, the Royal Navy was its own boss. The 30th Assault Unit used blanket authorization from Eisenhower to travel anywhere it wanted.[92] Toting a variety of British and captured German weapons, naval detachments ranged across the countryside in jeeps, lorries, and Humber scout cars. Specific targets were identified and seized according to a Black List, prepared previously in the Admiralty from captured documents, interrogations, and signals intelligence.[93] The 30th Assault Unit relied on speed and surprise to seize required installations. Often in front of the advancing military forces, the Royal Navy's detachments suffered surprisingly few losses. German prisoners of war at Bakum told Commander Patrick Dalzel Job, RNVR, leader of the 30th Assault Unit's fourth team, that 'they had not opened fire because we looked dangerous – an interesting comment on our tactics.'[94] The 30th Assault Unit's detachments brazenly raced through German lines towards ports and naval bases.

As a result, the 30th Assault Unit was at the forefront of the entry into German ports. On 26 April Job's team accepted the surrender of Bremen from the city's acting Bürgermeister, and then blitzed the dockyard to find sixteen Type XXI U-boats and two destroyers under construction in the Deschimag shipyard.[95] Taken completely by surprise, the Germans had no opportunity to implement destruction or scuttling measures. An American naval party, commanded by Captain V.H. Godfrey, USN, arrived in Bremen the next day to survey Bremen's port facilities.[96] With completion of this task, the naval detachment moved on to the next objective. Spotting Job again in the British advance column, General Sir Brian Horrocks, commanding British 30th Corps, gave his 'compliments, and would I please let the General enter Bremerhaven first?'[97] The 30th Assault Unit, which gained a reputation for audaciousness and force of purpose, proved a remarkably effective instrument in the capture of naval installations. German naval authorities generally preferred dealing with the Royal Navy rather than military forces. The 30th Assault Unit provided an early British naval presence.

The unexpected course of operations led some British naval authorities to make *ad hoc* arrangements. In an effort to trap German forces in Schleswig-Holstein and Denmark, British military forces crossed the Elbe River in a strong drive towards Lübeck.[98] Unfortunately, naval parties for Baltic ports were still in England. Deciding not to wait any longer for the Admiralty, Baillie-Grohman sent his intelligence staff officer, Lieutenant-Commander C. Blackler, RN, to make contact with the headquarters of Lieutenant-General Sir E.H. Barker's British 8th

Corps, established somewhere beyond the Elbe. Carrying two cardboard boxes of food obtained from a nearby London grocer and dressed in navy blues, Blackler unofficially travelled in a motor torpedo boat to Ostend, and then hitch-hiked to Germany, arriving in 8th Corp's operational area early on 25 April.[99] Pending Baillie-Grohman's arrival, Blackler advised Barker on all naval matters.

This unauthorized trip was fortuitous because British military forces captured ports on the Baltic before the end of hostilities. Late on 2 May Blackler entered Lübeck with advance units from British 11th Armoured Division against no active resistance.[100] He found the senior German naval officer dead in the port office from an apparent suicide. Although many U-boats, torpedo boats, and other ships were scuttled in Lübeck Bay, Allied prisoners of war from a nearby German camp guarded the dock and harbour facilities. A ghastly sight awaited Blackler in nearby Neustadt: British Typhoons sank the ships *Cap Arcona*, *Deutschland*, and *Athens* anchored in the harbour, drowning almost 7,000 concentration camp inmates, prisoners of war, and forced workers; the Germans then shot or clubbed the survivors to death.[101] Fregattenkapitän Heinrich Schmidt, the senior officer at Neustadt, blamed the act on the SS. Nonetheless, Baillie-Grohman, who arrived downstream at Travemünde on 3 May, recommended Schmidt's arrest.[102] The British flag officer controlled German warships and sailors in Lübeck and Travemünde with the assistance of cooperative German naval authorities and several British tanks until arrival of the main naval parties.

One by one, British naval parties departed from Bourg Léopold in convoys for designated ports. With the rapid advances of British military forces, preparations ceased for Operation 'Red Admiral', a planned airborne assault on the Kiel Canal.[103] The Royal Navy instead approached from land. In trucks and cars, naval parties drove for several days on congested and crowded roads. One British sailor described the journey as 'a real eye opener, such devastation everywhere.'[104] Strategic bombing had reduced many German cities to little more than rubble. On 1 May Waldock reported that most naval parties were under way and the Control Commission's headquarters staff was filling satisfactorily.[105] The activity was opportune because the Germans appeared ready to give up.

The British entered talks for the surrender of Hamburg, Germany's largest commercial port. On 3 May German military and naval representatives turned over the city to Lieutenant-General Sir Miles Dempsey and 2nd British Army.[106] Hamburg's important port facilities and docks were intact because Gauleiter Karl Kaufmann, the former Reichkommissar for sea transport, and Konteradmiral Hans Bütow, Hamburg's senior naval officer, refused to carry out Hitler's demolition orders. Captain Arthur Hoyer Alexander, RN, left his liaison position at

2nd British Army to become Hamburg's port superintendent.[107] Besides large numbers of wrecks, the harbour contained three *Sperrbrecher*, five fleet auxiliaries, and twenty-four merchant ships. In the meantime, the German High Command took advantage of the negotiations with Dempsey to send a delegation of senior officers to explore the possibility of an area surrender to the British.[108] Hamburg was the beginning of the end.

NOTES

1. OAB/NHC, Kirk, Series IV, Box 31, File 'Correspondence: Establishment of Command 1944', Announcement by Brigadier-General T.J. Davis, US Army, SHAEF Adjutant General, 'Temporary Appointment of Vice-Admiral A.G. Kirk, USN, as Allied Naval Commander Expeditionary Force', 16 Jan. 1945.
2. OHRO/Columbia, Transcript of Interviews with Admiral Alan Kirk, 1962, p. 225. BL, Cunningham, Add. Ms. 52578, Diary, 8 Jan. 1945.
3. NA, RG 331, SHAEF, Office of Chief of Staff, Secretary, General Staff, File 201, Message from ANCXF to AIG 514, COMNAVEU, Commander-in-Chief Rosyth, Commander-in-Chief Mediterranean, SHAEF Main, ANCXF(PH), ANCXF(BUCO), ANCXF(COTUG), Naval Advisor to British Embassy, Paris, 19 1848A Jan. 1945. Chandler and Ambrose, Vol. 4, p. 2436. Michael Simpson, ed., *The Somerville Papers: Selections from the Private and Official Correspondence of Admiral of the Fleet Sir James Somerville, GCB, GBE, DSO*, (Aldershot: Scholar Press, Navy Records Society, 1995), p. 627. PRO, ADM 199/628, Admiral Blake War Diary, Serial No. 340, 17 Jan. 1945.
4. CCAC, CUNN 5/2, Letter from Admiral Andrew Cunningham to Vice-Admiral Harold Burrough, 4 Feb. 1943. BL, Cunningham, Add. Ms. 52571, Letter from Admiral Andrew Cunningham to Admiral Geoffrey Blake, 9 May 1944.
5. Martin Stephen, *The Fighting Admirals: British Admirals of the Second World War*, (Annapolis: Naval Institute Press, 1991), p. 23. Burrough liked the appointment. BL, Cunningham, Add. Ms. 52578, Diary, 16 Jan. 1945.
6. IWM, DS/Misc/4, Admiral Harold Martin Burrough, RN, Notes for Press Conference given by Admiral Sir Harold Martin Burrough, ANCXF, 30 Jan. 1945.
7. NA, RG 331, SHAEF, ANCXF War Diary, 8 March 1945. The Admiralty had arranged Mansergh's departure before Ramsay's death. CCAC, RMSY 8/27B, Letter from Admiral Bertram Ramsay to Wife, 13 Dec. 1944.
8. PRO, ADM 1/18635, Memorandum from Rear-Admiral W.E. Parry to Secretary of Admiralty, 'Formation and Lift of "ECLIPSE" Parties', 22 Jan. 1945.
9. PRO, ADM 1/16186, Staff Minute by H.K. Oran, Director of Tactical and Staff Duties Division, 24 Jan. 1945.
10. PRO, ADM 1/16186, Staff Minute by H.R. Williams for Director of Plans, 8 Feb. 1945.
11. Christopher Duffy, *Red Storm on the Reich: The Soviet March on Germany, 1945*, (London: Routledge, 1991), p. 57.
12. Gerhard L. Weinberg, 'German Plans for Victory, 1944–45', *Central European History* 26(1993), p. 221.
13. PRO, ADM 205/44, Memorandum from First Sea Lord to Vice-Admiral G.C. Jones, RCN, 'Forecast of the U-Boat Campaign During 1945', 25 Jan. 1945. PRO, ADM 199/628, Admiral Blake War Diary, Serial No. 344, 1 Feb. 1945. Marc Milner, 'The Dawn of Modern Anti-Submarine Warfare: Allied Responses to the U-Boats, 1944–45', *Royal United Services Institution Journal* 134(1989), p. 67. The expected date of the German submarine offensive was later extended. CCAC, Commander H.J. Fawcett, RN, FWCT 2/4/6, 'Possibilities of Coming U/B Offensive during April '45'.

14. PRO, ADM 1/19125, Office Memorandum, 'Planning Date for End of German War. Revised Assumptions', 1 Feb. 1945.
15. NAC, RG 24, Vol. 11,752, File G38-2, Minutes of 64th Meeting U-Boat Warfare Committee, 26 April 1945.
16. CCS, Reel 3, Frame 235, Minutes of 186th Meeting Combined Chiefs of Staff, 6 Feb. 1945.
17. CCS, Reel 3, Frame 264, Minutes of 1st Tripartite Military Meeting at Yalta, 5 Feb. 1945. King thought that Kuznetsov was taunting the British, and he sarcastically asked what great achievements the Red Navy had achieved in the Baltic against the Germans. Ernest J. King and Walter Muir Whitehill, *Fleet Admiral King: A Naval Record*, (New York: W.W. Norton & Co., 1952), p. 589.
18. Chandler and Ambrose, Vol. 4, p. 2433.
19. CCS, Reel 3, Frame 223, Minutes of 184th Meeting Combined Chiefs of Staff, 1 Feb. 1945. Control of the American and British strategic air forces had reverted to the Combined Chiefs of Staff in Sept. 1944 through CCS 520/6.
20. CCS, Reel 3, Frame 153, CCS 774/3, 'U-Boat Threat During 1945', 2 Feb. 1945. John Terraine, *The Right of the Line: The Royal Air Force in the European War 1939–1945*, (London: Hodder & Stoughton, 1985), p. 680.
21. PRO, ADM 1/18996, Operations Division, Admiralty, 'Offensive Minelaying Northern European Waters and Mediterranean 3 Sept. 1939–5 May 1945,' 28 May 1945. Tom Burton, 'The Development of a British Air-Laid Ground Mine,' *Warship* 6(1978), p. 138.
22. G. Skinner, 'Aerial Minelaying: Possibly the Most Potent Sea Warfare Technique for the UK', *Royal United Services Institution Journal* 126(1981), p. 57.
23. Great Britain, *Royal Air Force: Final Reports on Operations – Night Raids* (hereafter RAF), (Wilmington, DE: Scholarly Resources Inc., 1977), Reel 4, Frame 492, Night Raid Report No. 556, 'Bomber Command Report on Night Operations 18/19 March 1944', 15 June 1944.
24. NAC, RG 24, Vol. 11,752, File G38-2, Minutes of 61st Meeting U-Boat Warfare Committee, 15 March 1945. Bomber Command laid 17,000 mines between August 1944 and the end of the war. NAC, RG 24, Vol. 11,752, File G38-2, Minutes of 65th Meeting U-Boat Warfare Committee, 10 May 1945.
25. L.R.N. Ashley, 'The Royal Air Force and Sea Mining in World War II', *Air University Quarterly Review* 14(1963), pp. 38–48. DHist, File 181.003(D488), 'Attacks on Targets Appertaining to Naval Warfare by Bomber Command Aircraft', 11 Jan. 1945. 'Enemy Casualties caused by British Mines during the War', *Naval Review* 34(1946), pp. 249–50.
26. CCAC, DENM 1, Captain Henry M. Denham, RN, 'War Narrative: Naval Attaché Stockholm', p. 100.
27. Bundesarchiv-Militärarchiv (hereafter BA/MA), Vizeadmiral Friedrich Ruge, N 379/244, 'Die Wirksamkeit der englischen Minenoffensive', 1950, pp. 6–7.
28. NA, RG 331, SHAEF, ANCXF War Diary, 30 March and 9 April 1945.
29. IWM, P. 34, Marshal of the RAF Sir Sholto Douglas, Box 6, 'Despatch by Marshal of the Royal Air Force Sir Sholto Douglas, GCB, MC, DFC, (Lord Douglas of Kirtleside) on the Air Operations Undertaken by Coastal Command from Jan., 1944 to May, 1945'.
30. Christina Goulter, 'The Role of Intelligence in Coastal Command's Anti-Shipping Campaign, 1940–1945', *Intelligence and National Security* 5(1990), p. 103. DHist 181.003 (D927), Coastal Command Intelligence Summary, 1 July 1945, pp. 5–6.
31. Christina Goulter, *A Forgotten Offensive: Royal Air Force Coastal Command's Anti-Shipping Campaign, 1940–1945*, (London and Portland, OR: Frank Cass, 1995), p. 260.
32. Ian Gooderson, 'Allied Fighter-Bombers Versus German Armour in North-West Europe 1944–1945: Myths and Realities', *Journal of Strategic Studies* 14(1991), pp. 211–13.
33. Piotr N. Pospelov, ed., *History of the Great Patriotic War of the Soviet Union*

1941–1945, (Wilmington, DE: Scholarly Resources Inc., 1985), Reel 5, Vol. 5, p. 233. The Soviet naval air arm disrupted German sea communications, supported amphibious landings with the Red Army, and attacked German warships. V.I. Achkasov and N.B. Pavlovich, *Soviet Naval Operations in the Great Patriotic War 1941–1945*, (Annapolis: Naval Institute Press, 1981), p. 249.

34. BA/MA, RM 7/850, Memorandum from Vizeadmiral Karl Hoffmann, Mrüst OKM, to Adm zbv beim ObdM; Chef Mrüst; 1/SKL; 2/SKL; Flotte; Kd Admiral U-Boote, 'Überblick über den Stand der Waffen- und Munitions Beschaffungslage', 15 April 1945.

35. Josef W. Konvitz, 'Bombs, Cities, and Submarines: Allied Bombing of the French Ports, 1942–1943', *International History Review* 14(1992), p. 43.

36. DHist, File 1650 – U-Boats 1945, Staff Officer Operational Records, Canadian Naval Mission Overseas, 'Report on German U-Boat Shelters Bay of Biscay Ports', 7 June 1945.

37. NA, RG 331, SHAEF, Office of the Chief of Staff, Secretary, General Staff, File 600.6, Memorandum by Major Donald F. Forbes, 'Air Attack against Submarine Pens at Bergen and Trondheim', 11 Nov. 1944. Wesley Frank Craven and James Lea Cate, *The Army Air Forces in World War II*, Vol. 3, *Europe: Argument to V-E Day January 1944 to May 1945*, (Chicago: University of Chicago Press, 1951), pp. 720–1. Chandler and Ambrose, Vol. 4, p. 2279. Stafford Cripps acknowledged 'that the liaison between the Admiralty and the Air Ministry on bombing naval targets required improving.', BL, Cunningham, Add. Ms. 52577, Diary, 19 Dec. 1944.

38. PRO, ADM 205/44, Memorandum from Assistant Chief of Naval Staff (U-Boat Warfare and Trade) to First Sea Lord, 'Intended Bombing of U-Boat Shelters and Building Slips and Installations', 24 Jan. 1945.

39. Great Britain Ministry of Defence (Navy), Günter Hessler, *The U-Boat War in the Atlantic 1939–1945*, (London: Her Majesty's Stationery Office, 1989), p. 94.

40. Great Britain Historical Section, Tactical and Staff Duties Division, Naval Staff, Admiralty, *Preliminary Narrative: The War at Sea*, Vol. 5, 1946, p. 544. OAB/NHC, US Naval Technical Mission in Europe, Series III, Box 26, Technical Report No. 222-45, Commander T.G. Springer, USN, and Lieutenant(jg) E.B. Hitchcock, USNR, 'Loss of the German Battleship Tirpitz 12 November 1944'. Love and Major, p. 173. Gerhard Wagner, 'Überlegungen der deutschen Marineführung zum Einsatz und Verlust der Schlachtschiffe während des Zweiten Weltkrieges', *Militärgeschichtliche Mitteilungen* 15(1974), p. 108. Michael Salewski, 'Das Ende der deutschen Schlachtschiffe im Zweiten Weltkrieg', *Militärgeschichtliche Mitteilungen* 12(1972), pp. 71–2.

41. W.M. James, *The British Navies in the Second World War*, (London: Longman's Green & Co., 1946), p. 202. RAF, Reel 5, Frames 727–8, Night Raid Report No. 887 'Bomber Command Report on Night Operations 9/10 April 1945', 1 June 1945.

42. PRO, ADM 205/49, Draft Letter from Secretary of Admiralty to First Sea Lord, 'Possible Breakout of the German Fleet', 19 March 1945. BL, Cunningham, Add. Ms. 52578, Diary, 20 March 1945. Holger H. Herwig, *'Luxury' Fleet: The Imperial German Navy 1888-1918*, (London: George Allen and Unwin, 1980), p. 248.

43. PRO, ADM 1/18989, Letter from Admiralty to Commanders-in-Chief Home Fleet, Nore, Portsmouth, Rosyth, Plymouth, Western Approaches, Air Officer Commander-in-Chief Coastal Command, Flag Officer Submarines, Flag Officer Naval Air Stations, 28 March 1945.

44. PRO, ADM 1/16180, Minute from C.H.M. Waldock to Director of Plans, 16 March 1945. Warships continued as legitimate targets, but Burrough curtailed bombing attacks against merchant ships because the British and Americans intended to use captured shipping in the Pacific. NA, RG 331, SHAEF, ANCXF War Diary, 20 April 1945.

45. BA/MA, RM 7/158, Message from Generaloberst Alfred Jodl, OKW WFSt/Ops to OKM 1/SKL, 'Die Anzeichen für mögliche Landungsabsichten des Engländers im

Raum von Emden', 19 1630 March 1945. OAB/NHC, German Naval Staff, Operations Division, Reel TM-100-P, Part A, 1/SKL Kriegstagebuch, 19 March 1945. Lack of naval fire support prevented the Royal Navy from undertaking amphibious landings on the Frisian islands. PRO, WO 205/704, 'Notes on Conference held at SHAEF between BGS (Plans), 21 Army Group and Army and Naval Representatives at SHAEF', 12 Dec. 1944.

46. V.E. Tarrant, *The Last Year of the Kriegsmarine: May 1944–May 1945*, (London: Arms & Armour, 1994), pp. 217–24.

47. BA/MA, RM 7/158, Message from Kapitän zur See Heinz Assmann, OKW WFSt/Ops to GKdos, 27 2255 March 1945.

48. Great Britain. Admiralty, *Fuehrer Conferences on Naval Affairs 1945*, (London: Admiralty, August 1947), p. 92. BA/MA, RM 7/850, Message from Generalfeldmarschall Wilhelm Keitel to 1/SKL Krokodil; Führungstab Nordküste, 07 1735 April 1945.

49. OAB/NHC, German Naval Staff, Operations Division, Reel TM-100-P, Part A, 1/SKL Kriegstagebuch, 10 March 1945. Percy Ernst Schramm, ed., *Kriegstagebuch des Oberkommandos der Wehrmacht (Wehrmachtführungsstab)*, Vol. 4/2, (Frankfurt am Main: Bernard und Graefe Verlag für Wehrwesen, 1961), p. 1162. PRO, ADM 1/18113, Memorandum from Admiral Harold Burrough to SHAEF, 'Enemy Raid on Granville', 24 March 1945. BA/MA, Ruge N 379/322, Letter from Vizeadmiral Friedrich Ruge to Commander M.G. Saunders, Historical Section, Admiralty, 'The Raid on Granville', 15 March 1952. Morison, Vol. 11, p. 308. The First Sea Lord adopted a nonchalant attitude towards Hüffmeier's raid: 'Betty Stark asked me if I was at all worried about raids from the Channel Islands. I think I rather shocked him by saying no.', BL, Cunningham, Add. Ms. 52578, Diary, 27 March 1945.

50. Charles W. Koburger, *Steel Ships, Iron Crosses and Refugees: The German Navy in the Baltic, 1939–1945*, (Westport, CT: Praeger, 1989), p. 80. BA/MA, Ruge, N 379/2, 'Bericht des Korv. Kapt. (Ing) Eggert, Kommandeur der 37. MEA über die Neuaufstellung der Abteilung in Gothafen'.

51. M.J. Whitley, *German Cruisers of World War Two*, (Annapolis: Naval Institute Press, 1985), p. 160.

52. Friedrich Ruge, *The Soviets as Naval Opponents 1941–45*, (Annapolis: Naval Institute Press, 1979), p. 52. Alfred M. De Zayas, *Nemesis at Potsdam: The Expulsion of the Germans from the East*, (Lincoln: University of Nebraska Press, 1988), pp. 74–5. Arthur V. Sellwood, *The Damned Don't Drown: The Sinking of the Wilhelm Gustloff*, (Annapolis: Naval Institute Press, 1996).

53. Salewski, *Seekriegsleitung*, Vol. 2, pp. 540–1. BA/MA, RM 6/113, 'Teilnahme des Ob.d.M. an der Führerlage am 16.3.1945 16,00 Uhr', 16 March 1945. NA, RG 242, T-1022, Reel 3438, File PG 31801f, Message from Grossadmiral Karl Dönitz to Admiral beim ObdM, 25 April 1945.

54. BA/MA, RW 17/79, Rotterdam Kommandanturbefehl Nr. 12, 23 March 1945.

55. BA/MA, RM 7/850, Memorandum from Chef 3/SKL to Chef SKL; 1/SKL; 1/SKL Ib; 3/SKL FL, 'Erfahrungen über Zerstörung bzw. Unbrauchbarmachung von Häfenanlagen', 13 April 1945. BA/MA, RM 7/851, Memorandum from Chef 3/SKL OKM to GKdos, 'Englische-amerikanische Anschauungen über die Wiederinbetriebnahme eroberter Häfen', 26 April 1945.

56. BA/MA, RM 6/113, 'Teilnahme des Ob.d.M. an der Führerlage am 23.3.45 16,00 Uhr', 24 March 1945. OAB/NHC, German Naval Staff, Operations Division, Reel TM-100-P, Part A, 1/SKL Kriegstagebuch, 20 March 1945.

57. PRO, ADM 1/18635, Memorandum from Rear-Admiral W.E. Parry to Secretary of Admiralty, 'Formation and Lift of ECLIPSE Parties', 22 Jan. 1945.

58. University of Victoria Archives and Special Collections (hereafter UVic), 21st Army Group, *Operation 'Eclipse': The Military Occupation of North-West Germany*, (Belgium: [s.n.], Jan. 1945).

59. PRO, ADM 1/17198, Letter from Rear-Admiral W.E. Parry to Secretary of Admiralty, 6 Feb. 1945.

60. PRO, WO 205/259, Letter from Admiral Harold Burrough to Secretary of Admiralty, 'ECLIPSE – Provision of Guards for Royal Navy in Germany', 2 March 1945.

61. PRO, ADM 1/17198, Letter from C.H.M Waldock to ANCXF, 15 March 1945. PRO, WO 205/259, Letter from Admiral Harold Burrough to Secretary of Admiralty, 'Guards for German Warships and Merchant Vessels', 30 March 1945.

62. NA, RG 331, SHAEF, General Staff, G-3 Division, Future Plans Section, File 17014/2/6, Commander US Naval Forces, Germany Operation Plan CTF 124, No. 1-45, 1 Jan. 1945. After initially occupying Bremen and Bremerhaven, 21st Army Group was to transfer responsibility to the US 9th Army and the US Navy. NA, RG 313, COMNAVEU, Series II, File 48, Memorandum from Vice-Admiral William Glassford to Admiral Harold Stark 'Twelfth Army Group ECLIPSE Operational Plan 1st Draft, dated 10 Jan 1945', 13 Feb. 1945.

63. Navy Department Library, Naval Historical Center (hereafter NDL/NHC), 'Administrative History, United States Naval Forces in Europe 1940-1946', Vol. 7, pp. 187–8.

64. NA, RG 331, SHAEF, G-4 Division, Plans Branch, File SHAEF/215/5/GDP-2 Bremen, Message from ANCXF(PH) to COMNAVFORFRANCE, 01 1815A Feb. 1945.

65. PRO, ADM 1/16186, Summary, 'Parties Required for Occupied Ports in Germany and Berlin Headquarters', 4 Feb. 1945.

66. PRO, ADM 1/18635, Memorandum from Rear-Admiral W.E. Parry to Secretary of Admiralty, 'Formation of ECLIPSE Naval Reconnaissance Parties', 18 Feb. 1945.

67. Alex H. Cherry, *Yankee R.N.*, (London: Jarrolds, 1951), pp. 492–5. PRO, FO 1038/126, Letter from Captain B.F. Adams to Brigadier C.A. Gueterbock, 'HQ – Port Parties: Training in the Naval Forces Division', 16 Dec. 1944.

68. OAB/NHC, Kirk, Series IV, Box 31, File 'Cragg, R.T. Lt., Flag Sec. 1944–1945: Correspondence, Misc.', Message from SHAEF Fwd signed Eisenhower to COMNAVEU, 08 1550A March 1945. PRO, ADM 1/18635, Staff Minute by J.L. Stovey, Director of Manpower, 6 March 1945.

69. NA, RG 331, SHAEF, Office of the Chief of Staff, Secretary, General Staff, File 381 Eclipse (Case No. 1) Misc., Memorandum from Commodore H.W. Faulkner to Lieutenant-General F.E. Morgan, 14 March 1945.

70. NA, RG 331, SHAEF, Special Staff, Adjutant General's Division, Executive Section, File 045-2, Message from ANCXF Main to SHAEF Fwd, 25 1645A March 1945. The naval parties required at least six weeks to form, train, and prepare. PRO, ADM 1/18635, Memorandum from Rear-Admiral W.E. Parry to Secretary of Admiralty, 'Provision of Personnel of ECLIPSE Naval Parties', 9 March 1945.

71. NA, RG 331, SHAEF, Special Staff, Adjutant General's Division, Executive Section, File 045-2, Message from ANCXF(PH) to ANCXF Main, EXFOR Main, 29 1738 March 1945. Ironically, the First Sea Lord was at the same time impressing on the Americans 'the necessity of opening the German northern ports & capturing them to hinder the U boat war...', BL, Cunningham, Add. Ms. 52578, Diary, 29 March 1945.

72. PRO, ADM 199/628, Admiral Blake War Diary, Serial No. 359, 30 March 1945.

73. IWM, Vice-Admiral Harold Tom Baillie-Grohman, RN, Memoirs, 'Flashlights on German Disarmament 1945/46', Vol. 3, p. 45.

74. IWM, Signalman John Knight, RN, 'Memories of a Miscreant', 17 Sept. 1984, pp. 88–90.

75. PRO, ADM 116/5300, ANCXF Post-Hostilities Planning Memorandum No. 14, 'Formation and Lift of Eclipse Naval Parties (British Only)', 5 Feb. 1945. PRO, WO 205/312, Memorandum from Commodore H.W. Faulkner to 21st Army Group Main, 'Placing Bids for Air Lift', 16 April 1945.

76. NAC, RG 24, Vol. 10591, File 215C1.(D383), Lieutenant-Colonel G.F.C. Pangman, GSO 1 Plans Main HQ 1st Canadian Army, 'Notes from a Conference at Headquarters 21 Army Group 1415 hours 28 March 1945', 29 March 1945. The

Admiralty previously promised to send naval parties by 23 March. PRO, ADM 1/19168, Message from Admiralty to 21st Army Group, 15 0059A March 1945.

77. PRO, ADM 1/16211, Commodore Hugh England, 'Commodore-in-Charge Hamburg's Orders', 7 April 1945. See also WO 205/260.

78. NA, RG 331, SHAEF, Special Staff Adjutant General's Division, Executive Section, File 381-8, 'Operation Eclipse – Revised Naval Plan', 10 April 1945. Also in PRO, WO 205/259.

79. NA, RG 331, SHAEF, Office of the Chief of Staff, Secretary, General Staff, File 381/3 Eclipse Vol. 1, Message from ANCXF Main to SHAEF Fwd, 11 1807B April 1945.

80. NA, RG 331, SHAEF, ANCXF War Diary, 10 April 1945. PRO, WO 205/274, Message from ANCXF Main to 21st Army Group, 10 2305B April 1945.

81. NAC, RG 24, Vol. 10,718, File 215C1.99(D17), Memorandum from Main HQ 21st Army Group to 1st Canadian and 2nd British Armies, 'Naval Liaison Officers', 29 March 1945. PRO, WO 205/274, Message from ANCXF Main to ANCXF (PH), 29 1215A March 1945.

82. IWM, Montgomery, Reel 11, BLM 126/73, 21st Army Group M.574 'Operational Directive for the Capture of Emden, Bremen, Hamburg and Lübeck', 22 April 1945. Bernard Montgomery, 'Operations in North-West Europe from 6 June 1944 to 5 May 1945', *Supplement to the London Gazette* (4 Sept. 1946), p. 4447.

83. NA, RG 331, SHAEF, Special Staff, Adjutant General's Division, Executive Section, File SHAEF/215/2/GDP-2, Message from SHAEF Fwd signed Eisenhower to ANCXF, 18 1300B April 1945.

84. NA, RG 331, SHAEF, ANCXF War Diary, 10 April 1945.

85. PRO, WO 205/259, Message from ANCXF Main to 21st Army Group, 19 1245B April 1945. The Royal Navy's presence amused the Belgians: 'Before the war we kept our horses there; the Germans conquered us and kept their prisoners there; the British liberated us and decided to live there.' IWM, 69/651, Lieutenant-Commander F.M. Savage, RN, Commodore, 'The Convoy must get through', *Royal Alfred Record*, Vol. 4, No. 6 (16 March 1946), p. 3.

86. John Pearson, *The Life of Ian Fleming*, (London: Jonathan Cape, 1966), pp. 122–33. PRO, ADM 223/500, Memorandum from Combined Operations HQ to Secretary, Joint Intelligence Committee, 'Formation of Special Intelligence Units', 31 July 1942.

87. Liddell Hart Centre for Military Archives, (hereafter LHC), Lieutenant-Commander Quinton Riley, RNVR, File 'Riley 30 Assault Unit', 'Minutes of Meeting to Discuss Intelligence Assault Unit (Special Engineering Unit No. 30 Commando) held at COHQ Room 412', 31 Dec. 1943.

88. LHC, Riley, File 'Riley 30 Assault Unit', Robert Harling, 'History of 30 A.U.', [n.d.]. J.A.C. Hugill, *The Hazard Mesh*, (London: Hurst & Blackett, 1947).

89. OAB/NHC, US Naval Technical Mission in Europe, Box 2, File 'US NavTechMisEU – Incoming Despatches (January–July 1945)', Message from COMNAVFOR-FRANCE to Chief of Naval Operations, 22 0300 Jan. 1945.

90. PRO, ADM 223/500, 'Summary of Conclusions Resulting from a Meeting held at ANCXF(Main) HQ on 27 January 1945'. NDL/NHC, Office of Chief of Naval Operations, 'Technical Mission in Europe', 1945, pp. 58–62. PRO, ADM 1/5300, ANCXF Post-Hostilities Planning Memorandum No. 24, 'Naval Intelligence', 9 May 1945.

91. NA, RG 331, SHAEF, ANCXF War Diary, 4 Feb. 1945.

92. A. Cecil Hampshire, *The Secret Navies*, (London: William Kimber, 1978), p. 237.

93. PRO, ADM 223/349, 30th Assault Unit, 'Target Lists for Operations in Germany', 15 Dec. 1944.

94. LHC, Commander Patrick Dalzel Job, RNVR, Memoirs, 'Special Service', p. 205.

95. NA, RG 331, SHAEF, ANCXF War Diary, 26 April 1945. BL, Cunningham, Add. Ms. 52578, Diary, 27 April 1945. Job was proud of the feat: 'When a Staff Officer arrived from 52nd Division and asked me to sign a receipt for the 16 submarines, it

was the last straw. I told the Royal Marines to put up a sign saying that the shipyard belonged to 30 A.U.', LHC, Job, 'Special Service', p. 216.

96. NDL/NHC, 'Administrative History, United States Naval Forces in Europe 1940–1946', Vol. 7, p. 192. Morison, Vol. 11, p. 327.

97. LHC, Job, 'Special Service', p. 223. Brian Horrocks, *A Full Life*, (London: Leo Cooper, 1974), p. 264.

98. PRO, ADM 234/363, BR 1736(37), Battle Summary No. 49, *The Campaign in North-West Europe June 1944–May 1945*, Historical Section, Admiralty Naval Staff, 1952, pp. 70–1.

99. When Blackler reported in Brussels with no papers, he was told to go back where he came from. IWM, Savage, Lieutenant-Commander C. Blackler, 'Twelve Months Ago – Almost', *The HMS Royal Alfred Record*, Vol. 4, No. 8 (1 April 1946), p. 4.

100. 'British Advance to Baltic', *The Times* (3 May 1945), p. 4.

101. FO/SU, 1946, Reel 30, Vol. 56890, Frames 10-11, Memorandum from Commodore R.M.J. Hutton to Secretary of Admiralty, 'Sinking of German Ships Off Neustadt on 3 May 1945', 8 April 1946. CCAC, John Burns Hynd, HYND 3/9, 'The Search for the Missing', *British Zone Review*, Vol. 1, No. 29 (26 Oct. 1946), p. 14.

102. OAB/NHC, King, Series IV, Box 31, File 'Helbig, J.J. Ylc USNR, Personal File 1944–45', Message from Admiral Harold Burrough to Chiefs of Staff, 06 2315B May 1945. Baillie-Grohman and a small party had flown from Brussels to Schleswig-Holstein on 2 May. IWM, Baillie-Grohman, 'Flashlights on German Disarmament 1945/46', Vol. 3, pp. 66-75.

103. NA, RG 331, SHAEF, 1st Allied Airborne Army HQ, File 322, HQ 1st Allied Airborne Army, 'Operation "Red Admiral" – Preliminary Planning Study for Airborne Operation to seize Bridges over KIEL Canal', 26 April 1945. NA, RG 331, SHAEF, Special Staff, Adjutant General's Division, Executive Section, File SHAEF/215/2/GDP-2, Message from SHAEF Fwd signed SCAEF to HQ 1st Allied Airborne Army, 28 April 1945.

104. IWM, 85/34/1, Signalman A. Vincent, Memoir, p. 82.

105. PRO, ADM 205/49, Memorandum from C.H.M. Waldock to Vice-Admiral Neville Syfret, 'State of Readiness – Germany', 1 May 1945.

106. LHC, General Sir Miles Christoper Dempsey, 2nd Army Intelligence Summary No. 334, 3 May 1945. DHist, 81/520/1650-DS, Vol. 33, Daily Summary of Naval Events No. 2068, 4 May 1945. German forces were ordered not to defend Hamburg. BA/MA, RM 7/854, Message from OB Nord West to ObdM; OKM SKL; OBDL, 02 1331 May 1945. Schramm, Vol. 4/2, p. 1470.

107. PRO, ADM 1/18422, Report of Proceedings from Captain A.H. Alexander to Commodore Hamburg, 12 May 1945. Kaufmann had declared Hamburg an open city before the surrender. BA/MA, RW 44I/9, Declaration by Karl Kaufmann.

108. PRO, ADM 205/47A, Report from Commodore Hugh England to Flag Officer Western Germany, 25 July 1945.

3

Surrender

The Royal Navy achieved victory after five hard years of struggle and sacrifice. Acknowledging Nazi Germany's total defeat, German plenipotentiaries signed instruments of unconditional surrender in early May 1945. The *Kriegsmarine* and its leaders assumed a prominent role in the capitulation to the Allied powers. While enjoying a great sense of accomplishment, the Royal Navy confronted the practical side of implementing and enforcing the surrender terms. Burrough issued the special naval orders to the German naval high command, warships surrendered at sea, and British naval parties arrived in ports within north-west Germany and the liberated countries. For the most part, the Royal Navy found German naval authorities cooperative and willing to follow British orders.

The *Kriegsmarine* was one of the few institutions to retain cohesion and authority in the Third Reich's chaotic collapse. Fighting spirit, loyalty, and a sense of cause only partly explains this remarkable achievement. The naval leadership lived with the shame of the mutinies within the German High Seas Fleet and the trauma of the October 1918 revolution.[1] Determined not to let down Germany again in its greatest hour of need, Grossadmiral Karl Dönitz, commander-in-chief of the *Kriegsmarine*, acted ruthlessly against any potential signs of disintegration within the navy. Legal measures increasingly replaced worn-out appeals to patriotism and service tradition.[2] Courts martial and special naval courts convened in large numbers. Naval judges awarded harsh penalties, including many sentences of death, for charges of desertion, defeatism, or *Wehrkraftzersetzung*, the peculiarly National Socialist version of subversion.[3] Judicial terror became the glue which held the *Kriegsmarine* together in the last months of the war.[4] On Helgoland, naval authorities summarily tried service personnel who suggested turning over the island to the British.[5] Arrests, convictions, and executions provided potent examples for other sailors. The auxiliary cruiser *Haussa*'s voluntary internment in Sweden at the end of April seemed an ominous sign.[6] Some were now giving up the struggle. In response, naval authorities further reinforced discipline.

The *Kriegsmarine*'s achievements and steadfast loyalty to the Nazi cause brought Dönitz increased responsibilities. On 20 April Hitler appointed Dönitz as commander-in-chief of the so-called 'Northern Redoubt'.[7] In addition to conduct of the sea war and evacuation efforts in the Baltic, Dönitz made preparations for the defence of north-west Germany. The naval high command moved its headquarters from Berlin to Plön, and from there to Flensburg.[8] Hitler's personal and professional admiration for Dönitz grew considerably in the last months of the war. Reichsfeldmarschall Hermann Göring and Reichsführer Heinrich Himmler, Hitler's most likely successors, compromised themselves by putting out peace feelers to the Western Allies.[9] Dönitz, on the other hand, remained politically reliable. On 30 April a wireless message from Nazi Party secretary Martin Bormann informed the naval commander-in-chief that Hitler, before his suicide in besieged Berlin, named Dönitz as president.[10] Although Hitler most likely expected resistance to continue, Dönitz concluded that Germany's strategic situation was untenable. Time, however, was still needed to withdraw forces facing the Red Army.[11] It was in this context that Dönitz decided to approach the British about the possibility of an area surrender.

The *Kriegsmarine* was well-represented on the delegation, which Dempsey sent forward to 21st Army Group's tactical headquarters at Lüneburg Heath. Generaladmiral Hans Georg von Friedeburg, Dönitz's faithful subordinate and the *Kriegsmarine*'s new commander-in-chief, headed the party.[12] His instructions were to secure a partial capitulation in order to allow German soldiers to withdraw from the east. Konteradmiral Gerhard Wagner, another member of Dönitz's staff, accompanied Friedeburg.[13] Montgomery received the two admirals under a pole flying the Union Jack. When Friedeburg introduced himself as head of the *Kriegsmarine*, the British field marshal replied that he had never heard of him, but asked what the delegation wanted.[14] Upon hearing the German requests, Montgomery demanded surrender of all forces opposite 21st Army Group in Holland, north-west Germany, and Denmark. Montgomery later wrote that Friedeburg wept after seeing a map with Allied and German dispositions on the western front.[15] The admiral returned to Flensburg to ask Dönitz and the German High Command for authority to sign a surrender agreement. Montgomery cabled London that the Germans would be likely to capitulate in the suggested areas because 'they are now quite clear as to the hopelessness of their situation.'[16]

The field marshal's optimism was justified. In a meeting with military and naval staffs at Flensburg early on 4 May, Dönitz recognized that further hostilities in the north-west region were pointless, and decided, over the objections of Generaloberst Alfred Jodl, chief of operations in the OKW, to accept the British terms in full.[17] Since the surrender seemed the best possible agreement in a bad situation, Dönitz took responsibility for the initial step in ending the European war. As a sign of good faith, he ordered all U-boats to cease hostilities immediately and return to port.[18] Friedeburg travelled back to Lüneburg Heath with a staff officer, who carried in a large leather briefcase confidential wireless codes and charts with the location of minefields in the North Sea. Late on 4 May Montgomery and the Germans signed a short document for 'the surrender of all German armed forces in Holland, in north-west Germany including the Frisian Islands and Helgoland and all other islands, in Schleswig-Holstein, and in Denmark', to take effect the next day.[19] Montgomery added in pen that the surrender included all naval vessels in these areas. The *Kriegsmarine* formally surrendered to British military forces. The German naval staff communicated the terms to the appropriate commands.[20] While Wagner remained at 21st Army Group, Friedeburg proceeded to SHAEF's headquarters in Rheims to negotiate an enlarged surrender.

The Royal Navy was busy in the interval between the signing of the armistice and when it became operative. Montgomery ordered 1st Canadian and 2nd British Armies to stop all offensive operations and stand firm.[21] This pause allowed the main naval parties to reach distant Allied front-lines. Naval operations continued off the coast of Norway because the surrender agreement with 21st Army Group excluded that country. Late on 4 May Martlet fighters and Avenger torpedo planes from three British escort carriers, supported by a covering force of cruisers and destroyers, sank a tanker and a U-boat depot ship with a submarine alongside at Kilbotn, north of Narvik.[22] The Home Fleet sortie was the last offensive action by the Royal Navy in the European war. The *Kriegsmarine*, on the other hand, no longer thought in offensive terms, but readied itself for the ultimate sacrifice.

Some German captains and crews decided to scuttle their warships and submarines before formal implementation of the surrender to 21st Army Group. Whether Dönitz and the German naval staff sanctioned these actions is unclear. On 30 April the naval high command had issued instructions to scuttle cruisers, destroyers, torpedo boats, fast motor torpedo boats, U-boats, and any new building upon receipt of the codeword '*Regenbogen*'.[23] Ships not engaged in evacuation work, minesweeping, or undergoing major repair were ordered to depart immediately for Norway. Even at this late hour, Dönitz probably had not abandoned entirely the idea of continuing the sea war from the Scandinavian country.[24] The large movement, however, attracted the attention of Allied aircraft operating in great numbers over the Baltic. On 3 May 2nd Tactical Air Force aircraft sank or damaged over seventy-five ships and U-boats departing in convoys from Kiel.[25] Since transfer to Norway was difficult and dangerous, many captains chose to scuttle their U-boats.

The German naval staff originally intended to leave as few submarines as possible to the British. Early on 5 May British intelligence staffs intercepted a wireless message from the German naval high command:

> IF POSSIBLE U-BOATS ARE TO GO TO NORWAY. ALL U-BOATS WHICH AT 0800/5/5 ARE IN GERMAN OR DANISH PORTS, ROADS OR BAYS OR ARE SOUTH OF LATITUDE 5510 NORTH WILL CARRY OUT 'REGENBOGEN', I.E. SCUTTLE IN AS DEEP WATER AS POSSIBLE, CREWS GOING ASHORE.[26]

There is some suggestion that Dönitz later countermanded the order. Nonetheless, an estimated 218 U-boats, including at least eighty-two Type XXI and twenty-nine Type XXIII, were scuttled during the night.[27] The number represented approximately two-thirds of available operational strength. Dönitz's fear that further scuttling might jeopardize the agreement with Montgomery prevented the destruction of more warships. Under Friedeburg's orders, remaining 'U-Boats in Norway are neither to be scuttled nor destroyed, because only in that way can hundreds of thousands of German lives in the east be saved.'[28] As surface vessels continued evacuations in the Baltic, preservation of the last U-boats assumed political significance.

Due to scuttling and last-minute transfers, British naval parties discovered only small numbers of operational warships in North Sea ports. Captain C.H. Petrie, RN, who entered Emden with Brigadier J.M. Rockingham's 9th Canadian Infantry Brigade in the early morning of 6 May, reported serviceable dock installations as well as twenty-five armed trawlers and patrol vessels.[29] Considerable evidence suggested that more naval units were present before the surrender. Wreckage littered the harbour and canal systems, and nominal returns from Kapitän zur See Axel von Blessingh, Emden's fortress commander, disclosed 17,000 naval personnel in barracks and scattered defence points.[30] In order to establish more effective control, the British and Canadians enclosed the main port area with barbed wire, and placed guards on all warships. Petrie, after commissioning the German hospital ship KMB 8 as HMS *Royal Prince*, oversaw operation of port and canal installations, disarmament of warships, collection of weapons, and removal of sailors to designated concentration areas.[31] The cooperation of Blessingh and his subordinates proved indispensable.

In a similar fashion, the British and Canadians secured areas surrounding Emden and the eastern Frisian Islands. At the naval munitions depot and training establishment in Aurich, Kapitän zur See Eberhard Jaehnke declared that three naval battalions under his command had disarmed and concentrated themselves, and he awaited further British orders.[32] Military forces took responsibility for considerable numbers of personnel in naval infantry brigades or manning coastal defences. Canadian officers, carried across on German minesweepers, accepted surrenders from Fregattenkapitän Dr. Erwin Duwe on Norderney and Fregattenkapitän Dr. Kurt Goebell on Borkum.[33] German authorities proved remarkably cooperative and efficient. Requested lists of materials on Norderney catalogued everything, right down to umbrella stands.[34] In keeping with the surrender terms, the Germans obeyed British and Canadian orders without question. Preparations began to transfer German naval personnel in garrisons on the outlying islands to the mainland.[35] Like Emden, the number of warships was small. Although Borkum served as an advance base with its own submarine shelter, only U-739, an older Type VIIC, was found operational. British naval authorities sailed the U-boat to Wilhelmshaven.

The *Kriegsmarine*'s main base on the North Sea was a major objective for the Royal Navy. Captain Edward Conder, RN, upon arriving in Wilhelmshaven with 1st Polish Armoured Division on 6 May, discovered all port installations intact and approximately 180 war and merchant ships immobilized for lack of fuel.[36] U-boats were scuttled in various harbours, but damage to the town and port, despite heavy Allied bombing, was relatively minor. The most pressing problem was the enormous number of naval personnel scattered around and inside Wilhelmshaven.[37] As a preventative measure, Conder immediately transferred surplus U-boat officers and ratings to barracks. Kapitän zur See Walter Mulsow, Wilhemshaven's fortress commander, directed staff officers to document and list all personnel and establishments in the general area.[38] Once Mulsow's work was completed, British naval authorities started large-scale transfers of personnel into concentration areas under Canadian control, keeping a reserve of 'frozen' personnel for ship maintenance parties and minesweeping. Conder formed a Port Executive Committee, comprising British naval and military representatives, to oversee the port's administration. Since the Admiralty intended to use Wilhelmshaven as the main collection point for German warships, effective control was essential.

The Royal Navy established satisfactory working relationships with German naval authorities in the North Sea area. At the headquarters of the *Marineoberkommando Nordsee* in nearby Sengwarden, Admiral

Erich Förste followed British instructions, although 'a fair amount of chaos reigned.'[39] The German staff attempted to impose order on confusion and disintegration. Women auxiliaries manned telephone and communications networks.[40] Förste preserved reasonable control and authority over scattered naval forces in the region. Muirhead-Gould allowed the German admiral to retain his position in return for absolute obedience under the surrender terms.[41] The practical arrangement relied largely on continued goodwill. On the island of Sylt, Captain Sir James F. Baget, RN, reported that Fregattenkapitän Carl Eugen Münzenmaier and his subordinates 'were most correct in their attitude and fulfilled all British orders with alacrity.'[42] The attitude of mind of German naval authorities at the time of the surrender was certainly curious. In the eagerness to follow orders and perform allotted tasks, they almost tried to impress the British. Even in defeat, the *Kriegsmarine* wanted to preserve honour and dignity. The desire caused some difficulties in Denmark.

The surrender in Denmark involved complex consultations between the British and the Danes. Since early 1945, the Admiralty had pursued secret talks with Vice-Admiral A.H. Vedel, Commander-in-Chief of the Royal Danish Navy and Director General of Denmark's Ministry of Marine.[43] The Royal Navy intended to help Denmark reconstruct the Danish fleet in the post-war period, with a view to a possible Scandinavian alliance. Commodore Reginald Vesey Holt, RN, the flag officer designate for Denmark, planned on the assumption that 'by helping to reconstitute the Danish state, we can, at low cost, obtain a real dividend from the Baltic.'[44] Assistance from Danish authorities was to offset the small size of the British naval party.

On the afternoon of 5 May Holt arrived in Copenhagen on a plane with Major-General Richard Henry Dewing, head of the SHAEF Mission to Denmark, and a company of 6th Airborne Division paratroops.[45] After addressing enthusiastic Danish crowds, the British established a temporary headquarters at the Hôtel d'Angleterre. Holt received permission from the Danish cabinet and King Christian to handle all naval matters directly with Vedel.[46] The Danish navy undertook to supervise most disarmament and minesweeping work. In staff talks with Holt, Vedel described the considerable German forces in Danish shore establishments and ports. By choice and necessity, the Royal Navy relied on Danish assistance.

A large portion of the *Kriegsmarine* surrendered in Denmark. Ships included the heavy cruiser *Prinz Eugen*, the light cruiser *Nürnberg*, the damaged light cruiser *Leipzig*, three flak cruisers and target vessels, thirteen large and medium destroyers, numerous minelayers, survey ships, naval auxiliaries, at least five U-boats, and over 100 merchant ships.[47] The majority had been involved in evacuation efforts in the Baltic. Consequently, tens of thousands of refugees and wounded soldiers also clogged Danish ports. In a message to naval authorities, Jodl ordered all forces in Denmark to maintain correct and disciplined behaviour, and to avoid actions which might provoke the Danes.[48] Since the Danish population was in a highly excited state after news of the surrender, the potential for friction was high. In discussions with Dewing and Holt, Generaloberst Georg Lindemann, commander-in-chief of armed forces in Denmark, took responsibility for sailors in shore establishments.[49] These naval personnel were disarmed and concentrated with German soldiers.

Danish attempts to board ships in Copenhagen harbour, however, encountered active resistance and sporadic gunfire. German naval authorities refused to recognize the Danes as victors, insisting that they had surrendered to the British. On 7 May Vizeadmiral Leo Kreisch, leader of destroyers flying his flag in *Prinz Eugen*, Kapitän zur See Waldemar von Fischer, sea commander for the Danish islands, and Kapitän zur See Max Freymadl, chief of staff to Admiral Hans Heinrich Wurmbach, the commanding admiral for the Skagerrak with a headquarters in Aarhus, appeared at the Hôtel d'Angleterre to discuss surrender arrangements with Holt.[50] The Germans wanted direction from the Royal Navy. Holt ordered an immediate standstill of all ships, provision of maintenance and care parties, and concentration of shore personnel into designated concentration areas.[51] Although compliant, the Germans interpreted these instructions in such a way as to ignore the Danes almost completely.[52] Vedel and Danish naval authorities were outraged. In this tense situation, Holt received welcome reinforcements.

The Royal Navy established an early naval presence in Denmark. After the 40th Minesweeping Flotilla cleared a channel through minefields in the Skagerrak and Kattegat, the cruisers HMS *Birmingham* and HMS *Dido* arrived in Copenhagen with the destroyers HMS *Zephyr*, HMS *Zealous*, HMS *Zodiac*, and HMS *Zest*, under the general command of Captain Herbert Wyndham Williams, RN.[53] The British warships provided Holt with the tacit firepower to enforce terms on the German fleet. As a result, the German attitude improved dramatically. Danish authorities assumed control over Copenhagen's port, and guarded German warships. Until naval parties for Danish ports arrived by road, officers from the British ships served on various surrender committees.[54] The work provided excellent opportunities for inspections. German officers gave Lieutenant-Commander R.M. Urie, RNVR, an officer from HMS *Dido*, an extensive tour of supply departments and store rooms on *Prinz Eugen*.[55] Under pressure from the Danish government, the Admiralty decided to transfer the largest warships from Denmark. The British cruisers HMS *Devonshire* and HMS *Dido*, accompanied by the destroyers HMS *Savage* and HMCS *Iroquois*, escorted *Prinz Eugen* and *Nürnberg* to Wilhelmshaven.[56] The naval surrender in Denmark was overtaken by the larger surrender of the German armed forces.

Circumstances finally forced German plenipotentiaries to concede defeat. Unlike Montgomery, Eisenhower refused to entertain a proposed area surrender.[57] Lacking authority to consider anything else, Friedeburg contacted Flensburg. Jodl duly arrived in Rheims with necessary powers to conduct further negotiations.[58] At this point, Dönitz wanted perhaps to shift the personal and institutional stigma for the unconditional surrender away from the *Kriegsmarine*. Jodl, in his capacity at the German High Command, represented the three armed services.[59] In contrast to Generalfeldmarschall Wilhelm Keitel, the Americans and British still considered Jodl an honourable soldier.

SHAEF's insistence on unconditional surrender, however, was firm. After Eisenhower threatened to close off the front and resume offensive operations, Jodl saw 'no other alternative – chaos or signature.'[60] With this dire assessment, Dönitz finally consented to unconditional surrender. Early on 7 May Jodl signed a document, which called for 'all forces under German control to cease active operations at 2301 hours Central European time on 8 May and to remain in the positions occupied at that time.'[61] The same paragraph prohibited scuttling or damage to German ships. On Eisenhower's behalf, Burrough issued to Friedeburg the special naval orders, approved by the Soviet naval staff in late 1944.[62] Jodl and Friedeburg then returned to Flensburg. Dönitz instructed naval authorities to obey Allied orders after 9 May.[63] In the meantime, the unconditional surrender required further formalities.

The Soviets insisted on final ratification of the unconditional surrender in Berlin. Burrough and Archer watched Friedeburg and representatives from the German High Command sign a modified unconditional surrender document, presented by Marshal Georgii Konstantinovich Zhukov, Commander-in-Chief of Soviet occupation forces in Germany.[64] The Germans were left with no illusions about the completeness of their defeat. Whatever the legal clarifications, Vizeadmiral Leopold Bürkner, who represented the Dönitz government during the Berlin ceremony, knew exactly what unconditional surrender implied.[65] The defeat of Nazi Germany kept the Western Allies and the Soviet Union united in a common purpose. The ceremony and subsequent banquet celebrated this collective achievement.

Announcement of Germany's unconditional surrender brought an immense sense of achievement within the Admiralty. Churchill's famous speech from 10 Downing Street, repeated over BBC radio, declared that

'The German war is therefore at an end', and finished with a rousing 'God Save the King!'[66] Sailors and officers joined joyous crowds in London streets as ships' whistles and horns wailed. Cunningham wrote that the principal business at the Board of Admiralty meeting on 8 May 'was drinking Waterloo brandy of which the First Lord produced a bottle.'[67] The German enemy – Cunningham's detestable Hun – was decisively defeated. In a radio broadcast to the United States, Burrough opened: 'The destruction of Nazi sea power is complete.'[68] Thereupon, he described the Royal Navy's major part in this achievement. The Admiralty conveyed a similar theme in a congratulatory message to the fleets: 'For the second time since the Battle of Trafalgar, sea power relentlessly applied has preserved and sustained our Nation and Commonwealth and led to the decisive defeat of Germany and her European associates.'[69] The Royal Navy saw itself as the main protector of Great Britain and a major player in the victory over the *Kriegsmarine*. It was a narrow win in the Battle of the Atlantic, but a win nevertheless.[70] The end of the Second World War was another high point for British sea power.

Of course, the British won the war in Europe in conjunction with allies. The Soviet ambassador in London delivered the following letter to the First Lord:

> I have the honour, on behalf of Marshal J.V. Stalin and myself, to express to you and to the valiant Royal Navy sincere congratulations on the great victory over our common enemy – German imperialism.
>
> Allow me to express to you my hope that the friendly cooperation between the peoples of Great Britain and the U.S.S.R., built up during the course of the war, will be successfully and happily maintained and developed in the postwar period.[71]

The Admiralty reciprocated the sentiments. In May 1945 the Royal Navy still regarded the Soviet Union as an ally rather than a potential enemy. Effective control and disarmament of the *Kriegsmarine* preoccupied British naval authorities.

The Admiralty made special arrangements for U-boats at sea. On 19 March the Commander-in-Chief Western Approaches had requested clarification on procedures and instructions for surrender of submarines and their internment at Loch Ryan and Lisahally.[72] In order to institute a uniform policy, Allied naval authorities needed proper guidance. Based upon a subsequent meeting at the Admiralty on 27 March, Horton suggested that German submarines surface, report their positions, fly a black or dark blue flag, jettison ammunition and torpedoes, and follow routes to selected Allied reception ports.[73] With minor adjustments and alterations, the Admiralty accepted these proposals under the code-name 'Adieu'. Since German captains were likely to ignore Allied transmissions, instructions for U-boats, drafted by Horton's staff, were added in two supplementary annexes to the special naval orders.[74] Acting through German naval authorities, the Royal Navy hoped that captains would cease active operations immediately.

Fortunately, Dönitz and the naval high command appeared amenable to the comprehensive special orders issued to Friedeburg. Late on 8 May the Royal Navy intercepted the following message:

> U-boat men. After an heroic fight without parallel you have laid down your arms. You have unprecedented achievements to your credit. You must now make the hardest sacrifice of all for your Fatherland by obeying the following instructions unconditionally. This casts no slur on your honour but will prevent serious consequences for your native land. The order to proceed on return passage to Norway ... is cancelled.[75]

Submarines were ordered to obey Allied orders without hesitation. At Burrough's direction, British naval authorities allowed German transmitters to continue broadcasting surrender instructions in code and plain language.[76] Whether U-boats on operations would actually follow the orders was still unknown.

After a short period of anxious waiting, U-boats at sea individually began to surrender in accord with the special orders. On the day of the unconditional surrender at Rheims, many submarines were still on station in the Atlantic or the North Sea.[77] U-boats surfaced and reported their positions. On 10 May U-249, a Type VIIC commanded by Kapitänleutnant Uwe Kock, arrived under the escort of the sloops HMS *Antelope* and HMS *Magpie* at Portland, the Royal Navy's main anti-submarine establishment.[78] Discipline and morale on the U-boat were high. When Commander H.J. Weir, RN, asked Kock if he was prepared to surrender the submarine, the German captain simply replied: 'I have to.'[79] In coming days, U-boats brought into British ports were put on public display or transferred to northern Ireland for internment under Operation 'Pledge'. Horton personally received the surrender of eight U-boats at Lisahally on 14 May.[80] Allied warships encountered other submarines still at sea. On 16 May the Norwegian destroyer HMNS *Stord*, carrying Rear-Admiral E.C. Danielsen, RNN, to northern Norway, intercepted fifteen U-boats, two depot ships, an accommodation ship, and a tanker from the 14th U-Boat Flotilla, in convoy from Narvik to Trondheim.[81] The submarines were diverted to Loch Eriboll under the escort of HMCS *Matane*. By 26 May forty-three U-boats were in British,

American, and Canadian ports.[82] The rest remained ominously silent.

Since individual U-boats were still capable of conducting offensive operations against Allied shipping, Allied naval forces remained vigilant. Coastal Command flew regular air patrols, and British ships continued 'for the present to observe full war-time precautions against attack by U-boat'.[83] Some submarines were certainly destroyed or badly damaged in previous operations. A report from the Canadian Naval Mission Overseas in London commented: 'Some U-Boats may yet be unaware of the surrender orders; the possibility that others will refuse to comply with them cannot be ignored.'[84] Several captains intentionally disregarded Allied and German directions. On 20 May Oberleutnant zur See Rolf-Werner Wentz scuttled U-963 off the coast of Portugal after local authorities refused supplies and assistance.[85] Neutral and other countries were generally unsympathetic. When U-530 and U-977 arrived off Mar del Plata, Argentinian officials detained the German crews.[86] Other submarines tried to sneak home unnoticed. Off Amrum island in the North Sea, a British boarding party narrowly missed death during an inspection of the recently abandoned U-979 when a petty officer asked: 'What do you make of that ticking?'[87] The crew, after setting a time fuse, had hoped to blend into the civil population, thereby avoiding delays associated with captivity and formal demobilization. Although evasion or contravention of the surrender terms was always a possibility, most naval authorities followed British and German orders.

The special orders required the *Kriegsmarine* to deliver information on minefields, vessels, shore establishments, personnel, and stocks to British commands within specified time periods. Carrying minefield charts of the Dutch and German coasts, Konteradmiral Erich Breuning left Rotterdam with two motor torpedo boats, S-204 and S-205, for HMS *Beehive*, the coastal forces base at Felixstowe.[88] The information was necessary for the safe entry of British warships and shipping into German and German-occupied ports. Vice-Admiral Edmund Rupert Drummond, RN, received a delegation, which arrived from Denmark in the minesweeper M-607, on HMS *Belfast*.[89] The admiral and his staff questioned Kapitän zur See Hugo Pahl, Wurmbach's representative, and Kapitän zur See Martin Saltzwedel, Kriesch's chief of staff, about reasons for the delay, locations of sea-mines, and preparations for demolitions in Danish ports. Since the location of Wurmbach's headquarters in Aarhus made contact with Holt difficult, Drummond ordered Pahl to deliver minefield charts to the Home Fleet at Scapa Flow. The information allowed the entry of the cruiser and destroyer force into Copenhagen. Other German naval authorities dealt directly with British parties in German ports after the capitulation.

An advance party arrived in Cuxhaven on 7 May, the same day as the unconditional surrender at Rheims. Captain Lionel Skipwith, RN, the Naval Officer-in-Charge at Cuxhaven, reported all port installations intact as well as 12,000 tons of oil fuel in reserve stocks.[90] Cuxhaven was a principal German operating base. The British found two destroyers – Z-15 (*Erich Steinbrinck*) and Z-33, four flak ships, twenty-two minesweepers, eight U-boats, and two merchant ships still afloat.[91] Unlike Emden and Wilhelmshaven, German naval authorities issued orders against scuttling. Nonetheless, two commissioned Type XVIIB hydrogen-peroxide driven submarines, were sunk in contravention of the surrender terms.[92] After learning of rumours about another planned scuttling, the Royal Navy decided to transfer remaining submarines and destroyers to Wilhelmshaven. With the assistance of Korvettenkapitän Heinrich Bleichrodt and British soldiers, Lieutenant-Commander P.J.H. Bartlett, RN, a submarine officer attached to Muirhead-Gould's command, paraded and removed German crews.[93]

British authorities established effective control over the port and large numbers of naval personnel in the town. In due course, Skipwith removed Kapitän zur See Kurt Thoma, chief of the 5th Security Division, Vizeadmiral Gustav Kleikamp, commanding admiral of the Deutsche Bucht, and Vizeadmiral Fritz Lamprecht, commander of ferry services in the Elbe-Weser estuaries, but retained the cooperative Konteradmiral Rolf Johanneson 'to administer the Naval Section of [the] concentration area.'[94] The British used Cuxhaven to support minesweeping operations. Under Operation 'Dropkick', British minesweepers swept mines from the approaches to Cuxhaven and Hamburg.[95] German minesweepers continued clearance work after withdrawal of these minesweeping forces to the Far East.

On the other side of the Elbe River, the Royal Navy established control over naval forces in Brunsbüttel. Captain Charles Wheeler, RM, and a 30th Assault Unit team entered the port with 7th Armoured Division on the afternoon of 7 May to find functioning harbour installations, the severely damaged destroyer Z-31, the submarine escort vessel *Saar*, the flak cruiser *Arcona*, four U-boats, motor torpedo boats, R-class and M-class minesweepers, artillery lighters, landing craft, ferries, and various merchant ships.[96] In addition, Kapitän zur See Karlhans Heye, Brunsbüttel's fortress commander, administered approximately 141 officers and 3,000 sailors in shore establishments and coastal defence points. Commander P.W. Coombe, RN, the appointed senior British naval officer at Brunsbüttel, arrived with the main port party the next morning.[97] The Germans disarmed and disembarked ammunition from the warships under British supervision. Lieutenant-Commander W.N. Eade, RNR, a submarine officer from the Admiralty, inspected *Saar* and U-3532, an uncompleted Type XXI which the Germans had towed from Bremen before that port's capture.[98] In terms of technical intelligence, the British found little of interest in Brunsbüttel. Coombe ordered the removal and transfer of all crews to concentration areas.[99] Brunsbüttel's importance lay primarily in its being the terminus of the Kiel Canal into the North Sea. The British discovered lock gates and canal machinery virtually undamaged.[100] Responsibility for the canal's administration and control fell to the Flag Officer Kiel.

The Flag Officer Kiel took over the *Kriegsmarine*'s major naval base in the Baltic at the other end of the Kiel Canal. Baillie-Grohman rebuked Generaladmiral Oskar Kummetz in German for using the Nazi salute, and raised the White Ensign over the headquarters of the *Marineoberkommando Ostsee* on 8 May.[101] A certain amount of breakdown and confusion existed in Kiel from the Allied bombing. In order to curb further disintegration, Baillie-Grohman issued detailed orders, setting out clearly what the British expected throughout the Baltic area.[102] Naval officers were made personally responsible for immediate compliance with the given orders, provision of information on minefields, ships and personnel, removal of Nazi flags, safeguarding of munitions and warships, discipline among sailors, and food supply.

Although large numbers of naval personnel were in the immediate vicinity, only a small number of minesweepers, a motor torpedo boat, and two depot ships were operational in Kiel Bay. From his requisitioned headquarters ship *Milwaukee*, Baillie-Grohman remarked:

> Well, there we were in Kiel at last, the very heart, so to speak of the German navy. ... The whole of my career had been, in a way, dominated by the German threat. Now, 41 years later, I was in at the death of the German Navy! It was certainly a great moment for all of us![103]

The destruction at Kiel gave at least one Royal Navy officer immense satisfaction. While German naval authorities began concentrating sailors into designated camps, Baillie-Grohman and his staff surveyed docks, shipyards, and the wreckage in the harbour. New arrivals soon overwhelmed the small naval party.

Kiel bore the brunt of the *Kriegsmarine*'s last-minute evacuations in the Baltic. Through German and Danish sources, Baillie-Grohman learned that ships carrying an estimated 142,000 soldiers, wounded, and refugees were expected from Swinemünde at any time.[104] The news was alarming. Devastated Kiel simply did not have the resources to deal with such large numbers. Baillie-Grohman forbade disembarkation at Kiel from eastern Baltic transports or ships.[105] The order represented little more than wishful thinking since these desperate people really had nowhere else to go. Danish ports were full and return to Soviet-occupied territory was unacceptable. As German naval authorities pointed out, the fleeing Germans were prepared to use force to land in the British Zone. Shortly thereafter, the entire 6th Destroyer Flotilla, commanded by Kapitän zur See Heinz Peters, landing craft filled with fully armed soldiers, and various other ships carrying wounded and civilians arrived in Kiel Bay.[106] Their intimidating presence forced Baillie-Grohman to reconsider the situation. Between 11 and 15 May 18,899 soldiers, 2,715 wounded, and 3,529 refugees disembarked in Kiel.[107] The Royal Navy distributed the remainder among smaller British-controlled Baltic ports. Eckernförde, Lübeck, Travemünde, and Flensburg took the largest shares.[108] Reception of refugees, although an unexpected extra burden for naval parties in the Baltic ports, guaranteed willing cooperation from German naval authorities. The British were seen as saviours.

The *Kriegsmarine*'s general compliance with the surrender terms also arose from a sense of conviction and duty. At Kiel Korvettenkapitän Hans Blöse, upon decommissioning the destroyer Z-6 (*Theodor Riedel*), transmitted: 'Germany lives!'[109] The encouraging message provided a small glimmer of hope for sailors throughout the fleet. Bonds of wartime service between commanders and subordinates remained. Drawing upon this relationship, Vizeadmiral Hellmuth Heye, the commanding admiral for small battle units, asked officers and sailors to put down weapons for the sake of their country and families.[110] Now that Germany was defeated, the future was more important than the past. Heye, like most German officers, came to terms with the capitulation. The *Kriegsmarine* was not comprised of gangsters.[111] Defeat signified a formal end to resistance. Cooperation with the British was the best means to ensure an orderly surrender. Not all German naval authorities accepted the change so readily.

Garrisons on the Channel Islands were particularly defiant. Jodl ordered Hüffmeier to stop preparations for further raids planned against St. Malo and Granville on 7 May.[112] Dönitz, Friedeburg, and the naval staff were unsure whether the Channel fortresses would cease fighting because communications with Germany were poor. After initial scorn, Brigadier-General A.E. Snow, representing Southern Command, arranged a meeting with the Germans at sea off Guernsey.[113] For his part, Hüffmeier simply agreed not to fire on approaching British warships. On 8 May Snow and Rear-Admiral Charles Gage Stuart, RN, left in HMS *Bulldog* and HMS *Beagle* to accept a surrender on behalf of SHAEF.[114] The Royal Navy prepared to transport forces to the Channel Islands under an operation called 'Nestegg'. The movement, however, seemed in jeopardy when Hüffmeier's representative, Kapitänleutnant Arnim Zimmermann, refused to sign an unconditional surrender.[115]

Although the British made numerous threats, he returned to Guernsey to take further guidance from Hüffmeier. Late on 9 May the Germans finally signed the appropriate surrender document on *Bulldog*'s quarterdeck.[116] The British found harbour installations and shipping in the Channel Islands intact. German naval authorities played a dangerous game of bluff.

The Soviets called the German hand on Bornholm. The German High Command, which tried to claim that the Danish Baltic island was included in the surrender to 21st Army Group, told the island's commander, Kapitän zur See Gerhard von Kamptz, to await transport to Germany.[117] Nonetheless, Soviet motor torpedo boats arrived in the main port of Röhne with an ultimatum to surrender Bornholm. After Kamptz refused, the Soviets bombarded and assaulted the island.[118] The garrison could offer little resistance. Naval authorities had earlier concluded that Bornholm was indefensible.[119] The Soviets removed 12,000 Germans to the Soviet Union as prisoners of war. Kamptz remained in captivity until January 1954. During a subsequent visit to the island, Holt found the Soviets 'most cordial, but could not say how long they would be in Bornholm, nor what they were doing there, since all the Germans had left.'[120] The Admiralty suspected that the Red Navy coveted Bornholm as an advance naval base in the Baltic. The island's eventual return to Denmark in April 1946 involved complex diplomatic negotiations.[121] German stubbornness gave the Soviets a pretext for overstaying their welcome. Bornholm showed the consequences of defying the surrender terms.

The British encountered similar obstructionism from naval authorities on Helgoland. A company of Royal Marines from Cuxhaven occupied the strategic North Sea island on 8 May.[122] Although a bombing raid in April had devastated the port and coastal defences, seven operational U-boats were found in Helgoland's submarine shelter. On 11 May Muirhead-Gould and a company of Scots Guards arrived in R-boats from the 7th German Minesweeping Flotilla to accept a formal surrender from Kapitän zur See Alfred Roegglen, the island's fortress commander.[123] Roegglen was cooperative during the visit, but became recalcitrant towards supervisory officers left behind on Helgoland. Consequently, Lieutenant-Commander Charles Kenneth Seymour Aylwin, RN, the Naval Officer-in-Charge Helgoland, arrested and replaced Roegglen.[124] The British wanted quick transfer of German personnel from Helgoland to the mainland without complaints or impediments. Destruction of the island's main distilling plant left the large garrison and British naval party without a source of fresh water. By the end of May the Royal Navy evacuated Helgoland entirely.[125] The British demanded cooperation and obedience from German authorities.

The *Kriegsmarine*'s surrender in Holland encountered different problems.

Western Holland was still under German control at the time of the surrender. From 28 April onwards SHAEF representatives pursued talks with Generaloberst Johannes von Blaskowitz, commander-in-chief of fortress Holland, and Reichkommissar Artur Seyss-Inquart, the Nazi political representative in Holland, concerning food distribution to the starving Dutch population.[126] An informal truce between the Canadians and Germans preceded the surrender to 21st Army Group. On 6 May General Harry D.G. Crerar, commanding 1st Canadian Army, made Blaskowitz responsible 'for all German Armed Forces (including German Navy, Army, Air Forces), auxiliaries and civilians' within Holland and Germany west of the Weser River.[127] Two days later Canadian military units moved through German lines into western Holland.

Due to delays with the 'Eclipse' naval parties, 1st Canadian Army handled the initial surrender and disarmament of the *Kriegsmarine* in Holland. A 30th Assault Unit detachment, led by Captain Charles Cunningham, RN, accompanied the Canadians into Dutch ports.[128] Since this small team pursued specific technical targets, most supervision devolved to military authorities. At Ijmuiden a Canadian infantry battalion secured midget submarines and motor torpedo boats.[129] To a certain extent, German authorities anticipated what was expected. A Royal Navy control officer later reported that 'most of the Naval personnel had disarmed themselves before the Canadians arrived.'[130] The Germans awaited further direction. Since 21st Army Group told military authorities not to become involved in matters concerning the *Kriegsmarine*, the Canadians simply froze German naval formations until the Royal Navy's arrival.[131] The practical arrangement worked successfully in most Dutch ports, with one notable exception.

Trouble in Amsterdam caused the Canadians to intervene in German affairs. On 10 May German sailors 'aboard the tugs in the dock area fired upon some civilians who were crowding around the waterfront streets.'[132] In the interests of public safety, the Seaforth Highlanders of Canada Regiment collected naval personnel into makeshift concentration areas on the outskirts of Amsterdam. The action inadvertently involved the Canadians in the German naval command structure. On 13 May the Seaforth Highlanders assisted Fregattenkapitän Alexander Stein, Amsterdam's harbour commander, to execute deserters.[133] German authorities believed that courts martial and death sentences were necessary to preserve order and discipline. Lack of direction from the Royal Navy allowed the disreputable business to occur.

An Allied naval command gradually took form in Holland. Vice-Admiral Gerald Charles Dickens, RN, the Flag Officer Holland designate, entered the Hague on 10 May.[134] Naval parties for various Dutch ports were still en route from Belgium and Great Britain. Dickens, formerly a naval attaché to the Netherlands and principal British naval liaison officer for Allied navies, coordinated with Vice-Admiral J.T. Furstner, chief of the Royal Netherlands Navy and Holland's Minister of Naval Affairs.[135] As in Denmark, the Royal Navy intended to use Dutch assistance as much as possible in the control of German naval forces. Mixed Dutch, British, and American naval staffs arrived separately over the course of the next week.[136] The Flag Officer Holland's headquarters formally opened in the Hague on 16 May.

In the meantime, Dickens tried to contact senior German naval authorities. Vizeadmiral Rudolf Stange, the commanding admiral in the Netherlands, was ordered to proceed to the Hague.[137] Unfortunately, the Admiralty failed to inform Dickens that Stange was in London. At a meeting on 13 May Stange's chief of staff, Kapitän zur See Gustav Freiherr von Liebenstein, instead expressed gratitude for finally dealing with a British flag officer:

> Up to now, various and often contradictory orders had been given on the one side by the 1st Canadian Army through General BLASKOWITZ and on the other side by various local allied naval and military commanders. The obvious result is that confusion arises which makes it very difficult for the German Naval authorities to comply with the different orders and instructions and in general with surrender terms.[138]

The Germans were eager to cooperate, but they needed consistent direction from a single source. Dickens ordered Liebenstein to make an immediate list of all German ships, personnel, and naval war materials in Holland. Under instructions promulgated to naval and military authorities, Dickens worked through the German headquarters at Bloemendaal.[139] German naval authorities implemented orders under the supervision of appropriate British and Dutch control officers in the individual ports.

German naval personnel and warships remaining in Holland were the most immediate concern. Dickens instructed Liebenstein to send 14,000 sailors 'to nearest concentration areas forthwith except crews of minesweepers and sea-going naval craft who are to remain frozen and such administrative personnel as you consider necessary.'[140] German cooperation and good behaviour was essential because Allied naval supervision was limited. The Royal Navy relied on the Canadians to oversee disarmament and collection of naval forces in the motor torpedo boat base at Den Helder.[141] The variety and quantity of small warships in Holland was particularly demanding. There were harbour defence vessels, marine police boats, depot ships, torpedo recovery vessels, Siebel ferries, armed trawlers, R-class and M-class minesweepers, motor torpedo boats, and midget submarines.[142] The British, Dutch, and Canadians disarmed these vessels, and transferred crews to concentration areas. In addition, the sixty-four craft Rhine River Flotilla, which Fregattenkapitän August Nettelrodt had surrendered at Hellevoetsluis on 14 May, arrived in Rotterdam for disarmament.[143] With the large German naval presence, Dickens requested a British destroyer to show the flag and boost Dutch morale. HMS *Blencathra* took station in Rotterdam harbour to ensure that the surrender went smoothly.[144] Dutch ports gradually returned to regular commercial traffic. Rotterdam and Ijmuiden formally reopened on 31 May. The Royal Navy faced an even more complicated situation in Norway.

The potential for trouble in Norway was high. Anxious about a possible Allied invasion, the Germans had strengthened coastal defences and reinforced formations along the Norwegian coast.[145] Eisenhower's headquarters feared that the 350,000 well-armed, fresh German troops in Norway might continue resistance after Germany's surrender. General Sir Andrew Thorne, the commanding general for the Scottish Command, assumed responsibility for Norway's liberation on behalf of SHAEF.[146] Mixed British and Norwegian staffs planned, under the code-name 'Apostle', Norway's equivalent of 'Eclipse'. Rear-Admiral James Stuart Ritchie, RN, the Flag Officer Norway designate, made preparations for the naval component within Thorne's SHAEF Mission.[147] Despite the danger of continued German resistance in Norway, only small forces in Scotland were allocated for 'Apostle'. In an extreme emergency, SHAEF simply intended to transfer troops from Germany.[148]

Given the situation, Thorne believed that a strong Allied presence at the time of the surrender was critical. On 8 May Brigadier Richard Hilton, Thorne's chief of staff, and Commodore Per Askim, RNN, representing Ritchie, flew to Oslo in a Catalina sea plane.[149] After meeting with Norwegian representatives, Hilton proceeded to the German headquarters in Lillehammer. General Franz Böhme, commander-in-chief of armed forces in Norway, protested to the OKW about the 'unbearably severe' surrender terms, but the Western Allies did not have to invade Norway.[150] German authorities promised to follow British and Norwegian orders. Although paratroops from 1st Airborne Division secured Norwegian airfields on 10 May, the bulk of the SHAEF Mission to Norway came by sea.

Before any sea transport could take place, the Royal Navy wanted information from German naval authorities. In Oslo, Askim made contact with Admiral Theodor Krancke, the commanding admiral in

Norway. The *Marineoberkommando Norwegen*'s headquarters received instructions from Flensburg to cooperate fully with Allied naval representatives. A delegation left by air for Rosyth with minefield and navigational charts. In an audience with Drummond on HMS *Renown*, Kapitän zur See Gottfried Krüger, Krancke's representative, provided details about minefields, U-boats, communications, and the state of discipline among naval forces in Norway.[151] The German officers answered British questions to the best of their ability.

With this information, the sea lift of Allied forces to Norway commenced. On 13 May the cruisers HMS *Devonshire*, HMS *Apollo*, and HMS *Ariadne*, escorted by the destroyers HMS *Savage*, HMCS *Iroquois*, HMNS *Arendal*, and HMS *Campbell*, carried Crown Prince Olav, Thorne, Ritchie, and Rear-Admiral Elias Corneliussen, commander-in-chief of the Royal Norwegian Navy, into Oslo harbour under Operation 'Kingdom'.[152] The Flag Officer Norway's headquarters formally opened in Oslo on 14 May. At Burrough's suggestion, Moore and Whitworth sent destroyers with Naval Officers-in-Charge and naval disarmament parties to major Norwegian ports. Vice-Admiral Sir Rhoderick R. McGrigor, RN, commanding the Home Fleet's 1st Cruiser Squadron, arrived in Bergen on 17 May.[153] Additional destroyers were sent to Norway on a rotating basis as they became available. The warships provided a strong physical Allied presence during the capitulation.[154] Despite limited resources, the Royal Navy and the SHAEF Mission imposed control over far larger German naval forces.

Ritchie and his staffs in Norway faced a formidable job. The bulk of the *Kriegsmarine* was in Norwegian ports because of previous transfers and recalls. British and Norwegian naval parties found 570 warships of all types and 147 merchant ships over 500 tonnes displacement.[155] The Admiralty's post-hostilities planning completely overlooked this eventuality. Ironically, the country with the largest number of German vessels possessed the smallest naval parties. Captain B.D. Nicholson, RNVR, the Naval Officer-in-Charge Bergen, reported thirty-five U-boats in that port alone.[156]

Although German authorities maintained control over port facilities and shipyards, the activities of Norwegian resistance fighters and roaming Soviet prisoners of war caused turmoil. After McGrigor reported the situation at Bergen as extremely unstable, Moore sent the 10th Cruiser Squadron and the 54th Norwegian Motor Torpedo Boat Flotilla to Norway.[157] As a further safeguard, Moore recommended transfer of German ships as quickly as possible from trouble spots. On 24 May the Admiralty ordered all serviceable U-boats and merchant ships in Norway to depart for British ports.[158] Reductions in the number of vessels in Norway somewhat eased the burden on Ritchie's overworked port parties. Krancke's staff also reported 84,600 officers and sailors on ships and in shore establishments in Norway.[159] The large figure represented a significant proportion of the *Kriegsmarine*'s total strength. Under Norwegian and British supervision, German authorities disarmed and collected naval personnel.

Naval forces were dispersed in coastal defences, shore establishments, and ships along the long, jagged Norwegian coastline. Vizeadmiral Bruno Machens, commanding admiral for the Arctic coast, used the flak cruiser *Nymphe* to evacuate personnel from areas north of Narvik and Harstad.[160] The Royal Navy relied on the existing German chain of command to implement most primary disarmament work in Norway. At Trondheim Captain John Henry Ruck-Keene, RN, the Naval Officer-in-Charge, received lists and reports from the Germans describing their activities.[161] Warships were disarmed, crews were removed, large coastal guns were rendered harmless, and small arms were collected and stored. After meetings with Danielsen, Vizeadmiral Erich Schulte Mönting, commanding admiral for the Norwegian north coast, and Admiral Otto von Schräder, commanding admiral for the Norwegian west coast, transferred sailors from various sea commands into designated reservations.[162] German cooperation guaranteed efficiency and speed. By 25 May more than 70 per cent of all naval personnel in Norway were inside reservations.[163] Given the small British and Norwegian naval contingents in Norway, the achievement was certainly impressive. The Royal Navy used German naval authorities to facilitate the surrender, control, and disarmament of the *Kriegsmarine*.

NOTES

1. Daniel Horn, *The German Naval Mutinies of World War I*, (New Brunswick, NJ: Rutgers University Press, 1969).
2. Manfred Messerschmidt and Fritz Wüllner, *Die Wehrmachtjustiz im Dienste des Nationalsozialismus*, (Baden-Baden: Nomos Verlagsgesellschaft, 1987), p. 262. This process actually began much earlier. BA/MA, RM 22/8, Generaladmiral Walter Warzecha, 'Ansprache des Chefs des Allgemeinen Marinehauptamtes im OKM Vizeadmiral Warzecha, an die leitenden Marineoberkriegs- und Kriegsgerichtsräte auf der Marinekriegsrichtertagung in Berlin 1942'.
3. PRO, ADM 223/291, NID 1/Ta/N/41, 'German Naval Legal System', 15 March 1945. BA/MA, RM 7/854, Message from MOK Norwegen to OKM 1/SKL, 06 1205 May 1945. Franz W. Seidler, 'Die Fahnenflucht in der deutschen Wehrmacht während des Zweiten Weltkrieges', *Militärgeschichtliche Mitteilungen* 2(1977), p. 33. Manfred Messerschmidt, 'German Military Law in the Second World War', Wilhelm Deist, ed., *The German Military in the Age of Total War*, (London: Berg, 1985), p. 333. Joachim Philipp, 'Der Gerichtsherr in der deutschen Militärgerichtsbarkeit bis 1945,' *Militärgeschichte* 27(1988), p. 547.
4. Otto Hennicke, 'Über den Justizterror in der deutschen Wehrmacht am Ende des Zweiten Weltkrieges', *Zeitschrift für Militärgeschichte* 4(1965), p. 720.
5. BA/MA, RM 7/851, Message from Adm Deutsche Bucht to OKM 1/SKL, 19 1720

April 1945. A pencilled notation on the bottom indicates that the message was immediately forwarded to Dönitz.

6. 'Naval Diary of the War', *Naval Review* 33(1945), p. 239. 'New Signs of Collapse: Germans Surrender in Cruiser', *The Times* (1 May 1945), p. 4. Sailors attempted or made earlier escapes to Sweden. BA/MA, RM 7/158, Message from Seekdt Oslofjord to OKM 1/SKL, 18 1340 March 1945. OAB/NHC, German Naval Staff, Operations Division, Reel T-100-P, Part A, 1/SKL Kriegstagebuch, 18 March 1945.

7. NA, RG 242, T-206, Reel 1, File OKM/4, Letter from Adolf Hitler to Grossadmiral Karl Dönitz, 20 April 1945. BA/MA, RM 7/851, Message from Adm zbV beim ObdM to Chefs and GKdos, 21 April 1945. Schramm, Vol. 4/2, p. 1452. The OKW, which retained overall strategic responsibility in the west, coordinated with Dönitz. BA/MA, RM 6/115, Admiral zbV beim ObdM Kriegstagebuch, 27 April 1945.

8. Karl Dietrich Erdmann, 'Die Regierung Dönitz', *Geschichte in Wissenschaft und Unterricht* 14(1963), p. 365.

9. Walter Baum, 'Der Zussammenbruch der obersten deutschen militärischen Führung 1945', *Wehrwissenschaftliche Rundschau* (1960), pp. 249–52.

10. NA, RG 242, T-608, Reel 1, File OKM/40, Message from Martin Bormann to Grossadmiral Karl Dönitz, 30 April 1945.

11. BA/MA, Grossadmiral Karl Dönitz, N 236/15, 'Auszug aus Auftreten Dönitz im amerikanischen Fernsehen am 8. Mai 1965'. Dönitz, p. 449. Reimer Hansen, 'Die Kapitulation und die Regierung Dönitz', Winfried Becker, ed., *Die Kapitulation von 1945 und der Neubeginn in Deutschland*, (Wien: Böhlau, 1987), p. 33.

12. BA/MA, Generaladmiral Hans Georg von Friedeburg, N 374/8, 'Tagesniederschriften der Reichsregierung'. Friedeburg was previously commander-in-chief of U-boats.

13. BA/MA, Konteradmiral Gerhard Wagner, N 539/31, 'Niederschrift über die Kapitulations Verhandlungen im Mai 1945'. Wagner was Dönitz's admiral for special duties (the admiral's admiral). BA/MA, Dönitz, N 236/24, Letter by Gerhard Wagner, 'Die Beisetzung des Grossadmirals Dönitz', 7 Feb. 1981.

14. Nigel Hamilton, *Monty: Final Years of the Field-Marshal 1944–1976*, (New York: McGraw-Hill Book Co., 1987), p. 502. Bernard L. Montgomery, 'The German Surrender at Lüneburg Heath', *The Listener* (10 June 1954), p. 993.

15. Bernard Law Montgomery, *The Memoirs of Field-Marshal the Viscount Montgomery of Alamein, KG*, (London: Collins, 1958), p. 336.

16. IWM, Montgomery, Reel 11, BLM 126/76, Message from Field Marshal Bernard Montgomery to Field Marshal Alan Brooke, 03 1730B May 1945.

17. Peter Padfield, *Dönitz: The Last Führer*, (London: Victor Gollancz, 1984), p. 419. Jodl wished to retain Holland and Helgoland for later bargaining. NA, RG 242, T-1022, Reel 3438, File PG 31801, 1/SKL Kriegstagebuch, 4 May 1945.

18. BA/MA, RM 7/854, Message from Kapitän zur See Heinz Assmann, OKW WFSt/Ops to General der Infanterie Eberhard Kinzel, 05 1735 May 1945. Patrick Beesly, *Very Special Intelligence: The Story of the Admiralty's Operational Intelligence Centre 1939–1945*, (London: Hamish Hamilton, 1977), p. 251.

19. IWM, Montgomery, Reel 7, BLM 83/2, Copy of Instrument of Surrender, 4 May 1945. Bernard Law Montgomery, *Normandy to the Baltic*, (London: Hutchinson and Co., 1947), p. 223.

20. NA, RG 242, T-1022, Reel 3438, File PG 31801m, Message from SKL to MOK Nord; MOK Ost; Adm Niederlande; Adm Deutsche Bucht; Adm westl Ostsee; Adm Skagerrak; Flotte; FdZ; 6/SKL; AdK; Kmd Adm U-Boote; SKL Adm Qu III, 6 May 1945.

21. NAC, RG 24, C17 Vol. 13,676, Administrative Liaison Section, 1st Canadian Army War Diary, 5 May 1945.

22. BA/MA, RM 7/849, Message from Seekdt Harstadt to OKM, 04 2200 May 1945. The operation was code-named 'Judgment'. PRO, ADM 199/1440, Vice-Admiral R.R. McGrigor, RN, 1st Cruiser Squadron, Home Fleet to Secretary of Admiralty, 'First Cruiser Squadron War Diary 1 May–30 June 1945'. 'Blow at Shipping off

Norway', *The Times* (7 May 1945), p. 2.

23. BA/MA, RM 7/851, Message from OKM 1/SKL to GKdos, 'Eigenvernichtung von Kriegschiffen', 30 April 1945.

24. NA, RG 242, T-1022, Reel 3438, File PG 31801l, Message from OKW WFST/Ops to OKM SKL, 03 1850 May 1945. BA/MA, RM 7/854, Message from 1/SKL Ops to 2/SKL BdU Ops, 04 2325 May 1945. 'Doenitz clears out to Norway', *Daily Express* (5 May 1945), p. 1.

25. DHist, File 81/520/1650-DS Vol. 33, Daily Summary of Naval Events No. 2068, 4 May 1945. 'Shipping sailing north', *The Times* (4 May 1945), p. 4.

26. PRO, DEFE 3/744, Intercepted Message, NS to ID8G, 05 0150 May 1945.

27. Hessler, p. 101. Peter Cramer, *U-Boat Commander: A Periscope View of the Battle of Atlantic*, (Annapolis: Naval Institute Press, 1984), pp. 207–8. Recent research claims that eighty-six Type XXI and thirty-one Type XXIII were scuttled. Erwin F. Sieche, 'The Type XXI Submarine Part 1', *Warship* 17(1981), p. 7. Erwin F. Sieche, 'The German Type XXIII Submarine', *Warship* 19(1981), p. 161.

28. PRO, DEFE 3/744, Intercepted Message from Captain (U/B) West to 11th and 15th U/B Flotillas, U/Boat Base Stavanger, Training Group Horten, Training Group Stavanger, 08 0125 May 1945.

29. NA, RG 331, SHAEF, ANCXF War Diary, 6 May 1945. DHist, File 81/520/1650-DS Vol. 33, Daily Summary of Naval Events No. 2072, 8 May 1945.

30. NAC, RG 24, Vol. 10,698, File 215C1.98 (D270), Surrender Proforma Fortress Command Emden. Blessingh retained his authority in Emden for several months after the surrender. PRO, ADM 228/70, Memorandum from Rear-Admiral F.E.P. Hutton to Kapitän zur See Karl Smidt, 'Responsibilities of Senior German Naval Officers', 22 July 1945.

31. PRO, ADM 1/18422, Captain C.H. Petrie to Flag Officer Western Germany, 'Naval Party 1745 – Report of Proceedings from 6 May 1945, date of Entry into Emden, to 30 June 1945', 5 July 1945.

32. NAC, RG 24, Vol. 10,593, File 215C1.(D510), Surrender Proforma and Map – 739, 740, and 741 Fortress Battalions. Jeffrey Williams, *The Long Left Flank: The Hard Fought Way to the Reich 1944–1945*, (London: Leo Cooper, 1988), pp. 296–9.

33. NAC, RG 24, Vol. 10,593, Files 215C1.(D512), (D513), (D514), Surrender Proformae – Norderney, Juist, and Baltrum Islands. NAC, RG 24, Vol. 10,698, File 215C1.98(D271), Surrender Proforma – Borkum Island, 11 May 1945. BA/MA, RM 7/854, Message MOK Nord to OKM 1/SKL, 'Lagebericht vom 13.5. – 1800 Uhr', 14 0825 May 1945. A British war crimes court later sentenced Goebell to life imprisonment – commuted to thirty-two years – for his participation in the execution of an Allied flyer on Borkum. BA/MA, Ruge, N 379/88, 'Auszug aus namentliche Liste der in westlichem Gewahrsaminhaftierten Angehörigen des Heeres, der Marine, der Luftwaffe und der Waffen-SS', 20 June 1955.

34. NAC, RG 24, Vol. 10,699, File 215C1.98(D277), German Lists from Norderney, 14 May 1945.

35. BA/MA, RM 7/854, Message MOK Nord to OKM 1/SKL, 'Lagebericht vom 19.5. 1800 Uhr', 19 2400 May 1945.

36. DHist, 81/520/1650-DS Vol. 33, Daily Summary of Naval Events No. 2073, 10 May 1945. Lieutenant-Colonel L.M. Sebert, 'How the War Ended', *Canadian Military History* 4(1995), p. 90.

37. NAC, RG 24, Vol. 10,593, File 215C1.(D473), Surrender Proforma – Fortress Command Wilhelmshaven.

38. PRO, ADM 1/18422, Captain E.R. Conder to Flag Officer Western Germany, 'Progress Report, 6 of May–1 July 1945', 27 July 1945.

39. IWM, Commander Peter J.H. Bartlett, RN, Memoirs, Vol. 4 'March 1943–End of War', pp. 25–6.

40. Like the Royal Navy, the *Kriegsmarine* employed large numbers of women on headquarters staffs. While some women continued working after the surrender, the

majority were handed over to military authorities for disbandment. PRO, ADM 1/16195, Message from ANCXF (PH) to Flag Officer Wilhelmshaven, 09 1750 May 1945.

41. PRO, ADM 1/18422, Office of Flag Officer Western Germany, 'Report of Proceedings 7 May–30 June 1945', 30 June 1945.

42. PRO, ADM 1/18422, Captain Sir James F. Baget, 'Letter of Proceedings Naval Party 1744, Period up to 30 May 1945', 6 July 1945.

43. PRO, ADM 228/12, Message from Admiralty to Commodore Denmark, 23 1707B June 1945. Vedel was still in Denmark at the time: 'Vedel not only commands the Danish Navy operationally but is also Director of the Admiralty and thus controls all Naval administration and [is] in close contact with the heads of other Ministries', LHC, Major-General Richard Henry Dewing, Diary, 29 Jan. 1945. For later conversations between Vedel and the British Admiralty see ADM 205/67. Jukka Nevakivi, 'Scandinavian Talks on Military Cooperation in 1946–1947: A Prelude to the Decisions of 1948–1949', *Cooperation and Conflict: Nordic Journal of International Politics* 19(1984), p. 168.

44. PRO, ADM 1/19014, Memorandum from Commodore Reginald Holt to ANCXF(PH), 'Eclipse Naval Plan for Entry into Denmark', 28 Feb. 1945. The Admiralty cultivated ties with Denmark. CCAC, Alexander, AVAR 12/117, First Lord's Notes for Speech at the Danish Club, 26 Sept. 1943. A.D. Divine, *Navies in Exile*, (London: John Murray, 1944), p. 166.

45. IWM, Montgomery, Reel 11, BLM 126/77, Message from Field Marshal Bernard Montgomery to Field Marshal Alan Brooke, 05 2250B May 1945. Kurt Jürgensen, 'La fin de la guerre (1945) en allemagne du nord et au danemark', *Revue d'Allemagne* 25(1993), p. 122. During the previous week, Holt had visited Sweden to coordinate activities with the Swedish navy and to inspect Danish minesweeping flotillas training there. PRO, ADM 205/49, Memorandum from Captain Henry Denham to Director of Naval Intelligence, 26 April 1945.

46. NMM, Rear-Admiral Reginald Vesey Holt, RN, Folder 18, File 'Denmark 1945', Letter of Proceedings from Flag Officer Denmark to ANCXF, 20 May 1945. LHC, Dewing, '1st Week in Denmark', pp. 2–3.

47. NA, RG 331, SHAEF, ANCXF War Diary, 8 May 1945. 'Two German Cruisers await Surrender', *Manchester Guardian* (8 May 1945), p. 5. PRO, ADM 228/17, Flag Officer Denmark to British Naval Commander-in-Chief Germany, 'List of German Surface Ships and Naval Auxiliaries in Danish Waters on 7 May 1945', 24 Aug. 1945.

48. BA/MA, RM 7/854, Message from Kapitän zur See Heinz Assmann, WFSt/Ops to OKM 1/SKL, 5 May 1945.

49. BA/MA, RW 38/172F, Wehrmachtbefehlshabers Dänemark Kriegstagebuch, 6 May 1945. BA/MA, RM 7/854, Message from MOK Ost to OKM, 'Besprechungsergebnis Generaloberst Lindemann mit allierten Besatzungstruppen in Kopenhagen', 06 1330 May 1945.

50. BA/MA, RM 54/9, Führer der Zerstörer Kriegstagebuch, 7 May 1945. David Woodward, *The Tirpitz*, (New York: Berkley Medallion, 1953), pp. 167–8.

51. BA/MA, RM 7/854, Message from Stabschef Admiral Skagerrak to 1/SKL; MOK Ost, 08 1500 May 1945.

52. OAB/NHC, German Naval Archives, Box T-76, NID 1/GP/2 'Essay by Admiral Wurmbach on his Activities in Denmark as FOIC and Admiral Skagerrak from 29 March 1943–4 August 1945', 23 Jan. 1946, p. 4. Holt observed: 'The Germans are subservient, and willing to carry out instructions, but they affect to have no conception of the hatred which their behaviour has aroused. In general they take the attitude that the football match is over and we shall all be friends again.' NMM, Holt, Folder 18, File 'Denmark 1945', Letter of Proceedings from Commodore Reginald Holt to ANCXF, 20 May 1945.

53. NA, RG 331, SHAEF, ANCXF War Diary, 9 May 1945. The operation was code-named 'Cleaver'. CCAC, Captain Stephen Wentworth Roskill, RN, ROSK 5/80,

'Home Fleet Operations in the German Surrender'.

54. Great Britain. *Preliminary Narrative: The War at Sea*, Vol. 6, pp. 267–8. The main naval party arrived in Copenhagen on 19 May. NDL/NHC, 'Administrative History, United States Naval Forces in Europe 1940–1946', Vol. 7, p. 304.

55. PRO, ADM 199/443, Captain R.F. Elkins to Vice-Admiral R.R. McGrigor, 'Report on Preliminary Inspection of the Supply Department of the German Cruiser Prinz Eugen', 27 May 1945. 'German Fleet Taken Over: Disarmed at Copenhagen', *The Times* (23 May 1945), p. 4.

56. PRO, ADM 228/5, Message from ANCXF Main to Flag Officer Western Germany, 23 1556 May 1945. NAC, RG 24 Vol. 11,707, File SI 8375, Message from Canadian Naval Mission Overseas to Naval Service Headquarters, Ottawa, 25 1703B May 1945. The *Dido* sent a parting signal to Kapitän zur See Helmuth Giessler on *Nürnberg*: 'Auf Wiedersehen, until better days.' Thaddeus V. Tuleja, *Eclipse of the German Navy*, (London: J.M. Dent & Sons, 1958), p. 272.

57. NA, RG 242, T-1022, Reel 3438, File PG 31801m, German Notes on Surrender, 5–7 May 1945. Dwight D. Eisenhower, *Crusade in Europe*, (Garden City, NY: Doubleday & Co., 1948), p. 425. Stephen E. Ambrose, *The Supreme Commander: The War Years of General Dwight D. Eisenhower*, (Garden City, NY: Doubleday & Co., 1970), p. 662.

58. Francis De Guingand, *Operation Victory*, (London: Hodder & Stoughton, 1947), pp. 454–5. Bodo Scheurig, *Alfred Jodl: Gehorsam und Verhängnis*, (Frankfurt am Main: Propyläen, 1991), pp. 331–2.

59. Marlis Steinert, *Capitulation 1945*, (London: Constable, 1969), p. 160. Correlli Barnett, ed., *Hitler's Generals*, (London: Weidenfeld & Nicolson, 1989), p. 162.

60. Schramm, Vol. 4/2, p. 1481. Dwight D. Eisenhower, *Report of the Supreme Commander to the Combined Chiefs of Staff on the Operations in Europe of the Allied Expeditionary Force 6 June 1944 to 8 May 1945*, (London: His Majesty's Stationery Office, 1946), p. 145.

61. National Archives and Records Administration, *Germany Surrenders 1945*, (Washington, DC: National Archives Trust Fund Board, 1989), p. 16. IWM, Burrough, Letter from Admiral Harold Burrough to Lady Burrough, 11 May 1945. The SHAEF document was not the surrender instrument approved earlier by the European Advisory Commission. Robert Murphy, *Diplomat Among Warriors*, (Garden City, NY: Doubleday & Co., 1964), p. 241. David Eisenhower, *Eisenhower: At War 1943-1945*, (New York: Random House, 1986), p. 803.

62. NAC, RG 24, Vol. 11,752, File CS 638-3, ANCXF to Secretary of Admiralty, 'Special Orders By the Supreme Commander, Allied Expeditionary Force to the German High Command relating to Naval Forces', 7 May 1945. Payson Sibley Wild, ed., *International Law Documents 1944–45*, Naval War College International Law Studies, (Washington: United States Government Printing Office, 1946), pp. 228–41. BA/MA, RW44/I/55, 'Besondere Anordnungen des Oberbefehlshabers der Alliierten Streitkräfte für das Oberkommando der deutschen Wehrmacht in Bezug auf die Seestreitkräfte', 8 May 1945. 'Orders to German Fleet: Position of Ships to be reported', *The Times* (9 May 1945), p. 2.

63. NA, RG 242, T-1022, Reel 3438, File PG 31801m, Message from Grossadmiral Karl Dönitz to OKM SKL, 7 May 1945.

64. IWM, Burrough, 'The German Unconditional Surrender at Rheims and Berlin', p. 3. Georgii K. Zhukov, *The Memoirs of Marshal Zhukov*, (London: Jonathan Cape, 1971), pp. 627–8. IWM, 76/197/1, Admiral Sir Ernest Russell Archer, RN, Letter MM 12, 21 May 1945. Archer, who arrived from Moscow, was to sign the surrender document if the SHAEF delegation failed to appear. John R. Deane, *The Strange Alliance*, (New York: Viking, 1946), pp. 170–1.

65. NA, RG 242, T-206, Reel 1, File OKM/11, Memorandum from Admiral Wilhelm Meisel to Vizeadmiral Leopold Bürkner; Konteradmiral Gerhard Wagner, 'Rechtsnatur und Inhalt der am 8 Mai 45 erklärten bedingungslosen Kapitulation', 12 May 1945.

66. Norman Longmate, *When We Won the War: The Story of Victory in Europe, 1945*, (London: Hutchinson, 1977), p. 65.
67. BL, Cunningham, Add. Ms. 52578, Diary, 8 May 1945. Leslie Gardiner, *The British Admiralty*, (Edinburgh and London: William Blackwood & Son, 1968), p. 377. CCAC, Alexander, AVAR 5/10/11, Letter from Admiral Harold Stark to First Lord, Admiralty, 8 May 1945.
68. IWM, Burrough, Transcript of Broadcast by Admiral Harold Burrough, 8 May 1945.
69. IWM, Misc. 3 Item 25, Message from Admiralty to All Concerned Home and Abroad, 09 0416 May 1945. Burrough sent his own congratulations to naval forces on the continent. OAB/NHC, Kirk, Series IV, Box 31, File, 'Helbig, J.J. Ylc USNR, Personal File 1944-45', Message from ANCXF Main to British Flag Officers and Naval Officer-in-Charge, 07 2212B May 1945.
70. R.A. Bowling, 'Mahan's Principles and the Battle of the Atlantic', Timothy J. Runyan and Jan M. Copes, eds., *To Die Gallantly: The Battle of the Atlantic*, (Boulder: Westview Press, 1994), p. 232. David Syrett, *The Defeat of the German U-Boats: The Battle of the Atlantic*, (Columbia: University of South Carolina Press, 1994).
71. PRO, ADM 1/19064, Letter from Feodor Gousev to First Lord, Admiralty, 11 May 1945.
72. PRO, ADM 116/5202, Message from Admiral Max Horton to Admiralty, 19 1529A March 1945.
73. NAC, RG 24, Vol. 11,752, File CS 638-3, 'Minutes of Meeting at the Admiralty concerning arrangements for dealing with German U-boats after surrender, 27 March 1945.' DHist, File 1650-U-Boats-1945, Commander G.F. Todd, RCN, 'Interim Report on Plans for Surrender of German U-Boats', 29 March 1945.
74. DHist, File 1650-U-Boats-1945, Commander G.F. Todd, RCN, Naval Assistant (Policy and Plans), 'Third Interim Report on Plans for Surrender of German U-Boats', 17 April 1945.
75. DHist, File 1650-U-Boats-1945, Intercepted Message from Commander-in-Chief U-Boats to All U-Boats, 08 1930 May 1945. DHist, File 1650-U-Boats-1945, Message from ANCXF Main to Admiralty, 09 1300B May 1945. Arseni G. Golovko, *With the Red Fleet*, (London: Putnam, 1965), pp. 227–8.
76. PRO, WO 205/259, Message from ANCXF Main to Flag Officer Kiel, 09 2021B May 1945.
77. BA/MA, RM 7/849, 'Lage U-Boote am 7 Mai 1945, 0800 Uhr', 7 May 1945.
78. Great Britain. *Preliminary Narrative: The War at Sea*, Vol. 6, p. 347.
79. 'U-249', *Naval Review* 33(1945), p. 218. 'First Surrender in Home Waters', *The Times* (11 May 1945), p. 4. The response called into question the effectiveness of the Admiralty's earlier attempts to promote defeatism among U-boat crews through black propaganda campaigns. PRO, ADM 1/17366, Staff Minute by J.J. Clanchy, 8 April 1945. Cramer, p. 50.
80. W.S. Chalmers, *Max Horton and the Western Approaches: A Biography of Admiral Sir Max Kennedy Horton GCB DSO*, (London: Hodder & Stoughton, 1954), pp. 225–7. CCAC, Roskill, ROSK 5/65, Captain M.J. Evans, RN to Commander-in-Chief Western Approaches, 'Report of Proceedings Operation Pledge', 9 June 1945.
81. PRO, ADM 116/5512, Message from Admiralty to ANCXF, 17 1912B May 1945. BA/MA, RM 7/854, 'Lage Westraum am 17 Mai 1945 um 0800 Uhr', 17 May 1945. Great Britain. *Preliminary Narrative: The War at Sea*, Vol. 6, p. 349. Marc Milner, *The U-Boat Hunters: The Royal Canadian Navy and the Offensive against Germany's Submarines*, (Toronto: University of Toronto Press, 1994), p. 265–6.
82. DHist, File 1650-U-Boats, P/W Weekly Report 'Surrenders', 26 May 1945. Michael L. Hadley, *U-Boats Against Canada: German Submarines in Canadian Waters*, (Montreal and Kingston: McGill–Queen's University Press, 1985), pp. 298–9.
83. DHist, File 1650-U-Boats-1945, Message from Admiralty to British Admiralty

Delegation Washington, 28 0915B May 1945.

84. DHist, File 1650-U-Boats 1939–45 Vol. 2, Report No. 9 from Canadian Naval Mission Overseas to Naval Service Headquarters Ottawa, 'Report on U-Boat War for Period 1 May to 10 May 1945', 16 May 1945. '300 U-Boats are Held', *Daily Express* (24 May 1945), p. 1.

85. 'U-Boat Crew in Portugal', *The Times* (22 May 1945), p. 3. NA, RG 313, COMNAVEU, Series II, File 61, COMNAVEU War Diary – Technical Intelligence Section, 7 June 1945.

86. . Heinz Schaeffer, *U-Boat 977*, (New York: Bantam, 1981), pp. 174–82. Great Britain. *Preliminary Narrative: The War at Sea*, Vol. 6, pp. 352–4. Argentina had actually declared war against Nazi Germany on 28 March 1945. Schramm, Vol. 4/2, p. 1206.

87. IWM, Bartlett, Memoirs, Vol. 4 'March 1943–End of War', pp. 31–4. U-979's recovered war log indicated that the crew had been at sea for several weeks after the surrender.

88. BA/MA, RM 7/854, Message from SKL to MOK Nord; Adm Deutsche Bucht; Adm Niederlande; FdS, 10 May 1945. Peter Scott, *The Battle of the Narrow Seas: A History of the Light Coastal Forces in the Channel and North Sea, 1939–1945*, (London: Country Life, 1945), pp. 221–2.

89. PRO, ADM 1/18666, Admiral William Whitworth to Secretary of Admiralty, 'Conference with Admiral Skaggerak's Representatives held on Board His Majesty's Ship "Belfast" at 1030 on Monday, 14th May 1945', 15 May 1945. BA/MA, RM 7/854, Handwritten Message from SKL to Adm Skagerrak, 10 May 1945. Drummond represented the Commander-in-Chief Rosyth, Admiral William Whitworth, RN. IWM, P.95, Admiral Sir William Whitworth, RN, WJW 3, Letter from Richard Waltkin to Admiral William Whitworth, 18 July 1946.

90. OAB/NHC, Kirk, Series IV, Box 31, File 'Helbig, J.J. Ylc. USNR, Personal File 1944-45', Message from Admiral Harold Burrough to Chiefs of Staff, 09 2350B May 1945.

91. PRO, ADM 228/17, Captain L.P. Skipwith to British Naval Commander-in-Chief Germany, 'Report of German Warships, Naval Auxiliaries', 6 Sept. 1945.

92. Erwin Sieche, 'The Walter Submarine – 1', *Warship* 20(1981), p. 241.

93. PRO, ADM 1/18325, Lieutenant-Commander P.J.H. Bartlett to Flag Officer Western Germany, 'Report of Proceedings of Submarine Party attached to the Command of Flag Officer Western Germany', 30 May 1945. IWM, Bartlett, Memoirs, Vol. 4, 'March 1943–End of War', pp. 26–8. Cuxhaven's 5th Security Division disembarked 23 officers and 1,020 sailors from warships. BA/MA, RM 7/854, Message from MOK Nord to OKM 1/SKL, 'Lagebericht vom 19.5. 1800 Uhr', 19 2400 May 1945.

94. PRO, ADM 1/18422, Captain L.P. Skipwith to Flag Officer Western Germany, 'Report of Proceedings 9 May 1945–31 May 1945', 1 Aug. 1945.

95. Great Britain. *Preliminary Narrative: The War at Sea*, Vol. 6, p. 255. BA/MA, RM 7/854, OKM 1/SKL, 'Lagebericht vom 21.5. 1800 Uhr', 21 May 1945.

96. CCAC, Misc. 31, Captain Charles Wheeler, RM, 'Report on German Navy at Brunsbüttel', 7 May 1945.

97. PRO, ADM 1/18422, Commander P.W. Coombe to Commodore Hugh England, 'Report of Proceedings 8 May–31 May 1945', 2 July 1945.

98. PRO, ADM 228/8, Commodore-in-Charge Hamburg to Flag Officer Wilhelmshaven, 'Report from Brunsbüttel on Type XXI U-Boat and U-Boat Depot Ship', 19 May 1945.

99. BA/MA, RM 7/854, Message from MOK Nord to OKM 1/SKL, 'Lagebericht vom 16.5. – 1800 Uhr', 17 2000 May 1945.

100. NA, RG 331, SHAEF, ANCXF War Diary, 9 May 1945. BA/MA, RM 7/854, Message from MOK Ost to OKM SKL; Kdt Flensburg, 10 2115 May 1945.

101. PRO, WO 205/312, Message from Flag Officer Kiel to ANCXF, 09 01490 May 1945. Baillie-Grohman was fluent in German because his mother was Austrian.

Brock, p. 192.

102. NA, RG 242, T-1022, Reel 3383, File PG 31801a, Memorandum from Konteradmiral Hans Meyer, SKL to Mrüst; SKL Adm Qu VI, 'Befehle an die deutschen Dienststellen im MOK Ost Bereich', 9 May 1945.

103. He relished the scene of utter desolation: 'Personally, I had for some time, a very satisfactory start to each day, for while shaving at my cabin scuttle in *Milwaukee*, I could view the wrecks of seven submarines, while if I crossed over to the other side of the ship, I could see seven more.' IWM, Baillie-Grohman, 'Flashlights on German Disarmament 1945/46', Vol. 3, p. 84.

104. PRO, WO 205/259, Message from Flag Officer Kiel to ANCXF, 08 1400B May 1945. The German naval staff had previously sent destroyers to the eastern Baltic to transport refugees. BA/MA, RM 7/854, Message from OKM 1/SKL to Kdos, 03 2245 May 1945.

105. BA/MA, Friedeburg, N 374/8, 'Tagesniederschriften der Reichsregierung', 8 May 1945, p. 11.

106. Burrough, p. 195. Baillie-Grohman called the exodus a 'German Dunkirk'. IWM, Baillie-Grohman, 'Flashlights on German Disarmament 1945/46', Vol. 3, p. 86.

107. BA/MA, RM 7/854, Message from MOK Ost to OKM 1/SKL, 'Lage Ostsee am 17 Mai 1945, 0800 Uhr', 18 May 1945.

108. BA/MA, RM 7/854, Message from MOK Ost to OKM 1/SKL, 'Lage Ostsee am 18. Mai 1945, 0800 Uhr', 18 May 1945.

109. BA/MA, RM 7/854, Message from *Theodor Riedel* to Alle, 11 1020 May 1945.

110. BA/MA, RM 7/854, Message from Vizeadmiral Hellmuth Heye to Sailors, Small Battle Units, 13 1903 May 1945.

111. Jordan Vause, *U-Boat Ace: The Story of Wolfgang Lüth*, (Annapolis: Naval Institute Press, 1990), p. 200.

112. BA/MA, RM 7/854, Message from Generaloberst Alfred Jodl, OKW WFSt/Ops to MOK West; OKM 1/SKL, 5 May 1945.

113. IWM, 90/24/1, Commander O.M. Andrew, RN, Message from General Officer Commander-in-Chief Southern Command to Officer Commanding German Armed Forces Channel Islands, 07 2323B May 1945.

114. NA, RG 331, SHAEF, ANCXF War Diary, 8 May 1945.

115. 'Channel Islands Freed', *The Times* (11 May 1945), p. 2.

116. DHist, 81/520/1650-DS Vol. 33, Daily Summary of Naval Events No. 2073, 10 May 1945.

117. BA/MA, RM 7/854, Message from OKW WFSt/Ops(M) to Befehlshaber Bornholm, 10 May 1945. Schramm, Vol. 4/2, p. 1489.

118. Pospelov, Reel 5, Vol. 5, pp. 236 and 353. BA/MA, Dönitz, N 236/22, Letter from Karl Dönitz to Gerhard Bidlingmaier, 14 May 1966. 'Russian Control of Bornholm: Danes Seek Restoration of Communications', *The Times* (18 May 1945), p. 4. 'Mystery Isle Breaks Silence', *Daily Express* (17 May 1945), p. 4. Jürgensen, pp. 124–5. See also BA/MA, RW 44I/12. The Danes had earlier anticipated the Soviets' interest in Bornholm. LHC, Dewing, Diary, Vol. 3, 30 Jan. 1945.

119. BA/MA, RM 7/851, Message from MOK Ost to OKM 1/SKL, 23 0335 April 1945.

120. NMM, Holt, Folder 18, File 'Denmark 1945', Report of Proceedings from Flag Officer Denmark to British Naval Commander-in-Chief Germany, 11 Aug. 1945.

121. Knut Einar Eriksen, 'Great Britain and the Problem of Bases in the Nordic Area, 1945–1947', *Scandinavian Journal of History* 7(1982), pp. 141–3. FO/SU, 1945, Reel 18, Vol. 47964, Frames 46–8, Agenda for 'Terminal'. The British wanted to avoid any action which might encourage the Soviets to 'hang on to Bornholm.' BL, Cunningham, Add. Ms. 52578, Diary, 25 Sept. 1945.

122. Great Britain. *Preliminary Narrative: The War at Sea*, Vol. 6, p. 256. Helgoland's garrison included 890 officers, 21 officials, 473 non-commissioned officers, 1,737 ratings, and 42 women naval auxiliaries. BA/MA, RM 7/854, Message from Adm Deutsche Bucht to OKM 1/SKL; MOK Nord, 'Angaben über Helgoland', 10 0550 May 1945.

123. NA, RG 331, SHAEF, ANCXF War Diary, 11 May 1945.
124. PRO, ADM 1/18270, Lieutenant Commander C.K.S. Aylwin to Flag Officer Western Germany, 'Report of Proceedings of Occupation of Helgoland and Dune from 11 to 17 May 1945', 17 May 1945. 'Helgoland Commander under Arrest', *The Times* (18 May 1945), p. 4. BA/MA, RM 7/854, Message from Adm Deutsche Bucht to OKM 1/SKL; MOK Nord, 12 2330 May 1945.
125. PRO, WO 205/259, Message from ANCXF Main to SHAEF Fwd, 21 1940B May 1945. PRO, ADM 1/18422, Report of Proceedings from Captain E.P.G. Sandwith to Flag Officer Western Germany, 4 July 1945.
126. IWM, Montgomery, Reel 9, BLM 105/40, Message from SHAEF to Combined Chiefs of Staff, 29 April 1945. Bob Moore, 'The Western Allies and Food Relief to the Occupied Netherlands, 1944–1945', *War and Society* 10(1992), pp. 108–9.
127. NAC, RG 24, Vol. 10799, File 225C2.012(D4), Directive from General Harry Crerar to Generaloberst Johannes von Blaskowitz, 6 May 1945. Like Lindemann, Blaskowitz was ordered to maintain correct and disciplined behaviour among forces in Holland. BA/MA, RM 7/854, Message from Kapitän zur See Heinz Assmann, WFSt/Ops to OKM 1/SKL, 5 May 1945.
128. PRO, WO 205/1050, 'The Formation and Activities of First Canadian Army "T" Force', pp. 8–17. NAC, RG 24, Vol. 10,611, File 215C1.009(D52), Memorandum by Administrative HQ 1st Canadian Army, 'T-Force Targets: Holland and Germany', 5 May 1945.
129. DHist, File 145.2H1011(D1), Historical Report by Historical Officer, 1st Canadian Infantry Division, based on interview with Lieutenant-Colonel G.E.B. Renison, 'Aspects of an Infantry Battalion's Activities in Western Holland during the First Week of Eclipse', 2 June 1945.
130. IWM, 66/44/1, Commander R.P.C. Hawkins, RN, Report from Control Commander to Chief of Staff, Flag Officer Holland, 'Naval Intelligence', 13 June 1945.
131. PRO, WO 205/259, Message from EXFOR Main to 1st Canadian Army; 2nd British Army, 11 2130B May 1945.
132. NAC, RG 24, Vol. 15,258, Seaforth Highlanders of Canada Regiment War Diary, 10 May 1945. 'Liberation marred in Amsterdam: Crowds fired on by German Marines', *The Times* (11 May 1945), p. 4.
133. Chris Madsen, 'Victims of Circumstance: The Execution of German Deserters by surrendered German Troops under Canadian Control in Amsterdam, May 1945', *Canadian Military History* 2(1993), pp. 93–113.
134. LHC, Admiral Sir Gerald Charles Dickens, RN, File 'Dickens War Diary 1940–1945', Memoir, p. 42. IWM, 90/35/2, Admiral Sir Gerald Charles Dickens RN, File 'Correspondence 1940–1949', Letter from Vice-Admiral Gerald Dickens to Wife, 8 May 1945.
135. Gerald C. Dickens, 'The Royal Netherlands Navy at War and After', *Naval Review* 34(1946), p. 397. Furstner later visited the First Sea Lord 'to request that we would not remove our British control of the Dutch ports too quickly.' BL, Cunningham, Add. Ms. 52578, Diary, 5 June 1945. Gerke Teitler, 'Sea Power on the Decline: Anti-Americanism and the Royal Netherlands Navy 1942–1952', Rob Kroes and Maarten van Rossem, eds., *Anti-Americanism in Europe*, (Amsterdam: Free University Press, 1986), p. 73.
136. NDL/NHC, 'Administrative History, United States Naval Forces in Europe 1940–1946', Vol. 7, p. 284.
137. NAC, RG 24, Vol. 10,896, File 235C1.310(D8), Message from 1st Canadian Corps to 1st Canadian Infantry Division, 13 0930 May 1945.
138. IWM, Hawkins, 'Notes on Meeting of Flag Officer Holland with Chief of Staff to Admiral für die Niederlande at the British Legation, The Hague on Sunday, 13 May 1945 at 1030 hours, First Meeting', 14 May 1945.
139. IWM, Hawkins, Message from Flag Officer Holland to All Naval Officers-in-Charge, Royal Navy Officers; repeated Canadian Corps, Divisions, Brigades, 15

1009B May 1945.

140. NAC, RG 24, Vol. 10,896, File 235C1.013(D8), Message from Flag Officer Holland to 1st Canadian Infantry Division, 17 May 1945.

141. DHist, File 142.5M2011(D1), Historical Report by Historical Officer, 1st Canadian Infantry Division, 'The Concentration and Evacuation of Germans at Den Helder, 8 May–10 June 1945'. NAC, RG 24, Vol. 10,896, File 235C1.013 (D8), Message from Naval Liaison Officer, Flag Officer Holland to 1st Canadian Infantry Division, 17 2145 May 1945.

142. PRO, ADM 228/17, List from Senior British Naval Officer Holland to British Naval Commander-in-Chief Germany, 'German Vessels in Holland on Entry of Allied Forces', 19 Aug. 1945. The Royal Navy also found a considerable amount of new building. Besides completing previous Dutch construction, the *Kriegsmarine* had placed contracts for motor torpedo boats and trawlers with Dutch shipyards during the war. BA/MA, RM 22/4, Report from Vizeadmiral Karl Topp to Flag Officer Schleswig-Holstein, 'Überwasserkriegsschiffbau während des Krieges 1939–1945', 19 Feb. 1946. John D. Spek, 'The Dutch Naval Shipbuilding Program of 1939', *Warship International* 15(1988), p. 69.

143. IWM, Hawkins, Message from Flag Officer Holland to Naval Officer-in-Charge Rotterdam, Den Helder; Eclipse 'Q'; 1st Canadian Corps; 1st Canadian Division, 04 1901B June 1945.

144. Great Britain. *Preliminary Narrative: The War at Sea*, Vol. 6, p. 275.

145. Horst Boog, '"Josephine" and the Northern Flank', *Intelligence and National Security* 4(1989), p. 151.

146. National Army Museum, Chelsea (hereafter NAM), 8703-31, General Sir Andrew Thorne, 'HQ Allied Land Forces Norway After Action Report 13 September 44–14 July 1945'. Peter Thorne, 'Andrew Thorne and the Liberation of Norway', *Intelligence and National Security* 7 (1992), p. 302.

147. Love and Major, p. 187.

148. SHAEF also considered a request from the Norwegian government for Sweden to send forces into Norway. Henry Denham, *Inside the Nazi Ring: A Naval Attaché in Sweden 1940–1945*, (London: John Murray, 1984), p. 166.

149. LHC, Commander Douglas Capper, Chiefs of Staff Committee, COS(45)101, 'Weekly Resumé (No. 297) of the Naval, Military, and Air Situation from 0700 3 May to 0700 10 May 1945', p. 6. NAM, Thorne, List for 20th Anniversary, 'Liberation of Norway', May 1965.

150. Earl F. Ziemke, *The German Northern Theater of Operations 1940–1945*, (Washington, DC: Government Printing Office, 1976), p. 314. Schramm, Vol. 4/2, p. 1488. Frode Saeland, *Frigjoringen I Rogland*, (Stavanger: Statsarkivet i Stavanger, 1995), pp. 20–1. In his capacity as commander-in-chief, Böhme represented all German forces in Norway, including naval. BA/MA, RM 7/854, Message from OKW to OKM 1/SKL, 03 1715 May 1945.

151. PRO, ADM 1/18665, Admiral William Whitworth to Secretary of Admiralty, 'Notes on Conference with German Delegates from Norway held on Board His Majesty's Ship *Renown* on Friday, 11 May 1945', 13 May 1945. 'Minefield Secrets', *The Times* (12 May 1945), p. 4. *House of Commons Debates*, 5th Series, Vol. 411, 31 May 1945, Columns 393–4.

152. NA, RG 331, SHAEF, ANCXF War Diary, 13 May 1945. C.B. Koester, 'The Liberation of Oslo and Copenhagen: A Midshipman's Memoir', *The Northern Mariner* 4(1993), pp. 50–2. 'Liberation', *Naval Review* 33(1945), p. 213. 'Arrival of Prince Olav', *The Times* (14 May 1945), p. 3. Johs Andenaes, O. Riste, and M. Skodvin, *Norway in the Second World War*, (Oslo: Johan Grundt Tanum Forlag, 1974), p. 119.

153. PRO, ADM 199/1440, Vice-Admiral Rhoderick McGrigor to Secretary of Admiralty, 'First Cruiser Squadron War Diary – 1st May to 30 June 1945'.

154. NAM, General Sir Andrew Thorne, 'The Liberation of Norway: from the Point of View of the Commander-in-Chief Allied Land Forces Norway – A Report', p. 25.

155. NAM, Thorne, 'Supreme Headquarters Allied Expeditionary Force Mission (Norway) Final Report ending 13 July 45', Rear-Admiral J.S.M. Ritchie, Part II 'Naval Section', p. 1. PRO, ADM 228/17, Flag Officer Norway to British Naval Commander-in-Chief Germany, 'List of German Warships and Auxiliaries', 21 Sept. 1945. Ritchie ordered German naval authorities to take down German flags on all warships and merchant vessels. BA/MA, RM 7/854, Message from MOK Norwegen to Offen, 14 1734 May 1945.

156. PRO, ADM 116/5512, Message from Captain B.D. Nicholson to Admiralty, 16 1604B May 1945. Whitworth concluded: 'In view of the large and increasing number of U-boats in Norwegian Waters, the naval organisation as at present planned is inadequate to attend to their disarmament, inspection, and laying up.' NAC, RG 24, Vol. 11,752, File CS 638-3, Message from Admiral Whitworth to Admiralty, 09 1943B May 1945.

157. PRO, ADM 199/1440, Admiral Henry Moore to Secretary of Admiralty, 'Dispatch of the Commander-in-Chief, Home Fleet, Covering the Period 19 Dec. 1944 to the End of May, 1945', p. 57.

158. PRO, ADM 116/5512, Message from Admiralty to ANCXF, 24 2253B May 1945. PRO, ADM 228/5, Message from ANCXF to Flag Officers Kiel, Denmark, Norway, 24 1645B May 1945. NA, RG 331, SHAEF, ANCXF War Diary, 25 May 1945.

159. DHist, File 81/520/1650-DS, Vol. 33, Daily Summary of Naval Events Summary No. 2081, 18 May 1945.

160. BA/MA, RM 7/854, Message from MOK Norwegen to OKM 1/SKL, 'Nachmeldung zur Lagemeldung Nr. 2 vom 17/5', 18 0020 May 1945.

161. PRO, ADM 199/443, Letter from Captain J.H. Ruck-Keene to Flag Officer Norway, 'Information Collected from German Authorities', 15 June 1945.

162. BA/MA, RM 7/854, Message from MOK Norwegen to OKM 1/SKL, 'Lagemeldung Nr. 3 v. 18/5. 1600', 19 May 1945. BA/MA, RM 7/854, 'Lage Westraum am 21 Mai 1945 um 0800 Uhr', 21 May 1945.

163. NAM, Thorne, Letter from General Andrew Thorne to Lieutenant-General W. Bedell-Smith, 27 May 1945. Helmut Wolff, *Die deutschen Kriegsgefangenen in britischer Hand*, Vol. 11/1, Erich Maschke, ed., *Zur Geschichte der deutschen Kriegsgefangenen des Zweiten Weltkrieges*, (Bielefeld: Verlag Ernst und Werner Gieseking, 1962–74), p. 84.

4

Control and Disbandment

Between May and July 1945 Eisenhower's Allied headquarters remained in existence, pending transfer of responsibilities and authority in occupied Germany to an Allied Control Council. During the so-called 'SHAEF period', naval policy towards the defeated *Kriegsmarine* rested on the existing 'Eclipse' arrangements, but also displayed considerable flexibility and improvisation to meet particular circumstances. Control and disbandment of German naval forces was the Royal Navy's most immediate concern. Burrough decided to retain temporarily the German naval high command and its existing command structure to carry out the work. Under British direction, German naval authorities transferred, administered, and maintained naval forces before their demobilization. The arrangement, although not without problems, proved convenient and effective. The Royal Navy depended upon German collaboration to further the goal of complete naval disarmament.

As envisioned in the previous planning, British naval authorities took advantage of the existing command structure. The functional *Oberkommando der Marine* (OKM) maintained considerable control and authority over naval forces after the capitulation. German authorities issued Burrough's special orders, prohibited scuttling or sabotage, and followed British instructions. On 10 May Vizeadmiral Friedrich Ruge, Konteradmiral Eberhard Godt, and Kapitänleutnant Karl Kölzer arrived at Burrough's main headquarters, located at the Chateau d'Hennement in St. Germain near Versailles.[1] The delegation furnished mine and U-boat information requested, and answered questions from Burrough's staff. Ruge remained in St. Germain to provide liaison between British and German naval authorities.[2] Burrough and his staff officers simply issued orders and instructions to Ruge, who then relayed them to the OKM for distribution and implementation. Although the arrangement worked well on an interim basis, lack of direct supervision over the German naval headquarter's activities left open the possibility of evasion or non-compliance with the surrender terms.

Consequently, Burrough included naval officers in a SHAEF control party for the German High Command. On 12 May Captain G.O. Maund, RN, and Commander H.C.C. Ainslie, RNZN, arrived in Flensburg with Major-General Lowell W. Rooks.[3] The purpose of the control party was to impose Eisenhower's will on the German High Command after the unconditional surrender. An existing plan named 'Goldcup' envisaged creation of a tight control regime with a view towards suspension of the institution.[4] The SHAEF control party established a headquarters on the former Hamburg-Amerika liner *Patria* in Flensburg harbour opposite the former torpedo school. Rooks addressed Dönitz, dismissed Keitel, and appointed Jodl as head of the OKW.[5] The Germans already knew the basic intentions of 'Eclipse' because a copy of the plan had been captured during the Ardennes offensive. Jodl's cooperative attitude ensured general control over the German armed forces.

As Rooks pruned the German High Command to meet Allied needs, Maund and Ainslie interviewed naval officers at the OKW. Kapitän zur See Heinz Assmann, the *Kriegsmarine*'s representative since September 1943, and Vizeadmiral Leopold Bürkner, head of the foreign intelligence department, revealed that the OKM was not actually in Flensburg, but resided separately at a former naval school in nearby Glücksburg.[6] A staff car was provided to take Maund and Ainslie there.

The visit to the naval headquarters surprised the two Allied officers. Maund described Glücksburg as 'the city of refuge for every employed and unemployed German Admiral and other high ranking officers and it is presumed that someone will be sent here to interrogate these officers with a view to sorting out the wheat from the chaff.'[7] The intelligence potential was high because German naval authorities seemed anxious to supply information to the British. To a certain extent, the cooperative attitude was imposed. Ainslie remarked that Kapitän zur See Heinrich Gerlach, Friedeburg's chief of staff, was sincere in his collaboration, but the 'other officers, mostly, appear to comply with ANCXF's orders because they are ordered to do so from above.'[8] The seeds for resistance and opposition still remained, particularly once the German naval staff recovered from the initial shock of the unconditional surrender. Maund recommended immediate formation of a naval control party to exploit the OKM in this favourable situation.

The 'Eclipse' naval plan was notably vague on actual supervision over the naval high command. ANCXF intended to pass orders through German authorities, but had not dedicated specific staffs beyond those of the flag officers and naval officers-in-charge.[9] The British probably expected to impose control at the subordinate level, thereby by-passing the German naval headquarters completely. To make up the deficiency,

Burrough proposed drawing upon personnel from the Forward Interrogation Units, the 30th Assault Unit, and the US Naval Technical Mission to form a joint Anglo-American interrogation and technical party 'as the sole investigating authority with the OKM.'[10] Since the body would be directly responsible to ANCXF, Burrough hoped to avoid duplication and wasted effort. Rooks requested provision of no more than forty-seven officers and other ranks to oversee naval establishments under the existing 'Goldcup' plan.[11] The OKM was in Glücksburg because of shortages in accommodation and facilities within the general Flensburg area. Rooks consciously tried to keep the size of ministerial parties as small as possible, and to avoid independent and uncoordinated groups from converging on German establishments.[12] By doing so, SHAEF remained the overriding authority over the German High Command and its related service parts.

The Royal Navy deferred to Rooks' judgment. During a visit to ANCXF's main headquarters on 16 May, Maund was made personally responsible 'for all general policy relating to the control of the naval section of OKW and OKM.'[13] Maund coordinated with senior German naval officers, Rooks, and other parties. As well, Burrough appointed Captain Sir John Alleyne, RN, who arrived in Flensburg with a small naval staff, as 'my representative in all dealings between OKM and this Headquarters.'[14] Alleyne worked under Maund's general direction. In return for sole responsibility to approve visits to the naval headquarters on SHAEF's behalf, Burrough guaranteed that the total number of British and American naval supervisory personnel would not exceed 100.[15] Due to practical and organizational constraints, the Allied naval presence in Flensburg and Glücksburg remained small. An additional twenty officers and two ratings arrived in two flights from London on 21 May.[16] The naval party's limited size necessarily restricted the scope of supervision.

From the start, the naval control party dealt firmly with German naval leaders. During Maund's absence to St. Germain, a broadcast from a Flensburg radio transmitter disclaimed any knowledge about concentration camps in the Third Reich by the *Kriegsmarine*.[17] The German naval headquarters was the obvious source. At Friedeburg's direction, naval authorities circulated a similar message to officers and sailors within the *Kriegsmarine*.[18] The broadcast caused public outcries in Great Britain and the United States. During a SHAEF press conference, General Lucius Clay remarked that whether the German naval staff 'have any right to the claim to do so need not be discussed here, but they should not be permitted Pilate's gesture of calling for a basin and water.'[19] The *Kriegsmarine* was obviously trying to distance itself from the horrors of the Nazi regime. The Admiralty, seriously disturbed at the blatant political statement, told Burrough to curtail further transmissions.[20] Maund summoned and rebuked Friedeburg for the broadcast. Emphasizing that the British were in charge, he informed the German admiral that all orders from himself and Alleyne were to be carried out 'promptly and without exception'.[21] The Royal Navy and SHAEF took a dim view of the broadcast's political undertones. After the stern lecture, Friedeburg apologized, and promised to correct matters. The British prevailed in the first real test of authority.

The Royal Navy exercised general control over the German naval headquarters. Under orders issued by Burrough to German authorities on 15 May, the OKM remained responsible for administration of German naval forces, subject to instructions from individual Allied flag officers and their representatives.[22] Naval authorities simply carried out British and Allied orders. The OKM's three component parts remained functional in Glücksburg: the *Seekriegsleitung*, headed by Admiral Wilhelm Meisel, handled operations; the *Marinewehramt*, headed by Generaladmiral Walter Warzecha, dealt with administration and personnel; and the *Marinerüstung*, headed by Admiral Otto Backenköhler, oversaw material supply and maintenance.[23] The control party superimposed itself on the existing command structure. Since the Allied supervisory staff remained small, the arrangement relied largely on German goodwill and cooperation.

Why did German naval authorities willingly cooperate with the British? Although subject to British control and direction, they still ran the *Kriegsmarine*.[24] The threat of dismissal, removal, or worse sanctions was certainly a strong motivation. The navy was a career and a lifetime calling for most senior naval officers. Many knew nothing else. Consequently, individuals wished to remain in positions of authority. The Royal Navy allowed them to continue working as they had before. The departments and establishments in Glücksburg replicated the former naval headquarters in Berlin.[25] Work and responsibility permitted German naval officers to ignore defeat and put off an uncertain future for the time being.

The Soviets also showed an interest in the naval establishments at Glücksburg. Burrough made closure of any departments within the *Oberkommando der Marine* conditional upon 'the arrival of the Russian Ministerial Control Party and then only by tripartite agreement.'[26] British naval authorities initially intended to share the German naval headquarters with the Soviets. A Soviet ministerial control party from Zhukov's headquarters, headed by Major-General Truskov, arrived in Flensburg on 18 May.[27] Although prior arrangements confined the Soviet control party to examination of the OKW, Truskov inquired verbally about extension of visiting privileges for Soviet naval officers to the

OKM. Eisenhower's headquarters, however, decided to withhold access from the Soviets.[28] The Soviet control party's activities remained limited to the German Supreme Command.

SHAEF's policy was calculated rather than antagonistic. Despite Stalin's promises at the Yalta Conference and verbal assurances from General Aleksei Innokent'evich Antonov, the Red Army's deputy chief of staff, the Soviet Supreme Command repeatedly ignored requests by SHAEF and the Admiralty for inspections of captured naval installations in Gdynia, Danzig, Königsberg, Stettin, and Swinemünde.[29] Withholding access to the naval headquarters in Glücksburg appeared a good way to elicit more Soviet openness. Eisenhower tacitly hoped to attain reciprocal visits in Soviet-occupied areas.[30] At SHAEF's direction, Burrough authorized Maund to furnish information and charts on minefields in the Baltic, but he kept the OKM closed to the Soviets.

In the meantime, members of Truskov's party pursued informal contacts with German naval authorities. Maund saw the Soviets talking with and offering cigarettes to individual naval officers on the streets in Flensburg.[31] Despite the hatred between the two countries during the war, the Red Navy appeared to foster good relations with the Germans. These activities were understandable. Based on the previous amity in London and Moscow, the Soviets most likely expected the Royal Navy to grant visits to the OKM within a short time. Thus, SHAEF's denial of Soviet access, communicated to Truskov during a meeting on 21 May, came as quite a surprise. According to Maund, Soviet naval officers accepted the news 'in sullen gloom.'[32] The Soviet control party informed Moscow about the rebuff.

The Soviet Supreme Command quickly protested about the decision. Archer received a letter from Antonov, who asked Eisenhower to lift restrictions on the OKM.[33] Although official channels were now in use, SHAEF still refused access until Soviet authorities made some sign of opening Soviet-occupied ports to Allied inspections. Nonetheless, the problem was complex on the Soviet side. The Soviet naval staff supported British and American visits, but an over-bureaucratic Soviet officialdom and a xenophobic Red Army delayed issue of appropriate visas and authorizations. As Archer and other British officials in Moscow pointed out, it was just the Soviet way of doing business.

Unfortunately, Eisenhower's simplistic wish for some sort of *quid pro quo* locked the Royal Navy into a policy which purposely excluded the Soviets in Flensburg. Maund removed the *Kriegsmarine*'s liaison officer at the OKW for giving too much information to the Soviets.[34] Since obstacles to reciprocal visits persisted, the naval headquarters remained closed to Soviet inspection. The Soviet control party's naval contingent eventually left Flensburg disappointed.[35] Perceived secrecy indirectly raised Soviet suspicions about possible collusion between the Western Allies and the Germans. The Soviet control party's disappointment contributed to growing resentment and criticism over the acting German government.

Retention of Dönitz's services after the capitulation was an expedience which became increasingly untenable. The British believed that a central German authority was needed to ensure an orderly implementation of the unconditional surrender. Churchill, in particular, saw 'great advantages in letting things slide for a while.'[36] Eisenhower, who much preferred to terminate the acting government immediately, bowed to British pressure. According to a statement from SHAEF, Dönitz was not recognized as the legitimate head of state, but was only 'used temporarily under the instructions of the Allied Commanders, to carry out duties concerned with the feeding, disarmament and medical care of the German armed forces.'[37] SHAEF's restrictions gave the Soviets little stake in keeping the German administration. Truskov complained loudly about the arrangement, especially after several objectionable radio broadcasts from Flensburg disclosed the Dönitz government's political pretensions. For the Germans, a split between the Western Allies and the Soviet Union still appeared possible. Instead, strong press campaigns in Allied and Soviet newspapers demanded dissolution of the acting government and Dönitz's immediate detention.[38] Arguments for retaining Dönitz in office wore thin as public opinion turned against the regime. Eisenhower, acting upon the advice of his political advisers, ordered Rooks to arrest Dönitz and his entourage.[39] British authorities began elaborate preparations in Flensburg.

Operation 'Blackout', the formal closure of the Dönitz government and the OKW, occurred swiftly on 23 May. Captain John H. Lewes, RN, Burrough's staff officer for intelligence, arrived in Flensburg to coordinate the naval side of 'Blackout' with Maund. The British destroyers Zealous and Zodiac were transferred from Kiel to Flensburg for the operation.[40] With the two warships menacingly anchored in the harbour, armed troops from the British 159th Infantry Brigade, supported by tanks and armoured cars, surrounded German buildings. On board the Patria, Rooks, in the presence of Brigadier E.J. Foord, Truskov, and Maund, informed Dönitz that Eisenhower 'has decided, in concert with the Soviet High Command, that today the acting German government and the German High Command, with several of its members, shall be taken into custody as prisoners of war.'[41] At one stroke, the acting German government ceased to exist. According to Maund, Dönitz preserved a dignified bearing throughout the proceedings, but Jodl and Friedeburg 'showed signs of nervousness and disquiet.'[42] British soldiers arrested, collected, and searched German military and naval personnel at selected locations as 'a large number of the Press and other people were wandering about at will.'[43] Although accusations about British maltreatment and looting followed 'Blackout', only one significant incident marred the otherwise successful operation. Friedeburg, after returning to his quarters to collect personal belongings, evaded a British escort, and committed suicide by swallowing a poison capsule.[44] The sudden death of the *Kriegsmarine*'s commander-in-chief created some doubts about the continued reliability of the naval high command.

The Royal Navy was uncertain how German naval authorities would react to Dönitz's arrest and Friedeburg's suicide. The two men enjoyed considerable personal loyalty and respect within the *Kriegsmarine*, particularly within the U-boat branch.[45] Would the Germans still obey British orders? Maund, who visited Glücksburg with Baillie-Grohman immediately after 'Blackout', reported that 'a nervous excitement and a lack of tranquility was apparent.'[46] German naval authorities gloomily anticipated the OKM's early termination. Burrough, however, deferred a definite decision: 'Unless there is clear evidence that [the] German naval chain of command is being deliberately used to hinder our efforts I would prefer to retain it from OKM downwards.'[47] The naval headquarters still appeared the most economical and efficient means to control naval forces. Except for a few senior naval officers, individuals detained under 'Blackout' were quickly released.[48] British naval authorities tried to minimize the impact of the removals and arrests on the German naval command.

With Dönitz and Friedeburg gone, the Royal Navy required a new officer to take command. In Warzecha's absence, Backenköhler temporarily filled the position.[49] After 'Blackout', investigating and supervisory officers in Glücksburg noticed increased resentment on the part of German naval authorities towards the British. In an audience with Maund, Backenköhler warned that he was 'experiencing trouble amongst the officers and men of the *Kriegsmarine* and that it was becoming difficult to maintain discipline.'[50] He attributed the problems to Dönitz's arrest, closure of the OKW, discontent with press coverage over Friedeburg's suicide, rumours about the removal of decorations and service awards, and intermittent detentions by British naval authorities. Maund secretly suspected that Backenköhler encouraged passive opposition to British control. Despite some questions about political leaning, Burrough appointed Warzecha 'to take charge of the OKM under my orders from noon today Saturday 26 May.'[51] The British wielded arbitrary power to make appointments or dismissals. Warzecha was chosen based upon his organizational and administrative experience in the *Marinewehramt*. As Burrough pointed out, another naval officer of suitable rank could always be found if Warzecha proved unsatisfactory.[52] The Royal Navy was confident that the *Kriegsmarine* would continue to carry out British orders under Warzecha's leadership.

With the compliant Warzecha at the helm, the Royal Navy reconsidered the intended policy towards the *Oberkommando der Marine*. Previous planning envisioned gradual reduction of the naval headquarters over a period of time as personnel and departments became redundant. After discussions with Alleyne, Lewes, and Captain Arthur H. Graubart, USN, the US Navy's representative in Flensburg, Maund recommended closing it down in a single operation instead of piecemeal fashion.[53] While still within the bounds of the original 'Goldcup' plan, the proposed change allowed the British to benefit from the headquarter's unexpected functional integrity. At the same time, Waldock advised the First Sea Lord:

> We must be on guard against the continuance of OKM longer than is strictly necessary. As soon as sufficient control over German naval organisations is established in each locality, we ought to be able to do without any German Command and restrict our use of OKM to the administrative staff dealing with personnel and other records.[54]

Retention was a temporary convenience to maintain order and discipline among German naval forces. If handled carefully, the advantages outweighed the potential risks. Maund's apparent success so far with the OKM in large part persuaded the ANCXF staff.

The Allied naval headquarters at St. Germain liked Maund's proposal. After careful consideration, Owen advised Burrough to 'take no drastic action until D-Day and then cut down [the OKM] in one fell swoop to the minimum skeleton complement. This will keep them in blissful ignorance of their doom.'[55] The idea held a certain sardonic appeal; the British would use German naval authorities until no longer needed, and then chuck them aside. On 6 June Burrough established a three-phase policy for the OKM: retention of the current organization for transfer of personnel to concentration areas and performance of essential tasks; disbandment of all departments except those required for administration of naval forces under Allied control; and then complete dissolution.[56] The Royal Navy never entertained any thought of preserving the German naval command on a permanent basis. The question instead revolved around timing and method of reduction.

The Royal Navy's stance towards the *Kriegsmarine* necessarily had to accord with general occupation policy. A declaration regarding the defeat of Germany and assumption of supreme authority by the Allied powers, signed by the respective zone commanders in Berlin, required complete disbandment of the German armed forces as part of Germany's larger disarmament and demilitarization.[57] With this declaration, the days of the *Oberkommando der Marine* were clearly numbered. A corresponding statement established an Allied Control Council with a permanent coordinating committee and ancillary divisions, including a naval division. This council eventually became the main forum for the Allied powers to discuss and criticize policy decisions over Germany.[58] The Soviets claimed that the British unwittingly or intentionally maintained German militarism through continued operation of the naval high command. Burrough was certainly aware of the danger:

> While OKM exists, besides being a centre of co-operation, it may well be a centre from which anti-Allied doctrine might be formulated and distributed, and I am anxious to reduce it at the earliest possible date and finally, completely disband it.[59]

The naval headquarters was simply a convenient tool to fulfil the control, disarmament, and disbandment of the *Kriegsmarine*. British naval authorities dealt firmly with perceived resistance or defiance from the Germans.

Vague and sometimes contradictory orders allowed some authorities to test and push the limits of the Royal Navy's control. German and British naval officers worked through a parallel command structure within occupied Germany.[60] Individual authorities were directly responsible to British counterparts in flag commands and the respective ports. Nonetheless, Ruge, whom Burrough appointed chief of minesweeping forces, refused to acknowledge the orders of British supervisory officers in the minesweeping base at Friedrichsort, and sent a headquarters ship to replace Kapitän zur See Gerhard Schulz, Baillie-Grohman's appointed officer.[61] For the British flag officer, the action was a clear case of insubordination. After the ship's crew ignored several requests to muster, Commander A.H.R. Barton, RNVR, ordered two bursts from Bofors guns fired into the riggings:

> The effect was instantaneous. Men appeared from every door and hatchway, rushing to boats and rafts and some even jumping overboard to swim ashore. After this, they were fallen in on the jetty, and the British officer, quite rightly, was not yet satisfied. He made them double round the parade ground till dusk, under the encouraging eye of our Royal Marines. At dusk, all hands were battened down and received only bread and water, and at dawn, further drill was resumed, after which the German sailors

returned to their ships in a thoroughly chastened mood. There was no more trouble.[62]

Such demonstration of force was necessary to remind the Germans who was in charge. Commenting on the incident, the First Sea Lord countenanced even more drastic measures: 'I see Baillie-Grohman seems to be having trouble with the minesweepers (German) at Flensburg. I trust he will act firmly and if necessary shoot the leaders quickly.'[63] Although British naval authorities never took up Cunningham's advice, the threat was implied. Burrough arranged with the Admiralty for British destroyers to conduct a series of short visits to German ports to show the flag.[64] The warships and their guns provided an intimidating presence. The Royal Navy demanded absolute obedience to British orders. In return, German authorities retained remarkable powers over their personnel.

The *Kriegsmarine*'s ruthless disciplinary and judicial system remained in operation after the capitulation. Directed by Admiralrichter Dr. Joachim Rudolphi, 212 lawyers worked in sub-branches of the naval legal department – section IV within the *Marinewehramt* – at Glücksburg and various subordinate commands throughout the fleet.[65] These naval officers were principally engaged in convening and reviewing courts martial. A decree, issued by Warzecha on 10 May, reaffirmed the existing jurisdiction of *Wehrmacht* legal codes, and retained the death sentence for desertion because 'the current crisis demands harsh action to prevent a descent into chaos.'[66] Although minor adjustments were made for specific political offences, a Nazi-distorted military law, which had institutionalized judicial murder, remained in force. German naval authorities received corresponding directives from various German and British sources to maintain discipline and order.[67] Despite defeat, the *Kriegsmarine* was unable or unwilling to break from the previous wartime pattern. Faced with possible disintegration, naval authorities fell back on the familiar coercive power of military law and capital punishment.

German naval courts martial kept up a busy schedule after the unconditional surrender. Between 10 May and 31 August 1945 Rudolphi and his naval judges tried an estimated 1,646 cases of desertion in Schleswig-Holstein, western Germany, and Denmark.[68] Since prison facilities were limited, the punishment upon conviction was usually death. A civil court later tried Kapitän zur See and Kommodore Rudolf Peterson, leader of motor torpedo boats, Fregattenkapitän Herbert Max Schultz, Marineoberstabsrichter Adolf Holzig, and four other officers on a charge of crimes against humanity for executions related to desertion convictions after the surrender.[69] German sailors continued to die for a cause which no longer existed. Oberleutnant zur See Herbert Werner, a U-boat officer who witnessed a court martial and subsequent lynching in Norway, saw little hope 'when Germans kill Germans without qualms.'[70] Inside reservations and concentration areas, German authorities retained complete control over administration and discipline. The smallest sign of disorder, disobedience, or insolence was punished severely as a deterrent.[71] Interest in the maintenance of military values and order overrode any claim to moderation. In Norway, courts martial tried and convicted sailors on charges of desertion and absence without leave until July 1945.[72] The Royal Navy appeared completely indifferent to the apparent irony of the situation.

Previous post-hostilities planning had considered the question of German courts martial after the surrender. A meeting between representatives from the Control Commission's Naval and Legal Divisions in August 1944 decided that courts martial should continue to function for the purpose of maintaining discipline among German formations prior to their disbandment.[73] Proposed restrictions, including abolishment of the death sentence, were to limit the jurisdiction and sentencing powers of these courts. In Waldock's view, it was 'important to supervise the work of German naval courts martial, since German use of their disciplinary powers may have serious implications in the work of control.'[74] Nonetheless, the Admiralty's demand for economy made provision of large numbers of officers for legal work in occupied Germany unlikely. Instead, the Royal Navy planned to draw upon existing staffs from among the flag officer commands. As a member of the Legal Division commented, British naval authorities 'judging from the standard of their own British Naval Discipline Act may have underestimated the volume of work that will be cast upon them.'[75] The *Kriegsmarine* used courts martial to punish many offences, which the Royal Navy normally handled with summary punishment. British officers ignored the influence of Nazism in elevating particular military offences, such as desertion and subversion, into pseudo-political crimes.

Indeed, the Royal Navy showed far more interest in the preservation of German disciplinary and judicial powers rather than their limitation. The Legal Division intended to retain the German manual of military law and various disciplinary codes, subject to minor modifications.[76] The Royal Navy strongly supported the policy because naval planners regarded courts martial as an essential instrument to preserve order and cohesion. Parry declared 'that the maintenance of discipline among the German armed forces in the confused period prior to disbandment will be a matter of great difficulty and that it would be a mistake to interfere with the recognised processes of the German court martial procedure.'[77] It was recognized that the Royal Navy's intention to disband the

Kriegsmarine completely hampered German naval authorities from imposing lengthy terms of imprisonment. The German preference for death sentences, therefore, coincided with a British desire for a form of punishment with no subsequent commitments.[78] Executions were a quick and convenient means to encourage expected behaviour from German personnel. Baillie-Grohman even suggested issuance of a special instruction for punishment of individuals, who chose to desert or 'discard their uniforms in favour of civilian clothing prior to disbandment.'[79] British naval authorities were fully convinced that German courts martial should continue after the capitulation.

Unfortunately, the Royal Navy never established effective control or supervision over the *Kriegsmarine*'s post-surrender legal activities. Based upon previous requests, the Admiralty appointed two officers with legal training to work with the Legal Division: Captain (Sp) C.R.N. Winn, RNVR, in the Military Government Courts Branch and Commander R.B. Bodilly, RN, in the German Courts Martial Control Branch.[80] The latter was expected to oversee German courts martial on behalf of the Royal Navy. Military Government Law No. 153 and 21st Army Group Administrative Order No. 97, distributed to German, Canadian, and British commands in mid-May, abrogated questionable parts of German military legal codes, called for British permission before a court martial was convened, limited jurisdiction over certain offences, required written returns for review, and withheld right of confirmation on sentences over two years imprisonment.[81] These stipulations also applied to German forces under the Royal Navy's control. Rudolphi later claimed that he did not actually learn of the contents of Law No. 153 until 14 June 1945.[82] No dedicated British officer supervised the naval legal department's work because Bodilly was seconded as a president on military government courts, due to a shortage of qualified legal personnel in British-occupied Germany. In the absence of British direction, Rudolphi and his judges simply carried on business as usual.[83] Although guidelines were now in place, British naval authorities had absolutely no idea how many sailors came before courts martial or the types of sentences conferred after the capitulation. Local British staffs were too busy with other disarmament work to interfere in German affairs. As long as German naval authorities maintained order and discipline, the Royal Navy was satisfied.

The extraordinary arrangement resulted from an Allied change in the legal status of defeated German forces. For a variety of practical reasons, the British decided that they did not want to be bound by the provisions of the 1929 Geneva Convention in regards to large numbers of German service personnel at the end of the war.[84] The Royal Navy, in particular, planned to keep German authorities responsible for administration and food supply prior to disbandment. In Spring 1944 Captain Lloyd had approached the Americans through the European Advisory Commission with the idea of setting aside the obligations of international law over a specific time period for certain classes of captives.[85] In the Royal Navy's view, the circumstances demanded some flexibility. After considerable discussion in Washington and London, a decision had been made to hold German forces on the Continent as capitulated troops – labelled by the British as 'Surrendered Enemy Personnel' (SEP) – rather than prisoners of war. The new designation was not without precedent: the Germans had held defeated Polish, French, Belgian, and Yugoslavian soldiers from earlier in the war in a similar fashion.[86] Subsequent 'Eclipse' plans incorporated the SEP policy. Discretion to assign or withhold prisoner of war status from German forces rested with Eisenhower and his subordinates at SHAEF.[87] Although neither in the spirit nor the letter of the 1929 Geneva Convention, the SEP label furnished the Royal Navy with a convenient means to handle large, surrendered naval forces. British naval authorities treated virtually all members of the *Kriegsmarine* after the capitulation as 'frozen' or surrendered enemy personnel. Continued use of the German command structure, which the SEP label facilitated, was central to British control and disbandment arrangements.

Under British supervision, German authorities undertook large-scale transfers from Holland and Denmark to Germany. Blaskowitz submitted a plan to 1st Canadian Corps for movement of soldiers in large marching groups across the Zuider Zee causeway, commencing 25 May.[88] In addition, tank landing craft provided a ferry service from Den Helder to Harlingen. Although naval artillery and coastal defence units from Hoek van Holland marched to Germany, Stange received approval to transfer remaining naval personnel in German vessels.[89] The sea lifts included women auxiliaries, sick and wounded, and soldiers otherwise incapable of marching. Between 22 May and 20 June twelve convoys carried 21,000 naval personnel and 24,280 other persons from Den Helder, Ijmuiden, and Hoek van Holland to Wilhelmshaven.[90] British and Canadian authorities performed inspections for prohibited goods and plunder at points of departure, but left detailed staff work to the Germans. They were required to meet established deadlines.[91]

Evacuations from Denmark progressed in a similar fashion. At Lindemann's direction, long columns of troops began marching to the German border on 10 May.[92] The Germans handled all the arrangements. Coastal defence units and naval personnel in shore establishments accompanied the army.[93] Naval authorities received considerable responsibilities. Lindemann appointed *Kriegsmarine* officers in Frederikshaven, Esberg, and Aarhus to oversee remaining troops in those respective areas.[94] Warships and merchant vessels transported sailors, sick and wounded, and refugees to German ports. Although Dewing arrested Lindemann at Silkeborg on 5 June, Holt retained Wurmbach and his staff until early August.[95] More naval forces left Denmark in subsequent weeks. A small organization, under the supervision of Holt and Vedel, remained to perform minesweeping in Danish waters.[96] Swift personnel reductions in establishments and concentration areas took place within Holland and Denmark.

Transport difficulties and an unsettled situation prolonged transfer of German forces from Norway. By 10 July 70,052 naval personnel resided in reservations under German authority and cursory British supervision.[97] The rest were engaged in care and maintenance of ships, minesweeping, and various administrative duties. The sea was the only means of return transport because no direct land connection existed with Germany and Sweden refused transit privileges for German formations. Since redeployments to the Pacific theatre restricted Allied shipping space, Ritchie earmarked sixteen German merchant ships for evacuation work.[98] Nonetheless, 21st Army Group's reluctance to accept more personnel into overcrowded concentration areas within Germany caused delay. After several weeks of negotiations, Thorne finally secured approval to begin repatriation at the end of July.[99] As the Germans completed preparations for the large sea-lift, the British removed senior naval officers. At the request of the Norwegian government, Krancke was detained as a prosecution witness at the trial of Vidkun Quisling, the pro-Nazi Norwegian political leader.[100] Evacuation of German forces from Norway proceeded over the coming months. Ritchie's flag command in Norway ceased on 15 October 1945.

Upon arrival in German ports or completion of work under the surrender terms, most German naval personnel were handed over to British military authorities for screening and disbandment. With adjustments to the original 'Eclipse' plan, 21st Army Group established large concentration areas in the Emden-Wilhelmshaven peninsula and Schleswig-Holstein.[101] Sailors joined other members of the German armed forces. As surrendered enemy personnel, the Germans administered themselves, and drew upon food stocks from local resources. The British simply passed orders through designated German commanders and an artificially-imposed military structure, of which the *Kriegsmarine* formed a part. Within the concentration areas, naval officers remained responsible for administration and discipline. By 1 July 380,000 naval personnel were in concentration areas or prisoner of war camps within British-occupied Germany.[102] British military authorities began the large job of discharge.

Despite the overwhelming numbers, release of sailors under British control took place relatively quickly. Under Operation 'Blimp', the Royal Navy discharged directly 2,590 personnel for employment in German ports.[103] Acute labour shortages in key industries necessitated further disbandments. The British released German servicemen to gather the harvest of autumn 1945 under Operation 'Barleycorn' and to mine coal under Operation 'Coalscuttle'.[104] Remaining personnel went through a standard discharge process. With the exception of selected senior officers and individuals in automatic arrest categories, 21st Army Group (the British Army of the Rhine after 25 August) disbanded sailors from the British Zone as soon as possible.[105] Those men with residences in other parts of Germany faced a somewhat longer wait. The British and Americans exchanged naval personnel for discharge in their respective zones.[106] Others remained in captivity in Canada, Great Britain, and the United States. The British used German labour as an informal means of reparations. Several years of work in agriculture and on reconstruction projects preceded the return to civilian life.

Concurrently, the British naval command structure took form in occupied Germany. Eisenhower moved SHAEF's headquarters from France on to German soil. ANCXF's main headquarters reopened in a former Melitta paper factory at Minden in Westphalia.[107] The central location was within driving distance of Eisenhower's new headquarters at Frankfurt, the Control Commission's military and civil divisions at Hanover, and Montgomery's headquarters at Bad Oeynhausen. Requisitioning surrounding houses for accommodation, the Royal Navy transformed the industrial site into HMS *Royal Henry*.[108] Additional personnel, including a large number of Wrens, arrived from London to complete the staff. Parry, whom the Admiralty appointed as Burrough's deputy in Germany, and twelve officers from the ANCXF post-hostilities staff relocated to Frankfurt.[109] Meanwhile, the respective flag commands in Germany established permanent headquarters in Plön, Bremen, and Buxtehüde. Rear-Admiral F.E.P. Hutton, RN, the Flag Officer Belgium, became the Flag Officer Western Germany, after Muirhead-Gould suffered a fatal heart attack during a cocktail party on 26 June.[110] The naval command structure remained essentially the same upon SHAEF's dissolution on 13 July. As the Royal Navy became more organized in Germany, British naval authorities looked towards dispensing with the *Oberkommando der Marine*.

Inadequate supervision over the activities of the German naval headquarters was the primary impetus. After the SHAEF and Soviet control parties departed from Flensburg at the end of May a small staff under Brigadier H.R.B. Watkins and the naval control party stayed behind on the liner *Calabria*.[111] The Germans still predominantly ran their own affairs in Glücksburg. Captain Edward Hale, RN, Maund's successor, observed that British control over the OKM was 'nominal rather than practical and depends on German obedience of orders and fear of the consequences of disobedience.'[112] The relationship was certainly not sustainable for any length of time without some chance of non-compliance or opposition. At Burrough's direction, Hale ordered Warzecha to begin work on proposals to reduce and reorganize German establishments.[113] Although the British simply wanted the Germans to perform most of the work, the assignment inadvertently raised German expectations. During a meeting with the Flag Officer Western Germany, Warzecha asked whether the OKM would continue to exist for an indefinite period.[114] The British reply was non-committal. Burrough's intention to dissolve the German naval headquarters entirely was still unknown to German naval authorities.

Strong American disapproval forced the British to accelerate the planned reductions. During meetings between British and American naval officers in Minden, Commander E.W. Mantel, USN, told Burrough 'that the dissolution of OKM was not being carried out with sufficient speed and that too many German officers and men were congregated in one location entirely free to carry on any activities they desired.'[115] ANCXF's retention of the German command structure was in direct conflict with American occupation directives. Demanding immediate dissolution, Mantel described Warzecha's daily meetings, where officers openly debated the future of the German High Command and the German navy. American criticism certainly seemed justified; British supervision over the OKM was superficial. Burrough ordered Hale to hasten plans to reduce naval establishments and transfer responsibilities to a smaller organization to oversee minesweeping.

British naval authorities finalized arrangements for discontinuation of the OKM. During a meeting in Minden on 11 July Faulkner outlined existing policy, ANCXF's intention to close establishments in Glücksburg, and the proposed transition into a new organization called the German Minesweeping Administration (GM/SA).[116] The change started phase two in Burrough's previous guidelines. The proposals satisfied the Americans. Hale closed down the OKM on 21 July.[117] Henceforth, selected German naval authorities handled only administration, discipline, and supply of small minesweeping forces. A central naval authority ceased to exist. Since the British had involved Warzecha in the process, the action occurred relatively smoothly. Hutton took advantage of the opportunity to disband the *Marineoberkommando Nordsee* and replace Förste with Kapitän zur See Karl Smidt.[118] The 'one fell swoop' descended on the German naval high command without significant incident or protest. British naval authorities transferred redundant naval personnel to 21st Army Group for disbandment or detention in prisoner of war camps. With the shutting down of the OKM, the Royal Navy proceeded with disposal of the *Kriegsmarine*'s surviving warships.

NOTES

1. NA, RG 331, SHAEF, ANCXF War Diary, 11 May 1945.
2. NA, RG 242, T-77, Reel 863, File OKW/30, 'Zusammenarbeit der deutschen mit alliierten Kdo. Behörden', 12 May 1945. BA/MA, RM 7/854, Memorandum from OKM Amt Schiffe und Werften to Chef Mrüst, 11 May 1945.
3. PRO, ADM 228/71, Directive from Lieutenant-General W.B. Smith to Major-General Lowell Rooks, 'Supreme Headquarters Control Party (OKW)', 11 May 1945.
4. PRO, FO 1032/484, Notes on 4th Eclipse Planning Meeting, 20 April 1945.
5. BA/MA, RM 7/854, Minutes by Oberstleutnant Boehm-Tettelbach, WFSt/Einsatz-Abteilung (L), 'Unterredung zwischen dem Grossadmiral und Gen. Major Rooks in Flensburg auf der "Patria" am 13.5. 1945, 12.00 Uhr', 13 May 1945. Schramm, Vol. 4/2, pp. 1493–5. Wilhelm Keitel, *The Memoirs of Field Marshal Keitel*, (London: William Kimber, 1965), p. 234.
6. NA, RG 242, T-77, Reel 863, 'Unterbringungsübersicht für den Sonderbereich des Oberkommandos der Wehrmacht', 12 May 1945.
7. PRO, ADM 228/71, Letter from Captain G.O. Maund to ANCXF, 15 May 1945.
8. PRO, ADM 228/71, Letter of Proceedings from Commander H. Ainslie to ANCXF (PH), 20 May 1945.
9. NA, RG 331, SHAEF, Special Staff, Adjutant General's Division, Executive Section, File 381-8, ANCXF 'Operation Eclipse – Revised Naval Plan', 10 April 1945.
10. NA, RG 331, SHAEF, General Staff, G-3 Division, Post-Hostilities Planning Section, File GCT 091.711-1/GPS, Message from ANCXF Main to Admiralty; COMNAVEU, 14 1515B May 1945.
11. NA, RG 331, SHAEF, Office of the Chief of Staff, Secretary, General Staff, File 322.01/31, Message from SHAEF Control Party signed Rooks to SHAEF Fwd G-3 Ops, 14 May 1945.
12. NA, RG 331, SHAEF, Office of the Chief of Staff, Secretary, General Staff, File 322.01/31, Message from Major-General Lowell Rooks to ANCXF, 15 May 1945.
13. NA, RG 331, SHAEF, General Staff, G-3 Division, Post-Hostilities Planning Section, File GCT 091.711-1/GPS, Memorandum from ANCXF to Major-General Lowell Rooks, 'Command and Responsibilities at OKW and OKM', 17 May 1945.
14. NA, RG 331, SHAEF, Office of the Chief of Staff, Secretary, General Staff, File 322.01/31, Message from ANCXF Main to Captain G.O. Maund, 15 1717B May 1945.
15. PRO, ADM 228/71, Message from ANCXF Main to SHAEF Fwd, 17 2322B May 1945.
16. BA/MA, RM 7/854, Message from EINGAN to Captain G.O. Maund, 20 2216B May 1945.
17. PRO, ADM 228/71, Text of OKM Broadcast, 13 May 1945. PRO, ADM 116/5423, Telegram No. 75 from Foreign Office to Christopher Steel, British Political Adviser, SHAEF, 16 May 1945.
18. BA/MA, RM 7/854, Message from MOK Ost to FdZ; AdK; Seekmdt Schleswig-Holstein, 14 2058 May 1945.
19. 'Stern Military Regime for Germany', *The Times* (17 May 1945), p. 4.
20. PRO, ADM 116/5423, Message from C.H.M. Waldock to ANCXF, 17 1817B May 1945.
21. PRO, ADM 228/71, Letter from Captain G.O. Maund to ANCXF, 19 May 1945.
22. PRO, WO 205/259, Message from ANCXF Main to OKM, 15 1705 May 1945.
23. PRO, ADM 199/443, Letter and Enclosures from Commodore H.W. Faulkner to

Secretary of Admiralty, 'SHAEF Control Party at OKW Flensburg', 18 May 1945.

24. PRO, WO 205/259, Message from EXFOR Main to 2nd British Army; 1st Canadian Army, 21 1900B May 1945.

25. NA, RG 242, T-1022, Reel 4102, File PG 43405, 'Fernsprechverzeichnis: Oberkommando der Kriegsmarine', 22 May 1945.

26. NA, RG 331, SHAEF, Office of the Chief of Staff, Secretary General Staff, File 322.01/31, Message from ANCXF Main to Captain G.O. Maund, 15 1717B May 1945.

27. NA, RG 331, SHAEF, Office of the Chief of Staff, Secretary, General Staff, File 322.01/31, Message from SHAEF Fwd to ANCXF Main, 20 1925B May 1945.

28. PRO, ADM 228/71, Message from SHAEF Fwd to ANCXF Main; SHAEF Control Party, 20 1930B May 1945.

29. Stark advised Eisenhower to withhold visiting privileges for Soviet naval officers, 'pending more favourable action on the part of Russians for our teams in their zones'. FO/SU, 1945, Reel 3, Vol. 47848, Frame 172, Message from Admiral Harold Stark to General Dwight Eisenhower, 30 1614 March 1945.

30. Alfred D. Chandler and Couis Galambos, eds., *The Papers of Dwight D. Eisenhower: Occupation, 1945*, Vol. 6, (Baltimore and London: Johns Hopkins University Press, 1978), pp. 94–5. FO/SU, 1945, Reel 4, Vol. 47849, Frame 172, Message from SHAEF Fwd signed Eisenhower to Military Mission Moscow, 31 1625Z May 1945.

31. PRO, ADM 116/5423, Message from Captain G.O. Maund to ANCXF, 21 0938B May 1945.

32. PRO, ADM 228/71, Message from Captain G.O. Maund to ANCXF, 22 1227B May 1945.

33. PRO, ADM 228/71, Message from Rear-Admiral Ernest Archer to SHAEF Fwd for Eisenhower, 24 0920Z May 1945.

34. PRO, ADM 228/71, Letter from Captain G.O. Maund to ANCXF, 24 May 1945.

35. PRO, ADM 116/5423, Message from Captain G.O. Maund to ANCXF Main, 31 1624B May 1945.

36. Winston Churchill, *Triumph and Tragedy*, (Boston: Houghton & Mifflin, 1953), p. 756.

37. 'Stern Military Regime for Germany', *The Times* (17 May 1945), p. 4.

38. FO/SU, 1945, Reel 12, Vol. 47893, Frame 58, Political Warfare Intelligence Series 1/2/ No. 108, 'Russian Propaganda to and About Europe (14 May–21 May 1945)'.

39. Marlis G. Steinert, 'The Allied Decision to arrest the Dönitz Government', *The Historical Journal* 31(1988), pp. 658–60. Murphy, pp. 242–4. IWM, Montgomery, BLM 105/41, Message from EXFOR to SHAEF Control Party OKW, 19 1845B May 1945.

40. NA, RG 331, SHAEF, ANCXF War Diary, 23 May 1945. PRO, ADM 199/1440, 'War Diary of Commander-in-Chief Home Fleet for the Month of May 1945'.

41. 'Dönitz Group Arrested: Last of the High Command', *The Times* (24 May 1945), p. 4. PRO, ADM 116/5423, Message from Captain G.O. Maund to ANCXF, 23 1047B May 1945. Walter Lüdde-Neurath, *Regierung Dönitz: Die Letzten Tage des Dritten Reiches*, (Musterschmidt: Druffel-Verlag, 1953), p. 154. The First Sea Lord felt that Dönitz's arrest 'was due to SHAEF being rushed by the Russians. No one seems to have considered the consequences nor what will take its place. The PM and the Foreign Office have not been consulted.' BL, Cunningham, Add. Ms. 52578, Diary, 23 May 1945.

42. PRO, ADM 228/71, Letter of Proceedings from Captain G.O. Maund to ANCXF, 24 May 1945.

43. PRO, ADM 228/55, Report by Lieutenant-Colonel R.G. Kreyer, 1st Battalion, Cheshire Regiment, 29 May 1945. Cremer, p. 212.

44. PRO, ADM 228/55, Report by Captain H. Davies, 1st Cheshire Regiment, 29 May 1945.

45. PRO, ADM 223/42, Konteradmiral Eberhard Godt, 'Address to U-Boat Commanders', 14 June 1945.

46. PRO, ADM 228/71, Letter from Captain G.O. Maund to ANCXF, 24 May 1945.
47. PRO, ADM 116/5423, Message from ANCXF Main to Flag Officer Western Germany, 24 1928B May 1945.
48. IWM, Baillie-Grohman, 'Flashlights on German Disarmament 1945/46', Vol. 3, pp. 95–6. Vizeadmiral Heye and Vizeadmiral Wilhelm Meendsen-Bohlken remained under arrest. Great Britain, *Preliminary Narrative: The War at Sea*, Vol. 6, p. 264. NA, RG 331, SHAEF, ANCXF War Diary, 23 May 1945.
49. PRO, ADM 116/5423, Message from Captain G.O. Maund to ANCXF, 23 1836B May 1945. Warzecha was away from Glücksburg during Operation 'Blackout'.
50. PRO, ADM 228/71, Letter from Captain G.O. Maund to ANCXF, 25 May 1945.
51. NA, RG 331, SHAEF, Office of the Chief of Staff, Secretary, General Staff, File 322.01/31, Message from ANCXF to All Commands, 26 0948B May 1945. Baillie-Grohman reported rumours that Warzecha was an extreme Nazi.
52. PRO, ADM 116/5423, Message from ANCXF Main to Flag Officer Kiel, 26 0310B May 1945.
53. PRO, ADM 228/70, Letter from Captain G.O. Maund to ANCXF, 26 May 1945.
54. PRO, ADM 116/5423, Memorandum from C.H.M. Waldock to First Sea Lord, 'Admiral Doenitz', 27 May 1945.
55. PRO, ADM 228/70, Staff Minute by Commander H.O. Owen, 27 May 1945.
56. NA, RG 331, SHAEF, General Staff, G-3 Division, Post-Hostilities Planning Section, File GCT 091.711-1/GPS, Message from ANCXF Main to Captain G.O. Maund, 06 1815B June 1945.
57. United States. Department of State, *Documents on Germany 1944–1985*, (Washington, DC: Government Printing Office, 1985), pp. 33–8. CCAC, Hynd, HYND 3/2, Cmd. 6648, *Unconditional Surrender of Germany: Declaration and Other Documents issued by the Governments of the United Kingdom, the United States, and the Soviet Union*, (London: His Majesty's Stationery Office, 1945). IWM, Montgomery, BLM 85/5, 'Précis of Meeting held at Berlin 5 June 1945 between the Four Allied Commanders-in-Chief to sign and issue the Declaration on the Defeat of Germany and the Assumption of Supreme Authority with respect to Germany, in connection with the Inauguration of the Control Council', 5 June 1945.
58. Rolf Badstübner, 'Zur Tätigkeit des Alliierten Kontrollrats in Deutschland 1945 bis 1948', *Zeitschrift für Geschichtswissenschaft* 34(1986), p. 596.
59. PRO, ADM 228/70, Memorandum from ANCXF to All Flag Officers, 'Dissolution of OKM', 7 June 1945.
60. BA/MA, RM 7/854, Memorandum from SKL Adm Qu II to Chef SKL; Adm Qu M 1/SKL, 'Zusammenarbeiten deutscher und englischer Marinedienststellen', 28 May 1945. UVic, British Army on the Rhine, *30 Corps District Handbook*, HQ 30th Corps District, Aug. 1945, p. 38.
61. Conflicting orders also occurred on the German side. Warzecha 'reported trouble at HAMBURG owing to orders being given to the Navy by a German General and requested that Admiral Meisel be permitted to proceed to enforce discipline', PRO, ADM 1/18422, ANCXF Post War Diary, 19 June 1945. BA/MA, RW 17/24, Memorandum from Chief of Staff 8th Corps District to Armeestab Müller, 'Abschrift der Übersetzung Angehörige der deutschen Marine', 6 Aug. 1945.
62. IWM, Baillie-Grohman, 'Flashlights on German Naval Disarmament 1945/46', Vol. 3, p. 92. The incident resulted in part from differences between Burrough's staff and Baillie-Grohman about how to deal with the Germans. Ruge remained in the minesweeping position for a short time longer.
63. BL, Cunningham, Add. Ms. 52578, Diary, 15 June 1945.
64. IWM, 91/7/1, Lieutenant Lionel H. Blaxell, RNR, *Through the Hawse Pipe 1939–46: Memoirs of Lionel H. Blaxell OBE DSC*, (Chippenham, Wiltshire: Antony Rowe Ltd., 1990), p. 168. On 23 June a naval party from HMS *Vernon*, supported by the destroyer HMS *Obdurate*, conducted Operation 'Raspberry', a surprise raid at Kiel in search of hidden documents. German naval authorities complained about

the British resorting to such underhanded methods. Great Britain. *Preliminary Narrative: The War at Sea*, Vol. 6, p. 290–1.

65. NA, RG 242, T-1022, Reel 4102, File PG 43405, Organizational Chart and Personnel List, 'Marinerechtsabteilung', 24 May 1945.

66. Lothar Gruchmann, 'Ausgewählte Dokumente zur deutschen Marinejustiz im Zweiten Weltkrieg', *Vierteljahrshefte für Zeitgeschichte* 26(1978): pp. 477–8. The British armed forces, which set aside the death sentence for desertion in 1930, imposed varying terms of imprisonment. William Moore, *The Thin Yellow Line*, (London: Leo Cooper, 1974), p. 225. Great Britain, *Manual of Military Law* (1929), pp. 20–1.

67. BA/MA, RM 7/854, Message from Adm Deutsche Bucht to OKM Mwehr; OKM 1/SKL; MOK Nord, 16 2115 May 1945.

68. PRO, ADM 228/85, Letter from Kapitän zur See Heinrich Gerlach to Commodore Hugh England, 9 October 1945.

69. *Justiz und NS-Verbrechen*, Vol. 5, (Amsterdam: University Press, 1970), pp. 193–265. PRO, ADM 228/85, Letter from Acting Senior Control Officer, Office of Regional Commissioner, HQ Military Government to Captain D.K. Bain, GM/SA, 21 June 1947. The court acquitted two defendants, and convicted the rest.

70. Herbert A. Werner, *Iron Coffins*, (New York: Bantam, 1978), pp. 388–90. As with most memoirs, Werner's observations must be used with caution. Michael L. Hadley, *Count Not the Dead: The Popular Image of the German Submarine*, (Montreal and Kingston: McGill–Queens University Press, 1995), pp. 130–3.

71. BA/MA, RM 7/854, Message from MOK Norwegen to OKM 1/SKL, 20 1600 May 1945.

72. Heinz Hürten, 'Umbruch der Normen: Dokumente über die deutsche Militärjustiz nach der Kapitulation der Wehrmacht', *Militärgeschichtliche Mitteilungen* 2(1980), pp. 143–50. Although reports to the British covering the Trondheim area listed naval judges, German naval authorities simply stated: 'Nothing to report. Discipline is orderly.' PRO, ADM 199/443, Lists from Captain J.H. Ruck-Keene to Flag Officer Norway, 'Information from Trondheim', 25 May 1945.

73. PRO, FO 1060/1174, Brigadier Andrew Clark, Chief Legal Division to Captain C.K. Lloyd, 'Minutes of a Conference held in Room 213 at 1645 hrs 22 Aug 44', 23 Aug. 1944. The Admiralty regarded trial and punishment by British courts martial under the Naval Discipline Act as inappropriate. PRO, ADM 1/16125, Staff Minute by J. Lawson, Naval Law Branch, 12 Sept. 1944. Great Britain, *The King's Regulations and Admiralty Instructions for the Government of His Majesty's Naval Service*, Vol. 1, (London: His Majesty's Stationery Office, 1939), pp. 169–71.

74. PRO, ADM 1/16125, Staff Minute by C.H.M. Waldock, 12 Oct. 1944.

75. PRO, FO 937/25, Letter from Group Captain E.St.C. Harnett to Brigadier Andrew Clark, 'German Courts Martial. Carpet Establishment', 3 Nov. 1944.

76. PRO, FO 1060/1175, Group Captain E.St.C. Harnett, 'Lecture on German Courts Martial', 25 Jan. 1945.

77. PRO, FO 1060/1174, Letter from Rear-Admiral W.E. Parry to Brigadier Andrew Clark, Chief Legal Division, 'German Courts Martial', 26 Feb. 1945.

78. The Admiralty later opposed repeal of capital punishment in Great Britain because 'the death penalty for certain offences was a deterrent essential to the efficiency of the armed forces.', PRO, ADM 167/128, Minutes of Board of Admiralty, 12 Dec. 1947.

79. PRO, ADM 228/59, Memorandum from Rear-Admiral W.E. Parry to SHAEF (GI), 5 March 1945.

80. PRO, ADM 1/16125, Memorandum from Naval Division CCG(BE) to Secretary of Admiralty, 'RN Representation on Legal Division of the Control Commission for Germany', 28 April 1945. The Admiralty initially wanted to appoint Duckworth, who was 'something of an authority on courts martial procedure', but he was occupied with work on the Control Commission. PRO, ADM 1/16125, Staff Minute by C.H.M. Waldock, 22 Jan. 1945. PRO, FO 1032/24, Brigadier Andrew

Clark to Rear-Admiral Roger Bellairs, 'Minutes of a Conference held in Room 302, Norfolk House on 18 Nov. 44, at 1145 hours', 20 Nov. 1944.

81. NAC, RG 24, Vol. 10,611, File 215C1.009(D33), Memorandum from Brigadier W.B. Wedd, Adm HQ 1st Canadian Army, 'Discipline of the Disarmed Wehrmacht (Excl. PW) 21 Army Group Administrative Instruction No. 97', 17 May 1945. The Royal Navy contributed to earlier drafts of Law No. 153. PRO, ADM 228/81, Memorandum from Rear-Admiral W.E. Parry to Brigadier Andrew Clark, 'Proposals to be Embodied in the Ordinance Regulations – German Courts Martial', 31 Jan. 1945.

82. Gruchmann, p. 477.

83. PRO, ADM 228/92, Admiralstabsrichter Joachim Rudolphi, 'Memorandum for a conference relating to the organization of the courts in the remaining German navy', 19 July 1945.

84. *House of Commons Debates*, Series 5, Vol. 438, 17 June 1947, Columns 1785–6. Howard S. Levie, ed., *Documents on Prisoners of War*, (Newport, RI: Naval War College Press, 1979), pp. 178–200. The Germans also questioned the constraints of existing international agreements. When Hitler had suggested renouncing the 1929 Geneva Convention in February 1945, Dönitz advised that Germany should 'keep up outside appearances and carry out the measures believed necessary without announcing them beforehand'. NA, RG 242, T-206, Reel 1, File OKM/95, 'Teilnahme des Ob.d.M. an der Führerlage am 19.2. 17,00 Uhr', 20 Feb. 1945. Jak P. Showell, ed., *Fuehrer Conferences on Naval Affairs 1945*, pp. 50–1.

85. Richard D. Wiggers, 'The United States and the Denial of Prisoner of War (POW) Status at the End of the Second World War', *Militärgeschichtliche Mitteilungen* 52(1993), p. 98.

86. S.P. MacKenzie, 'The Treatment of Prisoners of War in World War II', *Journal of Modern History* 66(1994), pp. 498–502. Alan Rosas, *The Legal Status of Prisoners of War*, (Helsinki: Suomalainen Tiedeatkatemia, 1976), p. 78. Canadian Red Cross Archives, Box ICRC – History – WWII – POW – Medical Commission, René-Jean Wilhelm, 'Can the Status of Prisoners of War be Altered?', (Geneva: International Committee of the Red Cross, 1953), pp. 5–8.

87. Brian Loring Villa, 'The Diplomatic and Political Context of the POW Camps Tragedy', Günter Bischof and Stephen E. Ambrose, eds., *Eisenhower and the German POWs: Facts against Falsehood*, (Baton Rouge: Louisiana State University Press, 1992), pp. 59–61. NAC, RG 24, Vol. 10,611, File 215C1.009(D33), Memorandum from EXFOR Rear to Administrative HQ, 1st Canadian Army, 9 May 1945.

88. NAC, RG 24, Vol. 10,611, File 215C1.009(D44), Memorandum from Lieutenant-General Charles Foulkes to Generaloberst Johannes von Blaskowitz, 21 May 1945.

89. NAC, RG 24, Vol. 10,967, File 260C3.009(D14), Major R.D. Prince, 3rd Canadian Infantry Brigade, 'Notes on Evac Germans', 21 May 1945. Stange departed from Ijmuiden for Germany on 8 June. IWM, Hawkins, Message from Flag Officer Holland to Naval Officer-in-Charge Ijmuiden, 05 1823 June 1945.

90. IWM, Hawkins, Commander R.P.C. Hawkins to Flag Officer Holland, 'Report on Work of Control Staff Naval Party 1731 8 May–21 June 1945', 21 June 1945.

91. IWM, Hawkins, Message from Flag Officer Holland to 1st Canadian Corps; 1st Canadian Division; 3rd Canadian Infantry Brigade; German Naval Commander Bloemendaal, 09 1452B June 1945. Dickens dispensed with the German headquarters at Bloemendaal on 19 June. NAC, RG 24, Vol. 10,738, File 219C1.009 (D233), Letter from Flag Officer Holland to 1st Canadian Army, 19 June 1945.

92. BA/MA, RW 38/178, Oberstleutnant Toepke for Generaloberst Georg von Lindemann, 'Befehl Nr. 3 für die Raumung Dänemarks', 8 May 1945. 'Nazi Navy walks Home', *Daily Express* (23 May 1945), p. 1.

93. BA/MA, RM 7/854, OKM SKL Adm Qu mit Anschriftenübermittlung als Zusatz auf Fernschreiben, 17 May 1945.

94. BA/MA, RW 38/178, Wehrmachtbefehlshaber Dänemark Kriegstagebuch, 16 May 1945.
95. 'Lindemann Arrested: In British Custody in Denmark', *The Times* (6 June 1945), p. 3. NMM, Holt, Folder 18, File 'Denmark 1945', Flag Officer Denmark to Admiral Harold Burrough, 'Letter of Proceedings 21 May–31 July', 11 Aug. 1945.
96. BA/MA, RM 7/854, Message from Stabschef Adm Skaggerak to OKM SKL, 17 0115 May 1945. PRO, ADM 228/94, Commodore Reginald Holt to ANCXF, 'Memorandum on Minesweeping in Danish Command', 5 July 1945. Wolff, Vol. 11/1, p. 382–6.
97. NAM, Thorne, 'Supreme Headquarters Allied Expeditionary Force Mission (Norway) ending 13 July 1945', Rear-Admiral James Ritchie, Part II – Naval Section, (F. Disbandment).
98. PRO, 1/18422, ANCXF Post War Diary, 27 June 1945.
99. NAM, Thorne, Letter from General Sir Andrew Thorne to Lieutenant-General W. Bedell Smith, 22 July 1945.
100. NAM, Thorne, Letter from General Sir Andrew Thorne to Field Marshal Alan Brooke, 19 Aug. 1945. Krancke was sent to Great Britain on 30 Aug. 1945. An American war crimes court later acquitted Generaladmiral Otto Schniewind, a former naval commander in Norway, for alleged implementation of the Commando Order. 'The German High Command Trial', *Law Reports of Trials of War Criminals* 12(1949), p. 95. Schniewind then worked for the US Navy in occupied Germany. BA/MA, Wagner, N 539/3, Letter from Captain A.H. Graubart to Otto Schniewind, 1 Aug. 1951.
101. PRO, WO 205/1035, 'Brief Administrative History on Disbandment of the Wehrmacht', June 1945.
102. Great Britain, *Preliminary Narrative – The War at Sea*, Vol. 6, p. 292.
103. PRO, FO 1038/144, Office of British Naval Commander-in-Chief Germany, 'Naval Division Progress Report for the Period 31 July–31 August 1945', 13 Sept. 1945. 'Blimp' ceased in early Sept. 1945. BA/MA, RW 17/24, Wehrmachtstandortälteste Kreiskommandant Gr. Hamburg Standortbefehl Nr. 22, 1 Sept. 1945.
104. NAC, RG 24, Vol. 10,568, File 215C1.(D34), Memorandum from Military Government, 21st Army Group to 9th US Army Group and 15th US Army Group, 'Operation Barleycorn', 27 May 1945. PRO, WO 205/1025, Lieutenant-Colonel Sellor, 'Notes on the Administrative Activities of 21 Army Group during the Post-Surrender Period 5 May–31 July 1945', pp. 18–21. UVic, British Army on the Rhine, *30 Corps District Handbook*, HQ 30th Corps District, Aug. 1945, p. 47.
105. PRO, WO 205/1041, Memorandum from Brigadier A.S. Elsworth for Major-General I/c Administration 21st Army Group to 1st Canadian Army; 2nd British Army, 'Disposal of German Officers', 21 May 1945. BA/MA, RW 17/24, 'Übersetzung Ernteplan Britische Zone in Deutschland 1945'. NAC, RG 24, Vol. 13,583, Canadian Section 1st Echelon HQ 21st Army Group War Diary, 23 Aug. 1945.
106. LC, Microfilm Shelf 51445, Office of the Chief Historian, European Command, *Disarmament and Disbandment of the German Armed Forces*, Frankfurt-am-Main, 1947, p. 36.
107. PRO, WO 205/259, Message from ANCXF Main to SHAEF Fwd, 15 1735B May 1945.
108. IWM, 88/55/1, Lieutenant Howard B. Moyse, RNVR, Diary, pp. 2–31.
109. Parry and his staff moved to Berlin after the Frankfurt offices closed down on 23 July. PRO, ADM 1/18660, Naval Expeditionary Force Temporary Memorandum No. 60, 25 July 1945.
110. PRO, ADM 1/18422, ANCXF Post-War Diary, 26 June 1945. IWM, Bartlett, Memoirs, Vol. 4, p. 30. Minor name changes took place. The Flag Officer Wilhelmshaven became the Flag Officer Western Germany, and the Flag Officer Kiel became the Flag Officer Schleswig-Holstein. PRO, WO 205/259, Message from ANCXF Main to AIG 507, 500, 18 2243B May 1945.

111. 'Last Days at Flensburg: Lost Hopes of General Staff: Control Party Disperses', *The Times* (30 May 1945): p. 4.
112. PRO, ADM 228/70, Memorandum from Captain E. Hale to ANCXF, 'Future Policy Regarding OKM', 5 June 1945.
113. PRO, ADM 228/70, Letter from Captain E. Hale to Oberbefehlshaber der Kriegsmarine, 11 June 1945.
114. PRO, ADM 228/70, Memorandum from Flag Officer Western Germany to ANCXF, 'Control of OKM: Interview with General Admiral Warzecha', 15 June 1945.
115. NA, RG 331, SHAEF, General Staff, G-3 Division, Post-Hostilities Planning Section, File GCT 091.711-1/GPS, Memorandum from Commander E.W. Mantel to Vice-Admiral Robert Ghormley, 'Continued Operation of the OKM', 9 July 1945.
116. PRO, ADM 228/70, 'Minutes of a Meeting held at ANCXF HQ at Minden Wed, 11 July 1945 to decide final arrangements for setting up German Minesweeping Department', 18 July 1945.
117. PRO, ADM 228/70, Message from British Naval Commander-in-Chief Germany to Admiralty, 23 1414B July 1945.
118. PRO, ADM 228/70, Message from Flag Officer Western Germany to British Naval Commander-in-Chief Germany, 14 2246B July 1945.

5

Division of the German Fleet

Due to German transfers and activities at the end of the war, most surviving warships and merchant vessels fell under British control. The Admiralty, eager to avoid another experience like the embarrassing scuttling of the German High Seas Fleet at Scapa Flow in 1919, favoured quick decisions on destruction or distribution. At the Potsdam Conference, political leaders from Great Britain, the United States, and the Soviet Union agreed to divide German ships between the three countries. From August to December 1945 tripartite naval and merchant marine commissions met in Berlin to decide upon specific allocations. Division of the German fleet involved complex negotiations with the Americans and the Soviets. Although some differences remained outstanding, naval delegates achieved a final agreement. The work of the Potsdam Conference and the tripartite commissions denied Germany possession of any major warship or submarine.

The ultimate fate of the German fleet had been the subject of inter-allied discussions since the First Sea Lord's submission to the Combined Chiefs of Staff in early 1944. Although reluctant to discuss the topic without consulting the Soviets, the US Joint Chiefs of Staff suggested that, except for a small number of ships retained for experimental purposes, the entire German fleet be destroyed, preferably by sinking in deep water.[1] The Americans, with their large navy, maintained no interest in additional surface ships or submarines. Nonetheless, the Joint Chiefs of Staff agreed with the British that none should be left in Germany. If destruction proved impossible for political reasons, Fleet Admiral William Leahy, USN, stated that American officials should insist on being awarded at least a one-third share across all ship classes, to be sunk in due course by the US Navy. Roosevelt, who personally favoured complete destruction, hoped that steel from the warships could be salvaged or ships scuttled for peaceful purposes as breakwaters in harbours.[2] In November 1944 the American representative on the

European Advisory Commission circulated a draft directive, which advocated wholesale scrapping of the German fleet.

The Admiralty received the American proposal with quiet approval. Until then, the Royal Navy gave little thought to final disposal of the German fleet because British naval planners were preoccupied with drafting the special orders and similar instruments of immediate control. Waldock acknowledged that destruction was 'in the best interests of the Royal Navy and of the United Nations.'[3] The proposed scrapping of warships offered to remove any justification for a German navy or related maritime industries, and hence accorded with the Admiralty's disarmament plans. Recognizing that final disposition of the German fleet was a political matter to be settled between the interested Allied governments, Waldock instead worried that:

> If, at the outset, we disdain any desire to add German units to the British Fleet and advocate destruction, the Russians and French may say that as neither we nor the U.S. require German warships, the simplest solution will be to give the whole lot to the U.S.S.R. and to France, with possibly one or two to the Dutch or other Allies.

Some European countries were expected to claim parts of the German fleet as compensation for sacrifices and losses during the war. Open support for destruction, therefore, offered a potentially weaker British bargaining position. Although preferring destruction, the Admiralty officially decided not to support the American proposal. The British played a waiting game until the intentions and demands of other Allied countries were more fully ascertained.

The Soviet Union was the largest unknown. British officials strongly suspected that the Soviets wanted a portion of former German warships, perhaps along similar lines to the earlier decision concerning the Italian fleet. During a weekly meeting with Rushbrooke in London on 30 April 1944 Kharlamov had inquired about arrangements for the German fleet's surrender.[4] The Soviets obviously expected warships to fall under their control during the advance into Germany. Based upon the Admiralty's previous dealings with the Red Navy, Waldock also believed that the Soviet Union would submit claims for ships found beyond the Soviet sphere of control in a peace settlement. The Italian fleet was the obvious precedent. The matter rested on whether the British government held outright objections to distribution of warships to the Soviets and if the demand for destruction could 'only be pressed at the risk of arousing the suspicion that it is antagonism to the USSR which prompts our policy.'[5] Privately, Waldock hoped that the Germans would scuttle all their warships, thereby avoiding awkward wrangling with the

Soviets. Nevertheless, he cautioned against such wishful thinking because the problem was too large 'for us to be able on that account to defer making up our minds.' The Royal Navy needed to adopt a definite policy towards a Soviet share of the German fleet sooner rather than later.

The Admiralty's chosen policy stressed political and disarmament concerns over actual acquisition of warships. After considering the surrendered fleet's future, Captain Guy Grantham, RN, the Director of Plans, concluded:

> If the U-Boat fleet was destroyed and German war-making industry obliterated, I do not think there would be any harm in letting the Russians have what remains afloat of the German surface fleet. With no spares, the ships would be a fairly rapidly wasting asset and there will be very few of them.[6]

The Admiralty was prepared to give the Soviet Union all remaining German ships as long as the Royal Navy achieved comprehensive disarmament measures in occupied Germany and secured destruction of submarines. In other words, British interest in ownership, other than outright denial to the Germans, was minimal. Waldock preferred that the surface ships 'went to the Russians than some of the Western Allies, who had much better stick to British types.'[7] The reconstruction period after the war offered the British a unique opportunity to promote cooperation and dependence among the Dutch, Danish, Norwegian, and French navies. Retention of German warships impeded the leadership role, to which the Royal Navy aspired in terms of training and equipment. The Admiralty, on the other hand, expected the Red Navy to return to its pre-war pattern of isolation and indigenous building under a new five year plan.

The Soviets actually possessed much larger ambitions. The war with Nazi Germany interrupted Stalin's plans to turn the Red Navy into a blue-water battleship and cruiser fleet by January 1943.[8] The Soviets ceased work on warships laid down under the third five year plan's existing shipbuilding programme, and concentrated scarce resources on smaller strike-craft and submarines. Soviet naval operations during the war mainly supported the Red Army with amphibious landings, protected Soviet sea communications, and conducted limited attacks against German shipping.[9] By necessity and choice, the Red Navy adopted a defensive and cautious naval strategy. Conserving Soviet naval strength, Stalin and Kuznetsov looked towards renewed expansion in the post-war period.[10] Prestige appeared the main motivation. The Soviet Union needed a large navy to match its emerging economic and political power. During a visit to the Admiralty, Archer told the First Sea Lord that the Soviets were 'determined to be a great naval power'.[11] British influence in this development could only be negligible. An order of the day from Stalin on the occasion of Red Navy Day in July 1945 declared: 'The Soviet people wishes to see its Navy still stronger and mightier.'[12] Although the Red Navy received wide praise, no reference whatsoever was made to the Royal Navy's leading role in the sea war against Germany. The oversight was intentional.[13] The Soviets felt that British naval power was waning. With projected new building programmes, the Red Navy would supplant the Royal Navy as the predominant navy in Europe and eventually share the world's oceans with the US Navy.

Before full realization of this lofty ambition, the Soviets faced a difficult time of recovery and build-up. Their industries suffered widespread dislocation and devastation from the war against the Germans.[14] Other economic and military priorities took precedence over a larger Red Navy in the immediate post-war period. Kuznetsov was eventually removed from his post for pressing ahead too quickly with plans for a large oceanic surface navy.[15] Shipbuilding capacity and naval armaments production expanded unevenly. The large submarine force in the mid-1950s was due in large part to the Red Navy's concentration on certain ship types.[16] Submarines were cheaper and faster to build in large numbers than cruisers and destroyers. As a stop-gap measure, the Soviets intended to use appropriated German warships until newer building became available. For the British, the Soviet Union's craving for the warships seemed more characteristic of a weak navy rather than a strong one. The Red Navy, however, considered their introduction as necessary for the on-going development of Soviet naval power.

Strong signs indicated that the Soviet Union would make a formal bid for a portion of the German fleet. Gousev, undoubtedly under instructions from Moscow, gave the American scrapping proposal a cool reception on the European Advisory Commission. Although not stated openly at the time, Soviet reluctance to endorse complete destruction suggested a strong desire for German ships. When Truskov candidly asked on 20 May 1945 how many warships and merchant ships were allocated to the Soviet Union, Rooks tactfully answered that the question was 'to be settled by the respective Governments.'[17] The impromptu Soviet approach left few doubts that the Soviet Union not only wanted, but expected some German ships as war booty.

The Soviet leadership pursued the matter at the highest political level. On 23 May Stalin sent almost identical messages to Churchill and Harry Truman, the new American President after Roosevelt's death the previous month, in which he asserted that the Soviet government could 'with good reason and in all fairness count on a minimum of one third of Germany's navy and merchant marine.'[18] Stalin, annoyed by the

Kriegsmarine's refusal to surrender a single operational warship to the Soviets, cited the precedent of the Italian fleet in support of the Soviet claim. The demand represented more than just a question of equality. Stalin implied that a minimum one-third share was needed to preserve good faith between the Western Allies and the Soviet Union. Stalin's quick intervention demonstrated how important the Soviet government and the Red Navy considered acquisition of German warships. The same telegrams informed the British and Americans that the Soviet naval high command had appointed Levchenko and a small staff to handle all matters concerning the German fleet.

Although non-committal, British and American replies were not adverse to the Soviet claim. Churchill thanked Stalin for his views, and stated that the German fleet's disposition was one of several subjects for discussion in a conference to take place between the victorious powers at the earliest opportunity.[19] Besides formalizing the European Advisory Commission's provisional proposals, the British desired a general settlement with the Soviets and Americans over the occupation of Germany. Churchill stressed the need for direct negotiations and tripartite agreement. During talks with Harry Hopkins on 27 May Stalin again reiterated a Soviet claim to part of the German fleet, warning that an outright rejection might have unpleasant consequences on further discussions.[20] The comment was a veiled threat. Hopkins, eager not to impede general progress over just one issue, assured Stalin that the United States and Admiral King maintained no long-term interest in the German fleet, but instead only desired technical examinations.[21] The American statesman then suggested that some sort of understanding between the major victors could guarantee the Soviets a share. In a subsequent message to Stalin on 30 May, Truman stated that the German fleet was 'an appropriate subject for discussion by the three of us at the forthcoming meeting at which time I am sure a solution which will be fully acceptable to all of us can be reached.'[22] Unlike Roosevelt, Truman held no particular penchant for destruction, and was open to transfer of some worn-out ships for the sake of a larger political settlement in Germany and continued good relations with the Soviet Union. On 1 June the British placed partition of the German navy and merchant marine on the agenda for the forthcoming three-power conference at Potsdam, near Berlin.[23]

Preparations for the Potsdam Conference, code-named 'Terminal', were extensive on the British side. The exchange of telegrams between Stalin, Churchill, and Truman gave sufficient warning that the German fleet's disposition would be raised at some point during the conference, most likely by the Soviets. The challenge was to be ready for the query and perhaps use the Soviet desire for ships to British advantage. A

Foreign Office brief, forwarded for the British delegation's guidance on 6 July, attached great importance to the subject:

> As we in fact hold all the undamaged ships, we are in a very strong position, and in fact this is about the best card we hold in our hand for Terminal. ... Experience in past negotiations suggests that the Russians would give us no real credit for spontaneously meeting their demand for the German ships at an early stage of the Conference, and that they would understand, and indeed respect us for it, if we drove a bargain.[24]

The paper advocated a type of carrot and stick approach. British negotiators should tantalize the Soviets with delivery of German ships in order to prise concessions in other areas of concern.

Whether scrapped or given away, the German fleet was expendable for diplomatic ends. A memorandum on the German fleet's disposal, submitted by the First Lord on 7 July, asked the Cabinet to endorse a policy of destroying the German fleet in 'the best interest of world security', or, if the Soviets insisted on division, claiming 'our full share' based upon relative naval losses during the war.[25] Since the Red Navy's active engagements during the war were fewer than the Western Allies, the Soviet Union stood to lose most from such a criterion. In due course, the proposal received approval from the Cabinet.[26] The Admiralty still appeared willing to give the Soviets most surface ships in exchange for destruction or British allocation of submarines.

With minor revisions, the Admiralty's proposal formed the basis for British efforts in three-power negotiations. The Ministry of War Transport, likewise, attempted to tie apportionment of merchant ships to reparations for wartime shipping losses, 'which would mean that we should get half and the Russians next to none.'[27] Whatever the situation, the British hoped to get the best possible deal from their superior position. A modest party from the Admiralty and the Ministry of War Transport, comprising the First Sea Lord, the Director of Plans, the Minister of War Transport, and various civilian and naval experts, accompanied the British political delegates to 'Terminal'.[28] Although British aims for the coming negotiations were clear and pragmatic, the Admiralty recognized that consistent American support was pivotal.

The Royal Navy's greatest worry, in the weeks prior to the conference, was that the United States might abandon Great Britain at the most difficult point in negotiations by wavering from the policy of scrapping, or ceding everything to the Soviets too early. Unlike the British, the Americans regarded disposal of the German navy and merchant marine as primarily a military rather than a political problem.[29] The Department of State largely abdicated consideration of the issue to the Joint Chiefs of Staff. Civilian input and coordination was minimal because the military chiefs advised the President directly. On 10 July the Joint Chiefs of Staff recommended destruction of the entire German fleet as the preferred course of action, division into equal parts for the four major powers if scrapping was not possible, and even relinquishing the American share to the Soviets 'to obtain the best bargain possible in the light of over-all assistance in the war against Japan.'[30] The Americans had already secured temporary employment of captured German merchant shipping in the Pacific theatre, and a few unwanted warships seemed a small price to pay for Soviet intervention against the Japanese.

The British, forewarned of the last recommendation through Admiral James Somerville, RN, the Admiralty's representative on the Combined Chiefs of Staff in Washington, were hardly enthusiastic. The intention to throw the American share on the table as an inducement conflicted with the British plan to drive the hardest possible settlement with the Soviets, particularly since the legitimacy of the Soviet claim represented, in their view, the best point of negotiation. The end was the same, in the sense that both countries were ready to yield most of the German fleet, but the means were different. The British desired concrete concessions from the Soviets over a range of issues before anything was acknowledged or given away, whereas the Americans disregarded potential political consequences for short-term operational needs.

Even worse, the Americans were unpredictable and divided amongst themselves over the appropriate policy. On 11 July King sent a telegram to Truman, expressing his objection to the suggested transfer of the American share to the Soviets.[31] He had been outvoted by the other chiefs when considering the previous proposal. Beside personal reservations, King knew, through Stark and Somerville, that the British disliked the idea. Although King's stance was promising, the Admiralty still did not know where it stood with the Americans on the German fleet, especially with the enormous amount of decision-making placed in one person, President Truman.[32] Would Truman follow the advice of his military chiefs or embark on his own track? No one really knew. The Admiralty recognized that the new President pursued his own priorities and agendas, sometimes beyond apparent rhyme or reason.

'Terminal' formally opened in the Cecilienhof Palace at Potsdam on 17 July. As expected, the Soviets brought up disposal of the German fleet right from the beginning. During the first plenary meeting between the three state leaders, Stalin claimed that he and Truman had reached a previous understanding on the German navy, and then asked: 'Why does Churchill refuse to give Russia her share of the German fleet?'[33] The question, designed to put the British on the defensive, was intentionally provocative. Churchill's reply that the German fleet should be sunk or divided was qualified by the statement: 'All means of war were horrible things.'[34] The ambiguous answer played straight into the Soviet leader's hands. Stalin asserted that German warships were to be divided, and: 'If Mr. Churchill prefers to sink the navy, he is free to sink his share of it; I have no intention of sinking mine.'[35] Truman's silence during the dialogue indicated that the British could not rely on American support for full destruction. When Molotov forced discussion of the German navy and merchant marine at the first meeting of foreign ministers the next morning, Anthony Eden was evasive, but he 'promised that the fleet would not be sunk in the meantime.'[36] No support was forthcoming from James Byrnes, the American secretary of state, who wished to discuss larger problems, such as the authority of the Allied Control Council.

Since the Red Navy desperately wanted German warships, Soviet diplomats persevered. After securing Eden's general agreement on 19 July, Molotov tabled a Soviet proposal, which called for transfer of a third of all warships and merchant vessels to the Soviet Union and establishment of an expert commission with representatives from the three countries' navies to oversee distribution.[37] A tripartite naval commission represented a Soviet initiative, in support of the claim for a share. Division of the *Kriegsmarine* was placed at the top of the agenda for the next plenary meeting. The British, outmanoeuvred and abandoned, conceded to the Soviets in the initial exchanges.

British performance in subsequent talks slightly improved. Molotov presented the Soviet memorandum at the third plenary meeting on 19 July. After a long discussion about the legal definitions of booty and reparations, British naval losses to U-boats, employment of German merchant vessels against Japan, and alleged Romanian and Finnish ships in Soviet hands, Churchill agreed in principle that the Soviet Union should take one-third of German warships if all the submarines were destroyed or sunk because 'he would welcome the appearance of the Russians on the seas of the world.'[38] Stalin, doubting Churchill's sincerity, maintained that the Soviet share was a right instead of a gift. Explaining further the distinction between surface ships and submarines, Churchill made an emotional appeal for Stalin to

> appreciate the sensitiveness of the people of an island like Great Britain, which grew far less than two-thirds of its food. We had suffered greatly from U-boats in two wars, in a way that no other nation had suffered. Twice we had been brought to the brink of disaster by U-boat campaigns, and the U-boats were not a popular weapon with the British people. He would strongly urge that a considerable part of the U-boats should be sunk, and that the rest

1. Midget submarine crews march into captivity, 11 May 1945

2. German sailors being checked before leaving their ship

3. German sailors milling about the dockyard at Wilhelmshaven

4. An E-boat arrives back at Den Helder

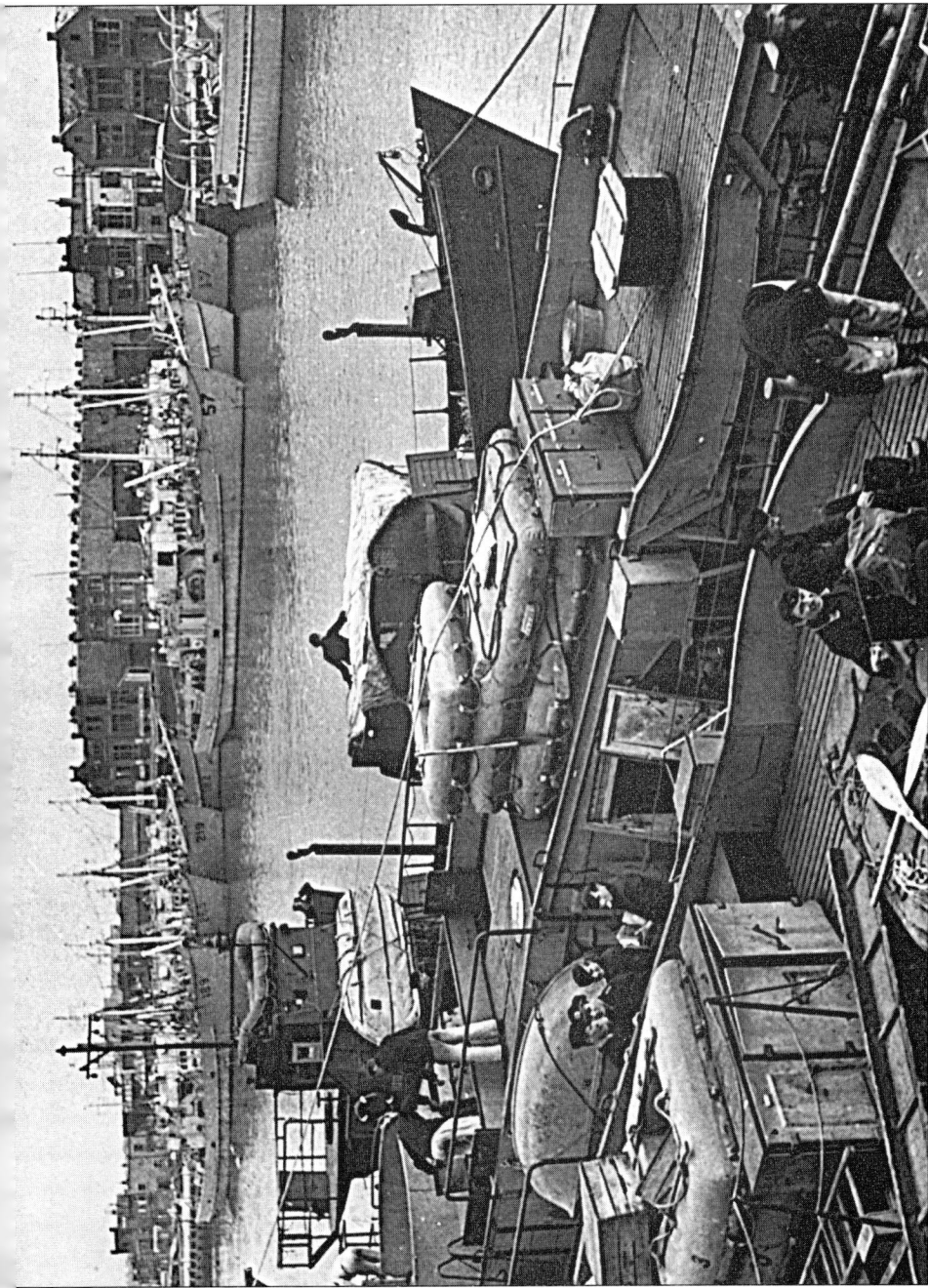

5. Armed trawlers and lighters collected in a Dutch port

6. The light cruiser *Köln* sunk at its moorings in Wilhelmshaven

7. An unfinished submarine pen damaged by Allied bombing

8. A prefabricated type XXI U-Boat section

9. The inner harbour at Emden, 7 May 1945

10. German and Canadian officers in a motor launch

11. Inspecting a midget submarine at Den Helder

12. Disarming German midget submarines

13. German and Canadian officers embark on a minesweeper to visit the Frisian Islands

14. Accepting the surrenders in the Frisian Islands, 8 May 1945

15. The heavy cruiser *Prinz Eugen* arrives at Wilhelmshaven, 26 May 1945

16. *Prinz Eugen* alongside HMCS *Iroquois*

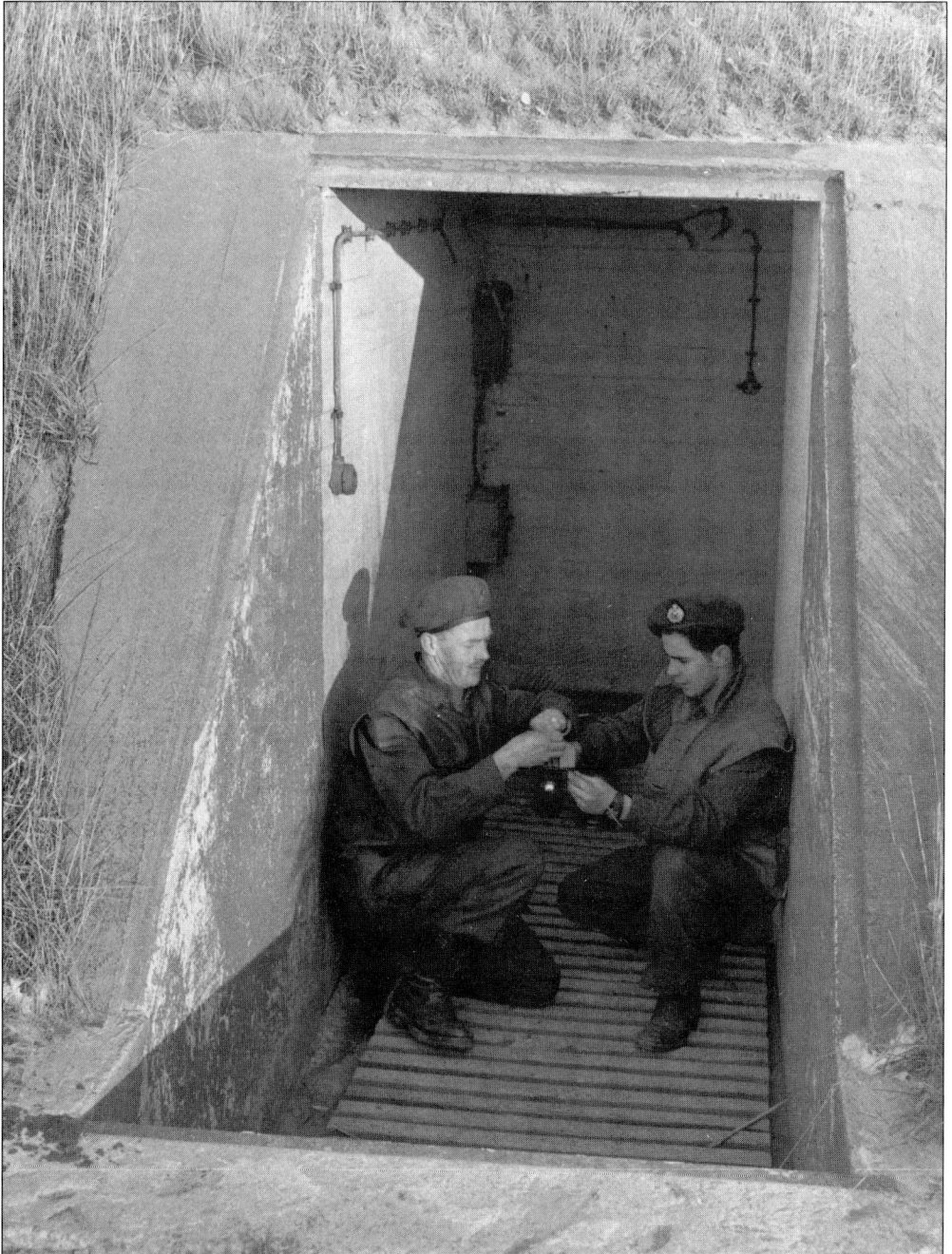

17. Royal Canadian Engineers prepare demolitions in coastal fortifications

18. Formalities at Borkum

19. Admiral Harold Burrough and A.V. Alexander visit Wilhelmshaven

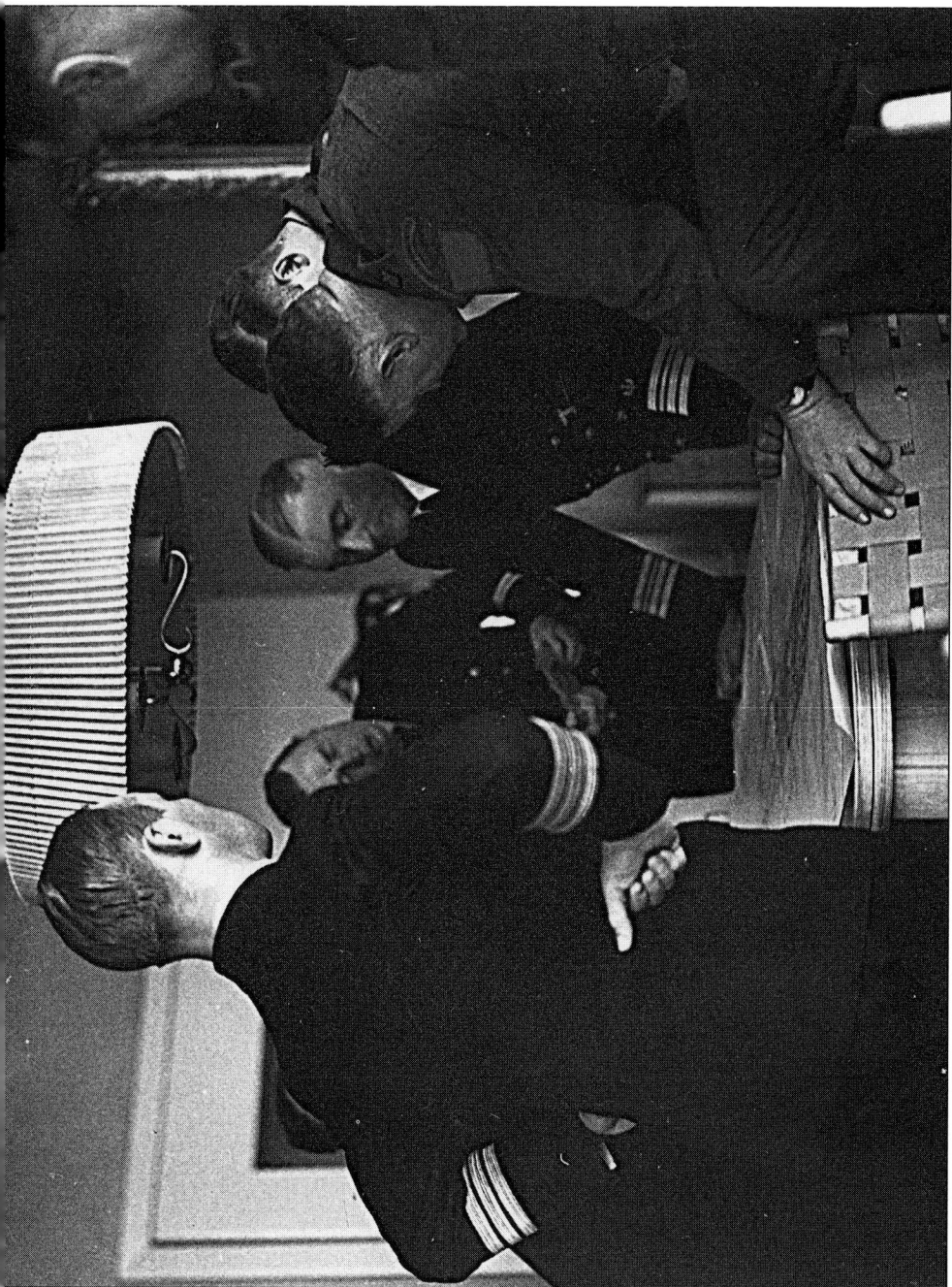

20. Former enemies confer on surrender plans

should be shared alike: the number kept by the Three Powers should be a token; more in order to spread technical knowledge than to keep large numbers in existence. As Great Britain had been subjected to terrible assaults by U-boats, we did not welcome any nation expanding in this form of naval construction.[39]

The British considered the submarine a despicable and illegal instrument of war, and demanded complete destruction. Faced with this resolute stand, Stalin assented to 'sinking a large proportion of the German U-boats', with which Truman also concurred. The British achieved their most important goal, a commitment to destruction of U-boats. The President deferred consideration of the German fleet until the end of the conference.

Despite this understanding in principle, the German fleet reappeared as a major question. The Soviets, who wished a more specific agreement, still exerted pressure. At Molotov's insistence, the foreign ministers placed the subject on the ninth plenary meeting's agenda on 25 July, but consideration was postponed because Truman and the American delegation were unprepared to discuss details.[40] In the meantime, a Labour Party victory in the British general election threw Churchill and Eden out of office. Clement Attlee and Ernest Bevin returned to 'Terminal' as Prime Minister and Foreign Secretary respectively.[41]

The change was wholly beneficial for British negotiations. Attlee, present since the start of the conference, was less volatile and better prepared than Churchill.[42] At least, Attlee read the briefing papers. During a British staff conference on the morning of 29 July, he stated that, in regard to the German fleet, the delegation 'should continue to stall on the final decision in the hope that it might still be possible to get some *quid pro quo*, particularly on reparations.'[43] The tactic echoed the Cabinet's previous intentions. A memorandum, prepared by the British delegation, suggested a share of the German fleet for France, destruction of all U-boats, inclusion of shipping taken by the Soviet Union from former Axis countries, and an adjusted timetable for transfers.[44] If the Soviets wanted to reopen the issue, the British might as well push for advantages. At the tenth meeting of foreign ministers on 30 July, Bevin proposed submission of the memorandum to a technical sub-committee.[45] As the British knew, a committee used up time in its deliberations. To Bevin's surprise, Molotov, who stated his own intention to forward a Soviet proposal, eagerly accepted the idea.[46] The three foreign ministers immediately appointed a technical sub-committee to consider disposition of the German fleet and merchant marine.

The sub-committee comprised representatives from each country:

Rear-Admiral McCarthy, William G. Weston, from the Ministry of War Transport, and Jack G. Ward, acting first secretary in the Foreign Office's Reconstruction Department, represented Great Britain; Vice-Admiral Charles M. Cooke, USN, King's chief of staff, and Donald Russell, special assistant to the Secretary of State, represented the United States; and Kuznetsov and Arkady Alexadrovich Sobolev, chief of the political section of the Soviet military administration in Germany, represented the Soviet Union.[47] Based upon a comparison of relative ranks, one must conclude that the Soviets took the sub-committee more seriously than the Western Allies. After visits to Allied naval commands in Germany and the torpedo experimental station at Eckernförde, Cunningham and King had returned to their respective countries, leaving behind subordinates at Potsdam.[48] Their absence left Kuznetsov as the most senior naval officer on the committee and the only naval commander-in-chief.

Since Kuznetsov made full use of his influence and position, the technical sub-committee's work clarified instead of solved outstanding problems. During a meeting on 31 July Kuznetsov shot down pleas by McCarthy and Weston for a four-part division to include France and provision of more merchant and coastal ships for the German peacetime economy. The Soviet admiral then asserted that the proposed number of submarines preserved for technical and experimental purposes was too small, and demanded at least thirty just for the Soviet Union.[49] Since destruction was already agreed upon at the political level, the British representatives found the last proposition most unpalatable. Still, Kuznetsov stood his ground.

Meanwhile, Stalin wanted to make final decisions on the German fleet at that day's plenary meeting. Byrnes, however, asked the heads of state to await the conclusions of the technical sub-committee.[50] Clearly dissatisfied, Stalin insisted on no further delays, even suggesting that the question could be put before the foreign ministers the next day. Attlee and Truman assented. Since the differences between Kuznetsov and the British naval representatives on the technical sub-committee left many issues unresolved, any agreement on the German fleet needed to come from the diplomatic and political level.

The foreign ministers resolved the disposition of the German navy and merchant marine quickly on 1 August. Byrnes raised the subject by stating that there were still differences of opinion, upon which Molotov invited the technical sub-committee members in for consultation.[51] Molotov had obviously received instructions from above to compromise on some points, and after a short adjournment, returned for serious negotiation. Bevin made a half-hearted plea for a French share in distribution, but finally acquiesced to Molotov's three-way division of the German fleet.

Submarines, however, were another matter. Broadening Churchill's earlier theme, Bevin told Molotov that if the Soviets 'asked for a big submarine fleet after what the British had suffered no statesman would survive.'[52] British public opinion and the Royal Navy strongly demanded destruction of U-boats. Bevin, an experienced trade union negotiator, proved more effective than Eden at convincing the Soviets that no leeway was possible on this point.[53] Since additional submarines were obviously unwelcome, Molotov agreed to retention of thirty, divided equally among the three countries for technical and experimental purposes. During ensuing discussions on the merchant marine, Bevin skilfully coaxed Molotov into accepting responsibility for Poland from the Soviet share, while the British and Americans took care of Holland, Norway, France, Greece, and Belgium. The foreign ministers referred the entire matter back to the Big Three.

The concluding discussions on the German navy and merchant marine at 'Terminal' were mere formalities. During the twelfth plenary meeting, the Soviet delegation formally withdrew its objection to Poland receiving ships from the Soviet share, thereby allowing adoption of the revised technical sub-committee's report and confirmation of a prepared decision.[54] Byrnes suggested that part of the report be issued later as a joint statement. When Truman inquired about the German fleet at the last plenary meeting in the evening, Stalin responded: 'There is an agreed decision; we have no amendments.'[55] With the conference at an end, the three countries now appeared in full unanimity. Attlee, recounting the day's events in a letter to Churchill, finished on a positive note: 'We have reached a satisfactory agreement on the German Fleet, especially on U-Boats.'[56] The British seemed satisfied with the results.

The official protocol issued at the end of the Potsdam Conference set out the agreed principles for disposal of the German navy and merchant marine: equal division between Great Britain, the United States, and the Soviet Union; completion of ships under construction or repair within prescribed time limits; destruction of U-boats with the exception of thirty retained for technical and experimental purposes; placement of merchant shipping under the control of the United Maritime Authority until the end of the war against Japan; provision of merchant ships for Poland from the Soviet share and for all other countries from the British and American shares; exclusion of German inland and coastal ships necessary for the German peacetime economy; and establishment of tripartite commissions, to begin deliberations by 15 August for the navy and 1 September for the merchant marine.[57] With possible scuttling in mind, the delegates decided to withhold public announcement of the agreement's details until after the two commissions finished their work.

In retrospect, the German fleet and merchant marine was a simple topic compared with reparations, Poland, and the future control of Germany. The question lent itself to an easy and lasting settlement.[58] The Soviets wanted German surface ships, which neither the British nor the Americans really cared about. The British, on the other hand, attained the desired commitment to destruction of most U-boats. Niggling over details was left to the tripartite commissions.

The Admiralty chose its representatives on the Tripartite Naval and Merchant Marine Commissions carefully. The appointees required expert knowledge, broad experience, tact, and the ability to undertake prolonged negotiations with difficult personalities. The combination was unusual in a naval officer. On 1 August Vice-Admiral Sir Geoffrey John Audley Miles, RN, received, during drinks at the Naval and Military Club, a telephone call from Rear-Admiral Claud Barry, RN, the naval secretary to the First Lord, to say that he 'might be off to Berlin in a fortnight'.[59] The admiral, resting after a period as flag officer commanding the western Mediterranean, was available and uniquely qualified. As head of the British naval mission in Moscow between June 1941 and March 1943 Miles had acquired an intimate knowledge of Soviet methods and the Red Navy.[60] This experience was important for the coming negotiations. McCarthy, upon returning from Potsdam, familiarized Miles with the decisions concerning the German fleet, in a meeting with Waldock.[61] The Admiralty felt that someone with extensive experience in the previous post-hostilities planning should assist Miles. After consulting with Burrough, Waldock and McCarthy decided that Parry would serve in a dual capacity as second representative on the Tripartite Naval Commission and deputy head of the Naval Division.[62] Miles was concurrently senior British representative on the Tripartite Merchant Marine Commission. The Admiralty accepted Sir Andrew Common, director of the Ministry of War Transport's Ship Management Division, as the other representative, while Peter Dalgleish was seconded as an assistant.

Detailed instructions for Miles and Parry established the parameters of the assignment. Waldock issued a directive for the Tripartite Naval Commission, setting out policy, priorities, expectations, and suggestions on how to handle the Soviets.[63] Although the Royal Navy maintained no interest in surface ships for operational use, Miles was to insist on allocation of the heavy cruiser *Prinz Eugen* to Great Britain for technical examination, obtain sufficient minesweepers for completion of clearance work in the North Sea and Baltic, and select the best destroyers and torpedo boats for later transfer to France. Of the thirty submarines retained under the Potsdam agreement, the Admiralty wanted U-1406 and U-1407 assigned to Great Britain and the United States. As for the hydrogen-peroxide development facilities, Waldock told Miles that he 'should, if possible, avoid discussing the subject with the Russians.'[64] Visits to German naval establishments by the Soviets were still strictly on a reciprocal basis. Waldock also directed Miles to argue that harbour equipment, including floating dry docks, cranes, dredgers, and tugs, was beyond the scope of the naval commission.

As far as possible, the Admiralty wanted most naval auxiliaries classed as merchant vessels. The corresponding directive for the Tripartite Merchant Marine Commission directed Miles to secure for Great Britain and its allies 'the maximum number possible of ships that can be brought into service quickly and are likely to give useful service for the next few years.'[65] Passenger liners, medium-sized cargo vessels, and tankers were in particular demand. The respective directives concluded with the same parting advice:

> The Russian delegation may be expected to drive the hardest possible bargain and concede nothing unless forced to do so. It is recommended that your tactics should be generally to hold out, so far as possible, on all points of importance to the Russians until essential British requirements have been met.

The Admiralty believed that a firm and uncompromising manner worked best with the Soviets. The British representatives were to give back whatever they received. After a long meeting with Cunningham, Syfret, McCarthy, and Waldock to clarify remaining points in the two directives, Miles confided in his diary: 'I am in for a tricky time.'[66] He and the Admiralty held no illusions about the tough negotiations ahead. Miles arrived in Berlin by air during the late afternoon of 13 August.

Over the next five months, the Tripartite Naval Commission and the Tripartite Merchant Marine Commission held twenty-seven and nine meetings respectively at the headquarters of the Allied Control Authority. Each commission comprised official representatives from the three countries, accompanied by requisite support staffs and technical experts: Miles, Parry, and Common represented Great Britain; Ghormley, Commodore H.J. Ray, USN, and Thomas F. Dunn, from the War Shipping Administration, represented the United States; and Levchenko, Engineer Rear-Admiral N.V. Alekseev, and Gospodin A.A. Affanasiev, deputy commissar of the Soviet merchant marine, represented the Soviet Union. Their purpose was to forward specific recommendations to the respective governments for allocation of the former German navy and merchant marine as agreed under the Potsdam Protocol.

The naval commission quickly started business. The first official meeting, which took place as scheduled on 15 August, dealt almost entirely with administrative details. Ghormley took the chair because the senior representatives rotated in alphabetical order. Levchenko wished to divide the German fleet straightaway, but Miles convinced him that the first task was to establish the exact number and types of warships through an agreed list.[67] Since verification required inspection and collation of information, the commission formed a sub-committee, consisting of Alekseev, Engineer Captain 1st Rank V.V. Golovin, Captain Arthur H. Graubart, USN, Lieutenant G.A. Ivers, USNR, and Lieutenant-Commander Geoffrey R.G. Watkins, RN. The delegates decided that the order of priority should be minesweepers, U-boats, surface vessels, and then naval auxiliaries. Each favoured the early allocation of minesweepers to support clearance operations in European waters. The third meeting, chaired by Rear-Admiral V. Melnikov in Levchenko's absence, agreed upon Miles' suggested classification of all warships into three categories: A (operational), B (repairable within six months), and C (non-repairable).[68] Only the first two were subject to allocation.

Joint inspection parties were to check the locations and conditions of particular warships. In keeping with the Admiralty's directive, Miles strived to limit the size and scope of these parties. He told Levchenko at the fourth meeting that the proposed Soviet itinerary, estimated at approximately three to four months, was too long and impractical.[69] If placement into the three broad categories was the intent, a short rather than a comprehensive examination should suffice. With Ghormley supporting Miles, Levchenko reluctantly conceded. The inspections, working from east to west, began after the sixth meeting's conclusion on 24 August.

The tripartite inspection parties covered an enormous amount of territory in a remarkably short period of time. The three senior delegates made arrangements with relevant authorities to extend facilities and access.[70] For the British, the most interesting opportunity was a tour, organized through Levchenko and the Red Navy, to Pillau, Königsberg, Danzig, Swinemünde, and Stettin. The official side of the inspection exposed mostly wrecked and uncompleted warships: the stripped heavy cruiser *Seydlitz*; the sunken battle-cruiser *Gneisenau*; the internally smashed aircraft carrier *Graf Zeppelin*; and numerous scuttled hulls. Miles confirmed that 'there is nothing but junk in the Soviet area.'[71] Nonetheless, more ships had been present at the time of the surrender. Conversations with Polish workers disclosed that the Soviets had removed eleven unfinished U-boats from Danzig.[72] Since the Red Navy previously reported no submarines in Soviet hands, the oversight required explanation from Levchenko. Miles also commented on the miles of barges at Stettin, loaded with every imaginable object from locomotives to furniture, ready for transfer to the Soviet Union: 'How they propose to tow them away before the winter I cannot imagine, but it may explain why Levchenko is so keen on getting his hands on ex-German tugs.[73] The Royal Navy gained a better appreciation of Soviet objectives after the visits to Soviet-occupied ports.

Similar inspections took place in areas under American and British control. At Copenhagen on 29 August Captain Arthur M. Knapp, RN, commanding officer of HMS *Diadem*, joined Alekseev and Lieutenant-Commander S.K. Brown, USN, on a tripartite party to Denmark and Norway.[74] In a hurried manner, the group examined warships at scattered ports and fjords. Like Miles, the Soviets found many ships missing from or additional to the lists provided by Burrough's staffs. Unfortunately, British naval authorities had relied on provided German information without checking for accuracy. Maund, the British representative on the tripartite party which inspected warships in western German ports, attributed criticism to the over-zealousness of his Soviet counterparts, Captain 1st Rank Bubnov and Engineer Captain Golovin.[75] Nonetheless, this party worked under perhaps the most restrictions. The Royal Navy denied entry to the main fleet units at Wilhelshaven and the naval experimental establishments at Kiel, the former for fear of German scuttling and the latter for security reasons. If the British intentionally withheld things, how could they expect anything better from the Soviets?

Relations in the tripartite naval party in Great Britain were far from smooth. The United Kingdom Tripartite Board first met in London on 28 August, and began inspections the next day.[76] At the outset, the British tried to be friendly. Archer, having returned from Moscow, escorted the tripartite party through German warships in various British ports and anchorages.[77] Nevertheless, the Admiralty's restrictions on what the party could see and the thoroughness of certain Soviet naval officers provoked resentment on both sides. During an inspection of M-class minesweepers at Port Edgar on 13 September German sailors described how the Soviets frantically rushed around to see everything on board, while the British and Americans leisurely smoked cigarettes on the after deck.[78] Warned of possible Allied duplicity, Soviet naval officers asked awkward technical questions, and persisted in efforts to see more ships, particularly submarines. The behaviour gradually wore down British patience.

In contrast to Great Britain, the tripartite parties across the Atlantic achieved a fairly congenial and business-like atmosphere. A Tripartite Naval Board for the Western Hemisphere, consisting of Rear-Admiral Frank H. Braisted, USN, Rear-Admiral John W.A. Waller, RN, and Engineer Rear-Admiral A.A. Yakimov, deputy chief of the Soviet government purchasing commission since April 1943, convened in Washington, DC on 29 August.[79] Under the board's authority, tripartite parties or delegated officers assessed the condition of surrendered U-boats and surface vessels in Canadian, American, Caribbean, and South American ports. The board's report listed nine submarines, of which only U-889 in Halifax was fully operational, and two destroyers, T-35 and Z-39.[80] Thus, the board dealt with fewer warships than in Great Britain. The small number allowed systematic material examinations and opportunities for Soviet amendments afterwards.[81] In general, the deliberations lacked the impression of haste which was so characteristic of the European inspections. Since Yakimov and his subordinates dealt with the US Navy and the British Admiralty Delegation over several years in Washington, the personalities also appeared compatible. The Tripartite Naval Board for the Western Hemisphere demonstrated that, given time and familiarity, tripartite efforts could achieve satisfactory results in the naval sphere.

Nevertheless, when the Tripartite Naval Commission resumed formal session in Berlin on 12 September, the senior British and Soviet representatives headed straight for confrontation. As the inspections concluded, the sub-committee tabled reports from the various parties. Much discussion centred on particular ships. For example, Levchenko argued that the crippled cruiser Leipzig, although requiring more than six months of repairs, be allocated because 'it seemed a pity to waste it.'[82] Miles stoutly opposed the argument, and the matter went before the sub-committee, which duly declared the cruiser to be in Category C. Miles and Levchenko also clashed over boiler repairs to the destroyer Fredrich Ihn, classification of hulks used as depot ships, and reconversion of trawlers, formerly employed by the Germans as minesweepers, into fishing vessels.[83] Because neither admiral appeared willing to give ground, a standoff ensued.

In response, the Soviets resorted to diplomatic channels. Molotov sent an aide-memoire to Bevin on 28 September, accusing the British delegates, especially Miles, of impeding work on the Tripartite Naval Commission.[84] Were the British too intransigent for the Soviets? In a meeting at the Admiralty on 3 October Waldock, McCarthy, and Miles considered Molotov's complaints 'as rather a compliment, but naturally we have to refute the charges.'[85] They placed ulterior motives behind the aide-memoire. In Waldock's opinion, it was 'obviously a manoeuvre designed to shake Admiral Miles's confidence, particularly when they are about to get down to the real business of allocating warships.'[86] The Admiralty and the Foreign Office sent the Soviet ambassador in London a strongly worded reply, which denied completely the Soviet accusations. At the next tripartite meeting in Berlin, Miles found that 'Levchenko showed no signs of hostility so I behaved in the usual manner.'[87] The endless search for advantage was all part of the game.

Despite the tough posturing, the Tripartite Naval Commission reached significant agreement, sometimes in a lively and comical manner. The senior representatives settled specific questions one by one as the sub-committee forwarded agreed recommendations on minesweepers, submarines, flak cruisers, and motor torpedo boats.[88] To ensure no side took unfair advantage in selection, lots were drawn for three relatively equal groups of ships. In fact, the process seemed almost too simple. Waldock told George Wilson at the Foreign Office 'that for the last few weeks everything has been going very smoothly – so smoothly that he suspects there must be a catch somewhere, but he does not know what it is.'[89] Personal problems occasionally delayed the schedule. Sickness from a poor heart kept Levchenko away from some meetings as well as Parry's popular cocktail and dinner parties. Nevertheless, the Soviet admiral was always in true form during negotiations. Parry described a particular incident for his wife on 19 October:

> We had a terrific meeting with our Russian admiral this morning, and finally, after much bargaining about certain ships, he held up several cigarettes in his hand and asked if that was enough. Loud laughter, of course – particularly when he dropped the cigarettes on the table, they turned out to be bits of paper rolled up with nothing under them![90]

Humour diffused otherwise tense situations and helped bridge differences between the delegates. After a boisterous debate, Miles, Ghormley, and Levchenko 'parted on the best of terms. A pity the Quadripartite party can't conduct their meetings in a similar atmosphere.'[91] Indeed, the navies achieved something special in Berlin. Business was business, but the personal touch remained. Social drinking outside official hours partly accounted for the good relations. The Soviets liked British hospitality so much that they soon reciprocated with their own vodka parties. The Royal Navy, US Navy, and Red Navy drank together on frequent occasions in Berlin.

The delegates settled down to the serious business of drawing for cruisers and destroyers. Over the course of several meetings, the naval delegates vigorously debated the relative worth of *Prinz Eugen*. Miles argued that the heavy cruiser was equal to four Narvik-class destroyers, whereas Levchenko and Ghormley considered six Narviks more appropriate.[92] The Tripartite Naval Commission made a distinction between larger destroyers and smaller, more specialized torpedo boats. The former, particularly the war-built Type 26A, more closely resembled mini-cruisers, much like the British Tribal-class.[93] In keeping with his original directive, Miles claimed that the Royal Navy had a moral right to *Prinz Eugen* because of British naval losses against the Germans. The suggestion brought quick responses from Levchenko and Ghormley, who countered with Soviet deaths on the eastern front and American naval losses in the Pacific. While awaiting firm direction from the Admiralty, Miles blocked allocation, although the technical sub-committee put forward three equitable groupings – X: *Prinz Eugen* and six destroyers (one Narvik); Y: *Nürnberg* and ten destroyers (four Narviks); and Z: thirteen destroyers (eight Narviks).[94] Both the Soviets and Americans pushed for immediate division. Levchenko was 'prepared to draw on the spot after saying he had a strong directive to obtain *Prinz Eugen*.'[95] Miles, however, still awaited direction from London. Early on 29 October the Admiralty finally agreed 'to grouping major units and to division by lottery.'[96] The draw could now proceed.

The British delegation arranged a surprise. During a meeting that same day, Miles 'announced that the great moment had arrived and put on a wonderful white yachting cap which belonged to Willi Vogel', and 'then offered it as the hat from which the draw would be made.'[97] Since both the British and the Soviets strongly desired *Prinz Eugen*, this allocation contained the most potential for trouble. Yet, as Parry recounted to his wife, the yachting cap worked wonders:

> Roars of applause from everybody, and I thought our tough old Russian admiral would never stop laughing! It really did tickle him; and when the draw went against him he was not in the least perturbed![98]

Chance intervened. Neither Levchenko nor Miles obtained *Prinz Eugen*. Ghormley, the luckiest of the three representatives, chose the much sought after group X. Ironically, the country which wanted the cruiser the least received the best prize.[99] Levchenko and the Red Navy received group Y, which included the light cruiser *Nürnberg*. The Tripartite Naval Commission cleared a major hurdle without discord.

Several questions before the Tripartite Naval Commission proved more contentious. The British delegation continued to make flimsy excuses for Admiralty decisions. At the twenty-first meeting on 9 November, Miles found Levchenko 'in one of his worst moods, deeply mistrustful of us and imputing the worst motives to me because we will not allow his officers to go on board the ships at Wilhelmshaven.'[100] The Soviets openly wondered what the Royal Navy had to hide. In a personal letter to Miles, Levchenko doubted 'the reasons, concerning sabotage by German crews on ships, and I don't see any other reasons.'[101] Miles empathized, but the main fleet units still remained off-limits to the Soviets.

Levchenko also protested against the Admiralty's proposed transfer of whalers to the Ministry of War Transport for the International Whaling Pool. The *Kriegsmarine* had designed, built, and purchased these ships in Norway during the war.[102] The Soviets argued that the whalers required allocation by the Tripartite Naval Commission. In point of fact, Levchenko wanted whale factory ships and whalers because the Soviet Union planned to expand its whale hunting operations.[103] Allocation through the naval commission was merely a subterfuge. To make matters more complicated, Norway, a leading commercial whaling power, also submitted claims on the ships.[104] The conflicting claims placed the British in an awkward situation. Miles and Common tried to limit discussion to the Tripartite Merchant Marine Commission.[105] The transparent attempt, however, simply left the Soviets more disgruntled. At Burrough's suggestion, Miles eventually told Levchenko to pursue negotiations with the Norwegians directly for payment or transfer because remaining German ships in Norway were now under Norwegian control.[106] In other words, the Royal Navy declined all responsibility. Of all the problems before the Tripartite Naval Commission, floating dry docks proved the hardest and most divisive.

In the face of American and Soviet opposition, the British adopted a firm stand on floating dry docks. The question revolved mostly around definition and appropriate disposition. Ghormley took the view 'that all floating cranes and floating harbour equipment which is part of German navy should be divided by the Tripartite naval commission but that sunken commercial equipment is part of harbour facilities and not of merchant marine.'[107] The Soviet position was even simpler. Levchenko regarded all floating dry docks, regardless of origin or type, available for allocation. Miles, on the other hand, contended that this equipment fell outside the Tripartite Naval Commission's jurisdiction, and instead constituted reparations.[108] Through such a definition, the British hoped to get a fairer deal. The Royal Navy took a strong stand because most floating dry docks were located in the British Zone.

As the British were well aware, floating dry docks were expensive and extremely useful items. Miles refused to be pressured by the other two delegates:

> A good deal of talk over floating docks in which both the Russians and Americans tried to get a snap decision. They are both very stupid and put up silly proposals to try to get an answer quickly as they both want to get away. I insist on getting the right answer and to hell with speed.[109]

Since the comparable worth of floating dry docks largely depended upon age and condition, Miles argued that an assigned monetary value, based upon expert assessment, was better than outright division. According to the British, floating dry docks were 'very valuable equipment and should not be divided by anybody by any arbitrary rule.'[110] The moveable docks constituted harbour equipment rather than part of the surface fleet. Although Ghormley and Levchenko made several appeals for allocation, Miles finally declared that 'the disagreement between the Soviet and American view on the one side and the British view on the other should be settled on a governmental level.'[111] The British admiral was not prepared to discuss the matter any further. The question of floating dry docks was left unresolved.

Despite apparent disagreement over floating dry docks, the Tripartite Naval Commission completed its work. In little more than four months since the Potsdam Conference, the Tripartite Naval Commission oversaw classification and allocation of all reported surface ships and selected submarines from the defeated *Kriegsmarine*. At the twenty-seventh meeting on 6 December, Miles, Ghormley, and Levchenko formally signed a final report, prepared by the technical sub-committee, after the Soviets accepted full responsibility for destruction of the aircraft carrier *Graf Zeppelin*.[112] The document, forwarded to the three respective governments for approval, reflected the efforts of the three navies, especially the Royal Navy, to reach an equitable division. Except for a British reservation on floating dry docks and harbour equipment, the naval delegates achieved complete consensus.[113] The British claimed other minor differences over the merchant marine. On 7 December Miles and Common signed the Tripartite Merchant Marine Commission's final report, but reserved government decision on the fishing fleet, port facilities, inland water transport, and compensation for use prior to delivery.[114]

As the British expected, negotiations over allocation of the German fleet and merchant marine were sometimes difficult. The Soviets, eager to get their hands on warships, drove a hard bargain. In the end, Miles could not say whether Levchenko's 'feelings lean more towards the Americans or us, but I am quite sure he likes us and respects us for our honesty and fair-dealing, however crooked a deal he may try himself to put over.'[115] Still, the Royal Navy worked together with the Red Navy and the US Navy to achieve division of the German fleet, a major component of German naval disarmament. With the work apparently finished, Miles departed for Great Britain, leaving behind Parry and a small staff in Berlin. While various government departments in London scrutinized the two reports, the Admiralty consented to the transfer of allocated ships.[116] Implementation of the Tripartite Naval and Merchant Marine Commissions' recommendations became the responsibility of the British Naval Commander-in-Chief in Germany.

NOTES

1. JCS, Reel 9, Part 1 1942–45: European Theatre, Frame 0173, Memorandum from Joint Chiefs of Staff, 'Policy for the Surrender of the German Fleet under RANKIN Case "C" Conditions', 16 May 1945.
2. JCS, Reel 9, Part 1 1942–45: European Theatre, Frame 0196, Memorandum from Franklin Roosevelt to Cordell Hull, 'Final Disposition of the Units of the German Fleet upon the Defeat of Germany', 21 Oct. 1944.
3. PRO, ADM 1/16076, Staff Minute by C.H.M. Waldock, 22 Jan. 1945.
4. PRO, ADM 116/5123, Letter from C.H.M. Waldock to First Sea Lord, 'Policy of Effecting Surrender of the German Fleet', 1 March 1944.
5. PRO, ADM 1/16180, Memorandum from C.H.M. Waldock to Director of Plans, 16 March 1945.
6. PRO, ADM 1/16180, Staff Minute by Director of Plans, 21 March 1945.
7. PRO, ADM 1/16180, Staff Minute by C.H.M. Waldock, 29 March 1945.
8. Evan Mawdsley, 'The Fate of Stalin's Naval Program', *Warship International* 27(1990), pp. 400–4. FO/SU, 1944, Reel 4, Vol. 43290, Frames 69–105, Report from Director of Naval Intelligence to V.F.W. Cavendish-Bentinck, Foreign Office, 6 July 1944. Eric Morris, *The Russian Navy: Myth and Reality*, (London: Hamish Hamilton, 1977), pp. 21–4.
9. I.S. Isakov, *The Red Fleet in the Second World War*, (London: Hutchinson & Co., 1947), pp. 15–20. Achkasov and Pavlovich, p. 363. The Red Navy appeared strongly influenced by the writings of the British naval historian/strategist Julian Corbett, in particular his ideas about the importance of secure sea communications and the 'fleet-in-being'. Of course, the Soviets could not embrace the bourgeois Corbett for ideological reasons, but instead attributed their strategy to careful study based upon Marxist-Leninist principles. Robert Waring Herrick, *Soviet Naval Theory: Gorshkov's Inheritance*, (Annapolis: Naval Institute Press, 1988), pp. 149–50.
10. Jürgen Rohwer, 'Alternating Russian and Soviet Naval Strategies', Philip S. Gillette and Willard C. Frank Jr., eds., *The Sources of Soviet Naval Conduct*, (Lexington: Lexington Books, D.C. Heath & Co., 1990), p. 108.
11. BL, Cunningham, Add. Ms. 52578, Diary, 8 June 1945.
12. The Foreign Office's representative in Moscow, commented that Stalin's order was the first 'issued to the Red Navy on the occasion of Red Navy Day, and it fits in with a number of other signs that the Soviet Government have begun to think in terms of a stronger fleet, which will mark the resurgence of Russia as a great naval power.' FO/SU, 1945, Reel 14, Vol. 47924, Frames 37–38B, Telegram No. 519 from Frank Roberts to Anthony Eden, Foreign Office, 7 Aug. 1945.
13. N.V. Nalumov, 'The Soviet View', Law and Howarth, pp. 555–6.
14. Susan J. Linz, 'World War II and Soviet Economic Growth, 1940-1953', Susan J. Linz, ed., *The Impact of World War II on the Soviet Union*, (Totowa, NJ: Rowman & Allanheld, 1985), pp. 21–2.
15. NMM, Admiral Sir Geoffrey John Audley Miles, RN, Box 2, File 'Moscow June 1941–March 1943', Report from Rear-Admiral W.E. Parry to Admiral Geoffrey Miles, 4 May 1948. In Feb. 1948 Kuznetsov and other senior Soviet naval officers were officially tried before a court of inquiry for being too friendly with the British during the war. After a reduction in rank and exile to the Pacific Fleet, Kuznetsov was rehabilitated to become the Red Navy's commander-in-chief again in July 1951. FO/SU, 1948, Reel 9, Vol. 71695, Frame 64, Memorandum from E.W. Harrison, Moscow to Ernest Bevin, Foreign Office, 21 Sept. 1948. Jan Kowalewski, 'The Russian Navy and the Revolution', Saunders, pp. 97–8. Norman Polmer, *Guide to the Soviet Navy*, 3rd edition, (Annapolis: Naval Institute Press, 1983), pp. 10–11.
16. Donald Macintyre, 'The Soviet Submarine Threat', Saunders, p. 169.
17. PRO, ADM 228/5, Message from Captain G.O. Maund to ANCXF, 20 1559 May 1945. Graubart told Truskov that the European Advisory Commission's draft

expressed the American view. PRO, ADM 228/5, Message from SHAEF Main signed Tedder to US Military Mission Moscow for Charles Deane, 22 1230 June 1945.

18. USSR, Ministry of Foreign Affairs, *Correspondence Between the Chairman of the Council of Ministers of the USSR and the Presidents of the USA and Prime Ministers of Great Britain during the Great Patriotic War of 1941–45*, (Moscow: Foreign Languages Publishing House, 1957), Vol. 1, pp. 359–60; Vol. 2, p. 238.

19. *Ibid*, Vol. 1, p. 360.

20. United States, State Department, *Foreign Relations of the United States Diplomatic Papers: The Conference of Berlin (The Potsdam Conference) 1945*, Vol. 1, (Washington, DC: Government Printing Office, 1960), pp. 33–4. Truman sent Hopkins to Moscow on a special mission to discuss outstanding points in Soviet-American relations, the United Nations, Eastern Europe, and the war against Japan. Herbert Feis, *Between War and Peace: The Potsdam Conference*, (Princeton, NJ: Princeton University Press, 1960), p. 333.

21. Peter Krüger, 'Die Verhandlungen über die deutsche Kriegs- und Handels-flotte auf der Konferenz von Potsdam 1945', *Marine Rundschau* 63(1966), p. 16-17.

22. USSR, Ministry of Foreign Affairs, *Correspondence Between the Chairman and the Council of Ministers of the USSR and the Presidents of the USA and Prime Ministers of Great Britain during the Great Patriotic War of 1941–45*, (Moscow: Foreign Languages Publishing House, 1957); Vol. 2, p. 239.

23. United States. *FRUS Berlin*, Vol. 1, p. 161.

24. Rohan Butler and M.E. Pelly, eds., *Documents on British Policy Overseas*, Series 1, Vol. 1, *The Conference at Potsdam July-Aug. 1945*, (London: Her Majesty's Stationery Office, 1984), p. 17.

25. The Admiralty was prepared to give the Soviet Union the light cruisers *Nürnberg* and *Leipzig*, the damaged aircraft carrier *Graf Zeppelin*, the uncompleted heavy cruiser *Lützow*, six destroyers, two E-boats, ten U-boats, and fifty minesweepers, with an additional two destroyers, two E-boats, and heavy cruiser *Prinz Eugen* after technical examinations. Butler and Pelly, Microfiche 10i, Memorandum from Brendan Bracken, First Lord of Admiralty to Cabinet, 'Disposal of the German Fleet', 7 July 1945.

26. Butler and Pelly, Vol. 1, pp. 229–31. BL, Cunningham, Add. Ms. 52578, Diary, 12 July 1945.

27. Butler and Pelly, Vol. 1, p. 333.

28. PRO, ADM 205/46, 'Terminal: Administrative Arrangements No. 2', 14 July 1945. IWM, Misc. 153 Item 2371, Lieutenant J.G. West, Pass for the Potsdam Conference, July 1945.

29. United States, *FRUS Berlin*, Vol. 1, p. 572.

30. United States, *FRUS Berlin*, Vol. 1, p. 574. JCS, Reel 9, Part 1 1942–45: European Theatre, Frame 0199, Memorandum by Joint Chiefs of Staff, 'Disposition and Distribution of the German Fleet', 5 July 1945.

31. United States, *FRUS Berlin*, Vol. 1, p. 574.

32. Charles L. Mee, *Meeting at Potsdam*, (New York: M. Evans & Co., 1975), p. 14. The President had already decided on division. OAB/NHC, Fleet Admiral William D. Leahy, Series I, Box 2A, File 19, 'Preparations for Agenda at Potsdam Conference – 1945'.

33. United States, *FRUS Berlin*, Vol. 2, p. 59. In a private talk after the session, Churchill stated that 'Britain welcomed Russia as a Great Power and in particular as a Naval Power. The more ships that sailed the seas the greater chance there was for better relations.' Stalin replied: 'As regards Russia's fleet it was still a small one, nevertheless, great or small, it could be of benefit to Great Britain.' Butler and Pelly, Vol. 1, p. 349.

34. United States, *FRUS Berlin*, Vol. 2, p. 59.

35. Robert Beitzell, ed., *Teheran, Yalta, Potsdam: The Soviet Protocols*, (Hattiesburg, MI: Academic International, 1970), p. 152.

36. United States, *FRUS Berlin*, Vol. 2, p. 71. During a briefing on the German fleet that afternoon, the First Sea Lord told Eden 'that he could not be expected to work miracles.' BL, Cunningham, Add. Ms. 52578, Diary, 19 July 1945.

37. United States, *FRUS Berlin*, Vol. 2, p. 971.

38. Butler and Pelly, Vol. 1, pp. 420–4.

39. Butler and Pelly, Vol. 1, p. 424. The First Sea Lord noted in his diary: 'P.M. in general was good about the German fleet but said it must be part of a general settlement. On the detail he was not quite so good.', BL, Cunningham, Add. Ms. 52578, Diary, 20 July 1945.

40. United States, *FRUS Berlin*, Vol. 2, pp. 382–3.

41. Dilks, p. 776.

42. Clement Attlee, *As It Happened*, (London: William Heinemann, 1954), pp. 148–9. Attlee was very familiar with post-hostilities problems. As Deputy Prime Minister in the wartime coalition government, he had served as chairman of the Armistice and Post-War Committee. Kenneth Harris, *Attlee*, (London: Weidenfeld & Nicolson, 1982), pp. 209–12.

43. Butler and Pelly, Vol. 1, Microfiche 450ii, Letter from Jack Ward, British Delegation Potsdam to Viscount Hood, Foreign Office, 29 July 1945.

44. Butler and Pelly, Vol. 1, pp. 1010–12.

45. United States, *FRUS Berlin*, Vol. 2, p. 492.

46. United States, *FRUS Berlin*, Vol. 2, pp. 976–7.

47. United States, *FRUS Berlin*, Vol. 2, p. 502.

48. BL, Cunningham, Add. Ms. 52578, Diary, 22 July 1945. Cunningham, pp. 646–7. LC, King, Box 20, File 'Conferences: Potsdam Conference July 1945', A.S. Dill, 'Outline of Potsdam Conference (Terminal) 16–26 July 1945.' King, pp. 611–17.

49. Butler and Pelly, Vol. 1, pp. 1102–4. United States, *FRUS Berlin*, Vol. 2, pp. 980–3.

50. United States, *FRUS Berlin*, Vol. 2, p. 524.

51. United States, *FRUS Berlin*, Vol. 2, p. 544.

52. United States, *FRUS Berlin*, Vol. 2, p. 558.

53. Alan Bullock, *Ernest Bevin: Foreign Secretary 1945–1951*, (London: Heinemann, 1983), p. 29.

54. United States, *FRUS Berlin*, Vol. 2, p. 576.

55. Beitzell, p. 307.

56. Butler and Pelly, Vol. 1, p. 1144.

57. United States, *FRUS Berlin*, Vol. 2, pp. 1487–8. NA, RG 38, Office of the Chief of Naval Operations/Commander-in-Chief US Fleet (Operations Division), Series III, Box 12, File 'Tripartite Naval Board/Western Hemisphere 1945', Telegram from Admiral Ernest King to Vice-Admiral Robert Ghormley, 14 1248 Aug. 1945.

58. Krüger, p. 88.

59. NMM, Miles, Box 4, Diary, 1 Aug. 1945.

60. NMM, Miles, Box 2, File 'Moscow, June 1941–March 1943', Report by Rear-Admiral G.J.A. Miles, Head of British Military Mission Moscow to the Chiefs of Staff Sub-Committee, 31 Dec. 1942. Miles impressed the British ambassador in Moscow, who recommended his promotion: 'I have nothing but praise for Admiral Miles whose conduct of 30 Mission, when he was its head, was marked by all the goodwill, patience and discretion that the situation demanded. He impelled the respect of the Russians and their confidence in him as an officer and a technician.' FO/SU, 1943, Reel 11, Vol. 36970, Frame 152, Telegram from Sir A. Clark to Viscount Halifax, Foreign Office, 21 Dec. 1943.

61. NMM, Miles, Box 4, Diary, 3 Aug. 1945.

62. NAC, RG 24, Vol. 11,752, File CS 638-3, Message from Admiralty to British Naval Commander-in-Chief Germany, 09 1025A Aug. 1945.

63. NMM, Miles, Box 2, File 'Tripartite Naval Commission Berlin 1945', C.H.M. Waldock to Vice-Admiral Geoffrey Miles and Rear-Admiral W.E. Parry, 'Directive to the Tripartite Naval Commission', 13 Aug. 1945. The American directive, issued to Ghormley on the same day, was not as detailed. NA, RG 38, CNO/

COMINCH(Ops), Series III, Box 12, File 'Tripartite Naval Commission/Western Hemisphere 1945', Telegram from Admiral Ernest King to COMNAVEU and COMNAVFORGER, 13 1839 Aug. 1945.

64. The US Navy had already made arrangements to ship U-1406 to Great Britain and then to New York. NA, RG 38, CNO/COMINCH(Ops), Series I, Box 8, File EF-30, Telegram from COMNAVTECHMISEU to CNO/COMINCH, 21 1613 Aug. 1945.

65. NMM, Miles, Box 2, File 'Tripartite Naval Commission Berlin 1945', C.H.M. Waldock to Vice-Admiral Geoffrey Miles, 'Directive to the British Representatives on the Tripartite Merchant Marine Commission', 6 Oct. 1945.

66. NMM, Miles, Box 4, Diary, 10 Aug. 1945.

67. NMM, Miles, Box 2, File 'Tripartite Naval Commission Berlin 1945', Report from Vice-Admiral Geoffrey Miles to Secretary of Admiralty, 8 Dec. 1945. Miles briefly assessed the day's meeting in a message to the Admiralty: 'Russian bowling so far only moderate but on usual sticky wicket. They appear to be chiefly interested in Minesweepers and Naval Auxiliaries, particularly Depot Ships.' PRO, ADM 228/19, Message from Vice-Admiral Geoffrey Miles to Admiralty, 15 1632 Aug. 1945.

68. Melnikov was head of the Soviet Naval Division in Berlin. PRO, ADM 116/5565, British Minutes of 3rd Tripartite Naval Commission Meeting, 18 Aug. 1945. These minutes are also in ADM 228/35.

69. PRO, ADM 116/5565, British Minutes of 4th Tripartite Naval Commission Meeting, 20 Aug. 1945.

70. PRO, ADM 228/19, Message from British Naval Commander-in-Chief Germany to All Flag Officers and Naval Officers-in-Charge in Germany, 23 1722B Aug. 1945.

71. PRO, ADM 228/19, Message from Vice-Admiral Geoffrey Miles to Admiralty, 17 1758C Aug. 1945.

72. PRO, ADM 228/19, Letter from Vice-Admiral Geoffrey Miles to Admiralty, 31 Aug. 1945. Stalin's order of the day for 30 March 1945 announced that the Red Army captured eight large U-boats at Danzig. House of Commons Debates, 5th Series, Vol. 410, 17 April 1945, Column 71. The Soviets later allowed a tripartite party to inspect these submarines at Libau. NA, RG 38, CNO/COMINCH(Ops), Series I, Box 8, File EF-30, Message from Vice-Admiral Robert Ghormley to COMINCH/CNO, 6 Oct. 1945.

73. BL, Cunningham, Add. Ms. 52572, Letter from Vice-Admiral Geoffrey Miles to Admiral Andrew Cunningham, 1 Sept. 1945.

74. NMM, Holt, Folder 18, Flag Officer Denmark to British Naval Commander-in-Chief Germany, 'Progress Report. Denmark Aug. 1945', 5 Sept. 1945. PRO, ADM 228/19, Telegram from Vice-Admiral Geoffrey Miles to Flag Officers Norway and Denmark, 25 Aug. 1945.

75. PRO, ADM 228/19, Letter from Vice-Admiral Geoffrey Miles to Flag Officers Schleswig-Holstein and Western Germany and Commodore Hamburg, 25 Aug. 1945.

76. NA, RG 38, CNO/COMINCH(Ops), Series III, Box 12, File 'Tripartite Naval Board/Western Hemisphere', Message from COMNAVEU to COMNAVFORGER, 28 1604 Aug. 1945.

77. IWM, Archer, PP1, 'Pacific Promenade No. 1', 6 Nov. 1945. The American members were Captain E.C. Forsyth, USN, Commander H.C. Stevenson, USN, Lieutenant A.A. Dach, USNR, and Lieutenant L.E. Hillsabeck, USNR. NA, RG 38, CNO/COMINCH(Ops), Series III, Box 12, File 'Tripartite Naval Board/Western Hemisphere', Memorandum from Director, Naval Division US Group Control Council to COMNAVEU, 'Names of Members of US Inspection Party', 20 Aug. 1945.

78. IWM, 84/45/1, Lieutenant Eric Harold Langridge, RNVR, Notebook, 'England fahrt ganz anders: Unserem Verbindungsoffizier in dankbarer Erinnerung an seine helfende Tätigkeit während der Minensuchvorführungen unseres Bootes im Firth of Forth von August bis November 1945'.

79. NA, RG 38, CNO/COMINCH(Ops), Series III, Box 12, File 'Tripartite Naval

Board/Western Hemisphere 1945', 'Notes on a Joint Meeting held at the Navy Department 9.30 a.m. Wednesday, 29 August, to consider the Inspection of Surrendered German Ships', 30 Aug. 1945.

80. NA, RG 38, CNO/COMINCH(Ops), Series I, Box 8, File EF-30, Report from Tripartite Naval Board Western Hemisphere to Tripartite Naval Commission Berlin, 'German Vessels in the Western Hemisphere – Inspection of by the Tripartite Naval Board for the Western Hemisphere', 25 Sept. 1945. PRO, ADM 228/26, Message from Vice-Admiral Geoffrey Miles to Admiralty, 16 1257A Nov. 1945. The US Navy took custody of the destroyers from the Royal Navy in Germany on 11 July, and they arrived in Boston on 7 August. NHC/OAB, NAVTECHMISEU, Series I, File 'Naval Task Group 120.6', Message from COMPHIBSUKAY to COMNAVEU, 11 0005 July 1945. NA, RG 38, CNO/COMINCH(Ops), Series I, Box 8, File EF-30, Message from USS DD939 to Commander-in-Chief Atlantic, 07 1725 Aug. 1945.

81. NA, RG 38, CNO/COMINCH(Ops), Series III, Box 12, File 'Tripartite Naval Board/Western Hemisphere 1945', 'Material Inspection Reports showing Corrections made by Soviet Board'.

82. PRO, ADM 116/5565, British Minutes of 8th Tripartite Naval Commission Meeting, 18 Sept. 1945.

83. PRO, ADM 116/5565, British Minutes of 9th Tripartite Naval Commission Meeting, 20 Sept. 1945. Mike Whitley, 'The Kriegsfischkutter', *Warship* 39(1986), p. 173.

84. Roger Bullen and M.E. Pelly, eds., *Documents on British Policy Overseas*, Vol. 2, *Conference and Conversations 1945: London, Washington and Moscow*, (London: Her Majesty's Stationery Office, 1985), pp. 454–5. PRO, ADM 1/18495, Aide-Mémoire from Vyacheslav Molotov to Ernest Bevin, 28 Sept. 1945.

85. NMM, Miles, Box 4, Diary, 3 Oct. 1945.

86. PRO, ADM 1/18495, Letter from C.H.M. Waldock to Jack Ward, Foreign Office, 5 Oct. 1945.

87. NMM, Miles, Box 4, Diary, 5 Oct. 1945.

88. PRO, ADM 116/5565, British Minutes of 13th Tripartite Naval Commission Meeting, 10 Oct. 1945.

89. FO/SU, 1945, Reel 5, Vol. 47857, Frame 136, Minute from George Wilson to Lord Hood, 30 Oct. 1945.

90. IWM, Parry, Box 10, Letter from Rear-Admiral W.E. Parry to Wife, 19 Oct. 1945.

91. NMM, Miles, Box 4, Diary, 19 Oct. 1945.

92. Miles earlier asked the Admiralty: 'If I can get seven or eight NARVIKS for the EUGEN would this suit our book better.' PRO, ADM 1/5513, Message from Vice-Admiral Geoffrey Miles to Admiralty, 10 1735B Oct. 1945.

93. M.J. Whitley, *Destroyer! German Destroyers in World War II*, (London: Arms & Armour Press, 1983), pp. 42–7. Michael Whitby, 'Instruments of Security: The Royal Canadian Navy's Procurement of the Tribal-Class Destroyers, 1938–1943', *The Northern Mariner* 2(1992), pp. 1–2.

94. The Admiralty's indecision put Miles 'in a hopeless position regarding the Prinz Eugen and I had to stall once more which was not popular with the other two.' NMM, Miles, Box 4, Diary, 22 Oct. 1945.

95. PRO, ADM 228/19, Message from Vice-Admiral Geoffrey Miles to Admiralty, 19 1638A Oct. 1945.

96. PRO, ADM 1/5513, Message from Admiralty to Vice-Admiral Geoffrey Miles, 29 0150 Oct. 1945.

97. NMM, Miles, Box 4, Diary, 29 Oct. 1945. Someone found the hat in Parry's requisitioned house the night before.

98. IWM, Parry, Box 10, Letter from Rear-Admiral W.E. Parry to Wife, 29 Oct. 1945. N.G. Kuznetsov, 'The War Years', *International Affairs* 12(1968), p. 102.

99. PRO, ADM 228/19, Message from British Admiralty Delegation Washington to Admiralty, 29 1717 Oct. 1945. Ghormley originally intended not to take part in the

draw, but the Admiralty interceded with King. Since the British and Americans agreed to share technical examinations if either won, the chances were better with two drawees. Pelly and Yasamee, Vol. 5, Microfiche 81ii, Minute from A.V. Alexander to Clement Attlee, 'Disposal of the German Fleet', 29 Oct. 1945.

100. NMM, Miles, Box 4, Diary, 9 Nov. 1945.

101. PRO, ADM 228/21, Letter from Admiral Gordei Levchenko to Vice-Admiral Geoffrey Miles, 10 Nov. 1945.

102. PRO, ADM 228/34, Message from Senior British Naval Officer Norway to Admiralty, 29 1630A Nov. 1945.

103. Before the war, the Soviet whale industry consisted of only small operations in the Behring Sea. Nonetheless, the Soviets participated in the 1946/47 Antarctic whaling season with the factory ship *Slava* (formerly the *Wikinger*), which was gained through German reparations in 1946. The smaller whalers served as catchers in support of the larger factory ship. FO/SU, 1948, Reel 10, Vol. 71712, Frame 10, Letter from H.W. Hollyer, Ministry of War Transport to M.Y. Watson, Joint Intelligence Bureau, 20 July 1948.

104. Pelly and Yasamee, Vol. 5, Microfiche 20iii, Letter from Lawrence Collier, British Embassy Oslo to Ernest Bevin, 15 Nov. 1945. The Norwegians intended to resume whaling as soon as possible after the war. Bjørn L. Basberg, 'Whaling or Shipping? Conflicts Over the Use of the Norwegian Whaling Fleet During World War II', *International Journal of Maritime History* 3(June 1991), p. 166.

105. PRO, ADM 228/34, Message from Admiralty to Vice-Admiral Geoffrey Miles, 05 0120 Dec. 1945.

106. PRO, ADM 228/19, Message from British Naval Commander-in-Chief Germany to Vice-Admiral Geoffrey Miles, 09 1214A Dec. 1945.

107. NA, RG 38, CNO/COMINCH(Ops), Series I, Box 8, File EF-30, Message from COMNAVFORGER to COMINCH/CNO, 02 1710 Oct. 1945.

108. The Ministry of War Transport advised the Admiralty that floating dry docks were properly part of port facilities. The British felt that the Soviets should request the docks as reparations through the Allied Control Council. FO/SU, 1945, Reel 3, Vol. 47844, Letter from E.W. Playfair to F.H. Keenlyside, 10 Sept. 1945.

109. NMM, Miles, Box 4, Diary, 13 Nov. 1945. During the meeting on 13 November, Ghormley and Levchenko suggested transfer of floating dry docks belonging to the *Kriegsmarine* before the war and all those built after 1939. PRO, ADM 116/5565, British Minutes of 22nd Tripartite Naval Commission Meeting, 13 Nov. 1945.

110. PRO, ADM 228/19, Message from Vice-Admiral Geoffrey Miles to Admiralty, 28 1820 Nov. 1945.

111. PRO, ADM 116/5565, British Minutes of 26th Tripartite Naval Commission Meeting, 1 Dec. 1945.

112. PRO, ADM 116/5565, British Minutes of 27th Tripartite Naval Commission Meeting, 6 Dec. 1945. PRO, ADM 228/19, Message from Vice-Admiral Geoffrey Miles to Admiralty, 06 1510A Dec. 1945.

113. PRO, ADM 116/5566, 'Report of the Tripartite Naval Commission Recommending the Allocation of the German Surface Navy and the German Submarine Fleet to the Government of the Union of Soviet Socialist Republics, the Government of the United Kingdom of Great Britain and Northern Ireland, the Government of the United States of America', 6 Dec. 1945. See also NMM, Miles, Box 1.

114. PRO, ADM 228/19, Message from Vice-Admiral Geoffrey Miles and Sir Andrew Common to Admiralty, 07 2019A Dec. 1945.

115. NMM, Miles, Box 2, File 'Tripartite Naval Commission Berlin 1945', Report from Vice-Admiral Geoffrey Miles to Secretary of the Admiralty, 8 Dec. 1945.

116. Pelly and Yasamee, Vol. 5, Microfiche 81ii, Memorandum from Cly Cardo, Admiralty to Jack Ward, Foreign Office, 16 Dec. 1945.

6

British Naval Commander-in-Chief Germany

After SHAEF's dissolution on 13 July 1945 Burrough was redesignated the British Naval Commander-in-Chief Germany. He and his subordinate staffs shouldered assorted duties for the control and disarmament of the *Kriegsmarine*. The Royal Navy used German naval personnel for minesweeping, clearance work, and maintenance parties. The arrangement, although temporary, provoked Soviet complaints that the Admiralty intentionally kept German forces under military command and discipline in contravention of Control Council laws. As the head British representative on the Naval Division and naval adviser to Montgomery, Burrough addressed this serious accusation at the Allied Control Council. The British Naval Commander-in-Chief Germany was also responsible for security, seizure, and transfer of the German surface fleet at Wilhelmshaven. Problems with the Tripartite Naval Commission's work precipitated sharp dialogue between Burrough and Soviet authorities. Yet, by the time the command of the British Naval Commander-in-Chief Germany ceased in March 1946, satisfactory resolution of outstanding differences had been achieved.

Upon termination of the OKM, the Royal Navy retained a smaller German administrative structure to supervise and support minesweeping. About 600,000 contact and ground mines remained in European waters after the war.[1] Under previous arrangements, the Admiralty coordinated clearance efforts. An International Mine Clearance Board convened in London to oversee work in specified zones.[2] The Royal Navy employed German minesweeping forces for several reasons: British minesweepers were redeployed to the Pacific; the West European navies were in various stages of rebuilding; the task was a residual obligation under the terms of surrender; and most importantly, minesweeping was extremely dangerous work. The predominant view within the Admiralty was that the Germans should be made to clean up the mess left over from the war, especially if there was a high risk of deaths. Preferring that German rather than British sailors died in this thankless work, the Royal Navy employed German minesweeping capabilities to the fullest extent possible. On 21 July Burrough designated Konteradmiral Fritz Krauss, the wartime chief of minesweeping forces, as administrator with Kapitän zur See Heinrich Gerlach as deputy administrator of the German Minesweeping Administration.[3] German naval authorities preserved considerable autonomy within this body, but worked under closer British supervision and restrictions than the OKM.

As naval staffs were drastically cut down through transfers or disbandment, Krauss chose senior officers from a British-provided list to fill the GM/SA's command positions. With the exception of Rudolphi, no section chief was above the grade of Fregattenkapitän. Hale used an enlarged control staff to oversee the activities of Krauss and the GM/SA at Glücksburg.[4] More than just a change in name, the reorganization tried to impose effective British control over naval forces retained for minesweeping work.

Burrough and his staffs were especially concerned that the GM/SA should not become a nucleus for continuation of the former *Kriegsmarine*. The British were aware that German naval officers manipulated minesweeping forces after World War I to circumvent restrictions in the Treaty of Versailles and preserve a talent pool for the reconstituted *Reichsmarine*.[5] The British intended to give the Germans no opportunity to do the same this time. After the recent war experience, Burrough felt 'it unsound policy for the British authorities to employ officers who have made names for themselves in the U-boat arm in any capacity whatsoever.'[6] The acquired skills and technical expertise in undersea warfare were completely different from those required for minesweeping.

The British tended to employ personnel whose previous service was principally in minesweepers. A surplus of willing executive officers permitted British naval authorities to pick and choose who should serve in the GM/SA.[7] Anyone found to be unsuitable or uncooperative was promptly replaced. In Holland, Korvettenkapitän Jürgen von Kleist, former chief of the 5th Security Flotilla, lost his GM/SA position after an anti-Dutch speech to minesweeping personnel.[8] Such interventions in the command structure – designed to stamp out potential opposition or insolence – reinforced the temporary nature of the arrangement. Whatever the aspirations of individual German naval officers, the GM/SA was merely a short-term expedience, of which the Royal Navy took advantage for the faster removal of sea mines in European waters.[9]

Under British auspices, German ships and personnel in the GM/SA worked in operational divisions within defined geographical areas. The largest were the first division, commanded by Konteradmiral Günther

Schubert, in Schleswig-Holstein, and the second division, commanded by Kapitän zur See Karl Smidt, in Western Germany. They undertook clearance work in the heavily-mined North Sea and western Baltic. Burrough approved formation of two main drafting pools, maintained at roughly ten per cent of the GM/SA's total strength, near Cuxhaven and Kiel.[10] These establishments provided sufficient personnel to support minesweeping within the two commands and additional areas: the third division in Denmark, the fourth division in Norway, the fifth division in Holland, and later a sixth division in the American Bremen-Bremerhaven enclave.

Initially, the clearance rate was painstakingly slow. Inexperienced crews, material deficiencies with ships and sweeping gear, as well as adverse weather delayed operations.[11] Work mostly involved clearing and widening demarcated channels for shipping. In the Kattegat, German minesweepers swept an average of ten mines per week. The small figure included fishing boats or minesweepers, which often had the misfortune to be sunk by mines. Minesweeping was always a tedious and dangerous occupation. As a result, the British encountered significant losses in personnel within the GM/SA.

Despite the efforts of British and German naval authorities, minesweeping became increasingly unpopular with many sailors. The threat to life and limb was apparent, and replacements were drawn primarily from draft pools through compulsion rather than on a voluntary basis. After a verbal report from Schubert, Baillie-Grohman disparaged those men 'whose only thought is to get out of the service, and, having no interest in their job, are a continual source of trouble.'[12] Irregular pay, low rations, and limited leave opportunities further exacerbated the situation. Pressed by local public opinion, foreign countries refused recreational and shore leave facilities for the GM/SA, insisting that crews stay on board ship or in fenced enclosures when ashore.[13] Even the most committed sailors recognized the lack of appreciation for their hard work. To alleviate discontent, the British Naval Commander-in-Chief Germany rotated units back to Germany for periods of leave, and instituted a compensation scheme for those personnel who were disabled or killed during minesweeping operations.[14] Although welcome, such measures failed to check growing morale and disciplinary problems. German naval authorities reported that sailors, tired of minesweeping and eager to go home, no longer trusted superiors and openly disobeyed orders.[15] Voting with their feet, some men decided to leave the service on their own initiative.

Desertions and absences without leave reached alarming proportions during late 1945. In a memorandum to Burrough, Krauss blamed pay stoppages, Communist propaganda, service conditions, and the presence of irresponsible elements for a rise in desertions and disorders.[16] British and German naval authorities recognized that a major motivational problem existed within the GM/SA. Although continued sea time might have satisfied executive or deck officers, the retention of technical specialists and engineering personnel – on whose skills the technically oriented GM/SA utterly depended – was much harder.[17] Promises of higher wages and bonuses in civil life, particularly from the Soviet Zone, furnished strong enticements for leaving. German naval authorities used courts martial as a deterrent, but the number of deserters actually recaptured was relatively small.[18] Unlike the American and French Zones, the British maintained no extradition agreement with Soviet authorities for the return of German nationals. The Soviets tied normalization of relations to a more general settlement of outstanding issues in occupied Germany. It was common knowledge within the GM/SA that the Soviet Zone was a safe haven beyond the reach of German and British naval authorities. The arrival of deserters in the Soviet sphere fuelled Soviet criticisms of British policy towards the German armed forces. They provided concrete proof that the British still maintained organized German formations.

The Royal Navy's operation of the GM/SA flouted statutes for the occupation and termination of the German armed forces. On 30 August Control Council Order No. 1 prohibited wearing of uniform by former members of the German armed forces.[19] Although British naval authorities contended that the order applied only to personnel after disbandment, other authorities adopted a stricter interpretation. British Military Government Ordinance No. 13, which became effective on 9 September, placed absolute restrictions on uniforms, decorations, and insignia.[20] In accordance with the regulation, Canadian and British soldiers forced German naval personnel in various ports to remove emblems and the *Kokarde*, the circular cap badge in existence since the days of Imperial Germany.

The unpopular action aggravated sagging morale and discipline among German sailors. Baillie-Grohman argued that Ordinance No. 13 encouraged desertion from the GM/SA, and asked Burrough for an exemption.[21] This recommendation was easier said than done. Subsequent discussions with the British Army of the Rhine encountered resistance from military authorities who insisted on a consistent policy throughout the occupation zone. In a meeting of the Control Commission's Legal Division, Commodore Hutton settled for deferred implementation of the regulations until after completion of particular tasks and the introduction of dyed uniforms.[22] Naval personnel immediately removed Nazi emblems bearing the swastika, but were still allowed to wear wartime medals, ribbons, and badges. Burrough informed his subordinate commands that no arrests would take place under Ordinance No. 13 before 15 October.[23] In this way, British naval authorities postponed application of regulations concerning uniforms to the GM/SA and other 'frozen' naval formations.

In fact, the Royal Navy claimed special treatment for German naval forces under British authority from the Allied Control Council. During a meeting of the Coordinating Committee on 17 September the British member, Lieutenant-General Brian Robertson, advocated an exemption clause for the GM/SA in a draft law eliminating and prohibiting military training.[24] He repeated the Royal Navy's contention that only disciplined and uniformed personnel could perform minesweeping and related naval tasks. Nonetheless, Y.A. Karasev, the Soviet representative on the Legal Directorate, questioned the appropriateness of such a clause, arguing that any exemption risked perpetuation of the German armed forces. The Red Navy performed its own mine clearance in the Baltic. Why could not the Royal Navy do the same? The Soviets wanted the provision deleted entirely and the British to fulfil their obligations to disband remaining German naval forces.

Despite mounting Soviet opposition, the British decided to retain German naval personnel in organized formations. In London, the Admiralty quickly rejected a Soviet proposal for 'the German navy to cease wearing uniforms forthwith.'[25] British naval authorities still required German labour for what was considered essential work. At the Coordinating Committee's meeting on 6 November General Vasillii Danilovich Sokolovsky refused to accept responsibility on the part of the Soviets for the GM/SA's control.[26] The organization, which the Soviets wished completely dissolved, functioned solely in the British and American Zones. On the advice of the Royal Navy, Montgomery, the British zonal commander-in-chief, directed that an exemption 'apply temporarily to such units or individuals of the ex-German Navy employed on services connected with minesweeping and with maintenance of ex-German warships and other essential work, as may be authorized by the British Naval Commander-in-Chief, Germany.'[27] British representatives in Berlin forcefully defended this position. Control Council Law No. 8, which took effect from 1 December, allowed German naval personnel under British control to wear existing uniforms without medals, decorations, and ribbons.[28] Although the Royal Navy gained a significant concession in the short-term, the exemption of German naval forces contributed to Soviet dissatisfaction over the sluggish pace of *Wehrmacht* disbandment.

The British faced a strong protest against their policy towards remaining German forces. In a letter to Montgomery on 20 November Zhukov accused British authorities of 'retaining organized German and other units in the British Zone contrary to the decisions of the Berlin Conference and the Declaration of the Defeat of Germany.'[29] The charge was certainly true, but the Soviets placed ulterior motives behind an arrangement which the British considered reasonable and necessary. British authorities viewed German personnel as primarily a convenient labour source rather than a reserve of armed troops for possible use against the Soviet Union. Commenting on Zhukov's letter, a Foreign Office official felt 'that the Admiralty are the main offenders in this respect, and attach perhaps exaggerated importance to maintaining intact the German minesweeping organization which they have built up.'[30] At the time, the Royal Navy kept approximately 45,000 officers and sailors in organized units under German naval discipline and administration.

Nonetheless, British authorities felt obliged to challenge the Soviet accusation because their integrity was in question. Montgomery dismissed Zhukov's claim that the British preserved over one million Germans under military training as 'quite absurd', and resolved that the British 'must be perfectly frank about the whole thing.'[31] British authorities, despite the Soviet rhetoric, were not acting in bad faith. They supported an American proposal to establish a tripartite commission to investigate the situation in all zones. In a message to the War Office, Montgomery described the exchange with Zhukov during a Control Council meeting on 30 November:

> Russians are deeply suspicious of our holding of 700,000 German troops and suspect our intentions. Zhukov himself is most friendly and the match has been played so far in a very good and amicable spirit. But he is undoubtedly under orders from Moscow. We are in good position to win the match. But everything depends on next shot and if the ball gets knocked off the green we may possibly lose the match.[32]

To allay Soviet fears, Montgomery recommended closing all German headquarters and immediately disbanding German service personnel remaining in concentration areas – including 225,000 held under the Cabinet's direction for future reparations labour in the United Kingdom. During a meeting of the Coordinating Committee on 3 December Robertson tabled a discharge plan 'to show the British readiness to fulfil at the earliest possible moment the undertaking of Field Marshal Montgomery at the preceding Control Council Meeting.'[33] British occupation authorities promised timely disbandment of German forces in the British Zone as a major conciliatory gesture towards the Soviets.

The Royal Navy showed less enthusiasm for the proposed changes. Robertson invited naval authorities to express their views before the

Coordinating Committee's next meeting.[34] Continued employment of German naval personnel remained the Royal Navy's chief concern. Under pressure from the Admiralty, the British Army of the Rhine excluded naval minesweeping forces from the plans to terminate and disband German formations within the British Zone by the target date of 20 January 1946.[35] The Royal Navy regarded continued use of German labour as fundamental to the goal of naval disarmament. Burrough wrote to Montgomery directly:

> It is essential, in order that I may carry out my responsibilities as British Naval Commander-in-Chief Germany, for me to maintain for the time being the British controlled organization which is known as the German Minesweeping Administration, and the German Naval personnel forming care and maintenance and steaming crews for the ex-German Fleet.[36]

For the Royal Navy, it was only proper that the Germans worked under the surrender terms, especially since British resources were limited or not available. Burrough asked Ghormley for American support, stating that 'any interference with this organization at this stage would, of course, be disastrous.'[37] Disarmament tasks and clearance work in adjoining waters would be impaired, thereby prolonging final disbandment of German naval forces or leaving important work unfinished. Paradoxically, the Royal Navy needed to keep German formations temporarily intact in order to destroy more fully German naval power and to address the damage which the *Kriegsmarine* had done during the war.

With German disarmament at stake, British naval authorities in Germany asked the Admiralty for assistance in retention of German forces. Burrough expected 'strong pressure to liquidate the present German Minesweeping Administration organization and unless powerful support is forthcoming I think there is little chance of maintaining it in its present form.'[38] Soviet criticism seriously tested British resolve, especially since the Soviets were absolutely correct about the Royal Navy keeping German formations intact and functional. As Zhukov's allegations on the Control Council persisted, the Royal Navy grasped for an opening from the Soviet side. In response to a long statement by Robertson on the naval position during a Coordinating Committee meeting on 17 December 1945 Sokolovosky stated that the 'Soviet delegation did not question [the] necessity for units carrying out special duties such as clearance of mines by land or sea.'[39] British naval authorities quickly read into this statement an invitation to maintain the GM/SA. The Admiralty informed Montgomery 'that Their Lordships regard the continued existence of the Administration to be of such importance that no decision to alter its organisation should be taken by the Control Council without reference to London.'[40] The Admiralty's intervention removed the entire issue from Montgomery's discretion. Unless the Soviets complained loudly, the Royal Navy intended to use the GM/SA and 'frozen' naval forces until completion of allotted tasks.

In addition to minesweeping, British naval authorities employed large numbers of personnel for care and maintenance of the remaining German surface fleet. Working parties and *Dienstgruppen* kept the numerous warships at Wilhelmshaven in good mechanical and physical condition, prior to allocation by the Tripartite Naval Commission. For this purpose, Rear-Admiral Hutton acknowledged the need for local German naval authorities 'to maintain discipline based on a logical and uniform system of command and administration.'[41] The British made full use of the existing naval command structure.

The willingness of senior German commanding officers to follow and enforce the Royal Navy's orders was paramount. The British found reliable partners in Konteradmiral Kurt Weyher, former sea commander of the East Frisian Islands, and Konteradmiral Paul Willy Zieb, Wilhelmshaven's shipyard director, whose cooperation was 'quite possibly inspired by the hope of obtaining better conditions for themselves, and of avoiding internment, as much as loyalty to British officers.'[42] In spite of the obvious self-interest, the two admirals genuinely felt honour-bound to obey British commands to the utmost of their abilities. In Weyher's words, success in the work 'depended on the dutiful collaboration of every officer, every superior and – no less – every sailor, if necessary discipline shall be maintained mentally as well as in its exterior forms.'[43] The Royal Navy counted on absolute obedience to British orders. Although defeated, German naval officers found comfort and predictability in a common code of military service, which demanded efficiency and obedience. This dangerous impulse – the fear of civilian life – was part of what motivated earlier German soldiers and sailors to join para-military organizations after World War I. After a visit to Wilhelmshaven, Parry commented on the plight of Weyher and Zieb in a letter to his wife:

> What a pathetic sight it is to see these intelligent and efficient people, so like ourselves in many ways. They can have no future in their own trade, and one trembles to think what will happen to them. ... However it's no good being too sympathetic – for I'm afraid we must make sure there is no German Navy for many years to come. And they must suffer for the mistakes of their rulers.[44]

The goal of complete naval disarmament transcended individual careers. The British regarded the services of senior officers like Weyher and Zieb as expedient and useful for a limited time, particularly in preventing possible scuttling.

The Royal Navy took the threat of sabotage at Wilhelmshaven seriously. In 1919 German crews had scuttled the German High Seas Fleet in the British anchorage at Scapa Flow. The incident deprived the victorious Allied powers of expected war spoils, and later provided a focal point for a reborn German navy. The Admiralty naturally hoped to avoid another such experience. While the British removed troublesome elements from German crews, Weyher and Zieb assumed personal responsibility for the warships at Wilhelmshaven.[45] German naval authorities suppressed the slightest sign of misbehaviour among sailors. The Potsdam commitments for the fleet's division and the Tripartite Naval Commission's deliberations demanded preservation. Levchenko expressed concern that the Germans might try to sabotage warships before transfer to the Soviet Union.[46] The onus was on the Royal Navy to ensure that vessels existed for ultimate allocation. On Britain's behalf, Miles accepted responsibility for security of warships 'to the best of our ability, but have refused to give a hundred per cent guarantee.'[47] To fulfil this promise, British authorities took necessary precautions.

Preparations against possible sabotage and for eventual transfer of warships at Wilhelmshaven were extensive. In early September Burrough asked the Flag Officer Western Germany to begin detailed planning in anticipation of a handover to the Soviet Union.[48] To minimize the chance of interference, the British Naval Commander-in-Chief Germany favoured a single action, which would take place some time after conclusion of the Tripartite Naval Commission's work. British authorities prepared a three-stage plan called 'Caesar' to remove German maintenance crews into barracks on shore, guard warships in secured berths, and then sail them to designated countries.[49] The proposed operation counted on close collaboration between naval and military authorities. As an occupation commitment, 31st Anti-Aircraft Brigade and 3rd Canadian Infantry Division (Canadian Army Occupation Force) patrolled port areas and the surrounding town in Wilhelmshaven.[50] These troops were expected to seize warships in the event of sudden unrest. 'Caesar's Wife', an alternative emergency plan, allowed 'by show of force and by fire (to kill) if necessary, to prevent any unruliness, riot or mutiny on the part of the Germans being off-loaded.'[51] At the first sign of impending scuttling, British and Canadian soldiers were to shoot first and ask questions later. Protection of warships for allocation was the highest priority.

Despite the risk of sabotage, Levchenko wanted minesweepers transferred to the Soviets prior to 'Caesar'. The Admiralty was reluctant to take a strong stand against the request because the Soviets still refused to participate on the International Mine Clearance Board.[52] An outright

135

refusal might have led to further alienation. The Red Navy obviously needed minesweepers in the Baltic before the winter freeze-up. Burrough initially rejected separate transfers as an undue danger to the larger warships, but eventually accepted the political and operational reasons behind the Soviet request.[53] As Miles reported back to London, Levchenko abruptly reversed his position concerning sabotage in the German fleet during earlier Tripartite Naval Commission discussions. The Soviets now considered the risk of scuttling as negligible!

British and Soviet authorities made arrangements for transfers to the Soviet Union. The Tripartite Naval Commission apportioned minesweepers on 9 October.[54] Levchenko immediately asked when the Soviet share would be available for collection. At a conference in Minden on 11 October Burrough, Miles, and Levchenko decided to withdraw allocated minesweeping flotillas in stages from the GM/SA for transfer to Travemünde.[55] Secrecy was still important to prevent possible attempts at sabotage or scuttling with the larger surface ships. As a pretext for the reductions, Baillie-Grohman noted Schubert's earlier request for 'a large scale weeding out of the more unwilling ratings and has recommended that, if necessary, minesweepers should be laid up in order to do this.'[56] The British wished, as much as possible, to keep German naval authorities ignorant about the movement's true purpose.

Since the sight of Soviet steaming parties could reveal Allied intentions towards the German fleet and increase the likelihood of sabotage, the British approved use of German crews for the transfers. The decision carried its own risks. At Kiel, Baillie-Grohman informed the Germans about the dire consequences of subversion or interference with the planned transfer:

> Commanding officers and men will be held personally and collectively responsible if there is any attempt at scuttling, contrary to the terms of surrender, and that there will be no hesitation about using force against any ships' companies so involved, either at the time of the incident or subsequently in Military Court.[57]

The Royal Navy intended to deliver minesweepers to the Soviets with compliant German assistance. Schubert asked whether the Soviets might choose to keep crews, perhaps through coercion or duress.[58] The question was certainly perplexing. Besides the moral implications, the GM/SA could not afford further manpower losses. To counter this fear, Levchenko personally guaranteed prompt return of crews after arrival at Soviet-controlled ports.[59] Although afforded the opportunity to volunteer for Soviet service, German sailors remained under British control and responsibility.

Transfer of minesweepers to the Soviet Union took place in several stages. The operation, known alternately as 'Scram' and 'Bitumen', entailed the sailing of convoys to Travemünde for handover to Soviet naval authorities, and thence to Bornholm or Swinemünde under Soviet escort.[60] Since Kiel was the major staging point, Baillie-Grohman and his subordinates handled most matters on the British side. Escort officers received detailed instructions, based on extensive staff planning.[61] The Soviets, on the other hand, worked differently. Despite British objections, the Soviet naval staff sent Vice-Admiral Iurii Fedorovich Rall, commander-in-chief of the northern Baltic with his headquarters at Kronstadt, to supervise the Soviet side of the transfers.[62] Soviet naval authorities generally preferred improvisation to planning. During the first convoy, Commander Frank Mountifort Beasley, RN, found their methods 'maddening to anyone who liked to have a plan ready to meet certain eventualities.'[63] Convoys left when Rall decided to wake up in the morning, sometimes without Soviet escorts, and occasionally in the face of adverse weather. After a particularly severe storm near Bornholm which scattered Convoy No. 22, the Soviets shamefully tried to shift the blame onto British naval authorities.[64] At times, cooperation with the Soviets stretched British patience.

Despite attempts at genuine goodwill, minor problems inevitably arose at the points of destination. Technically, the ships were under Soviet control after departure from British-controlled ports. Rear-Admiral P.I. Kolchen, the senior Soviet naval officer at Swinemünde, intervened with the Soviet bureaucracy when officials wanted Royal Navy officers to sign receipts for delivered ships.[65] The British feared being held responsible for later defects. In other cases, Soviet sentries allowed German sailors to desert, and blocked the movements of British officers. Faced with British protests, the Soviets regularly introduced alcohol to get their own way. Supplied with a hefty glass of vodka by a Soviet liaison officer, Lieutenant-Commander D.A. Grant jettisoned 'surreptitiously the majority of my portion in a cigarette tin and when Commander Vassiliev was subsequently called away there was the unprecedented spectacle of four British Officers making a concerted dash to the heads to throw away their liquor and substitute water.'[66] The British quickly learned the advantages of negotiating with the Soviets in a sober state.

After inspections at Swinemünde, Soviet authorities declared that many transferred minesweepers lacked important equipment. Following a particularly strong protest from Levchenko, Burrough responded that the Soviets had no 'right to complain of the slowness of transfer at the same time as the alleged bad state of the craft.'[67] Spare parts and fittings to bring the ships up to operational standards were in short supply, even in the British Zone. Similar complaints accompanied the transfer of U-boats to the Soviet Union.

Based on the Tripartite Naval Commission's decisions, British naval authorities made arrangements for transfer of Soviet-allocated submarines. The Admiralty initially wanted British crews to take ten U-boats to a Soviet-controlled port in order to avoid 'difficulties and endless requests.'[68] Levchenko, however, expressed his intention to send Soviet crews for collection. As a compromise, a party of ten executive and engineer officers, headed by Captain 1st Rank Morosov, arrived in Great Britain.[69] Unfortunately, the Soviets experienced problems with hotel accommodation, interpreting, and access to the U-boats. Once inspections took place, deficiencies were discovered in the submarines' kit and equipment, particularly with escape apparatus and rubber products. Cataloguing the numerous complaints, Engineer Rear-Admiral A.E. Brykin, the head of the Soviet Naval Mission in London, received little satisfaction at the Admiralty. McCarthy allegedly told the Soviet delegation: 'You are unwelcome guests and must be content with that which we can provide.'[70] The British admiral then curtly declared that equipment was unavailable in Great Britain. Promising a generous provision from sources in Germany, the Admiralty informed Levchenko and Brykin that the U-boats would depart from British ports 'as is'.[71]

The intended transfer proceeded as planned. On 24 November Soviet-allocated submarines, with the exception of U-3514, which encountered engine problems, sailed to Libau in an operation known as 'Cabal'.[72] Although the Soviets may not have been entirely satisfied with the equipment situation, the British followed the spirit, if not the letter, of the Potsdam Protocol.

With the departure of the Soviet-allocated submarines, the Admiralty proceeded with the destruction of remaining U-boats, as agreed at Potsdam. In mid-November the Commander-in-Chief Rosyth drafted 'Deadlight', a plan for scuttling 110 U-boats from Loch Ryan and Lisahally in deep water off the coast of Ireland.[73] The operation reflected the depth of hatred for the U-boat within the Royal Navy. The Admiralty informed the Americans that 'no experiments or trials are being carried out during sinking of U-boats but opportunity is being taken for live practice with standard weapons.'[74] The submarines were towed to a central location, and then sunk by gunfire or depth charges. The Fleet Air Arm and Coastal Command earmarked thirty-six U-boats for air practice and bombing runs.[75] The entire display took the form of an immense psychological release. For the Royal Navy, 'Deadlight' was the final triumph over the U-boat.[76]

'Deadlight' encountered problems with secrecy under the Potsdam agreement. The First Lord deflected questions in the House of

Commons regarding use of scrap metal and electrical generators from the U-boats for civilian needs.[77] Officially, the fact that the submarines were to be sunk was still unknown to the general public. In a meeting at the Admiralty on 19 November Alexander asked a group of editors from national and regional newspapers to

> appreciate the serious complaint which our two Allies will have against me if unauthorized publication takes place unilaterally in the U.K. concerning this transfer, and the awkward political consequences which may ensue if sabotage subsequently takes place in other German units still to be transferred to our Allies.[78]

In return for exclusive opportunities to witness the sinkings, British editors promised to submit voluntarily to Admiralty censorship. But, when 'Deadlight' commenced on 25 November, the *Daily Express* and the *Evening Standard* broke the agreement by reporting the full details.[79] The breach brought several letters from companies and individuals interested in the submarines' scrap potential.

Despite numerous protests, the Royal Navy sank all surplus U-boats held in British ports by 14 January 1946. The sole exception was U-3515, which was held in reserve in case the Soviet-allocated U-3514 proved incapable of repair.[80] Complete destruction of the U-boats was important to the Royal Navy. With the mass sinkings, the Admiralty ensured that the *Kriegsmarine*'s submarines would never again pose a threat to British maritime interests.

Publicity over transfer and sinking of U-boats caused the Royal Navy to accelerate its timetable for the German surface fleet's division. With approval from the Cabinet and the Admiralty, Burrough intended to seize and transfer major warships under Operation 'Caesar' on 9 January 1946.[81] Until then, British naval authorities tried not to give the Germans any reason for sabotage or scuttling. Burrough continued to turn down requests by Zhukov and Levchenko for Soviet technical officers to inspect the warships at Wilhelmshaven before transfer.[82] Although the Soviets downplayed the threat of sabotage, the Royal Navy considered the possibility to be still very real. Burrough told Ghormley that the British 'could punish severely the officers and men concerned, but the damage would then be done, and it would merely be a case of closing the stable door after the horse had bolted.'[83] Since responsibility for custody was exclusively British, the British Naval Commander-in-Chief Germany wished to make sure operational warships remained for allocation. On 4 December Burrough cancelled 'Caesar', and expressed his 'intention to "pounce" with a British force on the major warships at Wilhelmshaven as soon as the necessary arrangements can be made and that Russian skeleton crews shall then take over their allocation of ships.'[84] Intelligence information suggested that the Germans might attempt to scuttle the major warships some time around Christmas. Keeping ultimate intentions secret was increasingly difficult due to press coverage surrounding the U-boats.[85] German naval authorities now certainly suspected, or knew, of Allied intentions towards the fleet. The British hoped to pre-empt any German action.

British naval and military authorities seized warships in the German surface fleet without serious incident. Hutton arrived in Wilhelmshaven to undertake arrangements with Conder and local army units. In keeping with Burrough's directive, a quick and decisive operation, known as 'Silver', aimed towards 'safe and timely delivery to the American and Russian Navies and to the British Home Fleet of their allocations of the German major warships, as completely refitted and stored as time and the materials available have permitted.'[86] Reinforcements bolstered existing establishments in Wilhelmshaven. On 13 December thirteen Royal Marine officers and 150 other ranks arrived from England.[87] The British attempted to conceal the extensive preparations for 'Silver' from German naval authorities. As a precaution, the heavy cruiser *Prinz Eugen* sailed – ostensibly for repairs – to Bremerhaven under British guard two days before the intended 'pounce'.[88] In the early Sunday morning hours of 16 December British naval officers boarded the remaining warships, ordered crews mustered, and then with the support of British and Canadian soldiers, removed sailors to barracks on shore.[89] The surprise seemed so complete that crews on some vessels were found still asleep. British authorities left no Germans on board, and moved the large warships to secured areas of the port under guard.

Transfer of the expropriated warships, the second part of 'Silver', took place just as smoothly. On the morning of 18 December Rall arrived in the submarine depot ship *Otto Wünsche* with 700 officers and ratings to take over Soviet-allocated warships.[90] Soviet parties replaced British guards, and German crews were allowed back on the ships. In an order of the day, Conder held German sailors responsible for any sabotage, 'whether dockyard workmen are on board or not, and all will suffer for any stupidity by one misguided fool.'[91] As incentive for good behaviour, he promised leave and possible disbandment after completion of the transfers. Much to British relief, no trouble accompanied the return of German sailors to warships under Soviet control.[92] The Soviets prepared to sail with German steaming parties. Burrough told the First Sea Lord that Levchenko was 'just as anxious as I am to get his ships away from Wilhelmshaven as soon as possible – we can arrange about stores later.'[93] Ice conditions in the Baltic would soon make movements more difficult. On 2 January 1946 the light cruiser *Nürnberg*, flying Rall's flag, led a collection of smaller warships through the Kiel Canal to

Libau.[94] Over the coming weeks, similar convoys departed from Wilhelmshaven for Soviet-controlled ports.

Under pressure from the Americans and Soviets, the British made concerted efforts to accelerate the transfer of warships. American-allocated ships left in convoys for the United States enclave under Operation 'Scoot'. A Combined US/British Ship Repair Committee gave the repair of warships highest priority.[95] Those requiring only minimal work sailed directly to Great Britain under British guard. Moreover, the scope of 'Scram' convoys to Soviet-controlled ports broadened to all remaining naval vessels, including motor torpedo boats.[96] Many ships inevitably left with missing equipment and fittings. As Burrough told the Naval Division:

> It is not always realised by our Allies that GERMANY is a completely defeated nation, which we occupied in a state of chaos, and that much of the equipment and stores necessary to bring ships up to a state of first class efficiency is either destroyed, expended or out of production.[97]

British naval authorities did the best they could do with the available resources. Completeness was often sacrificed for speedy transfer. On 6 February 1946 Hutton reported that transfer of the Soviet share of major warships from Wilhelmshaven was finished.[98] The operation was a significant achievement for the Royal Navy towards its goal of complete naval disarmament.

British naval authorities, for reasons largely beyond their control, were unable to sail all allocated warships before the deadlines set out by the Tripartite Naval Commission. Whereas some ships required more extensive repairs than anticipated, others could not be found or never existed in the first place. The Tripartite Naval Commission's final report contained a number of mistakes, and the British requested amendments to reflect actual numbers. The Soviets, however, flatly refused to consider revisions, claiming 'the Papal infallibility of the Red Book subsequent to their own ratification.'[99] Calling the Tripartite Naval Commission's final report their 'Bible', they contended that the final report was a binding legal document, which placed certain obligations on the British. At a meeting of the reconvened Tripartite Naval Commission on 16 February 1946 Vice-Admiral F.S. Sidelnikov, who sat in Berlin during Levchenko's absence from ill-health, refused to consider proposed amendments:

> The Report of the Tripartite Naval Commission, dated 6 December 1945, was accepted by his government as factual and authoritative, that consequently no errors can exist in the Report, and therefore there is no necessity to amend the Report.[100]

The uncompromising position was a classic example of bureaucratic obstinacy. The Soviets accepted additions to the report, but not losses. Sidelnikov instead argued that deficiencies in the Soviet allocation should be compensated out of the British share because British naval staffs had verified the accuracy of the original lists. The British considered Sidelnikov's suggestion unfair and completely unacceptable.

In an effort to resolve the matter, the British Naval Commander-in-Chief Germany held separate meetings with Soviet authorities. After presenting a letter of protest to Sidelnikov on 19 February 1946 Burrough frustratingly declared that the 'argument is about a lot of junk, pure junk … It is like a rich man arguing with a rag-and-bone merchant over a penny.'[101] Burrough obviously felt that he was the aggrieved party. In his opinion, the Soviets had already received the worthwhile ships. The remaining vessels, used mostly by the Germans as accommodation hulks, lacked engines and important machinery. In an obvious slight directed at Sidelnikov and the Tripartite Naval Commission, Burrough stated that he had his 'own opinion about the individuals, but I cannot express them.' Requesting such worthless ships was simply undignified. At a subsequent meeting with Zhukov on 21 February Burrough declared that Soviet 'suspicions were unjust and without foundation', and asked the Soviet marshal 'to give Russian representatives the power to consider amendments of the Red Book.'[102] The British had absolutely no intention of leaving any war potential in Germany. According to Burrough, the Soviets and British could reach a satisfactory agreement to complete the transfer with mutual confidence and goodwill.

Apparently, his arguments were persuasive because the Soviets agreed to several sets of amendments to the Tripartite Naval Commission's final report. Burrough informed the Admiralty that Zhukov seemed favourably disposed towards Soviet naval authorities at least studying the errors and proposed amendments.[103] Further guidance was required from Moscow. Sidelnikov disappeared for a full week from Berlin.[104] The British clearly held the trump card since deliveries could be stopped at any time. When the Soviets finally agreed to amendments, Burrough continued transfers of warships 'in view of the improved Russian attitude.'[105] Some ships were better than none, and the Soviets recognized the tangible benefits of cooperation. Delegates on the Tripartite Naval Commission signed a first supplement on 23 March, followed by a second supplement on 31 May.[106] These incorporated amendments to the Tripartite Naval Commission's final report. At a meeting in Minden on 9 April Levchenko thanked British naval authorities for the assistance given Soviet officers in the transfer of Soviet-allocated warships from the British Zone.[107] Remaining warships represented a matter for further negotiation. The Soviet government took a much longer time to ratify the additional supplements.[108]

While the British, Americans, and Soviets reached an amicable agreement over transfer of remaining warships, British authorities confronted renewed Soviet attacks on the Allied Control Council against German forces under British control. At the First Sea Lord's insistence, Burrough served as the acting British zonal commander-in-chief and military governor during Montgomery's vacation in Switzerland between 2 and 24 February 1946.[109] Although raising the prestige of the Royal Navy in Germany, the capacity involved the British Naval Commander-in-Chief Germany even more intimately in complicated quadripartite deliberations. When Burrough showed indignation at Soviet concerns about British disbandment efforts during a meeting on 11 February Zhukov stated that he had to criticize 'because the obligations contracted by you are not fulfilled. Friendships are important, but agreements are even more important.'[110] Unlike the British, the Soviets separated personal relationships from the business at hand. The word of a Royal Navy officer was simply not good enough. Zhukov wanted concrete signs of progress towards complete disbandment. Despite Montgomery's earlier commitments, the Royal Navy still employed large numbers of uniformed German personnel in disciplined formations. Successful transfer of most warships and minesweepers removed any vested Soviet interest in maintaining German forces, even on a temporary basis. The GM/SA became a prime target for Soviet accusations.

The actions of German naval authorities ultimately made the GM/SA untenable in its existing form. In late December 1945 the British moved the GM/SA's headquarters from Glücksburg to the Navy House in Hamburg.[111] In spite of this physical relocation, Krauss and his subordinates continued to work with considerable independence. The general feeling of Commodore Hugh England, Hale's successor at the GM/SA, was 'that there are still too many Germans in this administration, and that the sooner we can eliminate them the better.'[112] Only the necessity to sweep mines kept the organization in existence. Nevertheless, German naval authorities overstepped the bounds of British approval with advertisements in newspapers to increase the percentage of volunteers and the relentless pursuit of runaway sailors.[113] Both inevitably attracted Soviet attention. Schubert reported that the majority of German naval deserters now headed for the Soviet Zone.[114] These malcontent sailors seemingly confirmed Soviet charges that German militarism was alive and thriving in the British Zone. Soviet propaganda intensified after Rudolphi and naval authorities imprudently sent out letters, which notified former sailors of outstanding convictions and sentences by naval courts martial.[115] The Royal Navy was caught red-handed. Faced with strong Soviet condemnation, embarrassed British naval authorities instituted steps to reorganize the GM/SA and remaining 'frozen' forces.

The new bodies adopted minor changes in form rather than structure. Since the original directive given to Krauss no longer reflected existing circumstances, Burrough directed Commodore England to begin drafting a statement of function and organization for the GM/SA.[116] This mandate entailed a comprehensive review of the entire administration. At a conference on 25 February British naval authorities discussed introduction of new working dress, selection of senior officers, manning, and disciplinary arrangements.[117] Despite Soviet protests, German management was considered efficient and serviceable. Even German courts martial, the main focus of Soviet complaints, served the useful purpose of maintaining discipline.[118] The courts certainly would be abolished, but there was no question of dispensing with the services of naval personnel. The Admiralty favoured continued operational use of the GM/SA for mine clearance.[119] The object was reorganization rather than complete dissolution.

The reforms generally sought to work within the provisions of Control Council laws and directives. The Royal Navy organized remaining naval forces into two distinct categories: the GM/SA and *Marine Dienstgruppen*.[120] The latter performed specific technical tasks, such as port clearance, maintenance, and demolitions. Beginning from 1 May 1946 naval personnel adopted new working dress, consisting of blue blouses and trousers with distinctive emblems.[121] The working dress regulations eliminated all outward vestiges of the former *Kriegsmarine*. In appearance at least, the GM/SA and *Marine Dienstgruppen* were now separate entities, dependent upon British authority. Commodore England issued detailed British instructions to the GM/SA in mid-May 1946, setting out the new dress, command, and disciplinary arrangements.[122] For the time being, the changes blunted Soviet insinuations. The Royal Navy was even prepared to accept a draft law for termination of the German armed forces, later passed as Control Council Law No. 34, 'provided [the] British Legal Division can give the Naval Division assurance that the German Minesweeping Administration and the Naval *Dienstgruppen* will not thereby be open to future attack as regards their legality.'[123] Soviet sensitivity towards British employment of German personnel kept the Royal Navy honest.

With successful transfer of warships and reorganization of the GM/SA, the British naval command within occupied Germany underwent restructuring. The First Sea Lord demanded major reductions in establishments and personnel by April 1946.[124] Consequently, the position of British Naval Commander-in-Chief Germany officially came to an end. On 15 March Burrough handed over command to Vice-Admiral Sir Harold T.C. Walker, RN, who adopted the designation of Vice-Admiral Commanding British Naval Forces Germany.[125] The former looked back with great satisfaction. At a press conference, Burrough reviewed the Royal Navy's achievements in control and disarmament of the *Kriegsmarine* during his tenure as British Naval Commander-in-Chief Germany.[126] The German Minesweeping Administration swept mines on behalf of the International Mine Clearance Board; the surface fleet was safely secured at Wilhelmshaven; transfers of warships to the Soviet Union took place; and the majority of U-boats were sunk in deep water. By all accounts, this was a most productive and significant period for German naval disarmament. Despite Soviet accusations and protests, the Royal Navy worked actively towards the complete elimination of German militarism and naval power.

NOTES

1. Gerhard Freiherr von Ledebur, 'Die Räumung von Seeminen in den Gewässern von Nord-, West- und Osteuropa nach 1945', *Marine Rundschau* 67(1970), p.273.
2. PRO, ADM 116/5787, Minutes of Meeting held at the Admiralty concerning Post-War Mine Clearance, 2 Oct. 1945.
3. PRO, ADM 228/70, Instruction from Admiral Harold Burrough to Head of GM/SA, 21 July 1945.
4. CCAC, HYND 3/8, 'Mine Clearance in European Waters', *British Zone Review*, Vol. 1, No. 9 (19 Jan. 1946), p.14.
5. Salewski, *Seekriegsleitung*, Vol. 2, p.563.
6. PRO, ADM 228/56, Letter from Admiral Harold Burrough to Flag Officer Schleswig-Holstein, 19 Nov. 1945.
7. Eric C. Rust, *Naval Officers under Hitler: The Story of Crew 34*, (New York: Praeger, 1991), p.138.
8. PRO, ADM 228/56, Letter from Senior British Naval Officer Holland to British Naval Commander-in-Chief Germany, 13 Nov. 1945. PRO, ADM 228/91, Letter from Konteradmiral Fritz Krauss to Commodore Hugh England, 13 Feb. 1946. German minesweeping forces remained in Holland until mid-1946. Hermann Jung, *Die deutschen Kriegsgefangenen im Gewahrsam Belgiens, der Niederlande und Luxemburgs*, Maschke, ed., Vol. 12, pp.227–32.
9. BA/MA, Ruge, N 379/248, Arnim Zimmermann, 'Das Räumen der Seeminen nach dem Kriegs', 1954, p.5.
10. PRO, ADM 228/90, Memorandum from British Naval Commander-in-Chief Germany to Flag Officers and Captain E. Hale, 'Provision of Drafting Pools and Base Staffs for German Minesweeping Administration', 23 July 1945.
11. PRO, ADM 228/96, 'British Naval Commander-in-Chief Germany Weekly Minesweeping Summary No. 1', 6 Sept. 1945.
12. PRO, ADM 228/61, Letter From Rear-Admiral Harold Baillie-Grohman to British Naval Commander-in-Chief Germany, 29 Oct. 1945.
13. PRO, ADM 228/60, Memorandum from Admiral Harold Burrough to Flag Officer Norway; Flag Officer Denmark; Senior British Naval Officer Holland; Naval Attaché Paris, 19 Sept. 1945.
14. PRO, ADM 228/93, Memorandum from Kapitän zur See Heinrich Gerlach to GM/SA Administrators Schleswig-Holstein, Western Germany, and Denmark,

'Pensions for the German M/S Personnel', 23 Aug. 1945.

15. PRO, ADM 228/62, Letter from Fregattenkapitän Philipp Deutscher to Konteradmiral Fritz Krauss, 30 Oct. 1945.

16. PRO, ADM 228/85, Memorandum by Konteradmiral Fritz Krauss to Admiral Harold Burrough, 29 Sept. 1945.

17. PRO, ADM 228/90, Memorandum from Konteradmiral Günther Schubert to Flag Officer Schleswig-Holstein, 'Re-employment of Engine Personnel', 19 Dec. 1945.

18. PRO, ADM 228/92, Memorandum from Captain L.P. Skipwith to Flag Officer Western Germany, 'Desertions from German Minesweeping Administration', 13 Feb. 1946.

19. CCAC, William Harold Ingrams, INGS 1/8, Control Council Order No. 1, 'Prohibiting the Wearing of Uniform by Former Members of the German Armed Forces', 30 Aug. 1945.

20. PRO, ADM 228/59, Military Government, Germany, British Zone, Ordinance No. 13, 'Military Uniform and Insignia', 7 Sept. 1945.

21. PRO, ADM 228/59, Message from Flag Officer Schleswig-Holstein to British Naval Commander-in-Chief Germany, 26 1645A Sept. 1945.

22. PRO, ADM 228/59, CCG(BE) HQ, Legal Division, 'Minutes of a Conference Held on 28 Sept. 1945 at 1130 hours', 28 Sept. 1945.

23. PRO, ADM 228/59, Message from British Naval Commander-in-Chief Germany to All Flag Officers and Naval Officers-in-Charge, 08 0941A Oct. 1945.

24. Pelly and Yasamee, Vol. 5, Microfiche 56iii, CORC/M(45)8, Coordinating Committee, 'Minutes of 8th Meeting held in Berlin on 17 Sept. 1945 at 1500 hours'.

25. PRO, ADM 116/5609, Message from TROOPERS to British Naval Commander-in-Chief Germany, 27 1745Z Oct. 1945.

26. Pelly and Yasamee, Vol. 5, p.328. PRO, ADM 228/74, Message from Deputy Head of Naval Division to British Naval Commander-in-Chief Germany, 08 2035 Nov. 1945.

27. PRO, ADM 228/59, Memorandum from Field Marshal Bernard Montgomery to British Naval Commander-in-Chief Germany, 'Law on Elimination and Prohibition of Military Training in Germany', 10 Nov. 1945. Burrough had previously told the Admiralty: 'If this law were issued without some safeguard it is obvious that the maintenance of discipline in the German warships including minesweepers under my control would become impossible', PRO, ADM 116/5609, Message from British Naval Commander-in-Chief Germany to Admiralty, 27 1832A Oct. 1945.

28. PRO, ADM 228/59, Allied Control Authority, Control Council Law No. 8, 'Elimination and Prohibition of Military Training', 30 Nov. 1945. LHC, Lieutenant-Commander Leonard George Hart, RN, File 3, 'Three New Control Council Laws', *British Zone Review*, Vol. 1, No. 7 (22 Dec. 1945), p.16.

29. Pelly and Yasamee, Vol. 5, Microfiche 89ii, Message from Lieutenant-General Brian Robertson to Field Marshal Bernard Montgomery, 20 1930A Nov. 1945.

30. Pelly and Yasamee, Vol. 5, Microfiche 89ii, Staff Minute, 20 Nov. 1945.

31. IWM, Montgomery, Reel 11, BLM 127/40, Message from Field Marshal Bernard Montgomery to TROOPERS London, 22 0355A Nov. 1945.

32. IWM, Montgomery, Reel 11, BLM 127/43, Message from Field Marshal Bernard Montgomery to Sir Arthur Street, War Office, 01 0532 Dec. 1945.

33. Pelly and Yasamee, Vol. 5, Microfiche 89iii(a), Allied Control Authority, Coordinating Committee, 'Minutes of the 24th Meeting held at Berlin, 3 Dec. 1945, at 1500 hours', 3 Dec. 1945.

34. PRO, FO 1038/140, Message from Deputy Head of Naval Division to British Naval Commander-in-Chief Germany, 06 1427 Dec. 1945.

35. Pelly and Yasamee, Vol. 5, p.412.

36. PRO, FO 1038/140, Letter from Admiral Harold Burrough to Field Marshal Bernard Montgomery, 6 Dec. 1945.

37. PRO, FO 1038/140, Letter from British Naval Commander-in-Chief Germany to

Vice-Admiral Robert Ghormley, 6 Dec. 1945.

38. PRO, ADM 228/74, Letter from British Naval Commander-in-Chief Germany to Secretary of Admiralty, 'Russian Criticism of German Minesweeping Administration', 6 Dec. 1945.

39. PRO, FO 1038/140, Message from Deputy Head of Naval Division to British Naval Commander-in-Chief Germany, 17 1805A Dec. 1945.

40. PRO, FO 1038/140, Letter from P.N.N. Synnott, Admiralty to British Naval Commander-in-Chief Germany, 12 March 1946.

41. PRO, ADM 228/56, Message from Flag Officer Western Germany to British Naval Commander-in-Chief Germany, 10 1511B Aug. 1945.

42. PRO, ADM 228/21, Letter from Admiral Harold Burrough to Secretary of Admiralty, 'Report on Operation Silver', 13 Feb. 1946.

43. PRO, ADM 228/59, Letter from Konteradmiral Kurt Weyher to Captain E.R. Conder, 22 Oct. 1945.

44. IWM, Parry, Box 10, Letter from Rear-Admiral W.E. Parry to Wife, 9 Nov. 1945.

45. IWM, Burrough, Transcript of Press Conference given by Admiral Harold Burrough, British Naval Commander-in-Chief Germany, 14 March 1946.

46. PRO, ADM 228/21, Message from Deputy Head of Naval Division to British Naval Commander-in-Chief Germany, 22 1445 Aug. 1945.

47. PRO, ADM 228/21, Message from Vice-Admiral Geoffrey Miles to Admiralty, 15 1257C Sept. 1945.

48. PRO, ADM 228/21, Memorandum from Commodore R.M.J. Hutton for British Naval Commander-in-Chief Germany to Flag Officer Western Germany, 'Transfer of German Warships to Russian Government', 5 Sept. 1945.

49. NAC, RG 24, Vol. 10,978, File 260C8.009(D11), 31st AA Brigade, 'Operation Caesar', 30 Nov. 1945.

50. DHist, Report No. 174, Historical Section, Canadian Military Headquarters, 'The Canadian Army Occupation Force in Germany, May 1945 to June 1946', p. 19. UVic, Oral History Interview with Major Charles Elsworth Goodman, 16 Jan. 1980, Reel 2 Side 1.

51. DHist, File 581.009(D103), 31st Anti-Aircraft Brigade, 'Guard Battery – Muhlenweg Bks – Operation – Caesar's Wife', 27 Nov. 1945.

52. PRO, ADM 228/22, Message from Admiralty to Vice-Admiral Geoffrey Miles, 22 1243A Aug. 1945. The Soviets, Americans, and British disagreed over mine clearance on the River Danube.

53. PRO, ADM 228/21, Message from British Naval Commander-in-Chief Germany to Admiralty, 21 1714A Sept. 1945. PRO, ADM 228/22, Message from British Naval Commander-in-Chief Germany to Deputy Head of Naval Division/Miles, 07 1010A Oct. 1945.

54. PRO, ADM 1/5513, Message from Vice-Admiral Geoffrey Miles to Admiralty, 09 1530B Oct. 1945.

55. PRO, ADM 228/21, 'Conclusions reached at a Meeting held at 1115 on 11th October to discuss Problems relating to the Division of the German Navy', 11 Oct. 1945.

56. PRO, ADM 228/21, Memorandum from Flag Officer Schleswig-Holstein to British Naval Commander-in-Chief Germany, 5 Oct. 1945.

57. PRO, ADM 228/21, Memorandum from Rear-Admiral Harold Baillie-Grohman to British Naval Commander-in-Chief Germany, 18 Sept. 1945.

58. PRO, ADM 228/22, Message from Flag Officer Schleswig-Holstein to British Naval Commander-in-Chief Germany, 22 1641 Oct. 1945.

59. PRO, ADM 1/5513, Message from British Naval Commander-in-Chief Germany to Flag Officer Schleswig-Holstein, 11 1802A Oct. 1945. PRO, ADM 228/21, Letter from Admiral Gordei Levchenko to Admiral Harold Burrough and Vice-Admiral Geoffrey Miles, 10 Dec. 1945.

60. PRO, ADM 228/22, Memorandum from Flag Officer Schleswig-Holstein to Naval Officers-in-Charge Kiel, Lübeck, 'Transfer of M/S to Russians', 15 Oct. 1945. The

two operations proceeded under the cloak of the operational transfer of minesweepers to the Soviets for use in the Baltic. PRO, ADM 1/5513, Message from British Naval Commander-in-Chief Germany to Vice-Admiral Geoffrey Miles, 26 1526 Oct. 1945.

61. PRO, ADM 228/22, Memorandum from Rear-Admiral Harold Baillie-Grohman to Commander F.M. Beasley, 23 Oct. 1945.

62. PRO, ADM 228/22, Memorandum from Vice-Admiral Geoffrey Miles to British Naval Commander-in-Chief Germany, 'Transfer of Russian Share of German Minesweepers to USSR', 19 Oct. 1945. The British argued that an officer of such high rank should not have been sent. PRO, ADM 223/256, Memorandum from Sub-Lieutenant (Sp) Chaplin, RNVR, Staff Officer (Intelligence), Naval Officer-in-Charge Lübeck to Director of Naval Intelligence, 'Operation Scram', 9 Jan. 1946.

63. PRO, ADM 228/42, Rear-Admiral Harold Baillie-Grohman to British Naval Commander-in-Chief Germany, 'Transfer of German M/S to Russians – Report on First Convoy', 11 Nov. 1945.

64. PRO, ADM 228/42, Flag Officer Schleswig-Holstein to British Naval Commander-in-Chief Germany, 'Report on Scram Convoy No. 22', 25 Feb. 1946. Levchenko had been anxious to hasten the transfer of small craft before weather deteriorated in the Baltic. PRO, ADM 228/21, Message from Flag Officer Schleswig-Holstein to British Naval Commander-in-Chief Germany, 30 1608A Oct. 1945.

65. PRO, ADM 228/42, Lieutenant P.S Parmenter, RNR, Senior British Naval Officer *Tanga* to Chief of Staff, Flag Officer Schleswig-Holstein, 'Report on Scram Convoy No. 13', 20 Dec. 1945.

66. PRO, ADM 228/42, Lieutenant-Commander D.A. Grant to Flag Officer Schleswig-Holstein, 'Report on Scram Convoy No. 17', 7 Jan. 1946. Canadian soldiers also learned about the Soviet propensity for alcohol. UVic, Oral History Interview with Lieutenant-Colonel Lawrence S. Henderson, 14 Jan. 1982.

67. PRO, ADM 228/38, Letter from Vice-Admiral Geoffrey Miles to British Naval Commander-in-Chief Germany, 12 Nov. 1945. Levchenko 'was careful to explain that these were more in the matter of reporting facts for necessary action than complaints.' PRO, ADM 228/21, Message from British Naval Commander-in-Chief Germany to Admiralty, 12 1008A Nov. 1945.

68. PRO, ADM 228/21, Message from Admiralty to Vice-Admiral Geoffrey Miles, 17 2250 Oct. 1945.

69. PRO, ADM 1/5513, Message from Admiralty to Captain Submarines Lisahally, 15 2305 Nov. 1945.

70. PRO, ADM 228/21, Letter from Admiral Gordei Levchenko to Vice-Admiral Geoffrey Miles, 23 Nov. 1945. PRO, ADM 1/19112, Letter from A.V. Alexander to Ernest Bevin, 22 Nov. 1945.

71. PRO, ADM 228/38, Message from Flag Officer Submarines to Admiralty, 19 10512 Nov. 1945.

72. PRO, ADM 1/5513, Message from Admiralty to Commanders-in-Chief Home Fleet, Nore, Portsmouth, Plymouth, Rosyth, 14 1135 Nov. 1945.

73. PRO, ADM 1/18537, Memorandum from Commander-in-Chief Rosyth to Secretary of Admiralty, 'Operation Deadlight', 14 Nov. 1945. See also ADM 1/18994.

74. PRO, ADM 1/5513, Message from Admiralty to British Admiralty Delegation Washington, 23 0306 Nov. 1945.

75. PRO, ADM 1/18568, Headquarters No. 18 Group Operation Order No. 8/45, 'Operation Deadlight', 26 Nov. 1945.

76. IWM, Blaxell, *Memoirs*, p.176.

77. *House of Commons Debates*, Series 5, Vol. 416, 21 Nov. 1945, Column 541.

78. PRO, ADM 1/18689, C.H.M. Waldock, 'Meeting of Editors with First Lord in Admiralty House, 3 p.m. Monday 19 November', 19 Nov. 1945. Newspapers reported earlier leaks. 'Disposal of U-Boats', *Manchester Guardian* (10 Oct. 1945), p.5.

79. PRO, ADM 1/5513, Message from Admiralty to Commander-in-Chief Rosyth, 29 2034 Nov. 1945.

80. PRO, ADM 1/18689, Telegram No. 154, Foreign Office to Moscow, 14 Jan. 1946.

81. PRO, ADM 228/21, Memorandum from British Naval Commander-in-Chief Germany to Flag Officer Schleswig-Holstein and Flag Officer Western Germany, 'Outline Plan for Transfer of the German Warships at Wilhelmshaven to the Receiving Powers', 16 Nov. 1945.

82. PRO, ADM 1/5513, Message from British Naval Commander-in-Chief Germany to Assistant Chief of Naval Staff (Home), 12 1008 Nov. 1945.

83. PRO, ADM 228/21, Letter from British Naval Commander-in-Chief Germany to Vice-Admiral Robert Ghormley, 15 Nov. 1945.

84. PRO, ADM 228/21, Memorandum from British Naval Commander-in-Chief Germany to Flag Officer Western Germany, 'Revised Outline Plan for the Transfer of the German Warships at Wilhelmshaven to the Receiving Powers', 4 Dec. 1945.

85. PRO, ADM 1/19112, Letter from A.V. Alexander to Sir Alexander Cadogan, Foreign Office, 12 Dec. 1945.

86. DHist, File 581.009(D16), Rear-Admiral F.E.P. Hutton, Flag Officer Western Germany, 'Operation Silver', 8 Dec. 1945.

87. PRO, ADM 202/428, Report from Major I.M. MacLean, RM, to Colonel Fuller, 'Naval Party 1780 – Operation Silver', 29 April 1946.

88. PRO, ADM 228/21, Message from British Naval Commander-in-Chief Germany to Commander United States Naval Forces Germany, 09 1547A Dec. 1945. Helmut Raumann, 'Life as "Employed Enemy Personnel"', *Naval History* 3(1989), p.28. After inspections, the Americans used *Prinz Eugen* as a target ship during Operation 'Crossroads', the atomic bomb tests at Bikini Atoll in the Pacific Ocean. Erwin F. Sieche, 'The German Heavy Cruiser *Prinz Eugen*: A Career under Two Flags Part II', *Warship International* 27(1990), pp.283–7. Jonathan M. Weisgall, *Operation Crossroads: the Atomic Tests at Bikini Atoll*, (Annapolis: Naval Institute Press, 1994).

89. PRO, ADM 228/21, Report from Flag Officer Western Germany to British Naval Commander-in-Chief Germany, 'Operation Silver', 22 Jan. 1946. IWM, Hawkins, Commander R.P.C. Hawkins, 'Operation Silver', 16 Dec. 1945.

90. IWM, 84/54/, Sub-Lieutenant Lancelot Stephen Harris, RNVR, Box 1, File 'Silver', Rear-Admiral F.E.P. Hutton, 'Operation Silver: Orders for Tuesday 18 December 1945', 17 Dec. 1945. Erwin Schubert, 'Die letzten Fahrten des U-Boot-Begleitschiffes "Otto Wünsche"', *Marine Rundschau* 81(1984), p.77.

91. PRO, ADM 228/63, Rear-Admiral F.E.P. Hutton to British Naval Commander-in-Chief Germany, 'An Order of the Day from the British Naval-Officer-in-Charge, Wilhelmshaven', 28 Dec. 1945.

92. PRO, ADM 1/5513, Message from Flag Officer Western Germany to British Naval Commander-in-Chief Germany, 18 1511 Dec. 1945.

93. BL, Cunningham, Add. Ms. 525272, Letter from Admiral Harold Burrough to Admiral Andrew Cunningham, 18 Dec. 1945.

94. PRO, ADM 228/21, Kapitän zur See Helmuth Giessler, 'Report on the Transfer of Cruiser *Nürnberg* to Libau', 14 Jan. 1946.

95. PRO, ADM 228/14, 'Minutes of 5th Meeting Combined US/British Ship Repair Committee held at Bremen on 8 November 1945', 13 Nov. 1945.

96. PRO, ADM 1/5513, British Naval Commander-in-Chief Germany to Flag Officer Schleswig-Holstein, Flag Officer Western Germany, 18 1518 Dec. 1945. IWM, PP/MCR/306, Lieutenant-Commander H.D. Marquis, RNR, Memoirs, pp.181–2.

97. PRO, FO 1038/144, Office of British Naval Commander-in-Chief Germany, 'Naval Division Progress Report for the Period 1 January–31 January, 1946'.

98. PRO, ADM 223/256, Message from Flag Officer Western Germany to British Naval Commander-in-Chief Germany, 06 1441A Feb. 1946. IWM, Hawkins, Letter from Commander R.P.C. Hawkins to Parents, 31 Jan. 1946.

99. PRO, ADM 228/19, Message from Deputy Head of Naval Division to Vice-Admiral

F.S. Sidelnikov, 16 1902 Feb. 1946.

100. PRO, ADM 228/19, Rear-Admiral W.E. Parry to Secretary of Admiralty, 'Report of the Meeting of the Tripartite Naval Commission, held on 16 February 1946, to the Governments of the USSR, UK, and USA', 22 Feb. 1946.

101. PRO, ADM 228/40, 'Record of a Meeting between Admiral Burrough and Admiral Sidelnikov at Admiralty House, Berlin, Tuesday 19 Feb. 1946'.

102. IWM, Burrough, 'Record of a Meeting between Admiral Burrough and Marshal Zhukov at Babelsberg (Potsdam) on Thursday, 21 Feb. 1946'.

103. PRO, ADM 228/19, Message from British Naval Commander-in-Chief Germany to Admiralty, 22 1600A Feb. 1946. In a private letter to the First Sea Lord about the meeting with Zhukov, Burrough wrote: 'It's difficult to gauge the reactions of a crocodile whether you tickle it under the chin or stick pins into it, but I came away with the feeling that I had made a hole in some very thick ice!', BL, Cunningham, Add. Ms. 52573, Letter from Admiral Harold Burrough to Admiral Andrew Cunningham, 25 Feb. 1946.

104. PRO, ADM 228/19, Message from Deputy Head of Naval Division to Admiralty, 23 1227A Feb. 1946.

105. PRO, ADM 228/19, Message from British Naval Commander-in-Chief Germany to Flag Officers Schleswig-Holstein, Western Germany, 13 1823 March 1946.

106. PRO, ADM 116/5565, 'First Supplement to the Report of the Tripartite Naval Commission concerning the Allocation of the German Surface Navy and the German Submarine Fleet', 23 March 1946.

107. PRO, ADM 228/22, Memorandum from Vice-Admiral Commanding British Naval Forces Germany to Naval Officers in Charge, 10 April 1946.

108. PRO, ADM 228/19, Memorandum from Captain P.L. Saumarez to Secretary of Admiralty, 'Ratification of First and Second Supplements to the Report of Tripartite Naval Commission of 6 December 1945', 22 Dec. 1946. Representatives on the Tripartite Naval Commission signed a 4th supplement on 20 April 1948. PRO, ADM 116/5565, Flag Officer British Naval Forces Germany to Secretary of Admiralty, 'Fourth Supplement to the Report of the Tripartite Naval Commission concerning the Allocation of the German Surface Navy and the German Submarine Fleet', 25 May 1948.

109. BL, Cunningham, Add. Ms. 52573, Letter from Admiral Harold Burrough to Admiral Andrew Cunningham, 25 Feb. 1946. Burrough was still technically subordinate to Robertson. PRO, ADM 228/75, Staff Minute by NA(P), 'Reorganisation of Naval Division', 12 Jan. 1946.

110. IWM, Burrough, Transcript of Discussions at Tripartite Meeting, Control Commission in Berlin, 11 Feb. 1946.

111. PRO, ADM 228/74, Telegram from Commodore GM/SA to All Commands, 29 Dec. 1945.

112. IWM, Parry, Box 10, Letter from Rear-Admiral W.E. Parry to Wife, 2 Nov. 1945. BL, Cunningham, Add. Ms. 52578, Diary, 24 Sept. 1945.

113. PRO, ADM 228/90, Letter from Captain A.C. Behagne for British Naval Commander-in-Chief Germany to Flag Officer Schleswig-Holstein, 21 Jan. 1946.

114. PRO, ADM 228/92, Letter from Rear-Admiral Harold Baillie-Grohman to Commodore Hugh England, 'Desertions from the German M/S Service', 4 Feb. 1946.

115. PRO, ADM 228/83, Memorandum by Area Security Officer Schleswig-Holstein to Senior Naval Officer Schleswig-Holstein, 'Interrogation of Dr. Rudolphi, Schlegelberger and Reich', 8 June 1946.

116. PRO, ADM 228/74, Letter from Admiral Harold Burrough to Commodore Hugh England, 5 Feb. 1946.

117. PRO, ADM 228/56, 'German Minesweeping Matters: Minutes of a Conference held at Navy House Hamburg on Monday, 25 February 1946'.

118. PRO, ADM 228/82, Memorandum from Commodore R.M.J. Hutton for British

Naval Commander-in-Chief Germany to Legal Division Main HQ, CCG(BE), 'Discipline of MDG and GM/SA', 5 March 1946.

119. PRO, ADM 228/74, Letter from Admiralty to British Naval Commander-in-Chief Germany, 12 March 1946.

120. PRO, ADM 228/68, Memorandum from Vice-Admiral H.T.C. Walker, Vice-Admiral Commanding British Naval Forces Germany to All Commands, 'Reorganisation of German Naval Frozen Personnel', 4 April 1946.

121. PRO, ADM 228/59, British Naval Commander-in-Chief Germany, 'Orders for Wearing of Working Dress by German Minesweeping Administration and *Marine Dienstgruppen* Personnel', 21 March 1946.

122. IWM, 76/43/1, Rear-Admiral Hugh Turnour England, RN, 'Instructions to the German Minesweeping Administration', 15 May 1946.

123. PRO, ADM 228/65, Letter from Captain M.J. Evans, Naval Division HQ, CCG(BE) to Chief, Legal Division, 18 July 1946.

124. PRO, ADM 1/19016, Letter from Secretary of Admiralty to British Naval Commander-in-Chief Germany, 3 Oct. 1945.

125. CCAC, HYND 3/8, 'New British Naval C-in-C for Germany', *British Zone Review*, Vol. 1, No. 14 (30 March 1946), p.9. Walker was affectionately known within the Royal Navy as 'Hooky Walker' because he had lost a hand during the raid at Zeebrugge in 1918. IWM, 85/44/1, Captain F.S.W. de Winton, RN, Memoirs, 'Ships in Bottles', p.80. The two flag commands in Schleswig-Holstein and Western Germany terminated on 1 April 1946. IWM, Baillie-Grohman, 'Flashlights on the Final Elimination of German Sea Power, 1945–46', Vol. 3, p.111. IWM, Savage, 'The Admiral Sums Up Naval Party 1734: A Unique and Interesting Year', *The HMS Royal Alfred Record*, Vol. 4, No. 8 (1 April 1946), p.1.

126. IWM, Burrough, Transcript of Press Conference given by Admiral Harold Burrough on relinquishing his post as British Naval Commander-in-Chief Germany, 15 March 1946.

7

Scientists, Archives and Admirals

As part of the agenda for complete German naval disarmament, the Royal Navy adopted tough policies towards senior *Kriegsmarine* officers. The experience with Germany after World War I had demonstrated the ability of even a small nucleus to maintain a naval tradition and quickly rebuild a modern navy. The British foresaw no future for the German naval officer corps. Although a few individuals with specific skills found temporary employment in intelligence, scientific, minesweeping, and administrative work, most senior naval officers languished in prisoner of war camps until final British decisions about denazification and release. The Royal Navy's efforts undermined the institutional and morale basis of the German naval leadership.

The Admiralty, in conjunction with the US Naval Technical Mission in Europe, sent interrogation teams to Germany to collect technical and operational intelligence from senior German naval officers. Much of the work, such as an American request for details on naval operations during the Normandy invasion, was for historical purposes.[1] Information from the German side provided a fuller understanding to particular campaigns. Captain Gilbert Roberts, RN, a staff officer from Western Approaches, interviewed several leading submarine officers, including Godt and Fregattenkapitän Günter Hessler, about operations and tactics.[2] Recent advances in hull designs and propulsion interested the Royal Navy. According to German submariners, new U-boat types relied on high underwater speeds to approach convoys undetected and evade escorts.[3] British naval authorities, at the Admiralty's direction, used officers to locate such submarines. After a tour of investigation, Godt confirmed that two Type XVIIB U-boats were scuttled at Cuxhaven shortly after the surrender.[4] On an individual basis, some German naval officers provided valuable assistance to British naval authorities.

The Royal Navy's interrogations and investigations extended to specialized fields. Many senior naval officers and officials had been involved in wartime research and development, training, and related decision-making. Captain C.E. Horton, RN, the head of an Admiralty team which investigated the *Kriegsmarine*'s progress in radar, communications, and radio direction-finding under Konteradmiral Wilhelm Rhein, concluded that the Allies were definitely ahead, but the Germans were 'rapidly gaining momentum.'[5] Despite considerable support in terms of money and research facilities, German radar development had adopted too narrow a field of vision. Unlike the Royal Navy, the *Kriegsmarine* failed to appreciate the importance of centimetric wavelengths.[6] Consequently German radar sets still used relatively large aerials. The scientific controller at the *Bevollmächtigter für Hochfrequenzforschung* told British interrogators that 'technical policy had been dictated by either the manufacturers or the general staff, usually incorrectly.'[7] Poor policy decisions rather than research competence impeded work. The research infrastructure for naval work was actually well developed.

British naval authorities quickly secured key scientists, laboratories, and equipment within Germany. Under the Royal Navy's direction, civilian and naval specialists performed experiments with underwater explosions at the Dänisch Nienhoff research establishment near Kiel.[8] This temporary employment was justified by the need to study the effectiveness of minesweeping. British and American officers conducted surveys of minesweeping establishments and ships to examine German techniques and sweeping gear.[9] Existing equipment varied in quality and sophistication because small machine shops constructed most sweeps. The Germans, however, proficiently handled all types of acoustic, magnetic, and pressure mines.[10] Research had even been done in specialized fields. A scientist named Dr Gützmacher conducted extensive tests in underwater acoustics to study the relationship between speed and noise in triggering mines.[11] These findings confirmed or added to Allied research. British officers travelled throughout the zone to interview scientists and engineers.[12] Where appropriate, the Royal Navy removed selected persons to the United Kingdom for further interrogation or funded additional research. A German Hydrographic Institute was established in Hamburg, under Quadripartite control, 'to produce navigational aids and ... to suck the brains of the German scientists so that valuable information is not lost to the world.'[13] Exploitation of German scientists served British naval needs.

The Royal Navy took a special interest in Helmuth Walter, the creator of the so-called Walter closed-cycle propulsion system. Walter, a capable scientist with practical organizing skills and political connections, enjoyed 'the respect and support of the officers at the highest level of the German Navy.'[14] His work with Ingolene – concentrated hydrogen-peroxide – offered to revolutionize submarine warfare. German scientists had recognized the need for a fuel to provide increased speeds over those available from existing electric batteries. Experiments with compressed and liquid oxygen encountered serious problems with endurance, storage, and safety.[15] Instead, Walter refined hydrogen-peroxide until relatively high concentration levels were attained. Amassing a large production and research establishment with over 4,500 employees, he designed and built jet engines, torpedoes, and submarines which used Ingolene for motive power.[16] British naval intelligence investigated these developments quite closely. A 30th Assault Unit detachment, commanded by Commander Dunstan Curtis, RNVR, and SAS troops captured Walter's main research establishments in Kiel virtually intact.

For the next seven months, a combined British–American intelligence team, directed by Commander (E) I.C. Aylen, RN, and Captain A.L. Mumma, USN, investigated and controlled the *Walterwerke* and its workers. Walter initially proved less than cooperative, but became more open after a staff officer from Glücksburg instructed 'him that nothing whatsoever was to be withheld.'[17] The German naval high command's intervention worked to British advantage. Interrogators profitably interviewed research department heads, who handed over previously missing blueprints and design schematics. Although the original submarine prototypes were destroyed before the British arrived, technicians reassembled a working Ingolene engine from spare parts. Walter personally demonstrated its operation during the First Sea Lord's visit to Germany in July 1945.[18] The Royal Navy saw potential operational value in Walter's work. At last, submarines could travel underwater at high speeds for extended periods of time. Hydrogen-peroxide furnished a good energy return, and of course, required no external source of oxygen.

Despite significant technical problems, the Admiralty decided to pursue further research with Walter's team. Hydrogen-peroxide, which was extremely unstable and corrosive in high concentrations, reacted violently with dirt and most metals.[19] As the Germans had discovered in early trials, the resulting explosion usually meant loss of ship and crew. This obstacle needed to be overcome before full operational use. The Royal Navy brought Walter, several of his technicians, and a good deal of research plant from Germany to Great Britain. In cooperation with the British company Vickers-Armstrong, Walter worked under contract at Barrow in the research and production of hydrogen-peroxide turbines for the Royal Navy.[20] The Royal Navy hoped to gain a lead in alternative submarine technology and effective counter-measures. Since a German navy no longer existed, Walter's unique abilities would have otherwise been wasted or exploited by another naval power.[21] The former

Kriegsmarine scientist now worked under British auspices in British research establishments.

Although Walter's hydrogen-peroxide propulsion ultimately proved a technological dead-end, the Royal Navy exploited other German research and development. It examined, with considerable interest, designs for hydrofoil motor torpedo boats, assault helicopters, new midget submarines, semi-submersible craft, submarine-fired rockets, and mechanical computers for anti-aircraft guns.[22] Most projects were still at the drawing board stage, but available prototypes were sent to Great Britain. Post-war British submarines incorporated many design improvements, such as the schnorkel, hull streamlining, propellers, escape apparatus, and higher capacity electric batteries. Moreover, German progress in passive sonar and long-range hydrophones increased the Royal Navy's ability to detect submarines.[23] Better countermeasures were important because other navies also acquired German knowledge.

Like the Royal Navy, the Red Navy removed scientists, technicians, and research plant from Germany to the Soviet Union. Submarines received special attention.[24] Levchenko's earlier silence on the Tripartite Naval Commission towards U-boats was probably due to the fact that the Soviets possessed design schematics and a full-scale model for the Type XXVI, Walter's planned Atlantic submarine. It was believed that the Red Navy constructed a hydrogen-peroxide closed-cycle engine with German technical assistance at the Gorski shipyard, the Soviet Union's main submarine production centre.[25] The Soviets conducted further research with captured acoustic torpedoes, missile systems, and conventional diesel-electric submarines. The Soviet W-class, built in considerable numbers at the Sudomekh shipyard in the immediate post-war period, closely resembled the Type XXI in design.[26] The Royal Navy became even more determined to exploit German scientific and technical expertise after realizing that the Red Navy was doing the same in a big way.

The Royal Navy gained an enormous advantage with the capture of almost all the *Kriegsmarine*'s official records. At the end of April 1945 a 30th Assault Unit detachment seized the German naval archives at Tambach castle, near Coburg.[27] The find included older historical files, technical reports, operational accounts, and war diaries. Historians and archivists at Tambach had decided to use wood and gasoline set aside for destruction of the archives to keep themselves warm through the winter.[28] The Royal Navy's sudden appearance solved the difficult professional dilemma of whether the archivists, not very keen on the idea in the first place, should destroy the records by some alternative means.

The Royal Navy recognized the significance of the papers. After inspecting Tambach, Commander Fleming recommended sending all post-1933 records, along with Korvettenkapitän Dr. Peter Freiherr Handel-Mazetti, the chief archivist, to the Admiralty.[29] The Tambach papers were centralized in London with naval files found in other scattered locations within the American and British Zones. Through prior arrangements, all records were 'the joint property of the British and U.S. Navies in the custody and under the direction of the Director of Naval Intelligence.'[30] The Admiralty instituted an ambitious classification, examination, and translation project, based upon its existing captured documents filing system.

Given the vast quantity of records, the identification and selection of pertinent documents posed a major challenge. WRNS personnel from the Special Duties (Y) Section prepared brief summaries for circulation to various Admiralty departments, and then made written or oral translations of documents considered to be of further interest.[31] Technical and scientific topics generally received highest priority. For example, some documents provided valuable insights into German torpedo development.[32] The papers proved especially useful in interrogating naval officers and scientists. The written records provided background information, refreshed failing memories on particular details, and checked the accuracy of oral statements.

Other records dealt with naval policy, both before and during the war. Since military occupation aimed at the elimination of German naval power, John Mossop, a lawyer in the Admiralty's Military Branch, considered the material 'worth study with an eye to the future.'[33] Translated documents exposed German evasions of the Treaty of Versailles and secret naval rearmament under the Nazis. The Tambach archives furnished the major evidential source in the later prosecution of major and minor war criminals.[34] These written documents disclosed the extent to which German leaders actively planned and waged wars of aggression.

Capture of the naval archives presented a unique opportunity. The victor navies were in absolute possession of most surviving records from the *Kriegsmarine* and its predecessors. At the direction of Captain Dudley Knox, USN, in Washington, special teams at COMNAVEU's headquarters in Grosvenor Square began a large-scale registration and microfilm programme to obtain 'a reasonably complete set of archives (microfilm form) for general historical reference in the future.'[35] The Royal Navy and US Navy intended to use German sources in writing official and staff histories. In just under two years, the American teams produced 3,905 microfilm reels from records selected by Captain Roland Krause, USN.[36] The Admiralty, which retained the original documents in London, imposed strict restrictions on access. During the trial of major war criminals at Nuremberg, the Director of Naval Intelligence opposed defence requests to inspect documents and war diaries in order 'to prevent the Germans from exploiting the contents of the records with a view to resurrecting their capacity for a future war.'[37] Although eventually forced to provide limited access, the Royal Navy claimed proprietorial rights to the German naval archives. Unlike the inter-war period, German naval authorities could not make use of historical writing and records to preserve a naval tradition and rebuild German sea power.[38] The official written memory of the German navy was firmly under British control.

Supplemental to the archival records, the Admiralty selected senior naval officers to write essays dealing with various political, operational, and specialized topics from the war. The rationale served more than just historical purposes. Burrough suggested sending to Great Britain officers, 'who are considered to be of outstanding importance and who, if left in Germany, might use their great knowledge to the detriment of the United Nations.'[39] Officers busily employed in writing could not become potential impediments to naval disarmament. Lieutenant-Commander Ralph W.B Izzard, RNVR, and the Royal Navy's Forward Interrogation Unit cultivated a high level of confidence with many senior naval officers.[40]

The voluntary essays were a natural extension of this interrogation work. Some naval officers, such as Vizeadmiral Eberhard Weicholdt, chief of the naval instructional staff and former commander-in-chief in the Mediterranean, attempted to explain the *Kriegsmarine*'s defeat.[41] In Weicholdt's opinion, Germany lost the war because of overconfidence in its own military strengths, underestimation of Allied sea power, and poor coordination between the service branches. Heye reached similar conclusions, but 'had he shown himself to be more pro-Nazi and less critical of Admiral Dönitz, with whom he was not popular, he would have risen to great heights.'[42] The writing was an opportunity to settle old scores and set the historical record straight. Godt only wrote on the condition that his essay should not be used against German naval leaders in upcoming war crimes trials.[43] A clear agenda came across in some work. Hessler's account of the submarine war retreated into the campaign's technical side without considering seriously the moral and legal implications behind this type of warfare.[44] And, differences in opinion inevitably arose. In contrast to Ruge's disdain for the Red Navy's performance during the war, Kapitän zur See Otto von Baumbach, a former naval attaché in Moscow, emphasized the Soviet Union's enormous naval potential and its ability to 'achieve surprise by doing the seemingly impossible.'[45] The words presaged the Red Navy's remarkable growth in the following decades.

Providing a forum for personal soul-searching, the writing gave German naval officers a sense of worth, and distracted them from thoughts about an uncertain future. Into the bargain, the Admiralty gained helpful operational, intelligence, and historical material. In 1949 several individuals, including Ruge, Heye, Wagner, and Godt, found renewed employment in a naval historical team at Bremerhaven under the US Navy's auspices.[46] Nonetheless, the Royal Navy always viewed the essay writing as a temporary assignment rather than a prolonged task. When no longer considered productive, senior naval officers quickly outlived their usefulness and were handed over to the British army.

Continued employment in various administrative positions within the British Zone was comparable. According to Kapitänleutnant Carl-Friedrich Mohr, many officers withdrew into technical and occupational specialties after the twin shocks of defeat and the Potsdam Conference.[47] Hard work, even under military occupation, represented an important means of coping. Royal Navy authorities profited from the eagerness of certain officers to remain in positions of authority. Under British direction, Kapitän zur See Erwin Liebhard supervised the naval arsenal in Kiel.[48] Various departments handled stores, supplies, equipment, and finances. The *Kriegsmarine* held approximately 1.4 million Reichsmarks worth of credits with industrial firms in the form of loans and contracts through the naval arsenal.[49] These assets required liquidation or application towards current transactions.

Continued employment of German officers, however, occasioned criticism. Burrough expressed surprise 'at the number of Kapitäns-zur-See and higher German officers who according to the replies made to my signals ... are still employed or shown as Frozen Personnel.'[50] Reductions were obviously needed, particularly in Schleswig-Holstein. When questioned on the need for so many retained officers, Baillie-Grohman responded:

> The majority are either specialists in charge of Arsenals without a second in command or are so closely connected with war materials and provision of spare parts and equipment, or key administrative posts, as to be essential unless great delay in the provision of gear can be accepted.[51]

For the time being, he considered the services of such officers indispensable. In addition to Schubert in the GM/SA, flag officers under Vizeadmiral Karl Topp prepared, at the Admiralty's direction, surveys of planned and actual warship construction.[52] Baillie-Grohman suggested re-employing these officers in a civilian capacity. Burrough, however, castigated the 'ostrich-like' attitude of the Flag Officer Schleswig-

Holstein, who 'seems to think that as long as a German Admiral is not frozen by him it doesn't matter, but as far as the Russians are concerned, they aren't in the least interested whom he is frozen by.'[53] The number of retained German flag officers in the British Zone certainly appeared excessive. While Burrough requested permission from the Director of Naval Intelligence to dispense with Topp's party, Baillie-Grohman was to take 'no action pending decisions [by] Chiefs of Staff Committee which is now considering treatment of officers of this calibre.'[54] Senior officers surplus to immediate requirements were handed over to military authorities for disbandment or detention.

As a matter of policy, the British took most admirals and selected junior naval officers into custody. Following Friedeburg's example, some senior officers decided to commit suicide rather than enter captivity. British naval authorities found Schräder dead in his office at Bergen on 19 July 1945.[55] The majority, however, accepted their fate. Förste returned home on parole for a short period before reporting to British army authorities.[56] An indefinite period of imprisonment awaited most senior officers. Guidelines, outlined by Burrough in August 1945, specified detention of flag officers, accused war criminals, persons in automatic arrest categories, and individuals likely to arouse 'suspicion of their participation in activities directed against the Allied Control, or towards keeping alive the German Navy.'[57] This list included members and former members of the Nazi Party. The Royal Navy arrested Konteradmiral Wilhelm Matthies and officers in the *Wehrgeistiger Führungsstab*, the 'branch of OKM concerned with the inculcation of Nazi principles in the German Navy.'[58] Even officers of potential intelligence value were not immune. Burrough recommended that Korvettenkapitän Paul von Wahlert, the former naval attaché in Stockholm, be placed in the automatic arrest category as 'a potential long-term danger which should hardly be fostered.'[59]

On the other hand, the Royal Navy released a small number of senior officers, considered useful or harmless to military occupation authorities. German churches petitioned British authorities for early discharge of clergy from the *Kriegsmarine*.[60] These religious men were desperately needed for spiritual rebuilding within communities after the Nazi disaster. British military government also relied on German administrators. The Royal Navy offered no objections to the suggested discharge of Vizeadmiral Bernhard Rogge to serve as a provincial official in Schleswig.[61] Former officers who held strong democratic views actively co-operated with the British. Likewise, Baillie-Grohman sent home Konteradmiral Heinrich von Hennig, an elderly naval librarian in Kiel, because 'it appears to me to be rather lowering to our prestige to trouble to rope this type of person in.'[62] The Royal Navy was not vindictive. On an individual basis, British naval authorities showed a good deal of magnanimity towards some former enemies. Disposal of remaining senior officers awaited Cabinet and Control Council decisions.

The most controversial question was whether the equivalent of a General Staff existed within the *Kriegsmarine*. During the Second World War, no central high command directed the activities of the German armed forces, but instead the different services, under the direction of separate commanders-in-chief, assumed staff functions.[63] The arrangement formally kept the services isolated and independent. The *Kriegsmarine*'s leaders dealt directly with Hitler in his capacity as supreme commander of the armed forces.[64] Nonetheless, the British indicted service commanders-in-chief, their chiefs of staff, chiefs and planners in the OKW, and area or branch commanders-in-chief – approximately 130 officers in all – as belonging to a higher coordinating body. The International Military Tribunal at Nuremberg subsequently ruled that senior German officers lacked the necessary cohesion and common training to be legally defined as a group.[65] They faced individual rather than collective responsibility for specific crimes committed during the Nazi period. The German General Staff was not deemed a criminal organization.

In spite of this legal distinction, the Royal Navy was more interested in the function rather than the form of a German naval staff. The Admiralty had prepared an open list of officers, 'who owing to their having held high staff appointments, or having given distinguished services during the war, are likely to be the planners of a future war.'[66] Based upon background and experience, certain officers posed potential risks to the perpetuation of a German naval staff. Subsequent interrogations verified the appropriateness of internment. Upon transfer, army authorities automatically awarded all flag officers the status of prisoners of war instead of surrendered enemy personnel.[67] The process was completely arbitrary. Individuals above a particular rank or holding certain positions were singled out for imprisonment. In response, the Germans argued that neither special insignia nor designation differentiated a General Staff within the *Kriegsmarine*.[68] No such body existed, at least in name. The *Kriegsmarine*, like most navies, simply identified younger officers of potential promise and competent for higher command.[69] For the Royal Navy, the argument was a moot point. Among the stated aims of British military occupation was suppression and elimination of a General Staff, in whatever form, and the German officer corps.[70] Aside from prohibiting continued naval service, the Royal Navy did not know what to do with senior naval officers. Parry personally believed that they were 'not dyed with same brush as the

German Army; and indeed our evidence is that attempts to "Nazify" the German Navy were very unsuccessful.'[71] Yet, the admirals were a likely group to make plans for a secret General Staff or naval staff. Confinement became a necessary part of German naval disarmament.

Pending a final answer to the debate over the General Staff, German admirals stayed in British captivity. On 8 January 1946 a British Army of the Rhine directive, which superseded all previous orders on the subject, specified that officers above the rank of Konteradmiral and in automatic arrest categories were not to be discharged.[72] The British allowed limited releases on compassionate grounds. Corps districts received authority to free or transfer naval officers whose lives were endangered by detention as prisoners of war, incurables, chronic invalids, mental defectives, and individuals over the age of seventy.[73] Since confinement of such officers strained British resources, release made practical sense. British authorities increased the discharge rate in an operation known as 'Clobber'.[74] Soviet pressure for disbandment of naval personnel within the British area provided an additional incentive.

As yet, no agreement existed with the Soviets over final disposal of high-ranking officers. By British estimates, a total of eighty-six senior naval officers, including seventeen admirals, were in Soviet captivity.[75] Most were either retired or had held appointments in the Soviet Zone at the end of the war. The Soviets had expressed a wish to shoot General Staff officers, or at the very least, intended to hold on to admirals for a long time.[76] In comparison, senior officers expected earlier release from British captivity. After careful consideration, the Board of Admiralty declared 'no objection to treating German Admirals and Generals alike as provision for review ... will allow release of unobnoxious German Naval Officers in due course.'[77] Treatment and length of imprisonment depended upon Allied conclusions in Berlin concerning the training and outlook of admirals in relation to the General Staff. In a letter to Burrough, the Admiralty stressed the 'need for circumspection in dealing with all senior officers to avoid political repercussions in Control Commission, embarrassment to yourself in future discussion of the subject, or impossibility of performance on your part of whatever may be finally agreed by Control Commission.'[78] The sober advice encouraged continued incarceration of German flag officers.

The admirals were held as prisoners of war in camps for high-ranking German officers. After the arrest of Dönitz and his government, Wagner stayed in an American prison camp near Mondorf, Luxemburg, with other leading naval, military, and political figures.[79] The Allies investigated these persons for possible war crimes and complicity with the Nazi regime. In early October 1945 British army authorities converted a former ammunition depot and enlisted men's transit camp, located in a low-lying part of Belgium, into a special camp for senior officers, designated as Camp 2226.[80] A collection of wooden and stone buildings was divided into three separate compounds. Förste served as camp spokesman with Ruge as his assistant. Indeed, the *Kriegsmarine* was strongly represented within Camp 2226. Upon his arrival in late October 1945 Warzecha discovered 'in this camp all the admirals of the OKM who were transferred to Belgium in the middle of July and a great many other admirals, most of whom had been in leading positions and had cooperated with British Authorities without any friction up to the time of their arrest.'[81] Separated from family and friends, the admirals naturally wondered how long imprisonment would last. Conditions at Camp 2226, an installation never intended for long-term occupation, caused further concern.

Low rations, damp quarters, and a cold winter led to considerable hardship. Towards the end of November 1945 British military authorities reduced food inside Camp 2226 because of general shortages throughout Europe.[82] Senior officers, however, still received higher rations than the general civilian population. The recent historical debate over James Bacque's outrageous claims against Eisenhower misses the fact that conditions in some British camps were just as poor as American camps.[83] Abysmal conditions resulted from the situation and policy decisions rather than the prejudices of certain Allied commanders.

Due to low rations, prisoners of war in Camp 2226 began to lose considerable weight during a harsh time of year. In a letter to the British commandant on 7 December 1945 Förste noted the bad effect that the onset of winter had on the physical and morale state of the prisoners, particularly among older officers.[84] Excessive ground water and poorly constructed dwellings made keeping warm extremely difficult. A growing number of prisoners suffered from cold-related sickness and malnutrition.[85] The conditions proved too much for some officers. Vizeadmiral Heinz Nordmann and Konteradmiral Werner Schönermark died in Camp 2226 around Christmas time.[86] The deaths led to inspections by the Red Cross. As a result, the British built special warming huts and increased rations for officers over the age of fifty. Despite public declarations that all prisoners of war were treated according to the 1929 Geneva Convention, many officers were still undernourished and sick in Camp 2226.

The army's treatment of senior naval officers genuinely shocked the Royal Navy as conditions in Camp 2226 became known. Rumours and reports, spread through letters to family members and acquaintances about the state of affairs in Belgium, circulated within German naval circles. Fearing the impact on British prestige if these stories were true, Baillie-Grohman felt that 'if it is considered necessary to treat Senior

Officers in this way it is suggested that some other nation should take over the administration of the necessary camp.'[87] In his view, the British should absolve themselves completely from such objectionable policies. Indeed, Hutton could not believe 'that senior German Naval Officers should be subjected to the treatment described which savours of what we have so much condemned in German concentration camps.'[88] The situation was potentially embarrassing for the British armed forces, particularly the Royal Navy.

The British Naval Commander-in-Chief Germany's staff made inquiries with appropriate army authorities. Brigadier A.E. Elsworth, the military officer in charge of prisoners of war under British charge on the Continent, admitted to Lewes that some 'deaths might have been accelerated by the bad conditions of the camps', but he could only suggest that the Royal Navy 'should hold on to any officers we did not want subjected to these conditions for as long as practicable, and that he would welcome any reduction in the number being handed over to him.'[89] Most British prisoner of war camps on the Continent were overcrowded and lacked food; Camp 2226 was not the worst. Responding to accounts in newspapers and a question from the Lord Bishop of Chichester in the House of Lords, the Secretary of State for War declared that the British Army of the Rhine had established a court of inquiry in Belgium to investigate reports of irregularities.[90] Although sympathetic, military authorities coped with limited resources. Lack of any firm decision at the political level over disposal of senior officers prolonged the ordeal.

The Royal Navy shortly discovered first hand the extent of conditions inside Camp 2226. Lieutenant Surgeon T.M. Ball, RNVR, the British medical officer at Wilhelmshaven, examined and photographed Kapitän zur See Erich von Dresky, an officer released from Camp 2226 on 4 March suffering from severe malnutrition.[91] Down to a weight of thirty-five kilograms (seventy-seven pounds), Dresky resembled a concentration camp inmate. At this point, Hutton initiated a full investigation in the hope that

> it will result in some definite improvement as I feel that most British Naval Officers from Their Lordships downwards, would be somewhat disgusted at the way German Naval Officers are being treated. Moreover, I worry that 'public opinion' would react rather unfavourably if it became known that the British Army was treating prisoners à la Belsen.[92]

The reaction reflected a mixture of moral indignation and self-interest. The Royal Navy did not want to be sullied with charges that the British were deliberately mistreating prisoners of war. Walker accepted an army invitation to send an officer from his staff to inspect Camp 2226.[93] Commander D.W. Child, RNVR, a former prisoner of war in Poland and Silesia, who had lost a leg from terrible treatment during German captivity, volunteered for the assignment. After a visit on 15 April Child confirmed that conditions inside Camp 2226 were deplorable.[94] A fairer assessment could not be expected. British naval authorities demanded definite improvements from the British Army of the Rhine. In late September German admirals moved from Camp 2226 to Munsterlager, a better camp near Lüneburg in Lower Saxony.[95] The Royal Navy's intervention improved conditions for senior naval officers. The process of sorting the innocuous from the dangerous began.

A major aim of Germany's occupation was to eliminate Nazism and militarism. Drawing upon historical example, Lord Vansittart earlier in the war argued that both trends were deeply rooted in the German character.[96] The German people accepted and glorified war. Although rather simplistic and rife with stereotypes, Vansittart's ideas found fertile ground within British government circles and the armed forces. Cribbing directly from Vansittart, a contributor to the *Naval Review*, the Royal Navy's professional journal, stressed the need to keep Germany 'defeated and incapable of starting another war.'[97] In the interests of European peace and security, British demilitarization activities sought to break the perceived German propensity for aggression. The complementary concept of denazification developed along these lines rather than any apparent wish to punish or exact revenge on the Germans.[98] In contrast to the Americans, the British adopted a pragmatic and moderate stance towards denazification. Although necessarily carried along by the more zealous Americans during the existence of SHAEF, the British made sure that their views were taken into account. Eisenhower's Proclamation No. 1 to the German people declared: 'We [the Allies] shall eradicate that German Militarism which has so often disrupted the peace of the world.'[99] Of course, actual application of denazification within the British Zone, especially towards former senior officers, posed an enormous challenge.

The Royal Navy participated in the formulation of British denazification policy. As high-ranking members of the armed forces, German admirals were included in a target group.[100] They met the selected criteria: agents of German militarism; members of a possible General Staff; potential sources of opposition to military occupation; and likely planners of a future war against Great Britain and other European countries. Captain Martin James Evans, RN, represented the Naval Division on a denazification working party, which met on 11 March 1946.[101] It was agreed that senior officers required screening in conformity with Control Council Law No. 10 and the earlier general resolutions of the Potsdam Conference. A month later, Cly Cardo, a civil servant from the Admiralty, attended a meeting in London to consider the Control Commission's proposals for disposal of war criminals, Nazis, militarists, and potentially dangerous Germans.[102] The key features were quasi-legal tribunals to hear individual denazification applications and limitations on further employment, especially in the civil service. In response to a letter from Warzecha, British authorities declined to give German admirals 'any indication of their future until such time as the denazification policy and measures to be taken against dangerous personnel have been agreed on a quadripartite basis.'[103] Pending final decisions in London and Berlin, the British simply kept senior officers in custody.

Implementation of British denazification policy was somewhat subjective. Not surprisingly, most German officers denied any connections with Nazism during screening and subtle attempts at re-education.[104] To say otherwise only meant further incarceration. The Germans were not stupid. As British commentators jokingly remarked, there were suddenly no Nazis or militarists in Germany and the higher echelons of the German armed forces. This did not matter so much since the Royal Navy and British military authorities predominantly assessed senior officers on future potential risk, based upon previous background and activities during the war. Robertson endorsed releasing Admiralarzt Dr. Otto Tarnow since 'there appear to be no objections to him on grounds of security and his imprisonment, particularly as a sick man, serves no purpose.'[105] For practical and humanitarian reasons, the British discharged individuals, judged to be harmless or in a low risk category. British denazification policy instead concentrated on those considered likely to perpetuate the German navy as an instrument of aggression against Great Britain. Remaining senior officers appeared before British review boards prior to release.

The elaborate denazification review process, which most German admirals went through, had as much to do with keeping perceived high risk officers in custody as the release of more innocuous ones. British review boards worked on the assumption that senior officers posed a threat if released. The onus was on the individual applicant to prove otherwise. Förste, who appeared before the No. 13 British Review Board on 13 December 1946, argued against the assertion that 'if released you might constitute a possible danger to security, particularly in view of your naval record.'[106] Future intentions weighed more heavily than past political inclinations. In fact, British denazification efforts generally lacked overt references to Nazism or war guilt. Förste faced the far more difficult task of trying to convince the review board that he could not or would not engage in activities, which his background and qualifications predisposed him towards. In pleading his case, Förste stressed the importance of his family, supposed moderate political views, and respect for the British Empire.[107] German admirals were forced to justify themselves in terms other than naval career and wartime service. Förste must have pushed the right buttons because the British released him on 20 January 1947.

Those admirals unwilling to make at least the pretence of abandoning the German navy remained incarcerated until another British review board. If captivity drove home the magnitude of defeat and German naval disarmament, then review boards and denazification provided the subtle transition step into new political and vocational orientations in civil life. The uneven application of denazification by some British officials certainly led to discrimination against former naval officers, particularly in regards to higher education and the civil service.[108] Senior officers, however, were never a disenfranchised and isolated group. Many subsequently thrived in business, industry, law, politics, and other respectable fields of endeavour.

Despite the name, denazification really had very little to do with Nazism. In the case of German admirals, the Royal Navy and British military authorities simply wanted to make sure particular individuals did not again become threats to British security or entertain ideas about rejuvenating German naval power. German energies were channelled into other directions. Although historians note the lack of clearly defined aims in the overall British programme, denazification appeared to concentrate successfully on the most important and influential group in the *Kriegsmarine*.[109] The majority of officers were released from army concentration areas after a quick check of papers and settling of outstanding pay, but the admirals quite properly required thorough examination. High rank conferred responsibility and accountability. One-by-one, British review boards released remaining admirals into civil life. A small number of officers and sailors still faced prosecution and imprisonment for war crimes.

NOTES

1. NA, RG 313, COMNAVEU, Series II, File 53, Letter from Lieutenant-Commander Peter van der Poel, USNR, Head of Historical Section to Chief of Staff COMNAVEU, 18 May 1945.
2. PRO, ADM 1/17561, 'Report from Capt. G.H. Roberts, RN, on Visit to Germany May 1945, to Interrogate German Naval Officers on U-boat Operations', 30 May 1945. Mark Williams, *Captain Gilbert Roberts R.N. and the Anti-U-Boat School*, (London: Cassell, 1979), pp. 144–5.
3. OAB/NHC, US Naval Technical Mission in Europe, Series III, Box 30, Technical Report No. 287-45, Dr. M.S. Livingston, Technician, 'Tactical Planning for High Speed U-Boats', 11 Sept. 1945.

4. PRO, ADM 228/8, Memorandum from ANCXF to Secretary of Admiralty, 'Report on Investigation regarding Location and Condition of Type XVII U-Boats carried out between 24 and 30 June 1945'. The Admiralty showed a particular interest in the Type XVIIB and Type XXVI. PRO, ADM 116/5202, Staff Minute by M.R. Campbell for Director of Naval Intelligence, 15 March 1945.

5. PRO, ADM 223/713, Report from Captain C.E. Horton under the auspices of the Director of Scientific Research to DSD, DRE, CSASE, DNOR, DMWD, 'OKMITU (Oberkommando Kriegsmarine Interrogation and Technical Unit', 11 June 1945.

6. Derek Howse, *Radar at Sea: The Royal Navy in World War 2*, (London: Macmillan, 1993), pp. 66–70. Axel Niestlé, 'German Technical and Electronic Development', Law and Howarth, p. 441. Jerome A. O'Connell, 'Radar and the U-Boat', *United States Naval Institute Proceedings* 89(1963), p. 62.

7. IWM, Combined Intelligence Objectives Sub-Committee, File XXXII-87, Report No. 320, Target No. 1/718 Radar, Lieutenant-Colonel R.G. Friend, Major W.H. Maddison, Squadron Leader Devons, Squadron Leader Farvis, Lieutenant-Commander Rowlands, Mr. Soderman, Mr. Gottlieb, 'Interrogation of Prof. Scherzer of BHF (Munich, 14 May 1945', p. 6. Montgomery C. Meigs, *Slide Rules and Submarines: American Scientists and Subsurface Warfare in World War II*, (Washington, DC: National Defense University, 1990), p. 209.

8. PRO, ADM 228/25, Letter from Naval Officer-in-Charge Kiel to British Naval Commander-in-Chief Germany, 'Under Water Explosion Research at Dänisch Nienhoff', 26 Oct. 1945. This research continued earlier work under the auspices of the US Navy. OAB/NHC, US Naval Technical Mission in Europe, Series I, Box 2, File 'US NAVTECHMISEU – Incoming Despatches (Jan.–July 1945)', Message from ANCXF to NAVTECHMISEU, 06 1600 July 1945.

9. PRO, ADM 1/19149, Captain, HMS *Vernon* to Director of Torpedoes and Mining, 'Report of Visit to Kiel and Denmark by Officers of HMS *Vernon* M/S 8 June to 19 July 1945 in BYMS 2054', 4 Sept. 1945. OAB/NHC, US Naval Technical Mission in Europe, Series III, Box 30, Technical Report No. 288-45, Lieutenant (jg), J.W. Gould, USNR, and Lieutenant (jg) R.E. Navin, USNR, 'Organization of German Mine-Sweeping Command', 7 Sept. 1945.

10. BA/MA, Ruge, N 379/244, Diagrams of German Minesweeping Gear, 1950.

11. IWM, British Intelligence Objectives Sub-Committee, No. 208 Item No. 13, Target No. C13/36, G.J. Thiessen, National Research Council, Ottawa, 'Acoustics Laboratories of the Physikalische Technische Reichsanstalt Göttingen', 22 Oct. 1945.

12. IWM, 91/4/1, Mrs. M.W. Ackroyd, Letter 32, Gale Hale, 'Recollections of my Life in the WRNS, Special Duties 1941–1947'.

13. PRO, ADM 228/27, 'German Hydrographic Institute: Statement by Captain Evans', 25 Oct. 1945. British officers inspected other German research institutes. LHC, Riley, File 'Riley 30 Assault Unit', Lieutenant-Commander Quinton Riley and Dr. Brian Roberts, 'Report on Visit to Germany in connection with the Library of the Institut für Meereskunde and German Polar Research', 11 March 1946.

14. Walter joined the Nazi party in 1932. OAB/NHC, US Naval Technical Mission in Europe, Series III, Box 7, Letter Report No. 2-45, Lieutenant-Commander Edward C. Ives, USNR, 'Interrogation of Dr. Walter on the Ingolene Torpedo and U-Boat', 31 May 1945. During a visit to Germany, the American Secretary of the Navy, James Forrestal, described Walter as 'a typical unreconstructed Hun.' Walter Millis, ed., *The Forrestal Diaries*, (New York: Viking Press, 1951), p. 82.

15. OAB/NHC, US Naval Technical Mission in Europe, Series III, Box 26, Technical Report No. 214-45, Captain Harry D. Hoffmann, USN, 'German Naval Closed-Cycle Diesel Development for Submerged Propulsion', 27 Aug. 1945.

16. OAB/NHC, US Naval Technical Mission in Europe, Series III, Box 9, Letter Report No. 52-45, 'Advance Report on Walterwerke, Kiel', 16 May 1945.

17. PRO, ADM 199/2434, Report by Commander (E) I.C. Aylen DSC, RN (Engineer Overseer, Walterwerke to Director of Scientific Research, 'Walterwerke Kiel: History of the Occupation by the Allies from 5 May to 25 Nov. 1945 and General Activities', 12

Dec. 1945, p. 14. Emil Kruska and Eberhard Rössler, *Walter U-Boote*, (München: J.F. Lehmanns, 1969), p. 13.

18. BL, Cunningham, Add. Ms. 52578, Diary, 22 July 1945.
19. The Germans developed flexible plastic containers to store the hydrogen-peroxide. IWM, Combined Intelligence Objectives Sub-Committee, File XXXI-77, CIOS Target No. 22/1662, 'The Fabrication of Plastic Containers used for Storage of Hydrogen Peroxide on German Submarines', July 1945.
20. PRO, ADM 167/127, B.474, Memorandum circulated by First Lord, 'Submarine Building Programme – Development of Hydrogen Peroxide (HTP) Propulsion', 9 July 1946. Vickers-Armstrong built two hydrogen-peroxide propelled submarines from this research: HMS *Explorer* and HMS *Excalibur*. Michael Wilson, 'The Walter Submarine–2', *Warship* 20(1981), pp. 252–3.
21. John Gimbel, *Science, Technology and Reparations: Exploitation and Plunder in Postwar Germany*, (Stanford: Stanford University Press, 1990), p. 40.
22. OAB/NHC, German Naval Archives, Box T-77, NID 24/T21/45, 'Miscellaneous New German Naval Developments', 28 July 1945. D.K. Brown, *A Century of Naval Construction: The History of the Royal Corps of Naval Constructors 1883–1983*, (London: Conway Maritime Press, 1983), p. 201.
23. Willem Hackmann, *Seek and Strike: Sonar, Anti-Submarine Warfare and the Royal Navy, 1914–1954*, (London: Her Majesty's Stationery Office, 1984), pp. 291–300.
24. Wilhelm Hadeler, 'The Ships of the Soviet Navy', Saunders, pp. 143–4.
25. OAB/NHC, German Naval Archives, Box T-68, Kapitän zur See Erich Holtorf and Fregattenkapitän Alfred Behr, 'Defensive Measures against Enemy Type XXI and Walter Type U-Boats', 14 Feb. 1951.
26. K.J. Moore, Mark Flanigan, and Robert D. Helsel, 'Developments in Submarine Systems, 1956–76', Michael McGwire and John McDonnell, eds., *Soviet Naval Influence: Domestic and Foreign Dimensions*, (New York: Praeger, 1977), pp. 152–3.
27. OAB/NHC, US Naval Technical Mission in Europe, Series I, Box 2, File 'U.S. Naval Technical Mission Europe Reports 1944–45', Message from NTS G-2 SHAEF to Admiralty, COMNAVEU, ANCXF, 27 1518 April 1945. LHC, Job, Memoir, 'Special Service', p. 169. The German naval staff had evacuated the records from Berlin to Tambach to escape Allied bombing.
28. Charles Burdick, 'The Tambach Archives: A Research Note', *Military Affairs* 36(Dec. 1972), p. 125. Jonathan Steinberg, *Yesterday's Deterrent: Tirpitz and the Birth of the German Battle Fleet*, (London: Macdonald, 1965), p. 6.
29. OAB/NHC, US Naval Technical Mission in Europe, Series I, Box 2, File 'US Naval Technical Mission in Europe 1944–45', Message from SHAEF Main NTS G-2 to Admiralty, 06 01110 May 1945. Lieutenant H.P. Earle, USNR, and Lieutenant A. Penn, RNVR, upon arrival at Tambach on 12 June, moved the remaining 30,000 documents, weighing almost twenty tons, into two large locked rooms, searched surrounding fields and houses, crated records for evacuation, and politely heard grievances from the Countess of Ortenburg, the castle's still-resident owner. NA, RG 313, COMNAVEU, Series II, File 53, Letter from Commodore Tully Shelley, USN, Intelligence Officer to COMNAVEU, 3 July 1945.
30. NA, RG 313, COMNAVEU, Series II, File 53, Memorandum from Captain I.M.R. Campbell, Deputy Director of Naval Intelligence to All Sections, 'NID Captured Documents Library', 30 Aug. 1945. Once sorted and catalogued, each file was assigned a PG number, short for 'Pinched from the Germans'. Howard M. Ehrmann, 'The German Naval Archives (Tambach)', Robert Wolfe, ed., *Captured German and Related Records*, (Athens, OH: Ohio University Press, 1974), p. 158.
31. IWM, Ackroyd, Letter 27, Phyllis Whitmarsh, [n.d].
32. DHist, 181.009 (593), 'A Short Description of Torpedoes Types ZAUNBUTT and ZAUNWAL', 12 Dec. 1945.
33. PRO, ADM 199/443, Staff Minute by J.C. Mossop, 10 Sept. 1945.
34. PRO, ADM 116/5550, Access Register, 'Information from the Tambach Archives, September–October 1945'. Anthony K. Martienssen, *Hitler and His Admirals*, (New

York: E.P. Dutton, 1949), pp. 1–7.

35. NA, RG 313, COMNAVEU, Series II, File 53, Letter from Captain D.W. Knox to Commander T.B. Kittredge, 13 June 1945.

36. Ernest M. Eller, 'United States Navy Microfilm of the German Naval Archives', Wolfe, p. 169. See also OAB/NHC, German Naval Archives, Boxes T-136 and T-137.

37. PRO, ADM 116/5549, Memorandum from Director of Naval Intelligence to Military Branch, 31 Jan. 1946.

38. Keith Bird, 'The Origins and Role of German Naval History in the Inter-war Period 1918–1939', *Naval War College Review* 32(1979), p. 43.

39. NA, RG 313, COMAVEU, Series II, File 53, Memorandum from Captain W.A. Finn, USNR, Intelligence Officer to COMNAVEU Intelligence Officer, 'History of German Naval Warfare', 25 Aug. 1945.

40. CCAC, Miscellaneous 49, Report from Lieutenant-Commander Ralph W.B. Izzard to Captain J.H. Lewes to British Naval Commander-in-Chief Germany, 'Activities of Forward Interrogation Unit 17th November 1944 to 1st January 1946', Section X.

41. OAB/NHC, German Naval Archives, Box T-76, Vizeadmiral Eberhard Weichold, 'Why Germany lost the Second World War', [nd].

42. PRO, ADM 223/255, NID 1/GP/13, Vizeadmiral Hellmuth Heye, 'The Naval Aspects of the War', 15 Oct. 1945. Ironically, Heye, as a member of the West German *Bundestag*, later appealed to have Dönitz released from captivity. BA/MA, Ruge, N 379/88, Letter from Friedrich Ruge to Lord Ismay, Secretary-General NATO, 3 Dec. 1955.

43. OAB/NHC, German Naval Archives, Box T-67, NID 1/GP/17, 'Essay by Rear Admiral Godt on the War at Sea', 3 Nov. 1945.

44. OAB/NHC, German Naval Archives, Reel T-47, Fregattenkapitän Günther Hessler, 'The Submarine War from 1939–1945'.

45. PRO, ADM 223/255, Report from Justin Richardson, Deputy Assistant, Chief of Staff (Intelligence), British Naval Commander-in-Chief Germany to Director of Naval Intelligence, 'Interrogation of Kapitän zur See Otto von Baumbach', 27 Aug. 1945. N.G. Kuznetsov, 'Before the War', *International Affairs* 12 (1966), p. 97.

46. BA/MA, Wagner, N 539/3, 'First Meeting of the Naval Historical Team (NHT)', April 1949.

47. PRO, ADM 228/73, Flag Officer Schleswig-Holstein to British Naval Commander-in-Chief Germany forwarding a Report by Kapitänleutnant Carl-Friedrich Mohr, Liaison Officer to Naval Officer-in-Charge Kiel, 'Current Ideas on the Present Situation of German Naval Officers', 16 Sept. 1945.

48. IWM, Savage, File 'Dispersed Stores and Subsequent Centralization and Distribution', Detailed Summary from Marineintendantur, Chief Intendant Hans Kreplin to British Liaison Officer, 'Plan of Organisation of the Naval Arsenal Kiel', 29 Aug. 1945.

49. PRO, ADM 228/56, Letter from Marineintendantur Kiel to Staff Supply Officer, Senior British Naval Officer Schleswig-Holstein, 12 Sept. 1946.

50. PRO, ADM 228/57, Message from British Naval Commander-in-Chief Germany to Flag Officer Schleswig-Holstein, 07 1531 Jan. 1946. In early Sept. 1945 Burrough had requested lists of all retained officers under British command. PRO, ADM 228/56, Message from British Naval Commander-in-Chief Germany to all Flag Officers and Naval Officers-in-Charge, 02 1009B Sept. 1945.

51. PRO, ADM 228/57, Message from Flag Officer Schleswig-Holstein to Deputy Head of Naval Division for British Naval Commander-in-Chief Germany, 09 1957A Jan. 1946.

52. BA/MA, RM 22/5, Memorandum from Vizeadmiral Karl Topp, Amt Kriegschiffbau to Commander F.M. Beasley, Office of Flag Officer Schleswig-Holstein, 'Kriegschiff-bauplan 1945', 21 Feb. 1946. See also ADM 223/51.

53. PRO, ADM 228/57, Staff Minute by Secretary GS, 10 Jan. 1946.

54. PRO, ADM 228/57, Message from British Naval Commander-in-Chief Germany to Flag Officer Schleswig-Holstein, 03 1116A Feb. 1946.

55. PRO, ADM 228/56, Message from Flag Officer Norway to British Naval Commander-in-Chief Germany, 21 1124B July 1945.

56. BA/MA, Förste, N 328/19, Letter from Rear-Admiral F.E.P. Hutton to Admiral Erich

Förste, 24 July 1945.

57. PRO, ADM 228/91, Memorandum from British Naval Commander-in-Chief Germany to Flag Officers Western Germany and Schleswig-Holstein; British Naval Commander-in-Chief Germany (GM/SA), 'Disbandment and Control of the German Naval Forces', 14 Aug. 1945.

58. OAB/NHC, German Naval Archives, Box T-107, File 9, Intelligence Report 8-45, Naval Division USGCC to Chief of Naval Operations, 7 June 1945.

59. PRO, ADM 228/56, Message from British Naval Commander-in-Chief Germany to Admiralty, 21 1730B Aug. 1945.

60. PRO, ADM 228/54, Letter from British Naval Commander-in-Chief Germany to 21st Army Group, 'Disbanding Clergy in the German Armed Forces', 24 Aug. 1945.

61. PRO, ADM 228/56, Message from British Naval Commander-in-Chief Germany (GM/SA) to 312 Penal Detachment Military Government, 24 1234B Aug. 1945.

62. PRO, ADM 228/57, Message from Flag Officer Schleswig-Holstein to British Naval Commander-in-Chief Germany, 12 1339A Jan. 1946.

63. OAB/NHC, German Naval Archives, Reel T-9, Kurt Assmann, 'Relations between the Supreme Command of Armed Forces and the Naval War Staff'.

64. Martienssen, pp. 6–9. The Royal Navy criticized the relationship. M.G. Saunders, 'Hitler's Admirals: Reflections Inspired by their Memoirs', *Journal of the Royal United Services Institution* 104(1959), p. 327.

65. Peter Calvocoressi, *Nuremberg: The Facts, the Law and the Consequences*, (London: Chatto and Windus, 1947), pp. 94–9.

66. NA, RG 331, SHAEF, Office of Chief of Staff, Secretary General Staff, File 381/3 Vol. I, ANCXF Post-Hostilities Planning Memoranda No. 24 'Naval Intelligence', 5 May 1945.

67. PRO, WO 205/1041, Memorandum from Brigadier A.L. Elsworth for Major-General I/c Administration 21st Army Group, 'A' Rear 21st Army to 1st Canadian Army and 2nd British Army, 'Disposal of German Officers', 21 May 1945.

68. BA/MA, Förste, N 328/19, Memorandum, Glücksburg, ObdM, 'Why there was neither a General Staff of the Supreme Command nor a Special General Staff Corps or Admiral Corps in the German Navy', 4 July 1945.

69. OAB/NHC, German Naval Archives, Box T-88, File RES 12, ONI Intelligence Report 4-46, COMNAVFORGER to Chief of Naval Operations, 'List of Promising Young Naval Officers 7 Dec 1945', 11 Jan. 1946.

70. PRO, ADM 116/5609, JIC(CCG) 45/1 (Final), 'Suppression of the German General Staff and Officer Corps', 5 Sept. 1945. The Americans opposed a proposal before the Control Council that members of the General Staff and their families should be removed from Germany and divided between the Soviet Union, Great Britain, France, and the United States for detention. Jean Edward Smith, ed., *The Papers of General Lucius D. Clay: Germany 1945–1949*, Vol. 1, (Bloomington: Indiana University Press, 1974), p. 116.

71. IWM, Parry, Box 10, Letter from Rear-Admiral W.E. Parry to Wife, 22 Jan. 1946. Rust, p. 123.

72. PRO, ADM 228/57, Directive from Major-General, Chief of Staff BAOR, to HQ 1st, 8th, 30th, L of C Corps Districts, 8 Jan. 1946.

73. PRO, ADM 228/57, Directive from Major-General, Chief of Staff BAOR to Corps Districts, 14 Jan. 1946.

74. PRO, ADM 228/59, 'Minutes of a Conference held in Room 45, Tax House, Lübeck, on 7 Feb. 1946 to consider the Present Position relating to Ordinance 13', 8 Feb. 1946.

75. PRO, ADM 228/66, Memorandum from Captain J.H. Lewes to Deputy Head Naval Division, 'German Naval Officers in Russian Hands', 29 March 1946.

76. BA/MA, Ruge, N 379/86, Friedrich Ruge, 'Deutsche Admirale in russicher Hand', 1951.

77. PRO, FO 1038/136, Message from TROOPERS to BERCOMB, 02 0250Z March 1946. PRO, ADM 116/5609, Letter from Military Branch I, Admiralty to S. Granville Smith, Control Office for Germany and Austria, 25 Feb. 1946.

78. PRO, ADM 116/5609, Message from Director of Naval Intelligence to British Naval Commander-in-Chief Germany, 15 1826 March 1946.

79. BA/MA, Wagner, N 539/1, Letter from Konteradmiral Gerhard Wagner to War Office PW I, 28 Oct. 1946. Wagner remained in American captivity until 4 July 1947. Arnold Krammer, 'American Treatment of German Generals during World War II', *Journal of Military History* 54(1990), p. 45.

80. BA/MA, Förste, N 328/19, 'The Story of 2226 POW Camp', [nd]. Senior German officers were transferred from Camp 2224 near Ostend. IWM, Moyse, Diary, pp. 66–8.

81. PRO, ADM 228/67, Letter from Generaladmiral Walter Warzecha to British Naval Commander-in-Chief Germany, 12 Feb. 1945.

82. Matthew Barry Sullivan, *Thresholds of Peace: Four Hundred Thousand German Prisoners of War and the People of Great Britain*, (London: Hamish Hamilton, 1979), p. 380.

83. S.P. Mackenzie, 'Essay and Reflection: On the Other Losses Debate', *International History Review* 14(1992), pp. 720–1.

84. BA/MA, Förste, N 328/19, Letter from Admiral Erich Förste to Camp 2226 Commandant, 7 Dec. 1945.

85. BA/MA, Förste, N 328/19, Letter from Admiral Erich Förste to Colonel Lyall, 'State of Health', 6 April 1946.

86. PRO, ADM 228/67, Letter from Field Marshal Bernard Montgomery to Vice-Admiral Commanding British Naval Forces Germany, 31 March 1946.

87. PRO, ADM 228/67, Letter from Rear-Admiral Harold Baillie-Grohman to Admiral Harold Burrough, 26 Feb. 1946.

88. PRO, ADM 228/67, Letter from Rear-Admiral F.E.P. Hutton to Admiral Harold Burrough, 13 Feb. 1946. Reservations were raised about sending Weyher and Zieb, the two cooperative admirals at Wilhelmshaven, 'to such a place'. PRO, ADM 228/67, Letter from Captain E.R. Conder to Flag Officer Western Germany, 12 Feb. 1946.

89. PRO, ADM 228/67, Staff Minute by Captain J.H. Lewes, 26 Feb. 1946.

90. *House of Lords Debates*, 5th Series, Vol. 141, 30 May 1946, Column 631.

91. PRO, ADM 228/67, Memorandum from Naval Officer-in-Charge Wilhelmshaven to Flag Officer Western Germany, 28 March 1946.

92. PRO, ADM 228/67, Letter from Rear-Admiral F.E.P. Hutton, Flag Officer Western Germany to Vice-Admiral Commanding British Naval Forces in Germany, 31 March 1946.

93. PRO, ADM 228/67, Letter from Commodore R.M.J. Hutton for Vice-Admiral Commanding British Naval Forces in Germany to Flag Officer Schleswig-Holstein, 13 March 1946.

94. PRO, ADM 228/67, Memorandum from Vice-Admiral H.T.C. Walker to HQ BAOR, 'Visits to German POW Camps', 23 April 1946.

95. PRO, ADM 228/67, Report from Lieutenant-Commander G.A Feilman, RNVR, c/o 23 Disposal Control Unit, BAOR to Vice-Admiral Commanding British Naval Forces in Germany, 17 Oct. 1946.

96. Robert Vansittart, *Black Record: Germans Past and Present*, (London: Hamish Hamilton, 1941).

97. C.K.S.A., 'The Eternal Hun', *Naval Review* 33(1945), pp. 57–61. James Goldrick, 'Naval Publishing the British Way', *Naval War College Review* 45(1992), p. 96.

98. Jill Jones, 'Eradicating Nazism from the British Zone of Germany: Early Policy and Practice', *German History* 8(1990), pp. 147–8.

99. NAC, RG 24, Vol. 13,644, SD Eclipse Section HQ 1st Canadian Army, Supreme Commander's Proclamation No. 1, May 1945.

100. F.S.V. Donnison, *Civil Affairs and Military Government North-West Europe 1944–1946*, (London: Her Majesty's Stationery Office, 1961), p. 362.

101. PRO, FO 1038/136, Covering Letter and Report from Administrative HQ CCG (BE) to DCOS (Exec), 'Disposal of War Criminals, Nazis, Militarists and Potentially Dangerous Germans', 13 March 1946.

102. PRO, ADM 116/5609, 'Minutes of Meeting convened at Norfolk House at 1500 hours 8 Apr 46 to consider Paper HQ/06101/9/Sec P dated 29 March 46, submitted by the British Element of the Control Commission Germany', 8 April 1946.

103. PRO, FO 1038/136, Letter from Chief, Army Division to Naval Division, 'Release of Senior Officers', 14 May 1946.
104. Henry Faulk, *Group Captives: The Re-Education of German Prisoners of War in Britain 1945–1948*, (London: Chatto & Windus, 1977), p. 81.
105. PRO, FO 1038/137, Letter from Lieutenant-General Brian Robertson, Deputy Military Governor to N.L.C. Macaski, Chief Legal Division, 'Detention of Admiral Arzt Dr. Med. Otto Tarnow', 6 Sept. 1946.
106. BA/MA, Förste, N 328/19, Letter from C.S. Style, Chairman, No. 13 British Review Board to Admiral Erich Förste PW No. A 461 195, 30 Nov. 1946.
107. The Admiralty had decided not to try Förste as a war criminal in regards to his activities in Greece during the war. PRO, TS 26/150, Letter from J.C. Mossop to P.H.B. Kent, 12 June 1945.
108. Rust, p. 137.
109. Ian Turner, 'Denazification in the British Zone', Turner, p. 261.

8

War Crimes Trials

The Royal Navy showed a strong interest in investigating and prosecuting Germans accused of violating the laws and usages of war and existing international agreements. British military law furnished the legal right to punish violations by the vanquished enemy. Under the authority of a Royal Warrant, military courts convened in occupied Germany and the liberated countries for prosecution of alleged war crimes. The Royal Navy actively participated in several naval-related cases involving the deliberate killing of British and Allied sailors, breaches of the surrender terms, and perceived misconduct. Moreover, the *Kriegsmarine*'s two wartime leaders, Grossadmiral Erich Raeder and Grossadmiral Karl Dönitz, appeared as defendants before the International Military Tribunal at Nuremberg with other leading political, military, and industrial figures from the Third Reich. War crimes trials were an important aspect of the Royal Navy's work in occupied Germany.

The Admiralty's interest in the judicial trial of Germans for alleged war crimes evolved in an incremental fashion. Waldock and Mossop, the lawyers employed at the Admiralty during the war, predominantly defined the Royal Navy's war crimes posture. In 1936 both Great Britain and Germany had signed an additional protocol to the 1930 London Naval Treaty which placed restrictions on submarine operations.[1] Under the protocol, submarines were required to follow the same rules of visit and search as surface ships. Although the *Kriegsmarine* had adopted a sink-at-sight policy in late 1939, Waldock voiced 'some difficulty in actually charging U-boat Commanders with war crimes by reason of their attacks on allied merchant vessels, unless the attack was accompanied by some particularly brutal conduct.'[2] This reluctance arose from the fact that the Royal Navy likewise pursued unrestricted submarine warfare in reprisal. At the First Lord's direction, the Admiralty publicly condemned German disregard of the submarine protocol, but privately intended to 'treat all cases on their merits.'[3]

Hoping to keep the protocol in force after the war, the Admiralty only worried about sinkings before British adoption of sink-at-sight in 1940 and flagrant abuses of the 1907 Hague Conventions and the 1929 Geneva Convention.

Several notable incidents in the early part of the war attracted the Admiralty's attention. On 3 September 1939 U-30, under the command of Kapitänleutnant Fritz-Julius Lemp, sank the passenger liner *Athenia* without warning.[4] The Germans denied responsibility and accused Churchill, then First Lord of the Admiralty, of sinking the ship to turn neutral public opinion against Nazi Germany. The Admiralty kept an open docket on the *Athenia* until later investigations in the captured Tambach records and interrogations of senior officers revealed that the German naval staff had deliberately tried to conceal the sinking by falsifying U-30's war diary.[5]

Conduct during the Royal Navy's seizure of the pocket-battleship *Graf Spee*'s supply ship, the *Altmark*, in neutral Norwegian waters also received scrutiny. Although the *Altmark* attempted to ram the British destroyer *Cossack*, the Admiralty felt that no legal proceedings should 'be taken against Captain Dahl in respect of his attempt to defend his ship from boarding – indeed we should have expected similar action on the part of a British skipper if the positions had been reversed.'[6] Under the circumstances, his behaviour was considered appropriate. Moreover, the Admiralty did not want to draw more attention to the fact that the Royal Navy's seizure of the *Altmark* had violated the international law of neutrality.

Other investigations involved alleged improper behaviour during and after battle. After sinking the SS *Sheaf Mead* on 27 May 1940 Kapitänleutnant Victor Oehrn was 'reported to have behaved in an exceptionally callous manner towards the men clinging to upturned boats and pieces of wood.'[7] Separating atrocities from normal combat was often a difficult task after the fact. In regard to a similar incident, Mossop acknowledged that shells and machine-gun fire from U-516 struck lifeboats near the stricken Brazilian ship *Antonica*, but 'they were directed primarily at the ship, and broadly speaking, I think the Board would feel that we have been guilty of so many sinkings of a rather similar character that we would not wish to be involved in a prosecution of a German for this kind of offence.'[8] The Admiralty recognized that a grey area existed in what was legally allowed and not allowed. Smashing and sinking ships during sea battles inevitably caused loss of life. Aside from outright disregard of the submarine protocol, the *Kriegsmarine* seemingly followed the existing rules during offensive operations against British and Allied shipping.

The Admiralty maintained a relatively good view of German activities

174

in the naval sphere until early 1944. Compared to brutal attacks on hospital ships and Allied sailors in World War I, the *Kriegsmarine* appeared to act correctly for the most part.[9] Although U-boats sank Allied ships in large numbers, German captains and crews avoided unnecessary suffering and even occasionally behaved in a chivalrous manner. The *Kriegsmarine*'s behaviour stood in stark contrast to the German army's misconduct on land, especially in eastern Europe and the Soviet Union.[10] Admittedly, the sea environment presented unique problems with the collection of evidence. U-boats may have committed atrocities, but ensured that no survivors remained to tell the tale.[11] War crimes at sea were harder to prove than war crimes on land because any trace quickly disappeared beneath the waves. Investigators could not uncover mass graves, exhume bodies, or examine the physical scene, but instead relied on eyewitness testimony, interrogations of prisoners of war, and captured documentary material.

Through such means, the Admiralty discovered serious improprieties by the *Kriegsmarine*. Reports from the Continent described summary executions under Hitler's notorious Commando Order in Norway and France.[12] Various independent sources substantiated earlier rumours concerning the fate of missing Allied sailors. The Admiralty asked the Foreign Office if a public warning could be issued to German commanders about the consequences of implementing the Commando Order. Meanwhile, American interrogations of captured U-boat captains disclosed transmission of an order that 'as part of total war, following sinking of enemy shipping all survivors are to be exterminated.'[13] Much to their credit, most German captains refused to carry out such a blatantly illegal directive. Nonetheless, the Admiralty soon confronted the actual killing of Allied sailors in lifeboats. After British aircraft forced U-852 to beach off the coast of Somalia, surviving crew members 'confessed that they machine gunned the crew of a Greek ship they torpedoed.'[14] The freighter *Peleus*, sunk by U-852 in the South Atlantic on 13 March 1944, had been in ballast from Freetown to the River Plate under Ministry of War Transport charter. Affidavits from wounded merchant mariners, who miraculously survived the vicious attack and twenty-seven further days in an open lifeboat, confirmed the incident.

As evidence of a definite pattern mounted, the Admiralty joined in general arrangements to investigate and eventually to prosecute accused war criminals. On 1 November 1943 the United States, Great Britain, and the Soviet Union had issued the Moscow Declaration, which stated the intention to try and punish German service personnel and members of the Nazi party who participated in war crimes, executions, and similar acts of atrocity. The British were instrumental behind the declaration and a proposed inter-allied war crimes organization. The Cabinet established a British war crimes investigation group to work within the framework of the United Nations War Crimes Commission.[15] The Admiralty forwarded relevant information to this body for central collection and compilation of war criminal lists. To overcome confusion which seemed endemic within the umbrella war crimes organization, Waldock and Mossop mostly worked through personal contacts with other civil servants in the Foreign Office, the War Office, and the Treasury Solicitor's Office. Sir Thomas Barnes, the Treasury Solicitor, was the legal adviser to the Admiralty. Specific charges were prepared under his direction for submission to the United Nations War Crimes Commission.

The Admiralty aspired to an active part in war crimes cases pertaining to the Royal Navy and British merchant marine. Waldock preferred military courts with naval members to deal with alleged war crimes.[16] Constituted on a national basis, these courts were to judge Germans accused of specific offences against British and Commonwealth subjects. A 1936 amendment to the British *Manual of Military Law*, which defined a war crime, had specified trial by 'military courts or by such courts as the belligerent concerned may determine.'[17] The War Office drew up applicable legal rules in consultation with the Attorney General and the Treasury Solicitor. Regulations, based largely on existing court martial procedure, were promulgated with a Royal Warrant on 18 June 1945.[18] The military court provided the Royal Navy and military authorities in British-occupied Germany with the legal means to arraign and prosecute minor war criminals.

The first British war crimes case completed under the Royal Warrant involved the *Peleus* killings. The chosen venue, the Curiohaus in Hamburg, hosted numerous war crimes trials in the immediate post-war period.[19] The British insisted on prosecution and implementation of sentences in Germany. According to Barnes, the *Peleus* trial was 'to impress upon the German people what is the result of committing crimes of this kind.'[20] If soldiers and sailors broke the established rules of war, then they were to be tried and punished as a deterrent to similar behaviour. U-852's commanding officer, Kapitänleutnant Heinz Eck, and four crew members faced charges of deliberate murder and unlawful wounding.[21] Opposite the defendants, the court comprised different services and nationalities. In addition to British army and naval officers, two Greek naval captains sat 'on this case which so closely concerns the interests of our two countries.'[22] Between 17 and 20 October 1945 the military judges heard evidence, testimony, and arguments from Colonel R.C. Halse for the prosecution and various legal counsel for the defendants. Eck, who denied knowledge of any verbal or written orders to kill sailors, stated that the decision to destroy the lifeboats was his alone.[23] Despite pleas of operational necessity and mitigating circumstances, the court found the defendants guilty, and sentenced Eck, August Hoffmann, and Walter Weisspfennig to death by shooting.

The verdicts in the *Peleus* case evoked a strong German reaction. Royal Navy intelligence officers reported that the so-called Cremer clique, a group of submariners associated with Godt and Hessler, was devastated.[24] Although Eck had certainly gone too far, his actions tainted the U-boat service and the larger *Kriegsmarine* with insinuations of criminality. Officers in the GM/SA refused to believe that an honourable German naval officer intentionally committed war crimes. In a petition for clemency, Krauss asked Montgomery, the confirming authority, to put aside questions of international law and politics, arguing that the killings were 'a secondary consequence of what he [Eck] believed an operational necessity.'[25] In the German view, Eck deserved the benefit of the doubt, particularly since the punishment was so absolute.

Several factors compelled the British to carry out the proscribed death sentences. The *Peleus* killings were a clear violation of existing laws and usages of war at sea. By deliberately firing on lifeboats, Eck and his subordinates had murdered in cold blood Allied sailors.[26] For British officials and the general public, the punishment was more than appropriate for the gravity of the crime. Even in an era of total war, Eck's actions seemed particularly callous. The Admiralty also initiated Eck's prosecution with the hope that his testimony would implicate more senior officers in the *Kriegsmarine*. Since Eck refused to do so, his usefulness was limited. The British resisted allowing Eck to appear as a witness at the upcoming war crimes trial of Raeder and Dönitz because he could in no way 'strengthen case for prosecution or affect result of trial.'[27] Only the defence counsel stood to benefit from Eck's firm denial of superior orders. After his trial, Eck told interrogators 'that he would have expected his superiors to regard his action as proper in view of the terms of the order but that the action he took was taken entirely on his own initiative and without reference to the order.'[28] The answer was not what the Admiralty wanted to hear. Was Eck a potential embarrassment to the prosecution at Nuremberg? The evidence strongly suggests that he was. Various appeals for clemency were turned down. The British executed Eck, Weisspfennig, and Hoffmann on 30 November 1945.[29] Whether punishment was justly deserved or a convenient way to silence an inopportune witness, Eck took the truth to the grave.

The Royal Navy located the officer who had instructed Eck and other U-boat captains to kill Allied crews. Korvettenkapitän Karl-Heinz Moehle, chief of the 5th U-boat Flotilla in Kiel, had briefed commanding officers before operational patrols.[30] Based on the earlier American reports, British officers interviewed Moehle in Germany after the surrender. He admitted that U-852 had been equipped at Kiel, but initially denied passing on any order to shoot Allied sailors.[31] At some point, Moehle realized that he was in serious trouble because his story changed dramatically upon subsequent interrogation. Moehle claimed that the Laconia Order, which the U-boat headquarters had issued on 17 September 1942, incited submarine commanders to destroy crews because 'Doenitz undoubtedly desired the total elimination of Allied forces at sea.'[32] Moehle allegedly sought clarification of the order in a conversation with Hessler or Korvettenkapitän Herbert Kuppisch on Dönitz's staff, at which time two examples were given of when it was appropriate to shoot shipwrecked survivors: downed British air crew on life-rafts in the Bay of Biscay and crews from American ships sunk near the Caribbean coast. While Hessler and Godt unequivocally disavowed Moehle's representation of Dönitz's intent, Godt told a Royal Navy interrogator that Kuppisch, who had died during active operations in the war, 'was given to making "snap" answers without considering their import too carefully.'[33] Whatever the source, Moehle gave the two examples if U-boat captains queried him on the order's meaning.

The Admiralty saw potential benefit in Moehle's version of events. Unlike Eck, Moehle fixed responsibility for the alleged order to kill shipwrecked survivors squarely with higher levels of the *Kriegsmarine*, possibly even with Dönitz. Waldock observed that Moehle was obviously trying 'to save himself by putting the blame on his superior officers.'[34] Regardless, the British felt that Moehle could strengthen the prosecution case against Dönitz. Verbal orders of this nature were exceedingly difficult to prove without such corroboration. The Admiralty arranged for Moehle to give evidence at Nuremberg.[35] He answered prosecution and defence counsel questions in an effective and credible manner. Certain Royal Navy officers even led Moehle to believe that in return for testimony against Dönitz, 'he would not have to face a trial himself.'[36] To Moehle's eventual surprise, the expectation proved incorrect.

Despite Moehle's cooperation at Nuremberg, the British followed through with trying and punishing the former flotilla chief for giving orders to captains to destroy ships and crews in contravention of the laws and usages of war. Since even Moehle agreed to the facts in the case, the Admiralty considered the offence sufficiently serious not to set aside. On 15 and 16 October 1946 Moehle appeared before a British war crimes court in Hamburg.[37] Halse drew upon Moehle's previous interrogation statements and testimony at Nuremberg to support the charge, while Dr. Otto Zippel, a civil lawyer engaged as defence counsel, presented Moehle as simply the conveyor of superior orders. Moehle was the sole witness during the proceedings. German naval officers, who apparently disapproved of Moehle's earlier disloyalty towards Dönitz, refused to speak on his behalf.[38] After weighing the evidence, the military judges, Lieutenant-Colonel J.A Gendinning, Major R.A. Readman, and Lieutenant-Commander N.H.B. Bloye, RNR, sentenced Moehle to five years' imprisonment. Despite numerous appeals, he served most of this sentence. The British released Moehle in November 1949 after Zippel petitioned that continued imprisonment caused undue hardship for his wife and children.[39] For the Royal Navy, Moehle's punishment seemed appropriate and necessary.

Based on the previous reports, the Admiralty also investigated incidents involving application of the Commando Order. Captured German documents strongly incriminated Admiral Johannes Bachmann, former naval commander-in-chief in western France, with the murder of two Royal Marines landed by HM submarine *Tuna* in Operation 'Frankton' off Bordeaux in December 1942.[40] Under Bachmann's instructions, a firing squad had executed the British marines shortly after their capture. In order to initiate prosecution efforts, British authorities within occupied Germany instituted a comprehensive search for the admiral. Investigations, however, discovered that Bachmann had died in military operations at the end of the war.[41] Although evidence of Bachmann's participation was overwhelming, no trial could take place for this particular crime because the accused was deceased.

The Admiralty diligently pursued other individuals connected with the criminal Commando Order. A former intelligence staff officer in Bergen disclosed that naval authorities had turned over, in conformity with the order, Norwegian and British sailors from the captured motor torpedo boat 345 to the SD in May 1943.[42] Although captured in uniform, the seven men were subsequently shot or perished in concentration camps. In early November 1945 the Admiralty forwarded a list of naval officers likely to be involved.[43] Further interrogations identified the responsible individuals.

The Admiralty was firmly committed to prosecution in the case of the MTB 345 killings. Murder charges were laid against nine former members of the SD in Norway.[44] The *Kriegsmarine* had played an ancillary rather than a direct part in the murders. In Oslo on 26 December a British military court, which included Commander E.P.G. Sandwith, RN, as a member, passed a death sentence, varying terms of imprisonment, and two acquittals.[45] After confirmation, British authorities executed Obersturmbannführer Hans Blomberg on 10 January 1946. Generaloberst Nikolaus von Falkenhorst, who had appeared as a defence witness during the trial in Oslo, later received a commuted term of life imprisonment for his own involvement in the MTB 345 and related commando killings.[46] The war crimes trials dealing with implementation of the Commando Order demonstrated the

Admiralty's strong interest in punishing Germans who killed British and Allied naval personnel outside of normal operations. The Royal Navy initiated investigations and participated in military courts. A sense of justice permeated these efforts.

War crimes trials involving scuttling of U-boats after the capitulation served a different purpose. At the end of the war, a small number of officers chose to disregard Allied and German instructions to surface and report to the nearest Allied port. British naval authorities charged Kapitänleutnant Johannes Meermeier, commanding officer of U-979, and Oberleutnant Heinrich Meyer, commanding officer of U-287, with disobedience of the surrender terms.[47] Both submarines were intentionally scuttled in German waters following the capitulation. A Royal Navy officer, who prepared one of the legal cases in Wilhelmshaven, cynically remarked that the captain would 'probably be shot, although his action is what the navy would expect of an Englishman in the same circumstances.'[48] Although sympathetic, British naval authorities adopted a hard line to prevent similar behaviour.

The Royal Navy made a clear example of at least one German naval officer. While serving on a guard ship in Cuxhaven on the night of 7 May Oberleutnant Gerhard Grumpelt opened the ballast tanks on U-1406 and U-1407, even though Kapitän zur See Kurt Thoma had issued an order prohibiting their scuttling.[49] The action angered the Admiralty because these two submarines were of the latest Walter design. After considering the evidence and the circumstances, the Legal Division recommended not prosecuting Grumpelt for a war crime because 'it would perhaps appear to be reducing a patriotically-minded German officer to the level of a Concentration Camp guard.'[50] Trial by military government court for a misdemeanour offence under occupation regulations appeared the preferable course. Burrough expressed his agreement with the Control Commission's advice. The Admiralty, however, insisted 'that with the transfer to the Russians of part of the German fleet imminent, it is essential that we should express our disapproval of scuttling by putting Grumpelt on trial.'[51] Prosecution became a deterrent to prevent any ideas about scuttling at Wilhelmshaven. On 13 February 1946 a British military court, which included Lieutenant-Commander Edward Hugh Cartwright, RN, and Lieutenant I.S.B. Crosse, RN, as members, sentenced Grumpelt to seven years' imprisonment.[52] Upon confirmation on 8 March 1946 the British commanding officer of the 8th Corps District remitted two years from the sentence.

In a subsequent case, the Admiralty initiated prosecution of Kapitänleutnant Ehrenreich Stever, who had scuttled U-1277 off the coast of Portugal on 2 June 1945. Since the major warships were now

180

transferred to the respective Allied countries, a strong deterrent against scuttling was no longer required. The Admiralty, however, approved prosecution for the sake of consistency with the previous Grumpelt case.[53] Stever's actions prior to the scuttling were certainly culpable. He knowingly ignored a wireless message and representations from U-1277's crew to proceed to an Allied port.[54] The Admiralty and the Judge Advocate General's Office felt that the case was easily proved. Stever was charged with scuttling U-1277 in contravention of the surrender terms.[55] The majority of evidence comprised statements and testimony from the submarine's dissatisfied crew. On 18 July 1946 a military court, which included Commander J.B. Herepath, RN, sentenced Stever to seven, commuted to five, years of imprisonment.[56] The Deputy Judge Advocate General recommended against a petition from Dr. Hans Radischat, a Hamburg civil lawyer who served as Stever's defence counsel. Nonetheless, Montgomery's successor, Air Marshal Sholto Douglas, later remitted three years from the original sentence.[57] Stever served the remainder of his sentence in British custody.

In regard to scuttling, the Royal Navy used war crimes trials to enforce proper behaviour from German naval personnel by highlighting the consequences of disobeying British orders. The crime was in a different class from those involving death or injury to Allied naval personnel. Notions of honour and duty usually motivated German officers to scuttle. After receiving a remittal of three more years, Grumpelt was released on 12 February 1948.[58] This willingness to excuse large parts of sentences at later dates reflected how British authorities regarded such offences. Although war crimes required punishment, the Royal Navy was understanding of particular circumstances.

The war crimes trial of the elderly Kapitän zur See Hellmuth von Ruckteschell underscored the discrepancy between a need to punish and respect for an honourable enemy. The case was among the earliest war crimes investigations undertaken by the Admiralty.[59] As captain of the auxiliary cruisers *Widder* (Ship 21) and *Michel* (Ship 28), Ruckteschell had intercepted Allied merchant ships in the South Atlantic and Indian Ocean. On several occasions, the warships allegedly continued to fire after British vessels had presented clear signs of surrender. Since such conduct contravened the existing laws of naval warfare, the Admiralty requested detention of Ruckteschell and former members of his crews for interrogation.[60]

Actually finding the German captain was another matter. At the end of the war, Ruckteschell was on the staff of the German naval attaché in Japan. His whereabouts were unknown to British naval authorities until late 1945:[61] Eventually located with other naval officers in an internment camp near Kobe, Ruckteschell was brought back to Germany for trial. According to the British charge submission to the United Nations War Crimes Commission, the evidence revealed 'at least one clear case of mass murder and several equally clear cases of the sinking of vessels whose crew were on the vessels when they were fired on, and were not picked up subsequently when on boats, rafts and in the water.'[62] As defence counsel, Ruckteschell hired Dr. Otto Zippel, the same Hamburg lawyer who had earlier represented Moehle.

During the trial in Hamburg between 5 and 21 May 1946 the defence tried to define the limitations of international law, called Vizeadmiral Bernhard Rogge as an expert witness, and questioned the recollections of British sailors. In closing, Zippel asserted that 'the law has recognized that in matters of sea even clever people are more liable to commit an error than in other walks of life.'[63] Although the prosecutor, Major A.E.E. Reade, paid tribute to Ruckteschell's exemplary character throughout the proceedings, the British military court convicted on three of five charges, and sentenced Ruckteschell to ten years' imprisonment.

The verdict against Ruckteschell indirectly raised concerns about further war crimes trials involving naval-related offences. Only one junior naval officer, Lieutenant C.C. Anderson, RN, sat as a judge during the trial. Upon appeal, Zippel asserted that in his opinion, 'a court composed of experienced sea officers would have arrived at a different judgment in the case.'[64] Army officers could not be expected to have a good knowledge of the technical and legal intricacies of naval warfare. The tendency towards less naval representation on the courts concerned British naval authorities. Royal Navy officers acknowledged 'that they have not been able to get the "Naval" side of the thing across sufficiently and that they fear that through ignorance or misunderstanding by the majority of the court, there is a very real chance of a miscarriage of justice taking place.'[65] As the Royal Navy's presence in Germany became progressively smaller, suitable officers to sit as members on military courts became harder to find.

As a result, British naval authorities actually discouraged further naval-related war crimes trials. After another petition from Zippel, Douglas remitted three years from Ruckteschell's sentence on 30 August 1947.[66] Individuals convicted of war crimes served various terms of imprisonment within the British Zone. Ruckteschell's was the last war crimes trial held under the Royal Warrant on behalf of the Royal Navy.[67] Grossadmiral Erich Raeder and Grossadmiral Karl Dönitz, on the other hand, were prosecuted with other leaders of the Third Reich.

The decision to try major war criminals resulted from intricate Allied deliberations. Churchill originally advocated summary execution of a select number of Nazi leaders from a Foreign Office compiled list, which included Keitel as the only military figure. Although the Cabinet backed the idea, opposition came from an unexpected quarter. Stalin firmly insisted on judicial proceedings against major war criminals. This demand did not arise from Soviet regard for due process or legal niceties. As the various purge trials of the late 1930s demonstrated, Soviet law generally considered defendants guilty until proven guilty.[68] A post-war trial instead represented an opportunity to expose the full extent of Nazi barbarity to the Soviet people and the world. As Waldock advised Alexander, the Americans also seemed 'squeamish about a mere decision to execute.'[69] During discussions with the Lord Chancellor in London, American representatives became increasingly convinced of the need for some sort of judicial proceedings. Listening to his advisers, Truman supported a legal trial of major war criminals.[70] The Americans presented definite proposals for prosecution of war crimes at the San Francisco Conference in early May 1945.

Gauging which way the political winds were blowing, the Admiralty anticipated eventual trial of the *Kriegsmarine*'s wartime leaders. Waldock instructed Burrough to detain Raeder and Dönitz 'until the question of their complicity in war crimes has been fully investigated', adding that the latter's 'succession to Hitler plainly may affect the attitude of Allied Governments towards him as a potential war criminal.'[71] Dönitz's position as the last political leader of the Third Reich played a significant part. Despite doubts within the Foreign Office and the Admiralty, the Americans placed Dönitz on a preliminary list of major war criminals prior to a legal conference in London to draft a charter for a proposed international tribunal.[72]

The British preference for summary executions disappeared when Attlee replaced Churchill at Potsdam. The Labour Party and the new Prime Minister strongly advocated judicial trial and inclusion of Germany's top military and naval officers among the accused.[73] By the end of the conference, Stalin, Attlee, and Truman agreed to establish an International Military Tribunal. The Admiralty supported Raeder's prosecution, but advised against charging Dönitz because existing evidence appeared insufficient to convict.[74] The Americans, however, considered differently. In London, Justice Robert Jackson insisted on Dönitz's indictment solely as Hitler's political successor.[75] Major-General I.T. Nikitchenko, the Soviet representative at the London Conference, forwarded Raeder's name on 28 August 1945. As one of only two likely candidates in Soviet captivity, Raeder was the Soviet Union's star war criminal. After consulting with Attlee, Sir Hartley Shawcross, the new Labour Attorney General, accepted both selections.

With the decision now made at the higher political level to arraign the *Kriegsmarine*'s leaders, the Admiralty assisted in the prosecution's preparations. The British War Crimes Executive wanted 'instances of things done – even if we cannot establish any direct proof that they were done by order of the German Admiralty – which were major in themselves and, in character, shocking – shocking to the conscience of the world.'[76] In court, impressions were important. Although a strong case could be made against Raeder for involvement in clandestine rearmament and planning wars of aggression against Poland and Norway, Dönitz held a subordinate operational command until his appointment as commander-in-chief in early 1943. This fact presented a problem. Mossop doubted whether a charge concerning the alleged order to kill shipwrecked sailors 'would succeed against them, and suggests that it would be unwise to muddy the waters by adding it to their indictment.'[77] The evidence was incomplete and open to interpretation. Waldock, however, adopted a different view towards Dönitz's responsibility:

> The instructions to U-boats are, on the face of them, highly improper. Apart altogether from the question whether they amount to an instruction to murder survivors, they plainly disregard a basic principle of humanitarian warfare which has long been part of the canon law of the sea. There is every justification for refusing to stop and pick up survivors when to do so would endanger the safety of the ship. I am quite sure that if I had been drafting Doenitz's instructions after the LACONIA incident, I would have stated plainly that the ground of the instructions was undue risk to U-boats. Doenitz, on the contrary, states the reason to be that to rescue survivors conflicts with the rudimentary demand of warfare to destroy them, and orders Commanding Officers to overcome humanitarian scruples by recalling bombing of German women and children; not a word about safety of U-boats.[78]

At the very least, Waldock felt that Dönitz should answer in court for the ambiguous order. Even so, the Admiralty hoped to focus on broader collusion with Nazi aggression rather than the legal technicalities of naval warfare. Waldock considered the tribunal's charter so generally drawn that he personally could not 'see how any of the persons can escape conviction.' In tandem, Raeder was the planner and Dönitz was the executor of aggressive naval war. Actual atrocities at sea simply compounded the illegality.

Dönitz and Raeder faced three principal charges under the International Military Tribunal's four-part indictment. Each allegedly conspired to prepare and plan wars of aggression, participated in wars of aggression in violation of international treaties, agreements, and assurances, and took part in specific war crimes in the naval sphere. Although the last resembled more closely the traditional definition of war crimes, the International Military Tribunal introduced certain innovations under international law in regard to the first two. The charges focused specifically on the culpability of higher political and military authorities in Nazi Germany for starting the war.[80] To this end, the process incorporated the established Anglo-American concept of conspiracy, expected compliance with pre-war international treaties, and retroactively extended certain laws to previous crimes. The International Military Tribunal constituted a hybrid political-legal trial, based upon a remarkable moral consensus among the victorious Allied countries immediately after the war against Nazi Germany.

The International Military Tribunal formally opened in the main court room of the Bavarian Central Courts of Justice in Nuremberg on 20 November 1945. In the absence of Montgomery and Alexander, Burrough represented the British occupation forces and the Admiralty on the first day.[81] Over the next eleven months, twenty-two defendants appeared before four judges and four alternates from France, Great Britain, the United States, and the Soviet Union.

The trial represented a major public event. Besides those employed in some connection with the trial, Royal Navy personnel in occupied Germany received passes to attend proceedings as spectators.[82] The trial was a chance to witness history in the making. A former Wren, stationed in Minden, remembered vividly the opportunity to see the former leaders of the Third Reich, 'all lined up in the dock like cartoon figures suddenly springing to life.'[83] Many were familiar villains from British wartime news and propaganda. Through text and cartoons in a letter to his young son, Sub-Lieutenant Lancelot Harris, RNVR, juxtaposed Raeder and Dönitz with the British judges, Sir Geoffrey Lawrence and Norman Birkett.[84] The best minds in the British legal system exposed the tyranny and worst excesses of the Nazi regime.

Raeder and Dönitz were key participants at the highest levels of the Third Reich. At Belsen, Commodore England had seen 'with my own eyes the extent of the cruelties which can be perpetrated by Germans.'[85] Claims by the German naval leadership to know nothing of these ghastly crimes certainly rang empty and false. Although considering the adoption of unrestricted submarine warfare as inevitable in modern war, an American naval officer at the trial remarked:

> Just as the student of naval affairs can scarcely believe that Dönitz as Flag Officer Submarines worked in an isolated political vacuum, so the student of government can scarcely credit his

statement that as Commander-in-Chief of the Navy he dealt solely with naval affairs. In a nation geared to the third year of total war, the Navy must have drawn to itself so large a share of the national effort that its affairs could not be isolated from the political whole.[86]

The purpose of the International Military Tribunal was to determine the extent of this association with the Nazis. Public opinion in the Allied countries demanded that the exercise take place.

The prosecution began argument against Dönitz on 14 January 1946. British counsel assumed the task because of Great Britain's obvious interest as the principal European naval power. Colonel Sir Henry Joseline Phillimore, the Continental Secretary of the British War Crimes Executive, described how Dönitz forged the *Kriegsmarine*'s submarine arm into an instrument of aggressive war with increasing ruthlessness against Allied shipping contrary to the 1936 Submarine Protocol, read incriminating passages from the admiral's own political speeches calling for a closer relationship with Nazism, presented evidence of widespread use of forced labour in ship construction, and attempted to draw a straight line between Dönitz and the *Peleus* killings.[87] Two witnesses, Moehle and Oberleutnant Josef Heisig, connected Dönitz with the alleged order to kill shipwrecked survivors. In summation, Phillimore described Dönitz as 'no plain sailor, playing the part of a service officer, loyally obedient to the orders of the government of the day; he was an extreme Nazi who did his utmost to indoctrinate the Navy and the German people with the Nazi creed.'[88] In keeping with the Admiralty's earlier advice, the prosecutors attempted to focus on generalities and political complicity. As reflected in the speech extracts read by Phillimore, Dönitz possessed a clear antipathy towards Jews.[89] Sharing the same attitudes and prejudices, the German admiral was a Nazi in all but name. The image was strong and persuasive.

In his defence, Dönitz focused on the naval side of the indictment. He chose Flottenrichter Otto Kranzbühler, a bright, young lawyer in Rudolphi's legal branch, as chief defence counsel.[90] German lawyers held their own views in regard to military necessity and the degree of latitude allowed an inferior navy. Admiralrichter Dr. Kurt Eckhardt contended that Germany's U-boat war was legally based upon the *Kriegsmarine*'s declaration of operational zones.[91] Differences in opinion existed between Great Britain and its continental neighbours in the interpretation of international law. The Germans especially resented the overriding British influence in the development of sea law over the past two centuries.[92] The area was in obvious need of redress after a German victory. Earlier in the war, the OKW established a committee, chaired by

Admiral Walter Gladisch, to consider rewriting the laws of war to reflect more strongly German interests.[93] Naval warfare received special attention. Although Nazi Germany's turn in fortunes frustrated the planned revisions, naval lawyers still emphasized the distinction between the German concept of the state's obligations under international law and the Anglo-Saxon interpretation of the individual's responsibility.[94] According to the former view, the *Kriegsmarine*'s leaders could not be held personally responsible for command decisions. During a subsequent interrogation by British officers, Dönitz 'launched into a passionate tirade on the inequity of his being considered a war criminal since he had never, throughout the war, done more than his duty as a naval officer and considered that the German Navy, at any rate, had fought a clean war.'[95]

Kranzbühler prepared to justify Dönitz and German submarine warfare on this basis. Phillimore requested the presence of Waldock or Mossop at Nuremberg during the defence 'as it looks very much as though they intend to fight us all along the line, including the "sink at sight" policy, although, as you know, we in no way emphasized this.'[96] A tribunal ruling required the Admiralty to provide access for Dönitz's defence lawyers to the captured German naval records. Fregattenkapitän Hans Meckel, Kranzbühler's assistant, travelled to London to examine relevant documents and war diaries. Although furnishing relevant extracts from the British 1938 *Defence of Merchant Shipping Handbook*, the Admiralty stoutly refused Kranzbühler's requests for confidential British fleet orders.[97] The potential for mischief was too high. The Admiralty feared that Kranzbühler might try to turn the case around into an attack on British policy during the war.[98] Dönitz, not the Royal Navy, was on trial at Nuremberg.

Defence submissions on Dönitz's behalf started on 7 May. Still in uniform, Kranzbühler showed himself as one of the most capable and articulate defence counsels during the entire trial.[99] As expected, he concentrated on German conduct at sea with expert testimony and documentation. Defence witnesses included Eckhardt, Wagner, Hessler, and Godt.[100] According to these officers, Germany's gradual implementation of unrestricted submarine warfare was in response to the British arming of merchant ships and integration of these ships into the overall Allied defence network. German captains attacked without warning for reasons of military necessity and self-preservation.[101] Submarines which followed existing rules of search and seizure only risked destruction. Taking the stand, Dönitz explained the inherent ruthlessness of modern economic warfare and his intended meaning behind the Laconia Order.[102] According to him, the latter involved a prohibition on rescue rather than destruction of shipwrecked survivors.

By far the biggest coup for Dönitz's defence was Kranzbühler's introduction of an affidavit from Fleet Admiral Chester Nimitz, USN, stating that the US Navy had adopted unrestricted submarine warfare against Japan immediately after the attack on Pearl Harbor.[103] The Allied navies pursued the same policy during the war for which Dönitz was now on trial.

Explanations from Dönitz about his political involvement – what the trial was really all about – were less effective. Commander Malcolm George Saunders, RN, the Director of Naval Intelligence's representative at Nuremberg, noted that plenty of evidence existed to show that Dönitz was an ardent supporter of the Nazi political system.[104] Utterances about the 'poison of Bolshevik Jewry' and Hitler as the 'only statesman of stature in Europe' certainly did not endear him to members of the court. In response to a question from Kranzbühler, Dönitz admitted to wearing the Nazi Golden Party Emblem from 30 January 1944.[105] He was noticeably vague about his relationship with Hitler and the Nazi bureaucracy. During cross-examination by Sir David Maxwell-Fyfe, the chief British prosecutor, Dönitz awkwardly answered questions about the *Kriegsmarine*'s use of slave labour in shipbuilding, his personal knowledge concerning concentration camps, and circulation of terror orders against sabotage in Denmark.[106]

The performance made a negative impression on the court and spectators alike. Joan Tutte, Shawcross' secretary, found Dönitz's 'answers most unconvincing.'[107] Indeed, Waldock remarked that the testimony almost guaranteed the grand admiral's conviction. Dönitz never fully grasped the true nature of the proceedings taking place at Nuremberg.[108] By an almost exclusive concentration on naval matters, his defence was weak on the political side, the more important of the two. In a closing statement on 15 July Kranzbühler asked the judges to apply 'the same standards, where the military appreciation and moral justification of the actions of these Germans is concerned, as the Tribunal would apply to admirals of their own countries.'[109] The impassioned plea worked to Dönitz's detriment. The tribunal judged the *Kriegsmarine*'s leaders by the same standards in the political sphere, and found them wanting.

The British prosecution encountered less trouble in presenting its case against Raeder. Major Frederick Elwyn-Jones, a Deputy Judge Advocate and Labour member of parliament for the constituency of Plaistow in East London, argued that Raeder 'more than anyone else, was responsible for transferring the loyalty of the German Navy to the Nazi Party, in whose main councils he was an active participant.'[110] The former naval leader oversaw rearmament in defiance of the Treaty of Versailles, welcomed the Nazi seizure of power, and helped plan the invasions of Poland and Norway. Under Raeder, the *Kriegsmarine* became 'an instrument of war to implement the Nazis' general plan of aggression.'[111] To support these contentions, Elwyn-Jones introduced a range of documentary material from the captured Tambach records. The most damning evidence as regards specific war crimes was Raeder's circulation of the Commando Order, which as stated previously, led to summary execution of Royal Marines at Bordeaux harbour on 10 December 1942.[112] The British prosecution forcefully showed that Raeder committed criminal acts under the terms of the International Military Tribunal's indictment.

Dr. Walter Siemer, a Hamburg civil attorney, countered these allegations. On the stand, Raeder explained the circumstances behind various naval decisions until his resignation as the *Kriegsmarine*'s commander-in-chief in January 1943. Cross examinations by Maxwell-Fyfe and Colonel Y.V. Pokrovsky, the Soviet deputy chief prosecutor, clarified particular details and events. Siemer called various witnesses on Raeder's behalf: Karl Severing, a former Social Democratic Minister of the Interior; Ernst von Weizsächer, previously Secretary of State in the German Foreign Office; and Vizeadmiral Erich Schulte-Mönting, Raeder's chief of staff between 1939 and 1943. The defence's questions were long and meandering. Birkett grew tired of Siemer going 'on endlessly, repeating himself over and over again.'[113] Overall, the lawyer failed to disassociate Raeder from Nazi-inspired aggression and war crimes. Moreover, written statements from Raeder's captivity in Moscow, introduced into evidence by Pokrovsky, described Dönitz's strong political inclinations and his alleged nickname – 'Hitler Youth Dönitz' – within the *Kriegsmarine*.[114] Raeder dragged down Dönitz as well. In spite of all Kranzbühler's hard work on the naval sphere, the political side haunted the two naval leaders. In the end, Raeder still appeared an active participant at both the political and military levels in the Nazi conspiracy to wage wars of aggression and to wage them ruthlessly.

The International Military Tribunal delivered its findings and verdicts on 1 October 1946. Dönitz, who the court found guilty of waging aggressive war and prohibiting rescue under the submarine protocol, received ten years' imprisonment.[115] The tribunal decided not to hold him accountable for the sinking of British armed merchant ships and the alleged murder order. As subsequent international lawyers have remarked, the judgment against Dönitz was rather vague on precise details.[116] Raeder, on the other hand, was found guilty on all three counts, and received life imprisonment. The verdicts and sentences astounded the two naval leaders. After hearing the tribunal's decision, Dönitz loudly smashed his headphones down on a court room table. For him, the judgment appeared a clear example of victor's justice.

Whatever one's particular views towards the process, it must be admitted that the *Kriegsmarine*'s leaders fared not badly under the International Military Tribunal. Outright acquittals for Raeder and Dönitz were never seriously considered by the majority of judges. During closed session, Nikitchenko, the Soviet chief judge, demanded death for both admirals. Indeed, their military counterparts, Keitel and Jodl, were hanged after conviction at Nuremberg.[117] Victor's justice was harsh, but appropriate for the magnitude of the crimes and the general mood of condemnation after the war against Nazi Germany's activities. Although the American chief judge, Francis Biddle, argued for Dönitz's full acquittal, the British and French judges demanded conviction on the last two counts, excluding the order to kill survivors.[118] Ironically, the Americans, who had forwarded Dönitz in the first place, were now unsure about convicting him as a war criminal. After the testimony at Nuremberg, the British felt no such pangs of conscience. The *Kriegsmarine* had clearly waged a ruthless war of aggression against Great Britain. The terms of imprisonment reflected a compromise among the Allied judges to find Dönitz and Raeder guilty primarily upon their political involvement with the Nazi regime.[119] The former naval leaders served their sentences at Spandau prison in divided Berlin.

The Royal Navy and British authorities received various appeals for the release of Raeder and Dönitz. In a petition addressed to the new First Sea Lord, Admiral Sir John Cunningham, admirals in Camp 2226 claimed that 'the German Navy as a whole conducted the war at sea in a fair and humane spirit and in accordance with the principles common to the sailors of all nations.'[120] Defence counsel tried to encourage the notion that the convictions of Raeder and Dönitz reflected badly on all members of the former *Kriegsmarine*. British naval authorities considered Kranzbühler's distribution of the defence's closing argument within the GM/SA to be 'reprehensible and the facts are submitted to the President of the Tribunal for such action as he may consider necessary.'[121] Even uncoached, many sailors still felt ties of loyalty and allegiance towards Raeder and Dönitz. A petition, signed by 257 officers in a POW camp in Northumberland, asked King George VI to intervene in mitigating the sentences, 'as the Sovereign of the country holding them in custody and at the same time, in Your capacity as the Senior Admiral of the Fleet of the Royal Navy.'[122] Former colleagues and friends gave the strongest support. Kranzbühler sent Walker a petition from eleven former German admirals on Raeder's behalf – incorrectly addressed to Andrew Cunningham as First Sea Lord – and a corresponding petition from twenty-two U-boat officers for Dönitz.[123] The chiefs of the American and French navies received similar appeals. Although forwarded to the British Military Governor, the petitions were rejected outright because only the Allied Control Authority possessed authority to consider pleas for clemency.

The British upheld the verdicts against Raeder and Dönitz. Responsibility for confirmation of the Nuremberg sentences belonged to the Allied zonal commanders-in-chief in occupied Germany. In regards to the petition from Camp 2226, Douglas declared that the conduct of the U-boat war was certainly not in accordance with the principles of humanity and fairness.[124] The British government, armed forces, and general public instead associated Raeder and Dönitz with ruthlessness and perfidy. These men caused the enormous loss of British lives in the Atlantic and on the world's oceans. A sympathetic editorial letter by Andrew Cunningham drew strong censure from the Admiralty.[125] Indeed, support for the German admirals was scarce within the Royal Navy. With a few exceptions, professional British naval officers were notably absent from the many letters of commiseration sent to Dönitz during and after his captivity.[126] The Royal Navy had experienced at first-hand the attacks and methods of the U-boats. Familiarity bred contempt. Although many American naval officers voiced opposition towards the verdicts against Dönitz and Raeder, the Admiralty was silent.[127] The punishment appeared appropriate from London. The British government advised Douglas 'that from a political point of view it would be an advantage if there were no alterations in the sentences.'[128] Douglas naturally took exception to this interference with his legal authority. In a melodramatic gesture, Raeder asked that a death sentence be substituted for his term of life imprisonment. Douglas and his colleagues, however, rejected appeals for Raeder and Dönitz, and confirmed the original sentences.[129]

Cynically, one can see the Royal Navy's interest in war crimes trials as a specific means to embarrass and weaken the German navy. The presence of Raeder and Dönitz in Spandau certainly endured as a black mark beside the *Kriegsmarine*.[130] Nevertheless, the images of sailors fired upon in lifeboats or summarily executed after capture in uniform also troubled the Admiralty. There was something wrong here. German actions went beyond the accepted means and sanctions of combat. War became an excuse for murder. The Royal Navy and the British government genuinely believed that clear violations against the laws and customs of warfare and complicity with the Nazi regime required punishment. As Lawrence stated after Nuremberg, the war crimes trials brought 'home to Germany and the world that a nation cannot with impunity resort to total warfare in defiance of International Law and the laws of war which have been recognized as part of International Law since the middle ages.'[131] The desire for legal redress was an understandable reaction to the horrors and excesses of a ruthless, ideological war.

NOTES

1. A. Pearce Higgins and C. John Colombos, *The International Law of the Sea*, (London: Longmans, Green & Co., 1943), p. 324. The protocol specified that a submarine first had to ensure the safety of passengers, crew, and ship's papers before any sinking. Natolini Ronzitti, ed., *The Law of Naval Warfare: A Collection of Agreements and Documents with Commentaries*, (Dordrecht: Martinus Nijhoff, 1988), p. 352. Wolff Heintschel von Heinegg, 'Visit, Search, Diversion, and Capture in Naval Warfare: Part I, The Traditional Law', *Canadian Yearbook of International Law* 29(1991), pp. 308–9.

2. PRO, ADM 116/5547, Staff Minute by C.H.M. Waldock, 19 Oct. 1943. OAB/NHC, German Naval Archives, Box T-105, File 1, NID 24/T164/45, 'Memorandum (15 Oct. 1939) sent by Raeder to Hitler on Intensification of U-Boat Warfare', 27 Sept. 1945.

3. PRO, ADM 116/5547, Letter from C.H.M Waldock to P.H.B. Kent, Treasury Solictor's Office, 28 Oct. 1943.

4. PRO, WO 311/616, Letter from J.C. Mossop to Lieutenant-Colonel V.A.R. Isham, 17 June 1945.

5. IWM, Ackroyd, Letter 12, Clare Baines (Boulter) to M.W. Ackroyd, 7 Nov. 1988. NA, RG 242, T-1022, Reel 4188, File PG 30027, U-30 Kriegstagebuch, 3 Sept. 1939. Although the British shot and killed Lemp in the water as he attempted to re-board U-110 on 9 May 1941, the Admiralty confirmed the *Athenia*'s sinking with former members of U-30's crew, who were prisoners of war in Canadian captivity at Lethbridge, Alberta. PRO, ADM 116/5548, Memorandum from Captain E.S. Brand, RCN, Director of Naval Intelligence and Trade, Ottawa to Director of Naval Intelligence, 'Sinking of the Athenia', 10 Aug. 1945. NAC, RG 24, Reel C-5415, Letter from Major-General A.E. Walford to Military District 13, 27 Aug. 1945.

6. PRO, ADM 1/18500, Staff Minute by J.C. Mossop, 30 Sept. 1945. C.H.M. Waldock, 'The Release of the Altmark's Prisoners', *British Yearbook of International Law* 24(1947), p. 219. Martin Gilbert, ed., *The Churchill War Papers: At the Admiralty*, Vol. 1, (New York: W.W. Norton, 1993), p. 775.

7. OAB/NHC, German Naval Archives, Box T-77, NID 24/T18/45, 'The Sinking of the *Sheaf Mead*', July 1945.

8. PRO, TS 26/150, Letter from J.C. Mossop to R.A. Beaumont, Foreign Office, 16 Dec. 1945. NA, RG 242, T-1022, Reel 3068, File PG 30554, U-516 Kriegstagebuch, 28 Sept. 1942. OAB/NHC, German Naval Archives, Box T-77, NID 24/T26/45, 'Sinking of Brazilian Vessel *Antonica* by Enemy Submarine 28 September 1942'. The *Kriegsmarine* claimed that British destroyers had fired upon sailors in the water during sea battles near Narvik in April 1940. 'Kommodore Bonte und seine Zerstörer', Germany *Die Kriegsmarine: Deutsche Marine Zeitung*, Vol. 1, (Hamburg: Verlag für geschichtliche Dokumentation GmbH, 1978), pp. 84–8. Alfred M. De Zayas, *The Wehrmacht War Crimes Bureau, 1939–1945*, (Lincoln: University of Nebraska, 1989), pp. 246–51. The Royal Navy's fighting instructions for destroyers are in ADM 234/132.

9. PRO, ADM 116/5547, Staff Minute by Captain Alfred C. Dewar, 11 Feb. 1944. In 1921 German courts at Leipzig tried German submariners for alleged atrocities connected with the sinking of the British hospital ships *Llandovery Castle* and *Dover Castle*. W.J. Fenrick, 'Legal Aspects of Targeting in the Law of Naval Warfare', *Canadian Yearbook of International Law* 29(1991), pp. 247–8. The British record in World War I was only slightly better. Alan Coles, *Slaughter at Sea: The Truth Behind a Naval War Crime*, (London: R. Hale, 1986). E.G. Trimble, 'Violations of Maritime Law by the Allied Powers during the World War', *American Journal of International Law* 24(1930), pp. 79–99.

10. Omer Bartov, *The Eastern Front, 1941–1945: German Troops and the Barbarisation of Warfare*, (Basingstoke, Hampshire: Macmillan, 1985), pp. 106–29. Mark Mazower, 'Military Violence and National Socialist Values: The Wehrmacht in Greece 1941–1944', *Past and Present* 134 (1992), p. 132. Detlev F. Vagts, 'International Law in the Third Reich', *American Journal of International Law* 84(1990), p. 696.

11. Robert M. Langdon, 'Live Men Do Tell Tales', *United States Naval Institute Proceedings* 78 (Jan. 1952), p. 18.

12. PRO, ADM 116/5547, Staff Minute by C.H.M. Waldock, 14 Dec. 1943. OAB/NHC, German Naval Archives, Box T-80, NID 24/T201/45, 'Order for the Ruthless Shooting of Commandos by Hitler, dated 18.10.1942', 11 Oct. 1945.

13. PRO, ADM 116/5548, Message from British Admiralty Delegation Washington to Admiralty, 17 1951Z May 1944.

14. BL, Cunningham, Add. Ms. 52577, Diary, 30 May 1944. OAB/NHC, German Naval Archives, Box T-107, File 5, OP-16-FA-4, 'German Naval Personnel involved in Violations of International Law', 4 May 1945.

15. United Nations War Crimes Commission, *History of the United Nations War Crimes Commission and the Development of the Laws of War*, (London: His Majesty's Stationery Office, 1948), pp. 120–4. Arieh J. Kochavi, 'Britain and the Establishment of the United Nations War Crimes Commission', *English Historical Review* 107(1992), p. 346.

16. PRO, ADM 116/5547, Memorandum from C.H.M. Waldock to Albert V. Alexander, 20 Nov. 1944.

17. Great Britain, *Manual of Military Law*, 7th edition, (London: His Majesty's Stationery Office, 1929), Amendment No. 12 (Jan. 1936), p. 84. The amendment, which took into account the new provisions of the 1929 Geneva Convention, superseded the outdated 1914 explication of the laws and usages of war in the published 1929 version.

18. PRO, WO 331/23, Royal Warrant/Army Order 81/1945, 'Regulations for the Trial of War Criminals', 18 June 1945. A.P.V. Rogers, 'War Crimes Trials under the Royal Warrant: British Practice 1945–1949', *International and Comparative Law Quarterly* 39 (1990), p. 789.

19. Walter Hasche, 'Britische Besatzungsgerichtsbarkeit in Hamburg 1945–48', *Archiv des Völkerrechts* 26(1988), p. 92. PRO, WO 311/646, Report from Deputy Assistant Legal Services to Adjutant General, 'War Crimes in Europe and the Far East', 23 Nov. 1948.

20. PRO, WO 311/219, Letter from Sir Thomas Barnes, Treasury Solicitor to Brigadier H. Shapcott, Military Deputy, Judge Advocate General, 23 Aug. 1945.

21. PRO, TS 26/177, United Nations War Crimes Commission Charge Sheet No. UK-G/A2, 'Eck'. 'U-Boat Crew Tried for Murder: Slaughter of Helpless Seamen', *The Times* (18 Oct. 1945), p. 3.

22. PRO, WO 311/616, Letter from R.D.J. Scott-Fox to Monsieur Jean A. Romanos, Greek Embassy, 24 Sept. 1945.

23. John Cameron, ed., *Trial of Heinz Eck, August Hoffmann, Walter Weisspfennig, Hans Richard Lenz and Wolfgang Schwender (The Peleus Trial)*, (London: William Hodge & Co., 1948), p. 55. See also WO 235/5.

24. PRO, ADM 228/56, Memorandum from Lieutenant-Commander Ralph W.B. Izzard to Captain J.H. Lewes, 'Situation Report of Conditions in the British Zone', 30 Oct. 1945.

25. PRO, WO 235/604, Petition from Konteradmiral Fritz Krauss to Field Marshal Bernard Montgomery, 'Kapitänleutnant Eck', 21 Oct. 1945.

26. 'U-Boat Men Sentenced: Appeal Lodged', *The Times* (22 Oct. 1945), p. 3.

27. PRO, WO 311/219, Message from EXFOR to TROOPERS, 10 1850A Nov. 1945.

28. PRO, ADM 116/5548, Letter from Colonel H.J. Phillimore, British War Crimes Executive to J.C. Mossop, 22 Nov. 1945.

29. PRO, WO 235/5, Message from EXFOR to Control Commission Germany (Legal Division, Penal Section); Judge Advocate General; CROWCRASS, 01 1815A Dec. 1945.

30. BA/MA, RW 44/I/55, Memorandum from Admiral zbV ObdM to OKM; 2/SKL BdU(Ops), 28 April 1945.

31. PRO, WO 311/272, Staff Officer Security to Flag Officer Schleswig-Holstein, 'Report on the Preliminary Investigation of the Case against Korvettenkapitän Moehle', 13 June 1945.

32. PRO, WO 311/272, 'Interrogation of K.K. Moehle, 5th U-Flotilla', 17 July 1945. Léonce Peillard, *The Laconia Affair*, (New York: Bantam, 1963), p. 158. OAB/NHC, German Naval Archives, Box T-77, NID 24/T27/45, 'Report on Korvettenkapitän Moehle with Reference to Orders alleged to have been given to the 5th U-Boat Flotilla', 20 July 1945.

33. PRO, ADM 116/5548, Memorandum from Director of Naval Intelligence to J.C. Mossop, 21 Aug. 1945.

34. PRO, WO 311/272, Letter from C.H.M. Waldock to Colonel R.C. Halse, 7 Nov. 1945.
35. PRO, WO 311/615, Message from War Office to British War Crimes Executive (E) Nuremberg, 20 1730 Nov. 1945.
36. PRO, WO 235/209, Petition from Dr. Otto Zippel, 28 Oct. 1946.
37. PRO, WO 235/209, 'Proceedings of a Military Court held at Hamburg on 15 and 16 October 1946 for the trial of Karl-Heinz Moehle, a German National in the charge of 98 Group, Pioneer Corps'.
38. Moehle remained alienated from the former German naval officer corps after his eventual release from prison. Reviewing an essay written by Moehle, Godt wrote: 'A judgment as to the value of his [Moehle's] personality is not given; it was and still is a debated subject among older and younger submarine officers.' OAB/NHC, German Naval Archives, Box T-66, Konteradmiral Eberhard Godt, 'Critical Review of *Die Unterseebootswaffe im Dritten Weltkrieg* by Korv. Kapt a.D. Karl-Heinz Moehle', 27 Nov. 1950.
39. PRO, WO 235/69, Letter from Major T.G. Coverdale, Private Secretary, UK High Commissioner to Brigadier Lord Russell of Liverpool, Deputy Judge Advocate General, HQ BAOR, 5 Nov. 1949.
40. PRO, WO 311/67, Message from Admiralty to British Naval Commander-in-Chief Germany, 05 0035A Sept. 1945.
41. PRO, ADM 1/18344, Letter from Colonel R.C. Halse to G.C.B. Dodds, Military Branch, 20 Feb. 1946.
42. PRO, WO 331/15, Statement by Korvettenkapitän Egon Drascher to Major R.H. Bryant, RA, 15 Aug. 1945.
43. PRO, WO 311/384, Letter from J.C. Mossop to Senior British Naval Officer Norway, 6 Nov. 1945. Waldock previously told the Foreign Office that he was glad 'to know that all possible steps were being taken to bring the culprits to justice.' PRO, TS 26/150, Letter from C.H.M. Waldock to Patrick Dean, Foreign Office, 3 May 1945.
44. PRO, TS 126/162, United Nations War Crimes Commission Charge No. UK – G/350, 'MTB 345'.
45. PRO, WO 235/30, 'Proceedings of a Military Court held at the Law Courts, Oslo, Norway on Thursday, 29 November, 1945 upon the Trial of Obersturmbannführer Hans Wilhelm Blomberg, Obersturmbannführer Hans Keller, Obersturmbannführer Georg Ludwig Werner Oppel, Untersturmführer Alfred Kreutz, Untersturmführer Erwin Lang, Rudolf Hermann Theodor Kapp, Willi Friedrich Reinhold Tiege, Oberscharführer Georg Ebert and Hauptscharf Friedrich Wilhelm Eisenacher'.
46. E.H. Stevens, ed., *Trial of Nikolaus von Falkenhorst*, (London: William Hodge & Co., 1949), pp. 240–1. A. Cecil Hampshire, *Undercover Sailors: Secret Operations of World War II*, (London: William Kimber, 1981), pp. 140–1.
47. PRO, ADM 1/16195, Office of Flag Officer Western Germany, 'Report of Proceedings 7 May to 30 June 1945'.
48. IWM, Moyse, Diary, p. 42. In April 1946 the Royal Navy court-martialled Lieutenant-Commander Rupert Philip Lonsdale, RN, and Lieutenant Trevor A. Beet, RN, for surrendering HM Submarine *Seal* to the Germans in May 1940. BL, Cunningham, Add. Ms. 52579, Diary, 12 March 1946. See also PRO, ADM 205/49 and CCAC, ROSK 4/85. C.E.T. Warren and James Benson, *Will Not We Fear: The Story of H.M. Submarine Seal*, (London: White Lion, 1973), pp. 219–25. The Admiralty considered the loss or surrender of British warships a serious matter. IWM, 66/26/1, Constructor Captain A.J. Merrington, RN, CAFO 3700, 'Losses of HM Ships – Investigation', 1940.
49. PRO, WO 235/632, Lieutenant A.J. Hunter-Edelston, RNVR, 'Interrogator's Report of Scuttling of Two German Submarines U1406 and U1407', 30 June 1945.
50. PRO, ADM 228/8, Memorandum from M.F.P. Herchenroder, Legal Advice and Drafting Branch, Legal Division CCG(BE) to SO(I) Executive Section, 12 Oct. 1945.
51. PRO, WO 311/277, Letter from J.C. Mossop to Colonel R.C. Halse, 6 Dec. 1945.
52. PRO, WO 235/64, 'Proceedings of a Military Court for the Trial of War Criminals held at the War Crimes Court, Hamburg, Germany on Tuesday, 12 February 1946 and Wednesday 13 February 1946 upon the Trial of First Lieutenant (Engineer) Gerhard Grumpelt'.

53. PRO, ADM 1/18293, Staff Minute, 18 March 1946.
54. PRO, ADM 1/18293, Report from Lieutenant-Commander M. Meiklejohn, Staff Officer Intelligence, Gibraltar to Director of Naval Intelligence, 'Interrogation of Survivors from U.1277', 19 June 1945.
55. PRO, WO 311/289, United Nations War Crimes Commission, Case No. UK – G/B 510, 'KptLt. Ehrenreich Stever'.
56. PRO, WO 235/127, 'Proceedings of a Military Court held at Hamburg on the 17 and 18 July 1946 for the Trial of Kapitänleutnant Ehrenreich Stever, an officer of the German Navy'.
57. PRO, WO 235/678, Letter from Brigadier H.W.R. William, Deputy Judge Advocate General to Penal Branch, Legal Division 'Ehrenreich Stever', 16 Oct. 1947.
58. PRO, WO 235/64, Certificate of Remittal by Air Marshal Sholto Douglas, 18 June 1947.
59. PRO, ADM 116/5547, Staff Minute by J.C. Mossop, 16 Nov. 1943.
60. OAB/NHC, German Naval Archives, Box T-77, NID 24 'Ship 21', 30 June 1945.
61. PRO, TS 26/150, Message from Admiralty to Commander-in-Chief British Pacific Fleet; Commander-in-Chief East Indies, 03 2113A Nov. 1945.
62. PRO, TS 26/176, United Nations War Crimes Commission Charge Sheet, No. UK – G/A1, 'Schiff 21'.
63. PRO, WO 235/364, 'Proceedings of a Military Court held at No. 1 War Crimes Court, Curiohaus Rothenbaumchausse, Hamburg on Monday, 19 May 1947, Tuesday, 20 May 1947, Wednesday, 21 May 1947 for the Trial of Hellmuth von Ruckteschell, a German national in the charge of No. 98 Group, Royal Pioneer Corps', Twelfth Day, p. 17.
64. PRO, WO 235/364 Part 3, Petition from Dr. Otto Zippel to General Officer Commander-in-Chief, British Zone, 2 June 1946.
65. PRO, WO 311/191, Letter from Flag Officer Commanding British Naval Forces Germany to Major-General W.H. Stratton, Chief of Staff HQ BAOR, 2 June 1947.
66. PRO, WO 235/723, Memorandum from Brigadier H.S. Brant to General Officer Commander-in-Chief, BAOR, 22 Aug. 1947.
67. The British Military Governor announced that 1 September 1948 was the last date to try war crimes under the Royal Warrant, except those involving murder. Anthony Glees, 'War Crimes: The Security and Intelligence Dimension', *Intelligence and National Security* 7(1992), p. 254.
68. Mira Traynina, 'A.N. Traynin: A Legal Scholar under Tsar and Soviets', *Soviet Jewish Affairs* 13(1983), pp. 50–1.
69. PRO, ADM 116/5547, Memorandum from C.H.M. Waldock to A.V. Alexander, 12 April 1945.
70. Bradley F. Smith, *The Road to Nuremberg*, (New York: Basic Books, 1981), p. 207.
71. PRO, TS 26/150, Directive from C.H.M. Waldock to Admiral Harold Burrough, 2 May 1945.
72. United States, Department of State, *Report of Robert H. Jackson, United States Representative to the International Conference on Military Trials: London 1945*, (Washington, DC: Government Printing Office, 1949).
73. Denis Nowell Pritt, *War Criminals*, (London: Labour Monthly, 1944), p. 31. Arieh J. Kochavi, 'The Moscow Declaration, the Kharkov Trial, and the Question of a Policy on Major War Criminals in the Second World War', *History* 76(1991), p. 409.
74. PRO, ADM 116/5548, Letter from C.H.M. Waldock to Patrick Dean, Foreign Office, 18 Aug. 1945. Robert E. Conot, *Justice at Nuremberg*, (New York: Harper & Row, 1983), pp. 412–13.
75. Telford Taylor, *The Anatomy of the Nuremberg Trials: A Personal Memoir*, (New York: Alfred A. Knopf, 1992), p. 90.
76. PRO, ADM 116/5548, Letter from R.A. Clyde, British War Crimes Executive to Lieutenant-Colonel V.A.R. Isham, War Office, 12 June 1945.
77. PRO, ADM 116/5548, Staff Minute by J.C. Mossop for Head Military Branch, 5 Sept. 1945.
78. PRO, ADM 116/5548, Staff Minute by C.H.M Waldock, 19 Oct. 1945.
79. PRO, ADM 116/5548, Letter from Albert Alexander to Sir Hartley Shawcross, 1 Nov.

1945.

80. Hans Laternser, 'Looking Back at the Nuremberg Trials with Special Consideration of the Processes against Military Leaders', *Whittier Law Review* 8(1986), pp. 572–3.

81. PRO, ADM 116/5550, Message from CONCOMB to Sinclair, British War Crimes Executive, 16 1930A Nov. 1945. IWM, P161, Vice-Admiral Edmund Gerhard Noel Rushbrooke, RN, EGR/3, 'War-Crimes Trials Nürnberg Germany Nov 20 1945'. 'Great Nuremberg War Trial Opens', *The Times* (21 Nov. 1945), p. 4.

82. IWM, Parry, Box 6, International Military Tribunal Visitor's Pass No. 1125, 10 May 1946.

83. IWM, Ackroyd, Letter 9, Sybil Welch (Russell), 9 Dec. 1988.

84. IWM, Harris, Box 1, Letter from Sub-Lieutenant Lancelot Harris, RNVR, to his Son, Duigand, 3 April 1946.

85. IWM, Hawkins, Memorandum from Commodore Hugh England to Admiral Harold Burrough, 'Visit to German Concentration Camp 18 April 1945', 24 April 1945.

86. OAB/NHC, German Naval Archives, Box T-105, File 1, Commander Melvin F. Talbot, USN, to Captain R.F. Pryce, USN, 'Report on the Trials of Grand Admirals Erich Raeder and Karl Doenitz before the Military Tribunal Sitting at Nürnberg Germany', 12 July 1946, p. 117.

87. PRO, ADM 116/5549, British Trial Brief, 'Karl Doenitz'.

88. United Nations, *The Trial of German Major War Criminals: Proceedings of the International Military Tribunal sitting at Nuremberg Germany*, Part 4, (London: His Majesty's Stationery Office, 1947), p. 261.

89. Bodo Herzog, 'Der Kriegsverbrecher Karl Dönitz: Legende und Wirklichkeit', *Jahrbuch des Instituts für deutsche Geschichte* 15(1986), p. 482.

90. Otto Kranzbühler, 'Nuremberg: Eighteen Years Afterwards', *De Paul Law Review* 14(1965), p. 333. Numerous naval officers and legal experts assisted in the defence. Salewski, *Seekriegsleitung*, Vol. 2, p. 579.

91. NA, RG 242, T-77, Reel 863, File OKW/21, Memorandum from Admiralrichter Dr. Kurt Eckhardt to Konteradmiral Gerhard Wagner, 'U-Bootkriegsführung', 16 May 1945.

92. PRO, ADM 228/69, Radio Broadcast by Vizeadmiral Friedrich Lützow, 'The Freedom of the Seas', 14 1945 May 1941. See also BA/MA, RW 38/50.

93. BA/MA, RW 2/26, Memorandum from Admiral Walter Gladisch to Generalfeldmarschall Wilhelm Keitel, 'Arbeitsplan für einen Auschuss zur Vorbildung des Kriegsrechts', 3 Dec. 1940. See also NA, RG 242, T-77, Reel 863. Dieter Fleck, ed., *The Gladisch Committee on the Law of Naval Warfare: A German Effort to Develop International Law During World War II*, (Bochum: UVB-Universitätsverlag Dr. N. Brockmeyer, 1990), pp. 6–7. De Zayas, *Wehrmacht War Crimes Bureau*, pp. 122–6.

94. PRO, TS 26/150, Letter from J.C. Mossop to P.H.B. Kent, 9 May 1945.

95. OAB/NHC, German Naval Archives, Box T-66, Grossadmiral Karl Dönitz, 'The Conduct of the War at Sea', 15 Jan. 1946, p. 33.

96. PRO, ADM 116/5549, Letter from Colonel Henry Phillimore to G.C.B. Dodds, 31 Jan. 1946.

97. PRO, ADM 116/5549, Staff Minute by G.C.B. Dodds for Head Military Branch I, 2 March 1946. The handbook, distributed at the outbreak of the war, directed masters of merchant ships to fire upon or ram submarines which followed prize rules. PRO, ADM 234/188, BR 136, 'Defence of Merchant Ships: Masters and Officers Handbook', 1938. Sally V. Mallison and W. Thomas Mallison, 'Naval Targeting: Lawful Objects of Attack', Horace B. Robertson, ed., *International Law Studies 1991: The Law of Naval Operations*, International Law Studies, Vol. 64, (Newport, RI: Naval War College Press, 1991), p. 248.

98. PRO, ADM 116/5549, Staff Minute by G.C.B. Dodds for Head Military Branch I, 17 April 1946. The British prosecutors were sensitive to the Admiralty's concern. Frederick Morgan Maugham, *U.N.O. and War Crimes*, (London: John Murray, 1951), p. 115.

99. Georg Lintz, 'Vom Schiffsdirector zum Admiralstabsrichter: Über die Entwicklung der Laufbahn der Marinerichter', *Zeitschrift für Heereskunde* 46(1982), p. 68. The GM/SA's new uniform regulations required Kranzbühler to wear civilian clothes after 1 June 1946.

PRO, ADM 228/59, Letter from Captain J.H. Lewes for Vice-Admiral Commanding British Naval Forces Germany to Secretary of British Judges, International Military Tribunal Nuremberg, 21 May 1946.

100. PRO, ADM 116/5549, Message from British War Crimes Executive to Admiralty, 09 1400A March 1946.

101. William Thomas Mallison, *Submarines and the Law of Naval Warfare*, International Law Studies 58, (Newport, RI: Naval War College, 1968), p. 107. Bryan Ranft, 'Restraints on War at Sea before 1945', Michael Howard, ed., *Restraints on War: Studies in the Limitation of Armed Conflict*, (London: Oxford University Press, 1979), p. 54.

102. United Nations, *Trial of German Major War Criminals*, Part 13, pp. 236–8.

103. Kurt Assmann, 'Der deutsche U-Bootskrieg und die Nürnberger Rechtsprechung', *Marine Rundschau* 50(1953), pp. 7–8. Richard Dean Burns, 'Regulating Submarine Warfare, 1921–41: A Case Study in Arms Control and Limited War', *Military Affairs* 35(1971), pp. 60–1.

104. PRO, ADM 116/5549, Letter from Commander Malcom Saunders to Meyer, Military Branch I, 25 April 1946. Holger H. Herwig, 'The Failure of German Sea Power, 1914–1945', *International History Review* 10(1988), pp. 102–3.

105. United Nations, *Trial of German Major War Criminals*, Part 13, p. 242.

106. United Nations, *Trial of German Major War Criminals*, Part 13, pp. 257–8, 271–3.

107. Ron Brooks, 'Letters from Nuremberg: A Secretarial Perspective from the Correspondence of Miss Joan Tutte', *The Historian* 16(1987), p. 17.

108. Karl Dönitz, *Deutsche Strategie zur See im Zweiten Weltkrieg: Die Antworten des Grossadmirals auf 40 Fragen*, (Frankfurt am Main: Bernard und Graefe, 1970), pp. 181–4.

109. United Nations, *The Trial of German Major War Criminals*, Part 18, p. 353.

110. PRO, ADM 116/5549, British Trial Brief, 'Erich Raeder'. Lord Elwyn-Jones, *In My Time: An Autobiography*, (London: Weidenfeld & Nicolson, 1983), p. 112.

111. United Nations, *Trial of Major German War Criminals*, Part 4, p. 262.

112. United Nations, *Trial of Major German War Criminals*, Part 4, pp. 275–7.

113. H. Montgomery Hyde, *Norman Birkett: The Life of Lord Birkett of Ulverston*, (London: Hamish Hamilton/The Reprint Society, 1965), p. 518.

114. BA/MA, Grossadmiral Erich Raeder, N 391/3, 'Mein Verhältnis zu Adolf Hitler und zur Partei', p. 23. United Nations, *Trial of German Major War Criminals*, Part 14, p. 234. G.M. Gilbert, *Nuremberg Diary*, (New York : Farrar, Straus, & Co., 1947), p. 346.

115. United Nations, *Judgment of the International Military Tribunal for the Trial of German Major War Criminals Nuremberg*, Cmd. 6964, (London: His Majesty's Stationery Office, 1946), pp. 107–10.

116. H.A. Smith, *The Law and Custom of the Sea*, 3rd edition, (London: Stevens & Sons, 1959), pp. 212–13. Horace B. Robertson, 'Submarine Warfare', *The JAG Navy Journal* 10(1956), pp. 6–8.

117. United Nations *Trial of German Major War Criminals*, Part 22, p. 529. Walter Görlitz, *Generalfeldmarschall Keitel: Verbrecher oder Offizier?* (Göttingen: Musterschmidt-Verlag, 1961), p. 438.

118. Bradley F. Smith, *Reaching Judgment at Nuremberg*, (New York: Basic Books, 1977), pp. 261–2.

119. Taylor, p. 568.

120. BA/MA, Förste, N 328/19, Draft Letter from German Admirals POW Camp 2226 to Admiral Sir John Cunningham, 16 Aug. 1946. Walker felt that no 'useful purpose would be served by sending the document to the First Sea Lord.' PRO, FO 1060/1388, Letter from Vice-Admiral H.T.C. Walker to Commander-in-Chief and Military Governor, British Zone, 'German Senior Officers', 28 Aug. 1946.

121. PRO, ADM 228/64, Message from Vice-Admiral Commanding British Naval Forces, Germany to President, International Military Tribunal, Nuremberg, 30 0105 Aug. 1946.

122. BA/MA, Förste, N 328/20, Letter of Petition from Naval Officers in Camp 18, Haltwhistle/Northumberland to His Most Excellent Majesty George the Sixth, 1 Oct. 1946. Another petition was sent to the International Military Tribunal. Leonard W. Seagren, 'The

Last Fuehrer', *United States Naval Institute Proceedings* 80(1954), pp. 536–7.

123. PRO, ADM 228/64, Message from Vice-Admiral Commanding British Naval Forces Germany to BERCOMB, 12 1220A Oct. 1946.

124. PRO, FO 1060/1388, Letter from Air Marshal Sir Sholto Douglas to Vice-Admiral H.T.C. Walker, 9 Sept. 1946.

125. *Daily Telegraph*, 5 Oct. 1946.

126. H.K. Thompson, Jr. and Henry Strutz, eds., *Doenitz at Nuremberg: A Re-appraisal, War Crimes and the Military Professional*, (New York: Amber Publishing Co., 1976). M.G. Saunders, 'Hitler's Admirals: Reflections inspired by their Memoirs', *Royal United Services Institution Journal* 104(1959), p. 327.

127. William J. Bosch, *Judgment on Nuremberg: American Attitudes toward the Major German War-Crime Trials*, (Chapel Hill: University of North Carolina Press, 1970), p. 168. The US Navy's keen interest in prosecution of Japanese officers for alleged war crimes was an entirely different matter. George E. Erickson, 'United States Navy War Crimes Trials (1945–1949)', *Washburn Law Journal* 5(1965), p. 110.

128. PRO, 1060/1388, Message from John Hynd to Air Marshal Sholto Douglas, 07 2150Z Oct. 1946.

129. Sholto Douglas (with Robert Wright), *Years of Command: The Autobiography of Sholto Douglas, Marshal of the Royal Air Force Lord Douglas of Kirtleside GCB, MC, DFC*, (London: Collins, 1966), p. 343.

130. BA/MA, Wagner, N 539/3, 'Resolution on War Criminals', 14 July 1952.

131. Lord Oaksey, Presidential Address to the Holdsworth Club of the University of Birmingham, 'The Nuremberg Trials and the Progress of International Law', 21 June 1947.

9

Dumping, Demolitions and Dismantling

The Royal Navy's fixation with German naval disarmament transcended the *Kriegsmarine*'s immediate division and disbandment. As an advanced industrial nation, Germany maintained an extensive physical and economic infrastructure to sustain a modern navy. Naval bases, fixed coastal defences, factories, and associated maritime industries were the foundation on which German sea power was built. These components took many years to develop properly, and if left untouched, provided a base to rebuild naval forces relatively quickly. British naval authorities pursued a range of activities within occupied Germany to eliminate war potential as much as possible. With single-minded determination, the Royal Navy disposed of war materials, destroyed naval installations, dismantled facilities as reparations, and limited shipbuilding. These efforts proceeded in the face of other conflicting priorities and cutbacks in available resources. Before leaving Germany, the Royal Navy endeavoured to cripple its naval power for a long time.

The Admiralty collaborated in general Allied arrangements for disposal of German stocks, equipment, and munitions. Both the British and American navies accorded high priority to acquisition of selected items of naval and technological importance.[1] The two countries, therefore, worked jointly through a single body. The London Munitions Assignment Board, established by the Cabinet earlier in the war, became responsible for allocation of captured and surrendered enemy war materials from the British and American commands in Germany and Austria.[2] A Naval Assignment Sub-Committee within the board handled specific requests pertaining to naval materials. The Combined Chiefs of Staff directed destruction of war materials surplus to the London Munition Assignment Board's requirements, but Churchill deferred implementation within British areas of responsibility until the end of the Potsdam Conference.[3] Decisions in Berlin concerning provision of stocks for the divided German fleet further complicated the question of war materials. In early October 1945 the Naval Assignment Sub-Committee distributed a detailed wish-list of naval equipment wanted by the British, American, Canadian, and Australian navies.[4] The task of locating and forwarding the desired items fell mostly to British naval authorities.

The Royal Navy discovered a relative bonanza of naval war materials within Germany and the liberated countries. The chief difficulty involved too much rather than too little. Under the previous post-hostilities planning, British naval authorities were responsible for custody and disposal of naval war materials.[5] In addition to stocks on warships, large quantities of ammunition, stores, equipment, and armaments existed in scattered dumps and arsenals. The Germans had abandoned many locations after Allied air attacks. In Hamburg and Kiel, a British investigating officer found damaged submarine sections and spare parts littered around shipyards and wharves.[6] Special missions targeted other areas of recognized German expertise, such as optics, gunnery, and diesel engine development. Although the Admiralty remained the coordinating authority, the Canadian Naval Mission Overseas sent an officer to Germany to find suitable equipment for the Royal Canadian Navy.[7] Possession was the best means to guarantee subsequent ownership. To the victors went the spoils.

War booty really just represented a form of official pilfering. The British removed whatever seemed valuable from occupied Germany under the auspices of the London Munitions Assignment Board. Vickers-Armstrong hosted a major exhibition of captured naval ordnance and gunnery equipment in Crayford during mid-1946.[8] The event assumed the attributes of a trade show. Admiralty departments, Allied navies, marine companies, and universities were given opportunities to choose displayed objects for study and emulation. As well, the Admiralty filled requests from the Imperial War Museum and the Canadian War Museum for German naval relics – ranging in size from uniform badges to midget submarines – suitable for public display.[9] As tangible proof of the Royal Navy's triumph over the *Kriegsmarine*, captured war materials were small reward for substantial British and Commonwealth sacrifices during the war.

Appropriating war materials as a legal right, the Admiralty became the agent for sharing the loot. British naval authorities in Germany promptly met requests from the US Navy for surplus submarine battery cells.[10] The Admiralty made sure that everyone was looked after, but there were limits to its generosity. Faced with large Soviet and French demands for captured war materials, the British kept in mind 'the object of our presence in Germany, namely the complete demilitarisation and destruction of its war potential, and not allow ourselves to be hampered by quibbles over hypothetical future requirements.'[11] While the Admiralty generously distributed sample components and equipment to deserving benefactors for research, testing, and historical purposes, most war materials were earmarked for destruction.

The enormous quantities of munitions and armaments presented a significant problem. The Royal Navy located 85,000 tons of naval ammunition, including 10,000 tons previously acquired by the Germans from the French and Italians, in major depots at Tannenhausen and Fahrenkrug, 8,500 torpedoes and 5,900 warheads at Eckernförde and a series of minor depots in the principal ports, as well as 26,000 mines and 13,000 depth charges in depots at Jägersberg, Wilhelmshaven, Forst Neuenberg, Heinschenwalde, Oxstedt, Druhwald, and Stakshorn.[12] Physical condition varied considerably. Where properly looked after, munitions were usually safe to handle, but storage for extended periods of time, open exposure to the elements, and damage from air attacks made some potentially dangerous. Mines and depth charges, in particular, were prone to sweating and deterioration. Accidental explosions sometimes killed or seriously wounded Allied and German personnel.[13] Care and disposal of munitions required special training and a certain degree of luck. Employing mostly German labour, the Royal Navy destroyed, through controlled explosions and burning, small quantities of unstable ammunition and armaments, which posed immediate threats to the public and the occupation forces.

Naval war materials located in Allied countries posed other challenges. To effect economies, the British tried to delegate responsibility for destruction to Dutch and Norwegian naval authorities within their respective areas.[14] Although someone else other than the Royal Navy performed the dangerous work, a strong desire in both countries to keep German war materials and equipment for their own navies conflicted with the Combined Chiefs of Staff's earlier endorsement of complete destruction. Confronted with numerous practical and political complications, the Admiralty allowed retention of limited naval munitions and equipment in Norway to secure Norwegian cooperation in further destruction efforts.[15] The arrangement, though not ideal, was the best solution in a difficult situation. The British could hardly argue against a cheap means to improve the naval forces and defences of a close ally. At the very least, naval war materials under Norwegian control were denied to the Germans. The Royal Navy permanently disposed of remaining munitions at sea.

Working with British military authorities, the Royal Navy dumped several hundred thousand tons of ammunition in selected spots off the coasts of Germany. In the absence of an overriding policy, British naval authorities started limited sea dumping shortly after the surrender.[16] Despite problems with loading and transport, the method proved a convenient means of disposal. During the first meeting of a Continental

Dumping Committee at 21st Army Group's headquarters, Burrough proposed dumping surplus ammunition in the harbours of German naval bases, 'which it is our policy to destroy when no longer required for immediate purposes.'[17] Since these live munitions would be dangerous for many years to come, the idea offered an additional obstacle to the revival of German naval power. Nonetheless, on the advice of the Continental Dumping Committee, the Admiralty instead approved dumping in deep water outside the 300 fathom line and in designated bays.[18] Disposal at sea involved more than just discarding ammunition over the side. Besides proximity to ports of loading, the chosen areas tried to avoid busy shipping channels, fishing grounds, and underwater telegraph cables.[19] As well, the British encountered numerous technical problems. In Oslo, a barge loaded with ammunition exploded at the quays, killing German working parties and shattering windows throughout the port.[20] Transhipment of munitions from ships to smaller lighters proved especially hazardous in bad weather. British naval authorities resorted to sinking fully loaded hulks and barges. Former merchant ships carried over 100,000 tons of chemical weapons ammunition, including mustard and arsenic gases, to the bottom of the Skagerrak.[21] Despite later environmental concerns, sea dumping fulfilled the Royal Navy's immediate need to get rid of large quantities of dangerous munitions in the shortest possible time. War materials were effectively out of sight and out of mind beneath several hundred metres of water.

Surplus munitions and explosives also proved useful in demolishing coastal fortifications, warship shelters, and similar naval installations. A stated long-term objective in naval disarmament plans was the 'complete destruction of naval war structures and defences in Germany.'[22] For such an ambitious proposition, the Royal Navy drew upon assistance from British and Allied military authorities. Under the 'Eclipse' arrangements, 21st Army Group's estimates for engineers and sappers took into account naval demolition needs.[23] Naval authorities forwarded lists of submarine pens, coastal defence batteries, and underground storage sites. Although approval for demolitions rested entirely with the Royal Navy, military authorities supervised the actual work.[24] Naval structures, with the exception of a few radar, infra-red, and research establishments retained by the British for dismantling or further study, were designated for destruction. Submarine and small warship shelters, which had so effectively supported attacks against Great Britain and its sea communications, gained highest priority.[25] Built largely by slave labour, the large concrete bunkers directly threatened British naval security. Thus, on moral and strategic grounds alone, the Royal Navy demanded full destruction.

Intended demolitions of German-constructed bunkers and fortifications in formerly occupied Allied countries encountered obstacles. The British government adopted 'the view that the U-boat and E/R-boat shelters in France, Holland, Belgium and Norway can be considered as dangerous to this country [Great Britain] and of small use to the Allied forces of occupation.'[26] The Chiefs of Staff directed British naval and military forces to commence demolitions soon after the surrender. During July 1945 an inter-service delegation for the Destruction of Enemy Installations in Liberated Areas, or DEILA for short, toured and inspected coastal defence batteries and warship pens in Holland and Belgium to identify installations which posed a threat to Great Britain.[27] As the DEILA delegation noted, demolitions were easily achieved in most cases because structures were already damaged from Allied bombing, but newer concrete pens, under construction by the Germans at Ijmuiden, posed a significant technical problem. These shelters, like similar submarine pens in Norway, were of a smaller design, which incorporated thick prestressed reinforced concrete beams.[28] Full destruction could not be assured because their location in the middle of busy Allied ports prevented use of higher weights of explosives.

Moreover, the Dutch and Norwegian governments informally asked to retain concrete pens and coastal defences for their own navies or conversion into civilian use. Since British policy encouraged the two countries to defend themselves, the Royal Navy clearly could 'not convey the idea that we do not trust them.'[29] Thus, demolitions of former German naval structures, in which Allied countries expressed a strong interest, were postponed indefinitely. An application from the Dutch government to transfer Borkum to Holland as part of border rectifications with Germany further delayed destruction of coastal fortifications on that German island.[30] Within the limits of Allied sensibilities, the British pressed for the levelling of the naval structures. The Dutch and Norwegians generally saved the installations they wanted, and destroyed the rest. If British security rested largely on the ability of the small West European countries to defend successfully against a potential attack, then widespread naval demolitions in Germany diminished the base for future aggression.

British authorities initiated a comprehensive demolition programme within their zone of occupation. Due to limited resources and a multitude of tasks, demolition work initially lagged behind control and disbandment of naval forces. During an inspection tour of the Wilhelmshaven-Emden area, a Royal Navy officer was surprised to find coastal defences and naval war materials on Borkum and Norderney virtually untouched.[31] Apart from removal of blocks from guns and storage of ammunition immediately after the surrender, the imposing structures stood intact. It was easier to do nothing, and progress usually depended upon the diligence of local naval and military authorities. The Royal Navy ordered specific demolitions through corps districts' headquarters, according to an established priority list.[32] Submarine pens were priority II and coastal fortifications were priority III.

On the whole, the work was slow and methodical. Earlier experiments found that large, shaped hollow charges were most effective in destroying reinforced concrete.[33] Available German munitions were usually sufficient for the purpose. To be done properly, demolitions required extensive preparation by skilled explosives personnel. British military engineers laboured for more than two months to blow up submarine pens in Kiel.[34] In this particular case, proximity to the commercial port area demanded extra precautions. Larger and more complex jobs naturally took more time. Even so, demolition teams established regular schedules as much as possible. On behalf of the Royal Navy, engineers from 3rd Canadian Infantry Division (CAOF) systematically destroyed emplacements, bunkers, and coastal batteries on Norderney, Borkum, and Juist over the course of several months.[35] Consistent application of effort gradually achieved results. Over half of the naval fortifications within the British Zone were demolished before the end of 1945.[36] British naval authorities and military engineers persevered in the remaining work.

Despite conflicting demands, the Royal Navy firmly insisted on demolition of former *Kriegsmarine* installations. Under Allied Control Council Directive No. 22, submarine and warship shelters required destruction within eighteen months and naval bases within a further four years.[37] The Royal Navy was obligated to fulfil quadripartite agreements. Yet, at a time of severe housing shortages and a large influx of refugees to the British Zone, demolitions were unpopular with military government authorities. The Royal Navy allowed temporary exemptions to meet urgent accommodation and storage needs.[38] There was, however, a determination to resist prolonged retention. An officer on the demolitions staff asserted:

> The destruction of German Naval Installations is by far the most important disarmament work we have still to carry out in Germany ... We must harden our hearts to blowing up 'good' buildings, and while the housing situation in Germany is an acute problem, we must not allow it to hinder disarmament.[39]

Naval disarmament took first priority. Compelling reasons to save naval structures always existed. For example, planned demolitions in Emden brought a desperate appeal to spare former naval bunkers, which were leased as storehouses and considered 'almost vital to the town's well-being.'[40] The Royal Navy realized that demolitions would become more difficult over time as opposition increased and resources dwindled.

Dissolution of the flag commands and repatriation of army personnel drastically reduced available manpower for demolition work. Based on the rate of progress, the Control Commission estimated full completion by December 1955, stating that Directive No. 22 'should be considered a guide, and subject to alteration in the light of experience.'[41] Naval authorities found this complacency quite unacceptable. Swift destruction of coastal fortifications and concrete structures was established policy. When military engineers left projects unfinished, the Royal Navy's own demolitions staff pressed ahead with German working parties. As a result, all submarine pens within British-occupied Germany, with the exception of Helgoland, were destroyed by the end of 1946.[42]

Destruction of coastal fortifications and the submarine bunker on Helgoland assumed a particular importance for the Royal Navy. In 1890 the British government had exchanged the strategic North Sea island for Zanzibar and colonial concessions in German East Africa. Developed into a fortress and naval base, Helgoland provided an important advance outpost for the German navy during World War I. An inter-allied naval sub-commission, headed by a young Andrew Cunningham, had overseen destruction of harbour works, tunnels, moles, and fortifications on the island under the terms of the Treaty of Versailles.[43] Nonetheless, the *Kriegsmarine* subsequently rebuilt and improved these defences, turning Helgoland into a supportive base for sea offensives against Great Britain. The permanent neutralization of Helgoland's defences represented a major goal in plans for German naval disarmament.

The Royal Navy pursued complementary policies prior to demolition. Since damage from Allied bombing at the end of the war made Helgoland virtually uninhabitable, the garrison and civilian population were evacuated to the mainland. German labourers and the British naval party departed later that year.[44] Harsh weather during the winter months impeded clearance and demolition activities. Hoping to keep Helgoland uninhabited, the Admiralty prohibited civilians from returning to the island.[45] It was left abandoned and forsaken. The Royal Air Force received government approval to use the island as a range for bombing practice.[46] Naval authorities supported the idea because bombing drove away trespassers and would be likely to result in eventual destruction of most fortifications. Whether testimony to the ineptitude of British air power or the ruggedness of German design, the submarine pens and large coastal guns still stood defiant after nine months of heavy bomber attacks.[47] The Royal Navy decided to reoccupy the island to implement disarmament measures. Navigational aids were re-established on Helgoland for the benefit of shipping and fishing vessels.[48] Strategic and practical considerations dictated full destruction.

Despite protests, the Royal Navy decided to blow up fortifications on Helgoland with a single large explosion. In a petition to British naval authorities, a former island resident argued against the planned demolition, calling upon 'our duty towards the coming generations to try everything to save the wonderful island.'[49] Besides supporting thriving lobster and fishing industries, Helgoland boasted a world-renowned marine biological institute. These facilities had already suffered considerable bomb damage. People in Germany and Great Britain also worried about the impact of an additional large explosion on the thousands of migratory birds, which used the island as a resting place.[50] The Royal Navy, however, remained unmoved. Destruction was deemed necessary because Helgoland posed an appreciable threat to British naval security and European peace.[51] The Royal Navy was even willing to risk Helgoland's physical integrity; demolition experts feared that the explosion might break the predominantly sandstone island into two parts or undermine its high sea cliffs. Nonetheless, a sufficiently large explosion was required to destroy munitions in otherwise inaccessible deep underground tunnels and galleries.[52] Naval authorities prepared the explosives accordingly.

In fact, the Royal Navy turned the explosion on Helgoland into a major public event. The operation, code-named 'Big Bang', was billed as the largest man-made explosion ever undertaken by the Royal Navy.[53] In a single stroke, the British sought complete destruction of the fortifications and U-boat pens. Over several months, British demolition officers, assisted by German workers, wired 6,700 gross tons of explosives, which included large numbers of depth charge primers from the mainland.[54] To ensure simultaneous detonation, the wiring pattern, based upon a battleship's main ring system, used generators to provide continuous power wherever the electrical loop became disrupted. The Admiralty invited newspaper correspondents, film crews, and numerous dignitaries to observe the explosion.[55] Helgoland fittingly provided the showcase for the Royal Navy's German naval disarmament efforts.

'Big Bang' was an awe-inspiring success. In the early afternoon on 18 April Gunner (T) E.C. Jellis, RN, on board HMS *Lasso*, a safe distance away from the island, pressed the firing button as 'it being virtually his last task before his retirement from the Royal Navy and it was thought fitting that he should have the privilege of ending his career with a bang.'[56] He was not disappointed. After a bright flash, a dense cloud of smoke and dust rose from the island to an altitude of 400 metres with a central mushroom-shaped pillar; shock waves and a deafening roar followed forty seconds later. Onlookers compared the effect to the

American atomic bomb tests at Bikini Atoll in July 1946.[57] For the Royal Navy, 'Big Bang' represented the next best thing. Subsequent inspections revealed full destruction of the coastal guns and submarine shelter with only marginal damage to the island's surface.[58] Despite the earlier dire predictions, the island was still intact. Workers exploded leftover munitions, causing considerable consternation for naval authorities in nearby Cuxhaven.[59] After the demolition teams withdrew, Helgoland reverted back to a bombing range for the Royal Air Force. 'Big Bang' was more than just a dramatic means to eliminate war potential on the heavily-fortified island; the explosion was a potent symbol of the Royal Navy's obsession with German naval disarmament.

The desire to obliterate every trace of the *Kriegsmarine* was manifested in curious ways. The Royal Navy far exceeded commitments to demilitarization in the Potsdam decisions and Allied Control Council Directive No. 22.[60] Wherever possible, authorities destroyed any buildings and structures remotely related to naval activities. Formal policy was to leave nothing standing. Walker even ordered a stone monument at Kiel, which commemorated dead German submariners in World War I, to be destroyed because 'any Memorial to a branch of the Navy that so flagrantly disobeyed the rules of warfare is distasteful to me.'[61] The obelisk, however, won a narrow reprieve. The Regional Commissioner for Schleswig-Holstein, concerned about a possible outcry from the local population, persuaded the Royal Navy to remove only a swastika on top of the monument.

British naval authorities likewise renamed former *Kriegsmarine* establishments to avoid Nazi and militarist connections. The practice was a subtle form of denazification. Within German ports, harbours, piers, and buildings named after German admirals and Prussian political figures received different titles, usually British in origin.[62] Kitchener and Jellicoe replaced Bismarck and Tirpitz. Since the Royal Navy and British military authorities temporarily retained some buildings, the new names were appropriate. In contrast to the utilitarian dominance of the parade ground in British barracks, German naval barracks usually were modern in construction and tastefully set in landscaped surroundings with greenery, trees, and ponds.[63] The almost university-like settings were appealing. British naval authorities destroyed these establishments with mixed feelings. Emotional considerations aside, the Control Commission stressed no slow down in demilitarization efforts.[64] The Royal Navy embraced the ideal of complete German naval disarmament with considerable zeal and imagination.

A strange proposal for the Kiel Canal highlighted the Royal Navy's enthusiasm for demilitarization. Constructed and enlarged before 1914, the deep artificial waterway possessed considerable strategic value by reducing travel time between the Baltic and the North Sea.[65] Warships, from the largest battleships to submarines, used the Kiel Canal. The Admiralty's aspiration was to make the Germans block and fill in the whole canal since 'this would seem to be a most effective monument to the completeness of their military defeat.'[66] Nonetheless, the British recognized that other countries might not accept such a drastic measure. If the intent was to prevent strategic or naval use, then placing the Kiel Canal under international or quadripartite control appeared sufficient. The Soviet Union, in particular, wanted the canal open to commercial traffic.[67] The waterway provided an alternative outlet from the Baltic. Pending agreement between the major powers, German administrators, supervised by Lieutenant-Commander J.A.G. Pollard, RNVR, the Resident British Naval Officer-in-Charge, operated the Kiel Canal.[68] British warships and merchant vessels passed through the canal on a regular basis.

Nevertheless, as demilitarization reached an advanced stage, British authorities within Germany became anxious about a firm decision on the waterway. Was the Kiel Canal to be destroyed or handed over to civilian control? To answer this question, Burrough requested guidance from the Admiralty.[69] The perceived danger was long term rather than immediate. As long as the Allied control regime continued in Germany, adequate safeguards suppressed naval power. Mere internationalization, however, would not necessarily reduce strategic value. A strong and prosperous Germany or, as the Chiefs of Staff increasingly feared, a hostile Soviet Union could be expected to seize control of the Kiel Canal. The Admiralty replied that destruction was still preferred, if only to deny the canal to a potential aggressor.[70] Paradoxically, naval authorities realized that the canal, if filled in, was relatively easy to excavate with modern machinery. By the time the British government decided to save the Kiel Canal towards mid-1947, work had not even started.[71] The Royal Navy expected better returns in the disablement of naval bases.

Demolition and dismantlement of Wilhelmshaven, Germany's largest North Sea naval base, naturally received high priority. Founded in 1869 on reclaimed marshland purchased from the Duke of Oldenburg, the town and dockyard catered almost exclusively to the needs of the German navy.[72] Wilhelmshaven's shipyards built and maintained the largest German warships. War potential greatly outweighed commercial interests. British naval authorities planned to demolish the main dockyard and allow the harbour to silt up, 'in accord with our policy that no vestige of the German Navy shall remain, nor anything that might assist its revival.'[73] Wilhelmshaven, intimately associated with German naval power, was to cease as a viable port. British naval authorities discussed several proposals with the Control

Commission, including relocation of the town's entire population. Two civil engineers from the Admiralty visited Wilhelmshaven to recommend a final destruction plan.[74] After division and transfer of the surface fleet, Wilhelmshaven's port facilities became redundant. The Royal Navy declared the dockyard available for reparations after 15 April 1946.[75]

Despite conflicting claims, British authorities implemented Wilhelmshaven's planned dismantlement under an operation called 'Bailiff'. Great Britain was not the only country interested in Wilhelmshaven. The Soviets submitted a reparations request for all the machinery in the dockyard.[76] Although the devastated condition of port facilities within the Soviet Zone called for some courtesy, the Admiralty regarded the Soviet demand as remarkably greedy. The British, quite frankly, wanted most equipment themselves. Walker also objected that 'the presence of Russians in Wilhelmshaven will undoubtedly delay our plan for destruction of the port.'[77] While the Foreign Office resisted the Soviet claim, the Royal Navy proceeded to dismantle Wilhelmshaven's port facilities.

Equipment surplus to naval requirements was transferred to the Control Commission's Reparations, Deliveries, and Restitution Division. Perhaps the oddest asset was Wilhelmshaven's *Kriegsmarine*-owned railroad, which included locomotives and rolling stock.[78] The Royal Navy tried to place the unprofitable enterprise under Reichsbahn control through the Railways Branch of the Transport Division. 'Bailiff' systematically packed-up and demolished Wilhelmshaven's port. The headmaster of Prince Rupert, a school for children of the occupation forces located in the middle of the dock area, complained about the utter desolation after removal of steel piling, claimed by the Ministry of Supply.[79] Rejecting pleas to cease or modify 'Bailiff', naval authorities ruthlessly eliminated Wilhelmshaven's capacity as a naval base. Thorough disarmament was imperative. The Royal Navy continued demolitions, even as critics questioned the harshness of the policy.

Demolitions at Eckernförde attracted significant opposition. In addition to Wilhelmshaven, the Royal Navy was responsible, under an agreement with the Economic Division's Shipbuilding Branch, for all disarmament work at Eckernförde and the naval arsenal at Kiel.[80] Located in a sheltered bay with minimal tidal influences and currents, Eckernförde was the *Kriegsmarine*'s principal testing station for torpedoes and underwater research methods. The town relied entirely on the German navy's patronage, growing from little more than a small fishing village before 1914 into a large installation comprising three separate establishments with various firing points.[81] With the intention of returning Eckernförde to its original state, the Royal Navy commenced equipment removals and demolitions under an operation known as 'Plainfare'. Nonetheless, after a visit to the British Zone, Richard Stokes, the Labour member of Parliament for Ipswich, protested strongly against destruction of the buildings, which he contended were appropriate for civilian use.[82] The claim demanded some consideration. Large numbers of refugees were still without adequate housing in Schleswig-Holstein. During a question period in the House of Commons, Stokes asked John Hynd, the Cabinet Minister for occupied Germany, to 'take some steps to prevent the Navy [from] going completely mad in this matter and going round Germany blowing everything up.'[83]

The Royal Navy strongly opposed any representations to save the former naval establishments. Air Vice-Marshal Hugh Vivian Champion de Crespigny, the Regional Commissioner for Schleswig-Holstein, argued for retention of a hospital and other naval buildings, but naval authorities asked the Regional Demilitarisation Committee to 'accept the Naval view that these establishments must be entirely destroyed, in accordance with the liquidation plan prepared by [the] Disarmament Branch.'[84] Eckernförde's infrastructure posed an unacceptable strategic risk. Rear-Admiral Stephen Harry Tolson Arliss, RN, the Flag Officer Commanding British Naval Forces Germany, emphasized the importance of complete disarmament:

> A future generation of naval officers, unaware of the facts of the present controversy, and ignorant of the overriding power of the Military Government authorities in Germany, might with reason censure the present generation for their apparent laxity in leaving in existence the nucleus of the torpedo arm for the next Continental Power.[85]

Naval authorities believed that insufficient measures in the present would be likely to have adverse consequences tomorrow. A tough stand on demolitions was the best means to guarantee security. In London, the First Sea Lord obtained approval from the Chiefs of Staff Committee to carry through with full destruction.[86] The Royal Navy's preoccupation with German naval disarmament prevailed over humanitarian concerns at Eckernförde.

Disablement activities in Kiel, the largest German naval base on the Baltic, encountered similar resistance. On an interim basis, the Royal Navy administered Kiel's harbour and port facilities.[87] In addition to the naval arsenal, Kiel's war potential rested mainly in its three major shipyards. Citing Allied Control Council Directive No. 39 for elimination of plant directly connected to armaments production, British naval authorities submitted a plan for destruction of deep water berths, slipways, and quays to the Regional Demilitarization

Committee.[88] Although the plan excluded commercial facilities, civil and economic representatives contended that demolition of naval-related shipyards would cause unwarranted hardship and distress among Kiel's civilian population. The committee deferred the question to higher authorities. After several months, a firm decision finally became necessary when the Soviets insisted on demolition of the entire port by June 1948 under Directive No. 39.[89]

Disarmament appeared the only real safeguard against future German aggression. In correspondence with the Deputy Military Governor, the Royal Navy pressed, on security grounds, for removal of the main shipyards, objecting 'most strongly to any proposal for reprieving them.'[90] An entreaty by Champion de Crespigny to keep the deep water berths and wharves was especially alarming. Naval authorities feared that 'by retaining those facilities in the most famous German naval base we leave ourselves open to considerable criticism.'[91] Dismantling and destruction were the surest means to neutralize Kiel's war potential. Robertson promised Arliss that the Royal Navy's views would be taken into account before any major decisions on demilitarization in Kiel.[92] One shipyard was subsequently retained for repair work on merchant ships and fishing vessels. Demolitions in the other shipyards corresponded with the agreed level of shipbuilding capacity to be allowed to the Germans.

Through reparations and demolitions, the Royal Navy intended to limit shipbuilding in Germany. The industry, supported by generous government subsidies and loans, was modern and well-developed. In 1939 Nazi Germany had possessed the fifth largest merchant fleet in the world.[93] During the war, shipbuilding capacity was devoted almost entirely to conversion of merchant ships into auxiliary cruisers and new naval construction. The Royal Navy, therefore, regarded the elimination of shipbuilding as a key objective for German naval disarmament.[94] Since the German navy benefited from the industry, the Potsdam Protocol called for abolition of major shipbuilding enterprises and reductions in shipyards. The Admiralty sponsored, through the Board of Trade, a six-member reparations assessment team, headed by Horace Wilson, to appraise equipment in shipyards and marine engineering firms, under an operation called 'Trademark'.[95] This civilian team visited British-occupied Germany over a three-week period in December 1945.

The 'Trademark' inspections strengthened the Admiralty's bids for shipbuilding plant and machinery within the British share of reparations. Civil and naval usage was virtually indistinguishable since commercial shipyards had engaged in war production, especially submarine construction.[96] In a legalistic sense, this involvement opened most shipyards to consideration as reparations. The Admiralty was particularly interested in the large commercial port of Hamburg because 'the potential of German sea power is to a large extent wrapped up in the Hamburg shipyards.'[97] Until mid-1946 these yards were busy with repair, refit, and conversion work on minesweepers and fishing vessels. Naval authorities undertook no further jobs to ensure 'that the German shipyards should be closed down and disposed of without any further delay.'[98]

Shipbuilding and repair facilities beyond the minimal needs of the civil economy were designated for removal. Backed by the British shipbuilding industry, the Admiralty pushed for either delivery as reparations or outright destruction.[99] Besides eliminating a strategic threat, disarmament provided a convenient means to reduce foreign competition in the shipbuilding field. Although abandoning a bid for the Blohm and Voss shipyard in favour of the Wilhelmshaven dockyard, the Admiralty requested plant and equipment from Hamburg's MAN Werke.[100] After reparations and selective demolitions, naval authorities transferred responsibility for individual commercial shipyards to the Economic Division's Shipbuilding Branch. The British effectively transformed shipbuilding into a light industry.[101] Merchant ships of larger sizes were not again built in Germany until the mid-1950s.

As part of the downsizing of shipbuilding and repair facilities, the Royal Navy advocated size restrictions on new construction. Absolute prohibitions remained on warships and merchant ships, but small commercial vessels for fishing purposes were permitted.[102] Fish represented a convenient and cheap food source for the hungry civil population. British naval authorities, however, asserted that deep sea trawlers above 350 GRT were 'easily converted to minor war vessels and therefore unacceptable in large numbers.'[103] A suggestion to exclude German vessels from distant fishing grounds, thereby undermining the economic rationale for big trawlers, was deemed impractical for political reasons. The British instead decided to prevent the Germans from replacing existing larger vessels.[104] Although a seemingly simple solution, an agreed limit on new construction was more difficult to determine. If economic pressures pushed the ceiling up, then conservation and disarmament concerns kept the limit low. Citing the Potsdam Protocol, the Soviets also insisted on a maximum size of 350 GRT.[105]

Reductions in facilities and shipyards necessarily placed practical constraints on the fishing fleet. Following reparations, the Royal Navy proposed leaving not more than eight dry and graving docks in the British Zone for shipbuilding and repair work.[106] The Germans would be incapable of handling significant numbers of larger vessels. After prolonged discussion, the Naval Directorate endorsed an upper limit of 400 GRT, with further restrictions on quantities of specific sizes in new construction.[107] This compromise balanced the needs of the economy with the demand for naval disarmament. Concurrently, the Royal Navy supported a Dutch restitution claim for transfer of German trawlers to the Netherlands.[108] Restrictions, reduced facilities, and withdrawals decreased the availability of commercial vessels with possible war-potential.

Beyond shipbuilding and fishing, the Royal Navy's disarmament measures affected maritime-related manufacturing industries. In the Ruhr industrial region, a naval control unit, under Captain Herbert Arthur Cambridge Lane, RN, investigated factories which had engaged in production of naval war materials.[109] The British again could make a good case for war booty and reparations. The *Kriegsmarine* had invested heavily in companies through large loans, subsidies, and even outright ownership.[110] Naval contracts wholly sustained some industries. While Royal Navy officers sorted out the complicated contractual relationships, the Admiralty offered assistance to British manufacturers:

> as regards information of German methods and techniques in the Nautical Instrument Industry by making available to your members the reports of official investigations of the firms and equipment in which you are interested, or, by arranging for representatives of your Association to visit specific targets in Germany.[111]

German firms, commercial competitors of British companies before the war, manufactured high-quality precision instruments and optics. With little regard for patents or invention protection, the British plundered German industrial knowledge and expertise. An Admiralty-sponsored team visited Germany to find samples of anti-fouling and anti-corrosion marine paints for testing in Great Britain.[112] Similar missions targeted other fields of commercial and technical interest.

By mid-1946 the Naval Division cleared several hundred factories for renewed civilian production or reparations. The demand for naval disarmament influenced industrial capabilities. Manufacturers, who had often engaged in various types of production, made civil apparatus with potential military applications. Naval authorities asked the Trade and Industry Division to prohibit manufacture of certain marine equipment, such as gyroscopic compasses, underwater acoustic apparatus, and optical gear.[113] Industrial capacity and war potential were closely intertwined. Specialized maritime industries required ongoing investment in research and production to stay viable. Stringent bans on maritime production and restrictions on shipbuilding promoted conversion into other more profitable areas of civil manufacture.

Factories, which the British deemed appropriate for reparations, were dismantled. The Royal Navy shared maritime plant in the British Zone with Soviet naval authorities.[114] The Red Navy was particularly interested in acquiring tools and machinery. Until late 1947 a Soviet naval mission supervised shipments of reparations from British sources to the Soviet Union.[115] Soviet animosity towards the merging of the British and American Zones into a single economic unit, under the name Bizonia, eventually led to withdrawal of the naval mission. As part of a larger change in policy, the British turned from reparations to stimulation of German industrial production. The Germans took over responsibility for repair and shipbuilding work.[116] The Royal Navy had achieved the reduction, limitation, and redirection of German maritime industries. The industrial infrastructure necessary to support a modern navy was now severely diminished. The Royal Navy's disarmament measures effectively extinguished the real and potential capabilities of German naval power.

NOTES

1. NA, RG 313, Series II, File 59, Memorandum from Captain T.J. Doyle to COMNAVEU, 'Allocation of Captured or Surrendered German Resources', 16 May 1944. Simpson, p. 645.
2. PRO, CAB 109/93, Message from Combined Chiefs of Staff to USFET (Eisenhower); 21st Army Group (Montgomery), 20 1554Z July 1945.
3. CCS, Reel 3, Frame 293, Minutes of 197th Meeting Combined Chiefs of Staff, 20 July 1945.
4. PRO, CAB 109/94, Memorandum from J.J. Waudby, Secretary, Naval Assignment Sub-Committee, London Munitions Assignment Board to British Naval Commander-in-Chief Germany; Flag Officer Norway; Senior British Naval Officers Holland and Denmark; USFET(G-4 Division); COMNAVFORGER; AFHQ(G-3 Division), 'LMAB Requirements for German Naval Material', 2 Oct. 1945.
5. NA, RG 331, SHAEF, Office of the Chief of Staff, Secretary, General Staff, ANCXF Post-Hostilities Memorandum No. 7, 'Custody and Disposal of Naval War Material', 5 May 1945.
6. PRO, ADM 228/4, Lieutenant-Commander W.N. Eade, RNR, 'Report on U-Boat Sections and U-Boat Equipment', 24 May 1945.
7. NAC, RG 24, Vol. 11,722, File CS 122-1-1, Lieutenant-Commander (SB)(E) A.H. Simmons, RCNR, Staff Officer (Naval Ordnance) to Naval Assistant (Weapons and Equipment), 'Enemy Equipment required by the RCN', 17 Jan. 1946.
8. NAC, RG 24, Vol. 11,722, CS 122-1-1, List from Director of Naval Ordnance, Admiralty to Canadian Naval Mission Overseas, 9 Sept. 1946.
9. PRO, ADM 205/49, Letter from Imperial War Museum to Admiralty, 23 March 1945. NAC, RG 24, Vol. 11,722, CS 122-1-1, Letter from Deputy Naval Secretary to Secretary Canadian Naval Mission Overseas, 3 June 1946. IWM, Hawkins, Message from Flag Officer Holland to 1st Canadian Army, 01 0929B June 1945.
10. PRO, ADM 228/5, Letter from Vice-Admiral Commanding British Naval Forces Germany to British Liaison Officer, US Naval Forces Germany, 5 April 1946.
11. PRO, ADM 228/5, Staff Minute by ANCXF Main, 7 July 1945.
12. PRO, FO 1038/144, Office of British Naval Commander-in-Chief Germany, 'Naval Division Progress Report for the Period 31st July–31st August 1945'.

13. DHist, 142.31011(D1), Historical Officer, 1st Canadian Infantry Division, Interview with Captain J.M. Church, 'The CRA Group in the Surrender Operation, 8 May–8 June 45'. PRO, ADM 1/18422, ANCXF Post War Diary, 12 July 1945.
14. OAB/NHC, US Naval Technical Mission in Europe, Series I, Box 2, File 'USNavTechMisEU – Daily Personnel Situation Reports (1945)', D. Frothingham, Senior US Naval Officer Netherlands to COMNAVFORFRANCE, 'Weekly Report (Netherlands) for period ending 9 June 1945', 10 June 1945.
15. Pelly and Yasamee, Vol. 5, Microfiche 20iv, Memorandum by First Sea Lord, 'Disposal of German Naval Equipment in Norway', 11 Oct. 1945.
16. PRO, ADM 228/24, Memorandum from ANCXF to Flag Officers Kiel, Western Germany, Denmark, Holland, 'Enemy Ammunition Dumping at Sea', 9 June 1945.
17. PRO, ADM 228/24, Message from British Naval Commander-in-Chief Germany to Admiralty, 19 1047B July 1945.
18. PRO, ADM 228/24, Message from Admiralty to British Flag Officers and Naval Officers-in-Charge, 07 2255A Aug. 1945.
19. PRO, ADM 228/24, Message from Admiralty to British Naval Commander-in-Chief Germany, 05 1446 Nov. 1945.
20. NAM, Thorne, Letter No. 11 from General Andrew Thorne to Field Marshal Alan Brooke, 19 Aug. 1945.
21. PRO, ADM 228/24, Message from Vice-Admiral Commanding British Naval Forces Germany to HBNM Norway, 28 1442A Oct. 1946. 'Destroying Nazi War Plants', Manchester Guardian (22 Oct. 1945), p. 5. IWM, Savage, 'Operations', 'Buzz': The Magazine of HMS 'Royal Harold' Naval Party 1742, Vol. 1, No. 6 (Sept. 1946), p. 19.
22. PRO, ADM 116/5300, ANCXF Post-Hostilities Planning Memoranda No. 8, 'Naval Demolitions', 27 April 1945.
23. PRO, FO 1038/127, Memorandum from Naval Party 1734 to CCMS(N) Branch IV, 'Requirements of the 21st Army Group', 30 Oct. 1944.
24. PRO, WO 205/393, Letter from BGS to Naval Liaison Officer, 21st Army Group, 'Destruction and Demolition of Coastal Defences', 13 May 1945.
25. PRO, ADM 228/16, Memorandum from Major-General, Chief of Staff, 21st Army Group to HQs 1st Canadian and 2nd British Armies, 28 May 1945.
26. NA, RG 331, SHAEF, Office of the Chief of Staff, Secretary, General Staff, File 600.6, War Cabinet, JIC(45) 92(0)(Final), 'Demolition of Installations in Liberated Territories', 23 March 1945.
27. PRO, ADM 228/16, Captain H.B. Ellison, RN, 'Report of Visit to Holland and Belgium: DEILA Reconnaissance Party 17–30 July'.
28. PRO, ADM 214/19, A.L. Dobson, 'Report on U-Boat Pens (Norway) at Bergen and Trondheim', 17 Aug. 1945. OAB/NHC, US Naval Technical Mission in Europe, Series III, Box 30, Technical Report No. 278, Lieutenant G.R. Wernisch CEC, USNR, 'Prestressed Reinforced Concrete Trusses in Submarine Pens', 12 Sept. 1945.
29. PRO, ADM 228/16, Message from Senior British Naval Officer Holland to Admiralty, 04 1450 Aug. 1945. The Royal Navy transferred a number of German naval radio stations in Denmark to the Royal Danish Navy. PRO, ADM 228/12, Memorandum from Captain G.H. Peters for Flag Officer Denmark to ANCXF, 'Former German Naval Radio Stations in Denmark', 26 June 1945.
30. PRO, FO 1032/779, Letter from Chief of Legal Division, CCG(BE) to Major-General G.W.J. Erskine, DCOS(Policy), 'Island of Borkum', 26 July 1946.
31. PRO, ADM 228/1, Report from Lieutenant Wake, RN, to Staff Officer Naval Demolitions, 25 June 1945.
32. DHist 581.009(D47), Memorandum from Main HQ 30th Corps, 'Demolitions – Policy', 4 June 1945.
33. NA, RG 331, SHAEF, General Staff, G-3 Division, Operations 'A' Section, File GCT-600.6-1/Ops 'A', Letter from Lieutenant-General Walter Bedell-Smith to Director of Military Ops (MO.3), 'Experimental Demolition on Enemy Installations', 17 May 1945. PRO, ADM 228/1, Memorandum from Lieutenant-

Colonel J.R.G. Scott for Engineer-in-Chief to SHAEF, 27 May 1945.

34. CCAC, HYND 3/9, 'Kiel U-Boat Pen Destroyed', *British Zone Review*, Vol. 1, No. 30 (9 Nov. 1945), p. 17.
35. DHist 581.009(D47), Memorandum from A.S. Michell for Major G.K. Wade CRE, 3rd Canadian Infantry Division (CAOF) to HQ 30th Corps District, 'Demolitions', 10 Jan. 1946.
36. PRO, FO 1038/144, Office of British Naval Commander-in-Chief Germany, 'Naval Division, Progress Report for the Period 30 Sept.–31 Oct. 1945', 14 Nov. 1945.
37. PRO, ADM 228/1, Allied Control Council Directive No. 22, 'Clearance of Minefields and Destruction of Fortifications, Underground Installations and Military Installations in Germany', 6 Dec. 1945.
38. PRO, ADM 228/1, Letter from R.H. Bevan for Admiral Harold Burrough to Flag Officers Schleswig-Holstein and Western Germany, 14 Oct. 1945.
39. PRO, ADM 228/1, Staff Minute by N.E. Ricketts, Staff Officer Naval Demolitions, 5 Feb. 1946.
40. PRO, ADM 228/1, Letter from Naval Officer-in-Charge Wilhelmshaven to Vice-Admiral Commanding British Naval Forces Germany, 29 July 1946.
41. PRO, FO 1032/554, Secretariat CCG(BE), 'Appreciation of the Short-Term Aspects of German Demilitarisation as it affects the Army', 16 April 1946.
42. PRO, FO 1038/144, Office of Vice-Admiral Commanding British Naval Forces Germany, 'Monthly Progress Report 1–31 October 1946'.
43. BL, Cunningham, Add. Ms. 52583A, Captain A.B. Cunningham, RN's copy of Lieutenant-Colonel P.R. Warren, 'Demolition of Heligoland: Final Report dated 30 September 1921'. Cunningham, pp. 108–10.
44. PRO, ADM 228/9, Letter from Commander F.W. Sandwith to Flag Officer Western Germany, 27 Sept. 1945.
45. PRO, ADM 228/53, Letter from Admiral Burrough to Deputy Military Governor CCG(BE), 'Heligoland – Future Policy', 14 Feb. 1945.
46. PRO, ADM 205/47A, Letter from A.P. Shaw to Captain (S) J. Ellerton, Secretary to ANCXF, 19 June 1945.
47. PRO, ADM 228/53, Memorandum from Vice-Admiral Commanding British Naval Forces Germany to Deputy Chief of Staff (Policy), 'Future Policy with Regard to the Island of Heligoland', 1 Nov. 1946.
48. PRO, ADM 228/80, Memorandum from F.J.C. Halden for Vice-Admiral Commanding British Naval Forces Germany to Controller General, Ports Branch, Transport Division CCG(BE), 12 June 1946.
49. PRO, ADM 228/53, Memorandum by Dr. Med. Eduard Uterharck, 'Helgoland Remains Alive: But How?', p. 5.
50. Muirhead-Gould, after the earlier visit to Helgoland, noted that 'the absence of all birds, even seagulls, is particularly noticeable', PRO, ADM 228/53, Message from Flag Officer Western Germany to Admiralty, 09 0919B June 1945.
51. CCAC, HYND 3/9, 'Why Heligoland must be destroyed,' *British Zone Review*, Vol. 1, No. 22 (20 July 1946), p. 7.
52. PRO, ADM 228/48, Report by Mr E. Garratt, Armament Research Department, and Lieutenant-Commander (Sp) E. de W.S. Colver, RNVR, Laboratory Officer, Director of Armament Supply Staff, 'Demolition of Explosives at Heligoland', 17 Oct. 1946.
53. PRO, ADM 1/20734, Vice-Admiral H.T.C. Walker, 'Operation Orders for the Demolition of Fortifications on Heligoland: Nick-Name and Short Title: Operation Big Bang', 16 March 1947.
54. CCAC, HYND 3/11, 'Heligoland Fortifications (Preparations Almost Ready)', *British Zone Review*, Vol. 1, No. 41 (12 April 1947), p. 16.
55. PRO, ADM 228/48, Message from Flag Officer Commanding British Naval Forces Germany to Admiralty, 13 1208A March 1947.
56. IWM, 83/24/1, Commander F.T. Woosnam, RN, 'Demolition of the Fortifications on Heligoland: Unreported Events', March 1950, p. 3. 'Destruction Heligoland:

Fortifications Blown Up', *The Times* (19 April 1947), p. 4.

57. CCAC, HYND 3/11, 'Operation Big Bang', *British Zone Review*, Vol. 1, No. 42 (26 April 1947), p. 17.

58. PRO, ADM 1/20734, Report from Vice-Admiral H.T.C. Walker, 'Demolition of the Fortifications on Heligoland (Operation Big Bang)', 1 June 1947.

59. PRO, ADM 228/48, Report from Captain L.P. Skipwith to Vice-Admiral Commanding British Naval Forces Germany, 24 April 1947.

60. PRO, FO 1032/1578, Conference of the Deputy Military Governor, 40th Policy Meeting, 'Responsibilities of Service Commanders-in-Chief, Service Divisions and Other Divisions in connection with the Demilitarization of Germany', 7 March 1946.

61. PRO, ADM 228/76, Letter from Vice-Admiral H.T.C. Walker to Air Vice-Marshal H.V. Champion De Crespigny, Regional Commissioner Schleswig-Holstein, 16 July 1946. *House of Lords Debates*, 5th Series, Vol. 141, 15 May 1946, Columns 206–7.

62. PRO, ADM 228/76, Memorandum from Commodore Hugh England to Vice-Admiral Commanding British Naval Forces Germany, 'Changing the Names of German Naval Establishments', 3 April 1946.

63. PRO, ADM 214/20, E. Berry Webber, Architect, 'Report Upon the Inspection of German Naval Barracks July/August 1946'.

64. PRO, FO 1032/1578, Memorandum from Brigadier C.J. Dalen, Chief Army Division to Deputy Military Governor, 'Demilitarisation', 9 Oct. 1946.

65. CCAC, HYND 3/5, 'The Vital Kiel Canal', *British Zone Review*, Vol. 1, No. 12 (2 March 1946), p. 12.

66. PRO, ADM 228/72, Staff Minute by SOP(O), 6 Oct. 1944.

67. FO/SU, 1945, Reel 6, Vol. 47861, Frames 58–60, Letter from British Embassy Moscow to Northern Department, Foreign Office, 23 Oct. 1945.

68. IWM, Savage, 'The Canal', *'Buzz': The Magazine of HMS 'Royal Harold'*, Vol. 1, No. 1 (April 1946), p. 6.

69. PRO, FO 1032/1818, Letter from Admiral Harold Burrough to Secretary of Admiralty, 'The Future of Kiel Canal', 6 Feb. 1946.

70. PRO, FO 1032/1818, Memorandum from P.N.N. Synnott, Admiralty to Vice-Admiral Commanding British Naval Forces Germany, 18 June 1946.

71. PRO, FO 1038/53, Message from Admiralty to Vice-Admiral Commanding British Naval Forces Germany, 18 1426A June 1947.

72. LHC, Lieutenant-Colonel Kenneth Garside, I/3, Naval Intelligence Division, *Germany*, BR 529, Vol. 4, *Ports and Communications*, May 1945, pp. 16–22.

73. NA, RG 331, SHAEF, Office of the Chief of Staff, Secretary, General Staff, File 600.6, Letter from Admiral Harold Burrough to Secretary of Admiralty, 27 April 1945.

74. PRO, FO 1038/144, Office of British Naval Commander-in-Chief Germany, 'Monthly Progress Report 1–28 February 1946'.

75. PRO, ADM 228/27, Message from Vice-Admiral Commanding British Naval Forces Germany to Admiralty, 12 1830A April 1946.

76. BL, Cunningham, Add. Ms. 52578, Diary, 11 Oct. 1945. PRO, ADM 116/5617, Memorandum from C.H.M. Waldock to Director of Dockyards; Director of Naval Construction; Director of Naval Equipment; Director of Electrical Engineering; Director of Naval Ordnance; Civil Engineer-in-Chief; Engineer-in-Chief, 25 Oct. 1945. 'The Navy's Task in Germany', *Naval Review* 37 (1949), p. 28.

77. PRO, ADM 116/5617, Message from Vice-Admiral Commanding British Naval Forces Germany to Admiralty, 22 1200B April 1946.

78. PRO, ADM 228/41, 'Minutes of Meeting to Discuss Disposal of Marinebahn Railway held in HMS *Royal Rupert*', 6 Feb. 1947.

79. PRO, FO 1032/1576, Letter from Brownjohn to Vice-Admiral S.H.T. Arliss, 31 May 1948. *House of Commons Debates*, 5th Series, Vol. 449, 12 April 1948, Column 598.

80. PRO, ADM 228/1, Letter from J. Condon, DCG(Disarmament) to Disarmament

Secretariat, 10 Sept. 1946.

81. PRO, FO 1032/1575, Memorandum from Lieutenant-General Brian Robertson to Foreign Office/German Section, 'Demilitarisation of the German Torpedo Experimental Station at Eckernförde', 2 Aug. 1948.

82. PRO, ADM 116/5761, Memorandum from Mr Madden to Vice Chief of Naval Staff, 'Germany – Destruction of Naval Installations', 24 Sept. 1947. Stokes visited Germany with member of Parliament Nigel Birch and the well-known publisher Victor Gollancz. Ruth Dudley Edwards, *Victor Gollancz: A Biography*, (London: Victor Gollancz, 1987), pp. 433–9. John E. Farquharson, '"Emotional but Influential": Victor Gollancz, Richard Stokes and the British Zone of Germany, 1945–9', *Journal of Contemporary History* 22(1987), p. 518.

83. *House of Commons Debates*, 5th Series, Vol. 427, 9 Oct. 1946, Column 191.

84. PRO, FO 1038/155, Memorandum from Rear-Admiral Stephen Arliss, Flag Officer Commanding British Naval Forces Germany to Chairman, Zonal Demilitarisation Committee, 'Minutes of the Twelfth Demilitarisation Committee Meeting held on 12 September 1947', 29 Sept. 1947.

85. PRO, ADM 116/5761, Memorandum from Rear-Admiral Stephen Arliss to Secretary of Admiralty, 'Demilitarisation of the German Torpedo Experimental Station, Eckernförde', 20 Nov. 1947.

86. PRO, FO 1038/155, Chiefs of Staff Committee, COS(48)9, Memorandum from First Sea Lord, 'Demilitarisation of the German Torpedo Experimental Station at Eckernförde', 17 Jan. 1948.

87. PRO, ADM 228/97, Memorandum from Captain P.W. Brock to Vice-Admiral Commanding British Naval Forces Germany, 'Regulations for Kiel Harbour', 20 May 1946. 'Kiel Becoming the Graveyard of German Sea-Power', *Manchester Guardian* (29 Aug. 1945), p. 8. PRO, ADM 228/77, Memorandum from Captain P.L. Saumarez for Vice-Admiral Commanding British Naval Forces Germany to Senior British Naval Officer Schleswig-Holstein, 'Boarding of British and Allied Merchant Ships', 23 April 1946.

88. PRO, FO 1032/1816, 'Minutes of an Extraordinary Meeting of the Regional Demilitarization Committee, held at Headquarters Military Government, Schleswig-Holstein Region at 1000 hrs on 5 December 1946'. Naval authorities had already dismantled some establishments. OAB/NHC, US Naval Technical Mission in Europe, Series III, Box 26, Technical Report No. 215-45, Captain L.V. Honsinger, USN, Acting Chief, NAVTECHMISEU to Chief of Naval Operations, 'Equipment for Training German Naval Engineering Personnel in Damage Control, Marineschule, Kiel', 21 Aug. 1945.

89. PRO, FO 1032/1817, Memorandum from Major-General V.J.E. Westropp, Chief of Combined Services Division to Deputy Military Governor, 'The Future of the Port of Kiel', 27 Sept. 1947.

90. PRO, FO 1032/1816, Letter from Rear-Admiral Stephen Arliss to Deputy Military Governor, 'Future of the Kiel Shipyards', 15 Oct. 1947.

91. PRO, ADM 116/5761, Memorandum from Captain C.A.G. Nichols to Secretary of Admiralty, 'The Future of Kiel', 30 Oct. 1947.

92. PRO, FO 1038/53, Letter from Lieutenant-General Brian Robertson to Rear-Admiral Stephen Arliss, 'Future of Kiel Shipyard', 30 Oct. 1947.

93. LHC, Garside, Naval Intelligence Division, *Germany*, BR 529, Vol. 3, *Economic Geography*, Nov. 1944, p. 477. CCAC, HYND 3/11, 'German Shipbuilding and Ship Repairing Industry', *British Zone Review*, Vol. 1, No. 34 (4 Jan. 1947), p. 6.

94. PRO, FO 1038/131, Memorandum from H.W.W. Fisher, Assistant Secretary, Transport Division to Secretariat CCG(BE), 'Economic and Industrial Planning Staff: Report of Working Party on the German Shipbuilding Industry', 11 Dec. 1944. Alec Cairncross, *The Price of War: British Policy on German Reparations 1941–1949*, (Oxford: Basil Blackwell, 1986), p. 59.

95. PRO, ADM 116/5617, Letter from P. Branch II, Admiralty to Miss Chasanovitch, Board of Trade, 'Operation TRADEMARK', 19 Nov. 1945.

96. IWM, British Intelligence Objectives Sub-Committee, J.C. Richards, 'Shipbuilding: Notes on Visits to Blohm and Voss, Deutsche Werft, Germania Werft and Deschimag', Jan. 1946.

97. PRO, ADM 228/13, Minutes of Hamburg Ship Repair Committee, 12 Sept. 1945. When Stokes stated in Parliament that the Blohm and Voss graving dock was probably the best in the world for repair of ocean-going merchant ships, the Secretary of State for Foreign Affairs replied: 'Yes, but it also helped to build the Bismarck,' *House of Commons Debates*, 5th Series, Vol. 448, 17 March 1948, Column 2094.

98. PRO, ADM 228/33, Letter from Rear-Admiral W.E. Parry to Ministry of War Transport Representative, Germany, 20 Feb. 1946. Under special arrangements, German shipyards repaired British merchant ships. PRO, ADM 228/99, 'Notes on Meeting held in Hamburg on 22 September 1947 between Representatives of Shipbuilding Branch, Industry Division, FOCBNG, MOT, JEIA, and Legal Division', 22 Sept. 1947.

99. PRO, ADM 116/5617, Letter from A. Belch, The Shipbuilding Conference to A.J. Brailey, P. Branch II, Admiralty, 11 March 1946.

100. PRO, ADM 116/5617, Message from Admiralty to Vice-Admiral Commanding British Naval Forces Germany, 09 1808A May 1946. PRO, ADM 1/19025, Letter from H.A. Turner, P. II Branch, Admiralty to A. Belch, Shipbuilding Conference, 9 Oct. 1947.

101. CCAC, HYND 3/9, 'Schleswig-Holstein: Elimination of the War Potential', *British Zone Review*, Vol. 1, No. 30 (9 Nov. 1946), p. 16.

102. *House of Commons Debates*, 5th Series, Vol. 440, 14 July 1947, Column 3.

103. PRO, ADM 228/32, Message from British Naval Commander-in-Chief Germany to Admiralty, 03 1555A Jan. 1946.

104. PRO, ADM 228/32, 'Record of a Meeting held in Room 115 Norfolk House on Tuesday, 16 April at 11 am', 27 April 1946. Occupation authorities faced pressure 'to get the German fishing fleet to sea in order to supplement their own food rations without drawing on this country [Great Britain]', *House of Commons Debates*, 5th Series, Vol. 420, 14 March 1946, Columns 1282–3.

105. PRO, FO 1038/1816, 'Minutes of a Meeting held by the President, Economic Sub-Commission on 24 July 1946 to discuss Outstanding Questions on Shipbuilding'.

106. PRO, ADM 228/36, Allied Control Authority, Naval Directorate DNAV/P(46)19, 'Drydocking and Repair Ship Facilities to be left for Germany's Peace-Time Requirements', 21 May 1946.

107. PRO, ADM 228/32, Allied Control Authority Naval Directorate, DNVA/Memorandum (46)75, 'Removals from, and New Construction of Fishing Vessels to be permitted for the Restoration of the Capacity of the German Fishing Fleet', 18 Sept. 1946.

108. PRO, ADM 228/34, Letter from T.F. Griffin, Deputy Chief, Food and Agriculture Division to Economic Sub-Committee, HQ CCG(BE), 23 July 1947.

109. PRO, ADM 228/3, Memorandum from British Naval Commander-in-Chief Germany to General Officer Commanding 1st Corps, 'Naval Staff in 1st Corps District (Ruhr)', 25 Aug. 1945.

110. PRO, ADM 228/37, Memorandum from Captain P.W. Brock to British Naval Commander-in-Chief Germany, 12 Feb. 1946.

111. PRO, ADM 116/5617, Letter from J. Hancock, Admiralty to Secretaries, British Nautical Instrument Trade Association, 6 Nov. 1945. The Admiralty sent a mission to examine production methods and tools in the German chronometer and watch industries. PRO, ADM 228/7, A.G.N. Wyatt, Hydrographer, 'Instructions to Lt. Cmdr (Sp) E.A. Goodey (RNVR)', 24 Sept. 1945.

112. PRO, FO 1038/144, Office of British Naval Commander-in-Chief Germany, 'Progress Report 1–31 December 1945'. IWM, Moyse, Diary, p. 188.

113. PRO, FO 1062/83, Letter from Commander P. Bethell, Naval Liaison Officer, Trade and Industry Division to Brigadier H.E. Pike, Director General, Disarmament

Branch, Trade and Industry Division, 6 Dec. 1946.
114. PRO, FO 1038/139, Letter from Rear-Admiral W.E. Parry to Finance Division, Advance HQ for Chambers, 'Soviet Request for Equipment', 28 Sept. 1945.
115. PRO, FO 1032/998, Memorandum from Lieutenant-General W.C.D. Knapton, Deputy Military Governor to Deputy Regional Commissioner, Schleswig-Holstein, 'Alleged Soviet Mercantile Marine Division', 16 Oct. 1947.
116. PRO, ADM 228/43, Letter from Captain C.A.G. Nichols to Shipbuilding Branch, Economic Division, 15 April 1947.

Conclusion

By the latter part of 1947 British naval authorities in occupied Germany felt considerable satisfaction with the progress of disarmament. In spite of numerous restraints and conflicting priorities, the Royal Navy had gone a long way towards its goal of eliminating the personnel, material, and industrial underpinnings of German naval power. The *Kriegsmarine* no longer existed in any recognizable shape or form. During a visit to the Royal Navy's headquarters in Hamburg, a group of officers from the Imperial Defence College listened to talks on demilitarization, disposal of the German fleet, naval intelligence in Germany, and minesweeping commitments, followed by a tour of Hamburg's harbour and cocktails at Admiralty House.[1] The Royal Navy was justifiably proud of its achievements in occupied Germany. The experience was significant since some of these officers would later achieve high rank in the British and Commonwealth armed forces.[2] The Royal Navy made sure that German naval power no longer posed a serious threat to Great Britain's maritime security. The German navy, the Royal Navy's enemy in two world wars, was almost gone.

British naval authorities soon hoped to dispense with the remaining parts. Walker earlier recommended disbandment of the GM/SA by September 1947 because 'the continued existence of a large minesweeping force manned by Germans has proved to be a cause of suspicion and criticism by certain other nations of our speed of disarmament and demilitarization of the Germans.'[3] No one was more diligent than the Royal Navy in German disarmament. Accusations that British authorities were maintaining a 'Black *Reichswehr*' in the British Zone were unfounded.[4] German labour was necessary because large numbers of British minesweepers were now decommissioned. Captain Donald Keppel Bain, RN, replaced Commodore England at the GM/SA on 1 February 1947.[5] Although considerable minesweeping work still remained to be done in waters off the German coasts, disquiet during meetings of the Coordinating Committee in Berlin indicated that the

221

Soviets intended to renew protests against continued employment of the 944 officers, 11,640 ratings, and 60 officials in the British-run minesweeping forces and various *Marinedienstgruppen*. Still firmly convinced of the need to keep personnel under naval administration and discipline until completion of various tasks, Arliss asked the Admiralty to prepare a brief on the GM/SA for Bevin at the Council of Foreign Ministers meeting in Moscow during March and April 1947.[6] The Royal Navy promised to disband the formation by the end of the year.

Naval authorities progressively reduced numbers as minesweeping and other tasks were finished. About half the personnel in the GM/SA had previously disbanded and then volunteered because the British offered steady employment and wages.[7] Arrangements were made to turn over remaining work and responsibilities to civilian administrators. A meeting at the Royal Navy's headquarters in Hamburg on 8 September discussed transformation of the GM/SA into a small minesweeping section under the Frontier Control Service within the Control Commission, to take effect from 1 January 1948.[8] As minesweepers decommissioned, sailors were transferred to Munsterlager for documentation and release.

Except for normal replacement of essential personnel lost through injury, death, or desertion, recruiting for minesweeping ceased after 15 September. The authorized force level in Germany for the coming year was 54 officers and 543 ratings, of whom 36 and 415 had to be seagoing.[9] The Frontier Control Service acquired a much smaller minesweeping organization than the German Minesweeping Administration. From 27 November onwards British authorities no longer issued arrest warrants against absentees and deserters who showed no intention of returning to minesweeping service.[10] Dissolution of the GM/SA allowed the Royal Navy to fulfil its commitments towards demilitarization and disbandment of the German armed forces. There were no more grounds for complaint because the new organization was completely civilian under the Control Commission's authority. Aside from outstanding demolitions and transfer of port facilities to civilian control, the Royal Navy maintained no direct responsibilities towards naval disarmament after 1 January 1948.

The Royal Navy's interest in German naval disarmament after the Second World War was extremely focused. British naval authorities never wavered from the goal of completely eliminating the *Kriegsmarine* and Germany's naval potential. It is difficult to say exactly why this preoccupation was so prevalent within the Royal Navy. Certainly, the fact that British naval officers experienced two major wars against Germany in the same generation played a large part. For Bellairs, Ramsay, Cunningham, Baillie-Grohman, and other senior officers, the

Germans – more often called Huns in personal diaries and letters – were the Royal Navy's unquestioned enemy. If afforded the opportunity, the German navy would again challenge British maritime security. History and recent experience appeared to demonstrate a German inclination towards militarism and aggression. For British naval officers, German naval disarmament became not only desirable, but imperative if Great Britain and Europe wanted peace in the future. The motivations behind German naval disarmament were inseparable from the personal prejudices and attitudes of the key participants.

The role of individuals in driving forward the idea of German naval disarmament cannot be overemphasized. Through various governmental, service, and interallied planning bodies, the Royal Navy formulated and developed plans long before the end of hostilities. The British preferred to have many different overlapping authorities or commands essentially doing the same thing. The complex organizational arrangement worked because individuals provided continuity and interaction from one planning body to the next. A logical progression existed from initial planning under the Military Sub-Committee to detailed planning under the Control Commission, ANCXF, and various commanders-in-chief. Appropriate officers and commands received specific assignments in regards to the surrender and disarmament.

Although the distribution of duties largely sprang from the need for economy, the desire for German naval disarmament also took on a life of its own. British naval authorities sincerely believed that the work was important and necessary. Actually finding sufficient resources and manpower to do a proper job in Germany was a huge administrative problem, particularly with the dispatch of a British fleet to the Pacific and the US Navy's smaller than expected commitment to Germany's occupation. British officers inside and outside the Admiralty fought hard on behalf of German naval disarmament. Despite numerous constraints and commitments, no one in the Royal Navy ever seriously questioned the rationale behind complete disarmament or whether the ambitious goal was even possible. Cunningham and Syfret may have disagreed about allocation of resources and timing, but they fully accepted the need to remove every vestige of the *Kriegsmarine*. There was an institutional consensus that German naval disarmament was a sound idea. The question instead involved how best to reach the desired goal in the shortest possible time and with minimum drain on the Royal Navy's limited means.

To this end, British naval authorities went around or simply ignored inconvenient impediments. One can cite many examples: bypassing the European Advisory Commission to gain Soviet approval for the special naval orders; keeping the German command structure intact to implement the surrender terms; allowing naval courts martial to maintain discipline after the surrender; setting aside the 1929 Geneva Convention by holding sailors as Surrendered Enemy Personnel; maintaining the German Minesweeping Administration and *Marinedienstgruppen* despite existing Control Council laws and Soviet protests; trying Germans before war crimes courts for actions which British officers would have done in the same situation; dumping enormous quantities of ammunition at sea; and blowing up naval establishments and buildings desperately needed to house the German population. The goal of complete naval disarmament overrode legal, diplomatic, and practical concerns. British authorities knew exactly what they wanted to achieve in occupied Germany, and let nothing get in their way until demilitarization was achieved. The attitude sprang from an extreme confidence among British officers that the Royal Navy's activities were in the best interests of Great Britain's strategic security. The end justified the means.

Perhaps even more remarkable was the extent to which the Royal Navy actually realized almost complete German naval disarmament. In little more than two years after the end of the war, the *Kriegsmarine* was entirely disbanded, the Tripartite Naval Commission divided remaining surface ships among Great Britain, the United States, and the Soviet Union, the Royal Navy sank U-boats *en masse* in the North Atlantic under Operation 'Deadlight,' concrete coastal defences and U-boat shelters in Germany were systematically demolished, and maritime-related industries faced severe restrictions or wholesale liquidation. Often extending beyond the demilitarization dictates of Allied Control Council directives, the Royal Navy's disarmament measures were definitely comprehensive.

British naval authorities viewed the occupation as a splendid opportunity to disable German naval power for a long time. Wilhelmshaven, for example, was transformed from a major naval base and centre for shipbuilding into a minor port based upon light industry and tourism. The British may have muddled their way through much of the time, but as one observer remarked, 'for some centuries past the [Royal] Navy has been in the habit of delivering the goods.'[11] British naval authorities in occupied Germany lived up to a long tradition of success. The swift and thorough implementation of German naval disarmament reflected well on the Royal Navy's sense of purpose, especially given the significant manpower and fiscal constraints facing the service in the immediate postwar period.

This study has primarily focused on the Royal Navy's intentions and actions in occupied Germany rather than deliberations at higher political levels or in other government departments between 1942 and 1947.

Revisionist historians who have attempted to find the origins of the Cold War on the British side make many generalizations about Great Britain's early recognition of the Soviet Union as a major threat. Yet, the Foreign Office and Chiefs of Staff Committee records, on which most writers construct their arguments, must be kept in perspective. A tremendous amount of flux characterized international relations in the immediate postwar period. The British, who explored a number of different contingencies, strove to preserve a degree of flexibility in the rapidly changing situation and to keep their options open. The Soviet Union was still very much an unknown quantity. At the service level, the Royal Navy remained preoccupied with a resurgent Germany, the far more familiar enemy. The comprehensive project of German naval disarmament addressed this concern. Even after the British recognized the Soviet Union as a likely adversary and considered building up part of Germany within a western bloc, the Royal Navy vigorously eliminated German naval potential. Historians must take account of this apparent contradiction.

In reality, the transition in attitudes between the German wars and the Cold War took a long time to filter down through the British armed forces. The Royal Navy was just as confused and unsure about relations with the Soviet Union as everybody else. In occupied Germany, British naval authorities maintained a remarkable working relationship with their Soviet counterparts immediately after the war. As this study has shown, the British and Soviets cooperated on the Tripartite Naval Commission, tried major war criminals, and dismantled Germany's industries and dock facilities. Dealing with the Soviets was far from easy, but the British at least made a sincere attempt. The desire to extinguish German military and naval power provided a common bond between the two sides.

Although transferred German warships and submarines facilitated the Red Navy's later expansion, the Royal Navy completely underestimated Soviet naval potential at the time. The oversight was understandable. The Royal Navy, still the predominant European navy, could not imagine a serious Soviet naval threat in the near future. Having played only a small part in the sea war against Germany, the Red Navy was little more than a small coastal force, overshadowed by the dominant Red Army within the Soviet armed forces structure. The experience with Soviet naval authorities in occupied Germany only reinforced the misconception. Throughout the remainder of the 1940s, the Royal Navy really had no identifiable enemy because the US Navy, the largest navy in the world, was a friend and close ally.[12] In this strategic vacuum, Germany persisted as the most likely potential adversary. The growing American naval presence in the Mediterranean from mid-1946 onwards suggests that the US Navy considered the Soviet Union as possibly a major threat at the same time as the Royal Navy, if not earlier.[13] As the Soviet Union emerged as an economic and political superpower, Great Britain and the Royal Navy were powerless to prevent the rise of the Red Navy.

The relationship with the Soviets soon changed dramatically. Admiral Bruce Fraser's visit to Leningrad on the occasion of Red Navy Day in 1946 and the presence of a detachment from the British Mediterranean Fleet in Sevastopol the next year showed that the Admiralty still tried to pursue friendly relations with the Soviets.[14] The attempt became difficult after Kuznetsov's fall from grace within the Red Navy hierarchy and Soviet political structure. With Bizonia and introduction of the Marshall Plan, the Soviets took an increasingly bellicose and hard-line stance towards the British and the Americans. Optimism from Montgomery's visit to Moscow in January 1947 concerning a renewed Anglo-Soviet Treaty was replaced by mistrust and suspicion.[15] The Western Allies and the Soviet Union failed to resolve outstanding issues over Germany during meetings between their foreign ministers in Moscow and London. At the end of 1947 travel restrictions for Royal Navy personnel increased between the British and Soviet Zones.[16] The coup in Czechoslovakia and the Berlin Blockade signified the final breakdown of relations which led to the escalation of the Cold War.

By 1948 the Royal Navy and the rest of the British armed forces confronted the prospect of fighting the Soviet Union. An appreciable Soviet naval threat was still many years away, but the British worried about an invasion of Western Europe. Ironically, Great Britain began to support a West German contribution to the collective defence. German rearmament replaced German disarmament.[17] Actual formation of a West German navy involved several years of debate and negotiation at the national and international levels. The *Bundesmarine*, created in 1956, was predominantly a coastal defence force for deployment in the Baltic. Although drawing upon the experience and traditions of the former *Kriegsmarine*, the new service was built virtually from scratch in terms of warships and establishments. The Royal Navy and the *Bundesmarine* now worked as partners within the North Atlantic Treaty Organization. Old enemies became steadfast friends.

NOTES

1. PRO, ADM 228/21, Memorandum by Flag Officer Commanding British Naval Forces Germany, 'Visit of Imperial Defence College Students to the Royal Naval Headquarters, Hamburg', 25 July 1947.
2. T.I.G. Gray, *The Imperial Defence College and the Royal College of Defence Studies 1927-1977*, (Edinburgh: Her Majesty's Stationery Office, 1977), p. 19.

3. PRO, ADM 228/74, Memorandum from Vice-Admiral H.T.C. Walker to Secretary of Admiralty, 'Future Mine Clearance Policy', 29 May 1946.
4. FO/SU, 1947, Reel 1, Vol. 66279, Frames 5-6, Letter from R.M.A. Hankey to Brigadier C.E.R. Hirsch, 31 Dec. 1946.
5. PRO, ADM 228/74, Message from Captain D.K. Bain to All Concerned, 01 0900 Feb. 1947.
6. PRO, ADM 228/74, Message from Flag Officer Commanding British Naval Forces Germany to Admiralty, 21 1619A Feb. 1947.
7. PRO, ADM 228/91, Memorandum from Captain D.K. Bain to 'A' Branch, British Army of the Rhine, 'Disbandment of GM/SA Personnel', 28 Aug. 1947.
8. PRO, ADM 228/61, Memorandum from Captain G.O. Maund, Controller General, Frontier Control Service to Director of Organization, British Army on the Rhine, 10 Sept. 1947. The Frontier Control Service patrolled and controlled the British Zone's sea and land boundaries. CCAC, HYND 3/9, 'The Frontier Control Service', *British Zone Review*, Vol. 1, No. 30 (9 Nov. 1946), p. 6.
9. PRO, ADM 228/90, Memorandum from J. Maylin for Captain GM/SA to Naval Officer-in-Charge Cuxhaven, 'Base Staff of 1948 M/S Force', 15 Oct. 1947. Gerhard Freiherr von Ledebur, 'Die Räumung von Seeminen in den Gewässern von Nord-, West- und Osteuropa (II) 1948–1956', *Marine Rundschau* 67(1970), p. 341.
10. PRO, ADM 228/82, Letter from Captain D.K. Bain to Senior Naval Officer Schleswig-Holstein and Naval Officer-in-Charge Cuxhaven, 27 Nov. 1947.
11. Frederick Morgan, *Overture to Overlord*, (London: Hodder & Stoughton, 1950), p. 48.
12. Robert S. Jordan, 'Introduction: The Balance of Power and the Anglo-American Maritime Relationship', John B. Hattendorf and Robert S. Jordan, eds., *Maritime Strategy and the Balance of Power: Britain and America in the Twentieth Century*, (New York: St. Martin's Press, 1989), p. 15.
13. Edward J. Sheehy, *The U.S. Navy, the Mediterranean, and the Cold War 1945–1947*, (Westport, CT: Greenwood Press, 1992), p. 71.
14. FO/SU, 1947, Reel 18, Vol. 66407, Frames 56-7, Memorandum from P.N.N. Synnott, Admiralty to R.M.A. Hankey, 18 June 1947.
15. FO/SU, 1947, Reel 1, Vol. 66279, Frames 154–64, War Office to Secretary of State, Foreign Office, 'Address by Field-Marshal Montgomery to Officers of the War Office on 20 January 1947', 24 Jan. 1947. Wayne Knight, 'Labourite Britain: America's "Sure Friend"? The Anglo-Soviet Treaty Issue, 1947', *Diplomatic History* 7(1983), pp. 273–5.
16. PRO, ADM 228/100, Letter from Lieutenant-Colonel G.S. Hutchinson for Lieutenant-General Brian Robertson to Flag Officer Commanding British Naval Forces Germany, 5 Dec. 1947.
17. BA/MA, Ruge, N 379/6, Lecture Notes WS 63/64 V4/1, 'Strategie, Rüstung, Abrüstung 1945–1953'.

Bibliography

PRIMARY SOURCES

Archives, Museums, and Libraries:

GREAT BRITAIN

Public Record Office, Kew:

ADM	1	Admiralty and Secretariat
ADM	116	Admiralty and Secretariat
ADM	167	Board of Admiralty
ADM	177	Navy Lists
ADM	186	Admiralty Publications
ADM	199	War Histories
ADM	202	Royal Marines
ADM	205	First Sea Lord
ADM	214	Civil Engineer-in-Chief
ADM	223	Naval Intelligence
ADM	228	British Naval Commander-in-Chief Germany
ADM	232	Central Mine Clearance Board
ADM	234	Navy Reference Books: BR Series
CAB	79	Chiefs of Staff Committee: Minutes
CAB	80	Chiefs of Staff Committee: Memoranda
CAB	81	Chiefs of Staff Sub-Committees
CAB	109	London Munitions Assignment Board
CAB	118	Deputy Prime Minister
DEFE	3	Intelligence Signals
FO	937	Control Office: Legal
FO	1032	Control Commission for Germany (British Element): Planning Staff, Military Sections and Headquarters Secretariat
FO	1038	Control Commission for Germany (British Element): Military Divisions
FO	1060	Control Commission for Germany (British Element): Legal Division

FO	1062	Control Commission for Germany (British Element): Disarmament Branch
TS	26	Treasury Solicitor and HM Procurator General: War Crimes
WO	205	21st Army Group
WO	235	Judge Advocate General's Office: War Crimes
WO	311	Judge Advocate General's Office: War Crimes
WO	331	HQ Allied Land Forces Norway: War Crimes Investigation Branch

Imperial War Museum, Lambeth North:

Petty Officer M.W. Ackroyd, WRNS(Y)
Commander O.M. Andrew, RN
Admiral Sir Ernest Russell Archer, RN
Vice-Admiral Harold Tom Baillie-Grohman, RN
Commander Joseph Howell Bartlett, RN
Lieutenant Lionel H. Blaxell, RNR
Admiral Sir Harold Martin Burrough, RN
Combined Intelligence Objectives Sub-Committee
Admiral Sir Gerald Charles Dickens, RN
Air Marshal Sir Sholto Douglas (Lord Douglas of Kirtleside), RAF
Rear-Admiral Hugh Turnour England, RN
Admiral John Henry Godfrey, RN
Sub-Lieutenant Lancelot Stephen Harris, RNVR
Commander R.P.C. Hawkins, RN
General Sir Leslie Hollis, RM
Signalman John Knight, RN
Lieutenant Eric Harold Langridge, RNVR
Lieutenant-Commander H.D. Marquis, RNR
Constructor Captain A.J. Merrington, RN
Field Marshal Bernard Law Montgomery (Viscount Montgomery
    of Alamein)
Admiral Sir Henry Ruthven Moore, RN
Lieutenant Howard B. Moyse, RNVR
Admiral Sir William Edward Parry, RN
Vice-Admiral Edmund Gerard Noel Rushbrooke, RN
Lieutenant-Commander F.M. Savage, RN
Sub-Lieutenant Desmond P. Scarle, RNVR
Signalman A. Vincent
Admiral Sir William Jock Whitworth, RN
Vice-Admiral Sir Peveril William-Powlett, RN
Admiral of the Fleet Sir Algernon Usborne Willis, RN
Captain F.S.W. de Winton, RN
Commander F.T. Woosnam, RN
Miscellaneous Files

National Maritime Museum, Greenwich:

Admiral Sir Geoffrey Blake, RN

Vice-Admiral Harold Tom Baillie-Grohman, RN
Rear-Admiral Reginald Vesey Holt, RN
Admiral Sir Geoffrey John Audley Miles, RN
Admiral Lord John Cronyn Tovey, RN

British Library, Department of Manuscripts, London:

Admiral of the Fleet Andrew Browne Cunningham (Viscount
    Cunningham of Hyndhope), RN

Naval Historical Branch, Ministry of Defence, Whitehall:

Rear-Admiral Roger Mowbray Bellairs, RN

*Liddell Hart Centre for Military Archives, King's College, University of
London:*

Commander Douglas Capper
Major-General Sir Francis Wilfred De Guingand
General Sir Miles Christopher Dempsey
Major-General Richard Henry Dewing
Lieutenant-Colonel Kenneth Garside
Commander Patrick Dalzel Job, RNVR
Admiral Sir Gerald Charles Dickens, RN
Lieutenant-Commander Leonard George Hart, RN
Lieutenant-Commander Quintin Riley, RNVR

National Army Museum, Chelsea:

General Sir Andrew Thorne

Churchill College Archive Centre, Churchill College, Cambridge University:

Albert Victor Alexander
Admiral of the Fleet Andrew Browne Cunningham (Viscount
    Cunningham of Hyndhope), RN
Captain Henry Mangles Denham, RN
Admiral Sir John Edelsten, RN
Commander H.J. Fawcett, RN
Sir David Maxwell Fyfe (Earl of Kilmuir)
Admiral John Henry Godfrey, RN
John Burns Hynd
William Harold Ingrams
Lieutenant-Commander Ralph Izzard, RNVR
Admiral Sir Bertram Home Ramsay, RN
Captain Stephen Wentworth Roskill, RN
Admiral of the Fleet Sir James Somerville, RN
Admiral of the Fleet Sir Algernon Usborne Willis, RN

GERMANY

Bundesarchiv-Militärarchiv, Freiburg:

RM   6   Oberbefehlshaber der Kriegsmarine
RM   7   Seekriegsleitung
RM 22 Marinewehramt
RM 54 Führer der Zerstörer
RM 87 Befehlshabers der Unterseeboote
RW   2   Oberkommando der Wehrmacht:
           Wehrmachtrechtsabteilung
RW 17 Wehrmachtkommandanturen
RW 37 Wehrmachtbefehlshaber in den Niederlanden
RW 38 Wehrmachtbefehlshaber Dänemark
RW 44/I Oberkommando der Wehrmacht:
           Führungsstab Nord

Nachlässe (Personal Papers):

N 236   Grossadmiral Karl Dönitz
N 328   Admiral Erich Förste
N 374   Generaladmiral Hans Georg von Friedeburg
N 379   Vizeadmiral Friedrich Ruge
N 391   Grossadmiral Erich Raeder
N 539   Konteradmiral Gerhard Wagner

UNITED STATES

National Archives, Washington DC:

RG   38   Office of the Chief of Naval Operations/Commander-
          in-Chief United States Fleet (Operations Division)
RG 313 Commander United States Naval Forces in Europe
RG 331 Supreme Headquarters Allied Expeditionary Force
RG 242 Captured German Records
T-77   Oberkommando der Wehrmacht
T-608   Oberkommando der Kriegsmarine
T-1022 Records of the German Navy, 1850–1945

Library of Congress, Washington, DC:

Admiral Frederick Joseph Horne, USN
Fleet Admiral Ernest Joseph King, USN
Disarmament and Disbandment of the German Armed Forces

United States Naval Historical Center, Washington DC:

Operational Archives Branch

German Naval Archives, 1922–1945
Admiral H. Kent Hewitt, USN

Admiral Alan Goodrich Kirk, USN
Fleet Admiral William D. Leahy, USN
Rear-Admiral Clarence Edward Olsen, USN
Admiral Harold Raynsford Stark, USN
United States Naval Technical Mission in Europe
World War II Command Files
Admiral Harry Ervin Yarnell, USN

Navy Department Library

United States Naval Administrative Histories of World War II

Oral History Research Office, Columbia University, New York:

Admiral H. Kent Hewitt, USN
Admiral Alan Goodrich Kirk, USN

CANADA

National Archives of Canada, Ottawa:

Canadian Naval Mission Overseas
Army Central Registry Files
Navy Central Registry Files

Directorate of History, Department of National Defence Headquarters, Ottawa:

Canadian Naval Mission Overseas
Army Central Registry Files
Navy Central Registry Files

Judge Advocate General's Office, Department of National Defence Headquarters, Ottawa:

Law Reports of Trials of War Criminals

Canadian Red Cross Archives, Ottawa:

International Committee of the Red Cross – Prisoners of War

Special Collections, McPherson Library, University of Victoria, Victoria:

British Army of the Rhine, *30 Corps District Handbook*,
    [s.n.]: HQ 30 Corps District, August 1945.
21st Army Group, *Operation 'Eclipse': The Occupation of
    North-West Germany*, Belgium: [n.p.], Jan. 1945.

Oral History Interviews:

Major Charles Elsworth Goodman
Lieutenant-Colonel Lawrence S. Henderson

Published Documents:

Beitzell, Robert, ed., *Teheran, Yalta, Potsdam: The Soviet Protocols*, Hattiesburg, MI: Academic International, 1970.

British Army of the Rhine, *Administrative History of Operations of 21 Army Group on the Continent of Europe, 6 June 1944–8 May 1945*, Germany: [n.p.], November 1945.

Bullen, Roger and M.E. Pelly, eds., *Documents on British Policy Overseas*, Series I Vol. 2, *Conferences and Conversations 1945: London, Washington and Moscow*, London: Her Majesty's Stationery Office, 1985.

Butler, Rohan and M.E. Pelly, eds., *Documents on British Policy Overseas*, Series I Vol. 1, *The Conference at Potsdam July–August 1945*, London: Her Majesty's Stationery Office, 1984.

Cameron, John, ed., *Trial of Heinz Eck, August Hoffman, Walter Weisspfennig, Hans Richard Lenz and Wolfgang Schwender (The Peleus Trial)*, London: William Hodge & Co., 1948.

Chandler, Alfred D., and Stephen Ambrose, eds, *The Papers of Dwight David Eisenhower: The War Years*, Vol. 4, Baltimore: Johns Hopkins University Press, 1970.

Chandler, Alfred D. and Couis Galambos, eds, *The Papers of Dwight David Eisenhower: Occupation, 1945*, Vol. 6, Baltimore: Johns Hopkins University Press, 1978.

Combined Chiefs of Staff, *Wartime Conferences of the Combined Chiefs of Staff, 1941–1945*, Wilmington, DE: Scholarly Resources Inc., 1983.

Dilks, David, ed., *The Diaries of Sir Alexander Cadogan, 1938–1945*, London: Cassell, 1971.

Duckworth, Arthur Dyce, *An Introduction to Naval Court Martial Procedure*, Devonport: Hiorns & Miller, 1943.

Eisenhower, Dwight D., *Report by the Supreme Commander to the Combined Chiefs of Staff on the Operations in Europe of the Allied Expeditionary Force 6 June 1944 to 8 May 1945*, London: His Majesty's Stationery Office, 1946.

Germany. Kriegsmarine, *'Die Kriegsmarine' Deutsche Marine Zeitung*, 4 Volumes, Hamburg: Verlag für geschichtliche Dokumentation GmbH, 1978.

Gilbert, Martin, ed., *The Churchill War Papers: At the Admiralty*, Vol. 1, New York: W.W. Norton, 1993.

Great Britain. Admiralty, *Fuehrer Conferences on Naval Affairs*, 7 Volumes, London: Admiralty, August 1947.

—, *The King's Regulations and Admiralty Instructions for the Government of His Majesty's Naval Service*, 2 Volumes, London: His Majesty's Stationery Office, 1939–40.

—, *Preliminary Narrative: The War at Sea*, 6 Volumes, London: Historical Section, Tactical and Staff Duties Division, Admiralty Naval Staff, 1946.

Great Britain. Foreign Office, *British Foreign Office: Russian Correspon-*

dence (FO 371), Wilmington, DE: Scholarly Resources Inc. 1976–82:
1941–1945: World War II,
1946–1948: The Onset of the Cold War.

Great Britain. Ministry of Defence (Navy), Günter Hessler, *The U-Boat War in the Atlantic 1939–1945,* London: Her Majesty's Stationery Office, 1989.

Great Britain. Royal Air Force, *Royal Air Force: Final Reports on Operations – Night Raids, 1941–1945,* Wilmington, DE: Scholarly Resources Inc., 1977.

Great Britain. War Office, *Manual of Military Law,* 7th edition, London: His Majesty's Stationery Office, 1929.

Gruchmann, Lothar, 'Ausgewählte Dokumente zur deutschen Marinejustiz im Zweiten Weltkrieg,' *Vierteljahrshefte für Zeitgeschichte* 26 (1978), pp. 433–98.

Hattendorf, John B., Knight, R.J.B., Pearsall, A.W.H., Rodger, N.A.M., and Till, Geoffrey, eds., *British Naval Documents 1204–1960,* Aldershot: Scholar Press, Naval Records Society, 1993.

Hürten, Heinz, 'Im Umbruch der Normen: Dokumente über die deutsche Militärjustiz nach der Kapitulation der Wehrmacht,' *Militärgeschichtliche Mitteilungen* 2 (1980), pp. 137–56.

Justiz und NS-Verbrechen, Vol. 5, Amsterdam: University Press, 1970.

Kesaris, Paul, ed., *Records of the Joint Chiefs of Staff Part 1: 1942–1945 Meetings,* Frederick, MD: University Publications of America, 1981.

King, Ernest J., *U.S. Navy at War 1941–1945: Official Reports to the Secretary of the Navy,* Washington, DC: Department of the Navy, 1946.

Levie, Howard S., ed., *Documents on Prisoners of War,* International Law Studies 60, Newport, RI: Naval War College Press, 1979.

Loewenheim, Francis L., Harold D. Langley, and Manfred Jonas, eds., *Roosevelt and Churchill: Their Secret Wartime Correspondence,* New York: E.P. Dutton & Co., 1975.

Love, Robert W. and John Major, eds., *The Year of D-Day: The 1944 Diary of Admiral Sir Bertram Home Ramsay,* Hull: University of Hull Press, 1994.

Millis, Walter, ed., *The Forrestal Diaries,* New York: Viking Press, 1951.

National Archives and Records Administration, *Germany Surrenders, 1945,* Washington DC: National Archives Trust Fund Board, 1989.

Oaksey, Lord, 'The Nuremberg Trials and the Progress of International Law,' Presidential Address to the Holdsworth Club, University of Birmingham, 21 June 1947.

Pelly, M.E. and Yasamee, H.J., eds., *Documents on British Policy Overseas,* Series I Vol. 5, *Germany and Western Europe 11 August–31 December 1945,* London: Her Majesty's Stationery Office, 1990.

Pospelov, Piotr N., ed., *The History of the Great Patriotic War of the Soviet Union, 1941–1945,* Wilmington, DE: Scholarly Resources Inc., 1985.

Pritt, Denis Nowell, *War Criminals,* London: Labour Monthly, 1944.

Ronzitti, Natolini, *The Law of Naval Warfare: A Collection of Agreements and Documents with Commentaries,* Dordrecht: Martinus Nijhoff Publishers, 1988.

Ross, Graham, ed., *The Foreign Office and the Kremlin: British Documents on Anglo-Soviet Relations, 1941–45*, Cambridge: Cambridge University Press, 1984.

Rothstein, Andrew, ed., *Soviet Foreign Policy During the Patriotic War: Documents and Materials*, London: Hutchinson & Co., 1948.

Schramm, Percy Ernst, ed., *Kriegstagebuch des Oberkommandos der Wehrmacht (Wehrmachtführungsstab)*, 4 Volumes, Frankfurt am Main: Bernard und Graefe Verlag für Wehrwesen, 1961.

Showell, Jak P., ed., *Fuehrer Conferences on Naval Affairs, 1939–1945*, London: Greenhill, 1990.

Simpson, Michael, ed., *The Somerville Papers: Selections from the Private and Official Correspondence of Admiral of the Fleet Sir James Somerville, GCB, GBE, DSO*, Aldershot: Scholar Press, Navy Records Society, 1995.

Smith, Jean Edward, ed., *The Papers of General Lucius D. Clay: Germany 1945–1949*, Vol. 1, Bloomington: Indiana University Press, 1974.

Stevens, E.H., ed., *Trial of Nikolaus von Falkenhorst*, London: William Hodge & Co., 1949.

Union of Soviet Socialist Republics. Ministry of Foreign Affairs, *Correspondence Between the Chairman of the Council of Ministers of the U.S.S.R. and the Presidents of the U.S.A. and the Prime Ministers of Great Britain During the Great Patriotic War of 1941–1945*, 2 Volumes, Moscow: Foreign Languages Publishing House, 1957.

United Nations. *Agreement by the Government of the United Kingdom of Great Britain and Northern Ireland, the Government of the United States of America, the Provisional Government of the French Republic and the Government of the Union of Soviet Socialist Republics for the Prosecution and Punishment of the Major War Criminals of the European Axis signed London, 8 August 1945*, London: His Majesty's Stationery Office, 1945.

United Nations. International Military Tribunal, *The Trial of German Major War Criminals*, 22 Parts, London: His Majesty's Stationery Office, 1947.

—, *Judgment of the International Military Tribunal for the Trial of German Major War Criminals (with the Dissenting Opinion of the Soviet Member)*, London: His Majesty's Stationery Office, 1946.

United States. Department of the Navy. Naval Security Group Command Headquarters, *Intelligence Reports on the War in the Atlantic, 1942–1945*, Wilmington, DE: Scholarly Resources Inc., 1980.

United States. Department of State, *Documents on Germany 1944–1985*, Washington, DC: Government Printing Office, 1985.

—, *Foreign Relations of the United States Diplomatic Papers 1944*, Vol. 1, Washington, DC: Government Printing Office, 1966.

—, *Foreign Relations of the United States Diplomatic Papers: The Conference of Berlin (The Potsdam Conference) 1945*, 2 Volumes, Washington, DC: Government Printing Office, 1960.

—, *Report of Robert H. Jackson, United States Representative to the International Conference on Military Trials*, Washington, DC: Government Printing Office, 1949.

Vansittart, Robert, *Black Record: Germans Past and Present*, London: Hamish Hamilton, 1941.

Wagner, Gerhard, ed., *Lagevorträge des Oberbefehlshabers der Kriegsmarine vor Hitler 1939–1945*, Munich: Lehmanns, 1972.

Wild, Payson Sibley, ed., *International Law Documents 1944–45*, Naval War College International Law Studies, Washington, DC: Government Printing Office, 1946.

SECONDARY SOURCES

Bibliographies, Guides, Reference Works, and Finding Aids:

A Guide to the Holdings of the Churchill Archives Centre, Cambridge: Churchill College Archives Centre, Cambridge University, Sept. 1993.

Allard, Dean C., Martha L. Crawley, and Mary W. Edmison, *U.S. Naval History Sources in the United States*, Washington DC: Naval History Division, Department of the Navy, 1979.

Bird, Keith W., *German Naval History: A Guide to the Literature*, New York: Garland, 1985.

Cantwell, John D., *The Second World War: A Guide to Documents in the Public Record Office*, London: HMSO Publications, 1993.

Heimdal, William C. and Marolda, Edward J., *Guide to United States Naval Administrative Histories of World War II*, Washington DC: Naval History Division, Department of the Navy, 1976.

Hooper, Edwin B., *Partial Checklist: World War II Histories and Historical Reports in the U.S. Naval History Division*, Washington DC: Operational Archives, Naval History Division, April 1977.

Knight, R.J.B., ed., *Guide to the Manuscripts in the National Maritime Museum*, 2 Volumes, London: Mansell, 1977–80.

Law, Derek G., *The Royal Navy in World War II: An Annotated Bibliography*, London: Greenhill, 1988.

Lenton, H.T., *German Warships of the Second World War*, London: Macdonald & Jane's, 1975.

Lohmann, Walter and Hans H. Hildebrand, *Die deutsche Kriegsmarine 1939–1945*, 3 Volumes, Bad Nauheim: Podzun-Verlag, 1956–64.

Lynch, Barbara A. and John E. Vajda, *United States Naval History: A Bibliography*, Washington, DC: Naval Historical Center, Department of the Navy, 1993.

Mayer, S.L. and W.J. Koenig, *The Two World Wars: A Guide to Manuscript Collections in the United Kingdom*, London: Bowker, 1976.

Meister, Jürg, *Soviet Warships of the Second World War*, London: Macdonald & Jane's, 1977.

Methven, Patricia J., *Liddell Hart Centre for Military Archives Consolidated List of Accessions*, London: King's College, University of London, 1986.

—, *Liddell Hart Centre for Military Archives Consolidated List of Accessions: Supplement 1 August 1985–1 November 1990*, London: King's College, University of London, 1991.

Mulligan, Timothy, *Guides to the Microfilmed Records of the German Navy, 1850–1945: No.2, Records Relating to U-Boat Warfare, 1939–1945*, Washington, DC: National Archives Records Administration, 1985.

Range, Clemens, *Die Ritterkreuzträger der Kriegsmarine*, Stuttgart: Motorbuch Verlag, 1974.

Rasor, Eugene L., *British Naval History since 1815: A Guide to the Literature*, New York: Garland, 1990.

Rohwer, J. and G. Hümmelchen, *Chronology of the War at Sea, 1939–1945*, 2 Volumes, London: Ian Allan, 1974.

Showell, Jak P. Mallmann, *The German Navy in World War Two: A Reference Guide to the Kriegsmarine, 1935–1945*, London: Arms & Armour Press, 1979.

Smith, Myron J., Jr., *The European Theatre: World War II at Sea. A Bibliography of Sources in English*, New York: Metuchen, 1976.

Dictionary of National Biography, 1901–1989.

Books and Dissertations:

Achkasov, V.I. and N.B. Pavlovich, *Soviet Naval Operations in the Great Patriotic War 1941–1945*, Annapolis: Naval Institute Press, 1981.

Adams, Henry H., *Witness to Power: The Life of Fleet Admiral William D. Leahy*, Annapolis: Naval Institute Press, 1985.

Ahmann, R., A.M. Burke, and Michael Howard, eds., *The Quest for Stability: Problems of West European Security, 1918–1957*, London: The German Historical Institute, Oxford University Press, 1993.

Albion, Robert Greenhalgh, *Makers of Naval Policy 1798–1947*, Annapolis: Naval Institute Press, 1980.

Ambrose, Stephen E., *The Supreme Commander: The War Years of General Dwight D. Eisenhower*, Garden City, NY: Doubleday and Co., 1970.

Andenaes, John, Olav Riste, and M. Skodvin, *Norway in the Second World War*, Oslo: Johan Grundt Tanum Forlag, 1974.

Anderson, Terry H., *The United States, Great Britain, and the Cold War, 1944–1947*, Columbia: University of Missouri Press, 1981.

Appleman, John Alan, *Military Tribunals and International Crimes*, Indianapolis: Bobbs-Merrill, 1954.

Aronsen, Lawrence and Martin Kitchen, *The Origins of the Cold War in Comparative Perspective: American, British, and Canadian Relations with the Soviet Union, 1941–1948*, New York: St. Martin's Press, 1988.

Attlee, Clement, *As It Happened*, London: William Heinemann, 1954.

Bardens, Dennis, *Lord Justice Birkett*, London: Robert Hale, 1962.

Barker, Elisabeth, *Britain in a Divided Europe 1945–1970*, London: Weidenfeld & Nicolson, 1971.

—, *The British Between the Superpowers, 1945–50*, London: Macmillan Press, 1983.

Barnett, Correlli, *The Audit of War: The Illusion and Reality of Britain as a Great Nation*, London: Macmillan, 1986.

—, *Engage the Enemy More Closely: The Royal Navy in the Second World War*, London: Hodder & Stoughton, 1991.

—, eds., *Hitler's Generals*, London: Weidenfeld & Nicolson, 1989.

Bartlett, C.J., *The Long Retreat: A Short History of British Defence Policy, 1945–70*, London: Macmillan Press, 1972.

Bartov, Omer, *The Eastern Front, 1941–45: German Troops and the*

Barbarisation of Warfare, Basingstoke, Hampshire: Macmillan, 1985.

Baylis, John, *British Defence Policy: Striking the Right Balance*, New York: St. Martin's Press, 1989.

—, *The Diplomacy of Pragmatism: Britain and the Formation of NATO, 1942–49*, London: Macmillan, 1993.

Becker, Josef and Franz Knipping, eds., *Power in Europe?: Great Britain, France, Italy and Germany in a Postwar World 1945–1950*, New York: Walter de Gruyter, 1986.

Becker, Winfried, ed., *Die Kapitulation von 1945 und der Neubeginn in Deutschland*, Wien: Böhlau, 1987.

Beesly, Patrick, *Very Special Admiral: The Life of Admiral J.H. Godfrey, CB*, London: Hamish Hamilton, 1980.

—, *Very Special Intelligence: The Story of the Admiralty's Operational Intelligence Centre 1939–1945*, London: Hamish Hamilton, 1977.

Behrens, C.B.A., *Merchant Shipping and the Demands of War*, London: Her Majesty's Stationery Office, 1955.

Bell, P.M.H., *John Bull and the Bear: British Public Opinion, Foreign Policy, and the Soviet Union, 1941–1945*, New York: Edward Arnold, 1991.

Benton, Wilbourn E. and Georg Grimm, eds., *Nuremberg: German Views of the War Trials*, Dallas: Southern Methodist University Press, 1955.

Best, Geoffrey, *Humanity in Warfare: The Modern History of the International Law of Armed Conflicts*, London: Methuen, 1983.

Best, Richard A., *'Co-operation with Like-Minded Peoples': British Influences on American Security Policy 1945–1949*, Westport, CT: Greenwood Press, 1986.

Biddle, Francis, *In Brief Authority*, New York: Doubleday, 1962.

Bird, Keith W., *The German Naval Officer Corps and the Rise of National Socialism*, Amsterdam: B.R. Grüner, 1977.

Bischof, Günter and Stephen E. Ambrose, eds., *Eisenhower and the German POWs: Facts against Falsehood*, Baton Rouge: Louisiana State University Press, 1992.

Black, Thompson Jr., *Prize Law in World War II*, Ph.D Dissertation, Los Angeles: University of California, 1954.

Blackwell, Michael, *Clinging to Grandeur: British Attitudes and Foreign Policy in the Aftermath of the Second World War*, Westport, CT: Greenwood Press, 1993.

Bosch, William J., *Judgment on Nuremberg: American Attitudes Toward the Major German War Crime Trials*, Chapel Hill: University of North Carolina Press, 1970.

Brown, D.K., *A Century of Naval Construction: The History of the Royal Corps of Naval Constructors 1883–1983*, London: Conway Maritime Press, 1983.

Bryant, Arthur, *Triumph in the West 1943–1946*, London: Collins, 1959.

Bullock, Allen, *Ernest Bevin: Foreign Secretary 1945–1951*, London: Heinemann, 1983.

Burridge, T.D., *British Labour and Hitler's War*, London: Deutsch, 1976.

Buell, Thomas B., *Master of Sea Power: A Biography of Fleet Admiral Ernest J. King*, Boston: Little, Brown, 1980.

Busch, Fritz-Otto, *The Story of the Prinz Eugen*, London: Futura, 1975

(1958).

Butcher, Harry C., *My Three Years with Eisenhower*, New York: Simon & Schuster, 1946.

Cairncross, Alec, *The Price of War: British Policy on German Reparations 1941–1949*, Oxford: Blackwell, 1986.

Calvocoressi, Peter, *Nuremberg: The Facts, the Law and the Consequences*, London: Chatto & Windus, 1947.

Carver, Michael, *Tightrope Walking: British Defence Policy since 1945*, London: Hutchinson, 1992.

Chalfont, Alun, *Montgomery of Alamein*, London: Weidenfeld & Nicolson, 1976.

Chalmers, Malcom, *Paying for Defence: Military Spending and British Decline*, London: Pluto Press, 1985.

Chalmers, William Scott, *Full Cycle: The Biography of Admiral Sir Bertram Home Ramsay KCB, KBE, MVO*, London: Hodder & Stoughton, 1959.

—, *Max Horton and the Western Approaches: A Biography of Admiral Sir Max Kennedy Horton*, London: Hodder & Stoughton, 1954.

Cherry, Alex H., *Yankee R.N.*, London: Jarrolds, 1951.

Churchill, Winston, *Triumph and Tragedy*, Boston: Houghton & Mifflin, 1953.

Coles, Alan, *Slaughter at Sea: The Truth Behind a Naval War Crime*, London: R. Hale, 1986.

Conot, Robert E., *Justice at Nuremberg*, New York: Harper & Row, 1983.

Cooper, R.W., *The Nuremberg Trial*, New York: Penguin, 1947.

Courtney, Anthony, *Sailor in a Russian Frame*, London: Johnson, 1968.

Cramer, Peter, *U-Boat Commander: A Periscope View of the Battle of the Atlantic*, Annapolis: Naval Institute Press, 1984.

Craven, Wesley Frank and James Lea Cate, *The Army Air Forces in World War II*, Vol. 3, *Europe: Argument to V–E Day January 1944–May 1945*, Chicago: University of Chicago Press, 1951.

Creswell, John, *Sea Warfare, 1939–1945*, London: Longmans, Green & Co., 1950.

Crowe, W.J., *The Policy Roots of the Royal Navy 1945–63*, Ph.D Dissertation, Princeton: Princeton University, 1965.

Cunningham, Andrew Browne, *A Sailor's Odyssey: The Autobiography of Admiral of the Fleet Viscount Cunningham of Hyndhope*, London: Hutchinson & Co., 1951.

Davis, Vincent, *Postwar Defense Policy and the U.S. Navy, 1943–1946*, Chapel Hill: University of North Carolina Press, 1966.

De Guingand, Francis, *Operation Victory*, London: Hodder & Stoughton, 1947.

De Lupis, Ingrid Detter, *The Law of War*, Cambridge: Cambridge University Press, 1987.

Deane, Charles R., *The Strange Alliance*, New York: Viking, 1946.

Deighton, Anne, ed., *Britain and the First Cold War*, Basingstoke, Hampshire: Macmillan, 1990.

—, *The Impossible Peace: Britain, the Division of Germany and the Origins of the Cold War*, Oxford: Clarendon Press, 1990.

Deist, Wilhelm, ed., *The German Military in the Age of Total War*, London:

Berg, 1985.

Denham, Henry, *Inside the Nazi Ring: A Naval Attaché in Sweden 1940–1945*, London: John Murray, 1984.

Divine, A.D., *Navies in Exile*, London: Murray, 1944.

Dockrill, Michael, *British Defence since 1945*, New York: Basil Blackwell, 1988.

— and John Young, eds., *British Foreign Policy, 1945–56*, New York: St. Martin's, 1989.

Dockrill, Saki, *Britain's Policy for West German Rearmament 1950–1955*, Cambridge: Cambridge University Press, 1991.

Dönitz, Karl, *Deutsche Strategie zur See im Zweiten Weltkrieg: Die Antworten des Grossadmirals auf 40 Fragen*, Frankfurt am Main: Bernard und Graefe, 1970.

—, *Memoirs: Ten Years and Twenty Days*, London: Weidenfeld & Nicolson, 1959.

Donnison, F.S.V., *Civil Affairs and Military Government: Central Organization and Planning*, London: Her Majesty's Stationery Office, 1966.

—, *Civil Affairs and Military Government: North-West Europe 1944–1946*, London: Her Majesty's Stationery Office, 1961.

Douglas, Roy, *From War to Cold War 1942–48*, London: Macmillan, 1981.

Douglas, Sholto (with Robert Wright), *Years of Command: The Autobiography of Sholto Douglas, Marshal of the Royal Air Force Lord Douglas of Kirtleside GCB, MC, DFC*, London: Collins, 1966.

Duffy, Christopher, *Red Storm on the Reich: The Soviet March on Germany, 1945*, London: Routledge, 1991.

Edmonds, Robin, *Setting the Mould: The United States and Britain 1945–1950*, New York: W.W. Norton, 1986.

Edwards, Kenneth, *Seven Sailors*, London: Collins, 1945.

Edwards, Ruth Dudley, *Victor Gollancz: A Biography*, London: Victor Gollancz, 1987.

Ehrman, John, *Grand Strategy*, Vol. 5 and 6, London: Her Majesty's Stationery Office, 1956.

Eisenhower, David, *Eisenhower at War 1943–1945*, New York: Random House, 1986.

Eisenhower, Dwight D., *Crusade in Europe*, Garden City, NY: Doubleday & Co., 1948.

Ellis, L.F., *Victory in the West*, 2 Volumes, London: Her Majesty's Stationery Office, 1962 and 1968.

Faulk, Henry, *Group Captives: The Re-education of German Prisoners of War in Britain 1945–1948*, London: Chatto & Windus, 1977.

Feis, Herbert, *Between War and Peace: The Potsdam Conference*, Princeton, NJ: Princeton University Press, 1960.

Fenrick, William John, *Developments in the Law of Naval Warfare since World War II: The Potential Emergence of a Law of Naval Warfare for Limited Conflicts*, LLM. Thesis, Washington, DC: National Law Center, George Washington University, 1983.

Fleck, Dieter, ed., *The Gladisch Committee on the Law of Naval Warfare: A German Effort to Develop International Law During World War II*,

Bochumer Schriften zur Friedenssicherung und zum Humanitären Volkerrecht, Vol. 5, Bochum: UVB-Universitätsverlag Dr. N. Brockmeyer, 1990.

Foschepoth, Joseph and Rolf Steininger, eds., *Die Britische Deutschland- und Besatzungspolitik 1945–1949*, Paderborn: Ferdinand Schöningh, 1985.

French, David, *The British Way in Warfare 1688–2000*, London: Unwin Hyman, 1990.

Gardiner, Leslie, *The British Admiralty*, Edinburgh and London: William Blackwood & Son, 1968.

Gibb, Andrew Dewar, *Perjury Unlimited: A Monograph on Nuremberg*, Edinburgh: Wm. Green & Son, 1954.

Gilbert, G.M., *Nuremberg Diary*, New York: Farrar, Straus, & Co., 1947.

Gilbert, Martin, *'Never Despair': Winston S. Churchill 1945–1965*, London: Heinemann, 1988.

Gillette, Philip S. and Willard C. Frank Jr., eds., *The Sources of Soviet Naval Conduct*, Lexington: Lexington Books, DC Heath & Co., 1990.

Gimbel, John, *The American Occupation of Germany: Politics and the Military, 1945–1949*, Stanford: Stanford University Press, 1968.

—, *Science, Technology, and Reparations: Exploitation and Plunder in Postwar Germany*, Stanford: Stanford University Press, 1990.

Goulter, Christina J.M., *A Forgotten Offensive: Royal Air Force Coastal Command's Anti-Shipping Campaign 1940–1945*, London and Portland, OR: Frank Cass, 1995.

Golovko, Arseni G., *With the Red Fleet*, London: Putnam, 1965.

Görlitz, Walter, *Generalfeldmarschall Keitel: Verbrecher oder Offizier?*, Göttingen: Musterschmidt-Verlag, 1961.

—, *Karl Dönitz: Der Grossadmiral*, Göttingen: Musterschmidt-Verlag, 1972.

Gormly, James, *The Collapse of the Grand Alliance, 1945–1948*, Baton Rouge: Louisiana State University Press, 1987.

—, *From Potsdam to the Cold War: Big Three Diplomacy, 1945–1947*, Wilmington, DE: SR Books, 1990.

Gray, T.I.G., *The Imperial Defence College and the Royal College of Defence Studies 1927–1977*, Edinburgh: Her Majesty's Stationery Office, 1977.

Green, Leslie C., *Essays on the Modern Law of War*, Dobbs Ferry, NY: Transnational Publishers, 1985.

Grove, Eric, *Vanguard to Trident: British Naval Policy Since World War II*, Annapolis: Naval Institute Press, 1987.

Hackmann, Willem, *Seek and Strike: Sonar, Anti-Submarine Warfare and the Royal Navy, 1914–1954*, London: Her Majesty's Stationery Office, 1984.

Hadley, Michael L., *Count Not the Dead: The Popular Image of the German Submarine*, Montreal and Kingston: McGill–Queen's University Press, 1995.

—, *U-Boats Against Canada: German Submarines in Canadian Waters*, Montreal and Kingston: McGill–Queen's University Press, 1985.

Hamilton, Nigel, *Monty: Final Years of the Field Marshal, 1944–1976*, New York: McGraw-Hill Book Co., 1987.

Hampshire, A. Cecil, *The Royal Navy since 1945: Its Transition to the Nuclear Age*, London: William Kimber, 1975.

—, *The Secret Navies*, London: William Kimber, 1978.

—, *Undercover Sailors: Secret Operations of World War II*, London: William Kimber, 1981.

Hankey, Maurice, *Politics, Trials and Errors*, Oxford: Pen in Hand, 1950.

Harbutt, Fraser J., *The Iron Curtain: Churchill, America, and the Origins of the Cold War*, New York: Oxford University Press, 1986.

Harris, Kenneth, *Attlee*, London: Weidenfeld & Nicolson, 1982.

Hathaway, Robert M., *Ambiguous Partnership: Britain and America, 1944–1947*, New York: Columbia University Press, 1981.

Hattendorf, John B. and Robert S. Jordan, eds., *Maritime Strategy and the Balance of Power: Britain and America in the Twentieth Century*, New York: St. Martin's Press, 1989.

Herrick, Robert Waring, *Soviet Naval Theory and Policy: Gorshkov's Inheritance*, Annapolis: Naval Institute Press, 1988.

Herwig, Holger H., *'Luxury' Fleet: The Imperial German Navy 1888–1918*, London: George Allen & Unwin, 1980.

Higgins, A. Pearce and C. John Colombos, *The International Law of the Sea*, London: Longmans, Green & Co., 1943.

Hingorani, R.C., *Prisoners of War*, New York: Oceana Publications, 1982.

Hollis, Leslie, *One Marine's Tale*, London: Deutsch, 1956.

Horn, Daniel, *The German Naval Mutinies of World War I*, New Brunswick, NJ: Rutgers University Press, 1969.

Horrocks, Brian G., *A Full Life*, London: Leo Cooper, 1974.

— (with Eversley Belfield and H. Essame), *Corps Commander*, London: Sidgwick & Jackson, 1977.

Hough, Richard Alexander, *The Greatest Crusade: Roosevelt, Churchill, and the Naval Wars*, New York: William Morrow & Co., 1986.

Howard, Michael, ed., *Restraints on War*, Oxford: Oxford University Press, 1979.

Howard, Michael, Andreopoulos, and Mark R. Shulman, eds., *The Laws of War: Constraints on Warfare in the Western World*, New Haven: Yale University Press, 1994.

Howse, Derek, *Radar at Sea: The Royal Navy in World War 2*, London: Macmillan, 1993.

Hugill, J.A.C., *The Hazard Mesh*, London: Hurst & Blackett, 1947.

Humble, Richard, *The Rise and Fall of the British Navy*, London: Queen Anne Press, 1986.

Hyde, H. Montgomery, *Norman Birkett: The Life of Lord Birkett of Ulverston*, London: Hamish Hamilton/The Reprint Society, 1965.

Isakov, I.S., *The Red Fleet in the Second World War*, London: Hutchinson, 1947.

Ismay, Lord, *The Memoirs of Lord Ismay*, London: Heinemann, 1960.

Jaffe, Lorna S., *The Decision to Disarm Germany: British Policy towards Postwar German Disarmament, 1914–1919*, Boston: Allen & Unwin, 1985.

James, W.M., *The British Navies in the Second World War*, London: Longman's, Green, & Co., 1946.

Johnson, Franklin A., *Defence by Committee: The British Committee of Imperial Defence 1885–1959*, London: Oxford University Press, 1960.

—, *Defence by Ministry: British Ministry of Defence 1944–1974*, London: Duckworth, 1980.

Jones, Elwyn F. Lord, *In My Time: An Autobiography*, London: Weidenfeld & Nicolson, 1983.

Kecskemeti, Paul, *Strategic Surrender: The Politics of Victory and Defeat*, Stanford: Stanford University Press, 1958.

Keegan, John, ed., *Churchill's Generals*, London: Weidenfeld & Nicolson, 1991.

Keitel, Wilhelm, *The Memoirs of Field Marshal Keitel*, London: W. Kimber, 1965.

Kemp, Peter K., *Key to Victory: The Triumph of British Sea Power in World War II*, Boston: Little, Brown, & Co., 1957.

Kennedy, Paul M., *The Rise and Fall of British Naval Mastery*, London: Macmillan Press, 1983.

Keohane, Dan, *Labour Party Defence Policy Since 1945*, Leicester: Leicester University Press, 1993.

Kilmuir, Lord (David Maxwell-Fyfe), *Political Adventure: The Memoirs of Lord Kilmuir*, London: Weidenfeld & Nicolson, 1964.

King, Ernest J. and Walter Muir Whitehill, *Fleet Admiral King: A Naval Record*, New York: W.W. Norton & Co., 1952.

Kitchen, Martin, *British Policy Towards the Soviet Union During the Second World War*, London: Macmillan, 1986.

Koburger, Charles W., *Steel Ships, Iron Crosses, and Refugees: The German Navy in the Baltic, 1939–1945*, Westport, CT: Praeger, 1989.

Kramer, Alan, *Die Britische Demontagepolitik am Beispiel Hamburgs 1945–1950*, Hamburg: Verein für Hamburgische Geschichte, 1991.

Kroes, Rob and Maarten van Rossem, eds., *Anti-Americanism in Europe*, European Contributions to American Studies No. 11, Amsterdam: Free University Press, 1986.

Kruska, Emil and Eberhard Rössler, *Walter-U-Boote*, München: J.F. Lehmanns Verlag, 1969.

Lamb, Richard, *Montgomery in Europe 1943–45: Success or Failure?*, New York: Franklin Watts, 1984.

Law, Derek and Stephen Howarth, eds., *The Battle of the Atlantic 1939–1945*, Annapolis: Naval Institute Press, 1994.

Leahy, William D., *I Was There: The Personal Story of the Chief of Staff to Presidents Roosevelt and Truman based on his Notes and Diaries made at the Time*, New York: McGraw-Hill, 1950.

Lewis, Julian, *Changing Direction: British Military Planning for Post-War Strategic Defence, 1942–1947*, London: Sherwood Press, 1988.

Linz, Susan J., ed., *The Impact of World War II on the Soviet Union*, Totowa, NJ: Rowman & Allanheld, 1985.

Longmate, Norman, *When We Won the War: The Story of Victory in Europe, 1945*, London: Hutchinson, 1977.

Lüdde-Neurath, Walter, *Regierung Dönitz: Die Letzten Tage des Dritten Reiches*, Musterschmidt: Druffel Verlag, 1953.

MacIntyre, Donald, *Fighting Admiral: The Life of Admiral of the Fleet Sir*

James Somerville, GCB, GBE, DSO, London: Evans Brothers, 1961.
—, *The Naval War against Hitler*, London: Batsford, 1971.
Mallison, William Thomas, *Submarines and the Law of Naval Warfare*, International Law Studies 58, Newport, RI: Naval War College Press, 1968.
Martienssen, Anthony K., *Hitler and His Admirals*, New York: E.P. Dutton & Co., 1949.
Maschke, Erich, ed., *Zur Geschichte der deutschen Kriegsgefangenen des Zweiten Weltkrieges*, Bielefeld: Verlag Ernst und Werner Gieseking, 1962–74; Vol. 11/1: Helmut Wolff, *Die deutschen Kriegsgefangenen in britischer Hand: Ein Überblick*; Vol. 12: Hermann Jung, *Die deutschen Kriegsgefangenen im Gewahrsam Belgiens, der Niederlande und Luxemburgs*.
Maugham, Frederick Herbert, *UNO and War Crimes*, London: Murray, 1951.
McGwire, Michael and John McDonnell, eds., *Soviet Naval Influence: Domestic and Foreign Dimensions*, New York: Praeger, 1977.
McHugh, Michael Caldwell, *With Malice toward None: The Punishment and Pardon of German War Criminals, 1945–58*, Ph.D. Dissertation, Miami University, 1991.
McNeil, William Hardy, *America, Britain, and Russia: Their Co-operation and Conflict, 1941–1946*, London: Oxford University Press, 1953.
Mee, Charles L. Jr., *Meeting at Potsdam*, New York: M. Evans, 1975.
Meigs, Montgomery C., *Slide Rules and Submarines: American Scientists and Subsurface Warfare in World War II*, Washington, DC: National Defense University, 1990.
Messerschmidt, Manfred and Fritz Wüllner, *Die Wehrmachtjustiz im Dienste des Nationalsozialismus*, Baden-Baden: Nomos Verlagsgesellschaft, 1987.
Milner, Marc, *The U-Boat Hunters: The Royal Canadian Navy and the Offensive against Germany's Submarines*, Toronto: University of Toronto Press, 1994.
Mitchell, Donald W., *A History of Russian and Soviet Sea Power*, New York: Macmillan, 1974.
Montgomery, Bernard Law, *The Memoirs of Field-Marshal the Viscount Montgomery of Alamein*, London: Collins, 1958.
—, *Normandy to the Baltic*, London: Hutchinson & Co., 1947.
Moore, William, *The Thin Yellow Line*, London: Leo Cooper, 1974.
Moorehead, Alan, *Eclipse*, London: Hamish Hamilton, 1945.
—, *Montgomery: A Biography*, London: Hamish Hamilton, 1946.
Morgan, Frederick, *Overture to Overlord*, London: Hodder & Stoughton, 1950.
Morgan, Kenneth O., *Labour in Power, 1945–51*, Oxford: Clarendon Press, 1984.
Morison, Samuel Eliot, *History of United States Naval Operations in World War II*, Boston: Little, Brown & Co., 1956–57; Vol. 10: *The Atlantic Battle Won May 1943–May 1945*; Vol. 11: *The Invasion of France and Germany 1944–1945*.
Morris, Eric, *The Russian Navy: Myth and Reality*, London: Hamish

Hamilton, 1977.

Murfett, Malcom H., ed., *The First Sea Lords: From Fisher to Mountbatten*, Westport, CT: Praeger, 1995.

Murphy, Robert, *Diplomat Among Warriors*, Garden City, NY: Doubleday & Co., 1964.

Northedge, F.S., *British Foreign Policy: The Process of Readjustment 1945–61*, New York: Praeger, 1962.

North, John, *North-West Europe 1944–5*, London: Her Majesty's Stationery Office, 1953.

Ollard, Richard, *Fisher and Cunningham: A Study in the Personalities of the Churchill Era*, London: Constable, 1991.

Ovendale, Ritchie, *The English Speaking Alliance: Britain, the United States, the Dominions, and the Cold War 1945–51*, London: George Allen & Unwin, 1985.

Owen, Charles, *No More Heroes: The Royal Navy in the Twentieth Century: Anatomy of a Legend*, London: George Allen & Unwin, 1975.

Pack, S.W.C., *Cunningham: The Commander*, London: B.T. Batsford Ltd., 1974.

Padfield, Peter, *Dönitz: The Last Führer*, London: Victor Gollancz, 1984.

Palmer, Michael A., *Origins of the Maritime Strategy: The Development of American Naval Strategy, 1945–1955*, Annapolis: Naval Institute Press, 1988.

Parker, Sally Lister, *Attendant Lords: A Study of the British Joint Staff Mission in Washington, 1941–1945*, Ph.D Dissertation, College Park: University of Maryland, 1984.

Parkinson, Roger, *A Day's March Nearer Home: The War History from Alamein to VE Day based on the War Cabinet Papers of 1942 to 1945*, London: Hart-Davis, MacGibbon, 1974.

Pearson, John George, *The Life of Ian Fleming*, London: Jonathan Cape, 1966.

Peillard, Léonce, *The Laconia Affair*, New York: Bantam, 1983 (1963).

Pogue, Forrest C., *The Supreme Command*, Washington, DC: Office of the Chief of Military History, Department of the Army, 1954.

Polmer, Norman, *Guide to the Soviet Navy*, 3rd edition, Annapolis: Naval Institute Press, 1983.

Raeder, Erich, *My Life*, Annapolis: United States Naval Institute Press, 1960.

Raven, G.J.A. and N.A.M. Rodger, eds., *Navies and Armies: The Anglo-Dutch Relationship in War and Peace 1688–1988*, Edinburgh: John Donald, 1990.

Riste, Olav, ed., *Western Security: The Formative Years (European and Atlantic Defence 1947–1953)*, Oslo: Universitets forlaget AS, 1985.

Robertson, Horace B., Jr., ed., *International Law Studies 1991: The Law of Naval Operations*, International Law Studies 64, Newport, RI: Naval War College Press, 1991.

Rodger, Nicolas A.M., *The Admiralty*, Lavenham: T. Dalton, 1979.

Rosas, Alan, *The Legal Status of Prisoners of War*, Helsinki: Suomalainen Tiedeakatemia, 1976.

Roskill, Stephen W., *Churchill and the Admirals*, London: Collins, 1977.

—, *Naval Policy Between the Wars*, 2 Volumes, London: St. James' Place, 1968, 1976.

—, *The War at Sea, 1939–1945*, 3 Volumes, London: Her Majesty's Stationery Office, 1954–61.

—, *White Ensign: The British Navy at War 1939–1945*, Annapolis: United States Naval Institute, 1960.

Rothwell, Victor, *Britain and the Cold War 1941–1947*, London: Jonathan Cape, 1982.

Ruge, Friedrich, *Der Seekrieg: The German Navy's Story 1939–1945*, Annapolis: United States Naval Institute, 1957.

—, *In Vier Marinen*, Munich: Bernard und Graefe, 1979.

—, *The Soviets as Naval Opponents 1941–1945*, Annapolis: Naval Institute Press, 1979.

Runyan, Timothy J. and Jan M. Copes, ed., *To Die Gallantly: The Battle of the Atlantic*, Boulder: Westview Press, 1994.

Rust, Eric C., *Naval Officers under Hitler: The Story of Crew 34*, New York: Praeger, 1991.

Ryan, Henry Butterfield, *The Vision of Anglo-America: The US-UK Alliance and the Emerging Cold War 1943–1946*, Cambridge: Cambridge University Press, 1987.

Saeland, Frode, *Frigjoringen I Rogland*, Stavanger: Statsarkivet i Stavanger, 1995.

Salewski, Michael, *Die deutsche Seekriegsleitung 1935–1945*, 3 Volumes, München: Bernard und Graefe, 1975.

Saunders, M. G., ed., *The Soviet Navy*, New York: Frederick A. Praeger, 1958.

Saville, John, *The Politics of Continuity: British Foreign Policy and the Labour Government, 1945–46*, London and New York: Verso, 1993.

Scharf, Claus and Hans-Jürgen Schröder, eds., *Die Deutschlandpolitik Grossbritanniens und die Britische Zone 1945–1949*, Wiesbaden: Franz Steiner Verlag GmbH, 1979.

Scott, Harriet Fast and William F., *The Armed Forces of the USSR*, 3rd edition., Boulder: Westview Press, 1984.

Scheurig, Bodo, *Alfred Jodl: Gehorsam und Verhängnis*, Frankfurt am Main: Propyläen, 1991.

Schofield, Brian Betham, *British Sea Power: Naval Policy in the Twentieth Century*, London: B.T. Batsford, 1967.

Schweling, Otto Peter, *Die deutsche Militärjustiz in der Zeit des Nationalsozialismus*, Marburg: N.G. Elwert Verlag, 1977.

Scott, Peter, *The Battle of the Narrow Seas: A History of the Light Coastal Forces in the Channel and North Sea, 1939–1945*, London: Country Life, 1945.

Sellwood, Arthur V., *The Damned Don't Drown: The Sinking of the Wilhelm Gustloff*, Annapolis: Naval Institute Press, 1996.

Sharp, Tony, *The Wartime Alliance and the Zonal Division of Germany*, Oxford: Clarendon Press, 1975.

Sheehy, Edward J., *The U.S. Navy, the Mediterranean, and the Cold War 1945–1947*, Westport, CT: Greenwood Press, 1992.

Shulman, Milton, *Defeat in the West*, New York: Ballantine Books, 1968

(1947).

Simpson, B. Mitchell III, *Admiral Harold R. Stark: Architect of Victory, 1939–1945*, Columbia: University of South Carolina Press, 1989.

Smith, Arthur L., *Heimkehr aus dem Zweiten Weltkrieg: Die Entlassung der deutschen Kriegsgefangenen*, Stuttgart: Deutsche Verlags-Anstalt, 1985.

—, *Churchill's German Army: Wartime Strategy and Cold War Politics, 1943–1947*, Beverley Hills, CA: Sage, 1977.

Smith, Bradley F., *Reaching Judgment at Nuremberg*, New York: Basic Books, 1977.

—, *The Road to Nuremberg*, New York: Basic Books, 1981.

Smith, H.A., *The Law and Custom of the Sea*, 3rd edition, London: Stevens & Sons, 1959.

Smith, William P., *The Politics of British Defence Policy, 1945–1962*, Columbus: Ohio State University Press, 1964.

Speer, Albert, *Inside the Third Reich*, New York: Avon, 1970.

Stacey, Charles Perry, *The Canadian Army 1939–1945*, Ottawa: Edmond Cloutier, King's Printer, 1948.

—, *The Victory Campaign*, Vol. 3, *Official History of the Canadian Army in the Second World War*, Ottawa: Queen's Printer, 1960.

Stein, Harold, ed., *American Civil–Military Relations*, Birmingham: University of Alabama Press, 1963.

Steinberg, Jonathan, *Yesterday's Deterrent: Tirpitz and the Birth of the German Battle Fleet*, London: Macdonald, 1965.

Steinert, Marlis G., *23 Days: The Final Collapse of Nazi Germany*, New York: Walker, 1969.

Stephen, Martin, *The Fighting Admirals: British Admirals of the Second World War*, Annapolis: Naval Institute Press, 1991.

Sullivan, Matthew Barry, *Thresholds of Peace: Four Hundred Thousand German Prisoners of War and the People of Britain 1944–1948*, London: Hamish Hamilton, 1979.

Syrett, David, *The Defeat of the German U-Boats: The Battle of the Atlantic*, Columbia: University of South Carolina Press, 1994.

Tarrant, V.E., *The Last Year of the Kriegsmarine: May 1944–May 1945*, London: Arms & Armour, 1994.

Taylor, Peter J., *Britain and the Cold War: 1945 as Geopolitical Transition*, New York: Guilford, 1990.

Taylor, Telford, *The Anatomy of the Nuremberg Trials: A Personal Memoir*, New York: Alfred A. Knopf, 1992.

Terraine, John, *The Right of the Line: The Royal Air Force in the European War, 1939–1945*, London: Hodder & Stoughton, 1985.

Thomas, Charles S., *The German Navy in the Nazi Era*, London: Unwin Hyman, 1990.

Thomas, Edward John Francis, *The European Advisory Commission and Allied Planning for a Defeated Germany, 1943–1945*, Ph.D Dissertation, Washington, DC: American University, 1981.

Thomas, Hugh, *Armed Truce: The Beginnings of the Cold War 1945–46*, London: Hamish Hamilton, 1986.

Thompson, H.K. Jr. and Henry Strutz, *Doenitz at Nuremberg: A Reappraisal, War Crimes and the Military Professional*, New York:

Amber Publishing Co., 1976.

Tolley, Kemp, *Caviar and Commissars: The Experiences of a US Naval Officer in Stalin's Russia*, Annapolis: Naval Institute Press, 1983.

Trevor-Roper, Hugh, *The Last Days of Hitler*, New York: Macmillan, 1956.

Tucker, R.W., *The Law of War and Neutrality at Sea*, Washington, DC: Government Printing Office, 1955.

Tuleja, Thaddeus V., *Eclipse of the German Navy*, London: J.M. Dent & Sons, 1958.

Turner, Ian D., ed., *Reconstruction in Post-War Germany: British Occupation Policy and the Western Zones, 1945–55*, Oxford: Berg, 1989.

United Nations War Crimes Commission, *History of the United Nations War Crimes Commission and the Development of the Laws of War*, London: His Majesty's Stationery Office, 1948.

Waddington, C.H., *Operational Research in World War II: Operational Research against the U-boat*, London: Elek Science, 1973.

Warlimont, Walter, *Inside Hitler's Headquarters*, London: Weidenfeld & Nicolson, 1964.

Warner, Oliver, *Cunningham of Hyndhope: Admiral of the Fleet*, London: John Murray, 1967.

Warren, C.E.T. and James Benson, *Will Not We Fear: The Story of H.M. Submarine Seal*, London: White Lion, 1973.

Watt, Donald Cameron, *Britain looks to Germany: British Opinion and Policy towards Germany since 1945*, London: Oswald Wolff, 1965.

—, *Personalities and Policies: Studies in the Formulation of British Policy in the Twentieth Century*, Notre Dame: University of Notre Dame Press, 1965.

Webb, R.G., *Britain and the Future of Germany: British Planning for German Dismemberment and Reparations, 1942–1945*, Ph.D Dissertation, New York: University of New York, 1979.

Webster, Charles and Noble Frankland, *The Strategic Air Offensive against Germany*, Vol. 4, London: Her Majesty's Stationery Office, 1961.

Weisgall, Jonathan M., *Operation Crossroads: The Atomic Tests at Bikini Atoll*, Annapolis: Naval Institute Press, 1994.

Werner, Herbert A., *Iron Coffins*, New York: Bantam, 1978 (1969).

Wettern, Desmond, *The Decline of British Seapower*, London: Jane's, 1982.

Wheeler-Bennett, John and Anthony J. Nicholls, *The Semblance of Peace: The Political Settlement after the Second World War*, London: Macmillan, 1972.

Whitley, M.J., *Destroyer! German Destroyers in World War II*, London: Arms & Armour Press, 1983.

—, *German Cruisers of World War Two*, Annapolis: Naval Institute Press, 1985.

Williams, Jeffrey, *The Long Left Flank: The Hard Fought Way to the Reich, 1944–1945*, London: Leo Cooper, 1988.

Williams, Mark, *Captain Gilbert Roberts R.N. and the Anti-U-Boat School*, London: Cassell, 1979.

Wilt, Alan F., *War from the Top: German and British Military Decision Making during World War II*, Bloomington and Indianapolis: Indiana

University Press, 1990.

Winton, John, ed., *The War at Sea: The British Navy in World War II*, New York: William Morrow & Co., 1967.

Wolfe, Robert, ed., *Captured German and Related Records: A National Archives Conference*, Athens, OH: Ohio University Press, 1974.

Woods, Randall Bennett, *A Changing of the Guard: Anglo-American Relations, 1941–1946*, Chapel Hill and London: University of North Carolina Press, 1990.

Woodward, David, *Ramsay at War: The Fighting Life of Admiral Sir Bertram Ramsay KCB, KBE, MVO*, London: William Kimber, 1957.

—, *The Tirpitz*, New York: Berkley Medallion, 1953.

Woodward, Ernest Llewellyn, *British Foreign Policy in the Second World War*, 5 Volumes, London: Her Majesty's Stationery Office, 1976.

Zametica, John, ed., *British Officials and British Foreign Policy 1945–50*, New York: Leicester University Press, 1990.

Zayas, Alfred M. De, *Nemesis at Potsdam: The Expulsion of the Germans from the East*, Lincoln: University of Nebraska Press, 1988.

—, *The Wehrmacht War Crimes Bureau, 1939–1945*, Lincoln: University of Nebraska Press, 1989.

Zhukov, Georgii K., *The Memoirs of Marshal Zhukov*, London: Jonathan Cape, 1971.

Ziemke, Earl F., *The German Northern Theater of Operations 1940–1945*, Department of the Army Pamphlet No. 20-271, Washington, DC: Government Printing Office, 1976.

Zimmerman, David, *The Great Naval Battle of Ottawa*, Toronto: University of Toronto Press, 1989.

Articles:

Adamthwaite, Anthony, 'Britain and the World, 1945–49: The View from the Foreign Office,' *International Affairs* 61(1985), pp. 223–35.

Ambrose, Stephen, 'Eisenhower's Generalship,' *Parameters* 20(1990), pp. 2–12.

Ashley, L.R.N., 'The Royal Air Force and Sea Mining in World War II,' *Air University Quarterly Review* 14(1963), pp. 38–48.

Assmann, Kurt, 'Der deutsche U-Bootskrieg und die Nürnberger Rechtssprechung,' *Marine Rundschau* 50(1953), pp. 2–8.

—, 'Hitler and the German Officer Corps,' *United States Naval Institute Proceedings* 82(May 1956), pp. 508–20.

Badstübner, Rolf, 'Zur Tätigkeit des Alliierten Kontrollrats in Deutschland 1945 bis 1948,' *Zeitschrift für Geschichtswissenschaft* 34(1986), pp. 581–98.

Barkmann, Herbert, 'Die Hilfsbegleitschiffe der deutschen Schnellbootwaffe im Zweiten Weltkrieg,' *Marine Rundschau* 86(1989), pp. 163–70.

Bartlett, Merrill, and Robert William Love Jr., 'Anglo-American Diplomacy and the British Pacific Fleet, 1942–1945,' *American Neptune* 42 (1982), pp. 203–16.

Basberg, Bjørn L., 'Whaling or Shipping? Conflicts over the Use of the Norwegian Whaling Fleet During World War II,' *International Journal of Maritime History* 3(1991), pp. 165–76.

Baum, Walter, 'Der Zussamenbruch der obersten deutschen militärischen Führung 1945,' *Wehrwissenschaftliche Rundschau* (1960), pp. 237–66.

Baylis, John, 'British Wartime Thinking about a Post-War European Security Group,' *Review of International Studies* 9(1983), pp. 265–81.

Beaumont, Joan, 'Starving for Democracy: Britain's Blockade of and Relief for Occupied Europe, 1939–1945,' *War and Society* 8(1990), pp. 57–82.

Beauregard, Claude and Edwidge Munn, 'Les Troupes D'Occupation Canadiennes en Allemagne Juillet 1945–Juin 1946,' *Canadian Defence Quarterly* 22(May 1993), pp. 36–41.

Best, Geoffrey, 'World War Two and the Law of War,' *Review of International Studies* 8(1982), pp. 67–78.

Bird, Keith, 'The Origins and Role of German Naval History in the Inter-War Period 1918–1939,' *Naval War College Review* 32(1979), pp. 42–58.

Boog, Horst, '"Josephine" and the Northern Flank,' *Intelligence and National Security* 4(1989), pp. 137–60.

Brand, G., 'The War Crimes Trials and the Law of War,' *British Yearbook of International Law* 26(1949), pp. 414–27.

'British Law Concerning Trials of War Criminals by Military Courts,' *Law Reports of Trials of War Criminals* 1(1947), pp. 105–10.

Brooks, Ron, 'Letters from Nuremberg: A Secretarial Perspective from the Correspondence of Miss Joan Tutte,' *The Historian* 16(1987), pp. 15–17.

Burdick, Charles, 'The Tambach Archive: A Research Note,' *Military Affairs* 36(Dec. 1972), pp. 124–6.

—, 'Vom Schwert zur Feder. Deutsche Kriegsgenfangenen im Dienst der Vorbereitungen der amerikanischen Kriegsgeschichtsschreibung über den Zweiten Weltkrieg. Die organisatorische Entwicklung der Operational History (German) Section,' *Militärgeschichtliche Mitteilungen* 10(1971), pp. 69–80.

Burns, Richard Dean, 'Regulating Submarine Warfare, 1921–41: A Case Study in Arms Control and Limited War,' *Military Affairs* 35(1971), pp. 56–63.

Burrough, Sir Harold Martin, 'The Final Stages of the Naval War in North-West Europe,' *Supplement to the London Gazette* (6 Jan. 1948), pp. 191–9.

Burton, Tom, 'The Development of a British Air-Laid Ground Mine,' *Warship* 6(1978), pp. 136–8.

Collins, J.O., 'War Crimes Trials,' *The JAG Navy Journal* 2(April 1948), pp. 12–14.

Conover, Denise O'Neal, 'James F. Byrnes and the Four-Power Disarmament Treaty,' *Mid-America* 70(1988), pp. 19–34.

Cowles, Willard B., 'Trials of War Criminals (Non-Nuremberg),' *American Journal of International Law* 42(1948), pp. 299–319.

Deighton, Anne, 'The "frozen front": The Labour Government, the Division of Germany and the Origins of the Cold War, 1945–47,' *International Affairs* 63(1986–87), pp. 449–65.

Dunbar, N.C.H., 'Military Necessity in War Crimes Trials,' *British*

Yearbook of International Law 29(1952), pp. 442–52.

Ebner, H.O., 'Bundesgrenzschutz See und Kriegsmarine,' *Marine Runschau* 52(1955), pp. 118–21.

Edmonds, Robin, 'Yalta and Potsdam: Forty Years Afterwards,' *International Affairs* 62(1986), pp. 197–216.

Eichelberger, C.A., 'The Law and the Submarine,' *United States Naval Institute Proceedings* 77(July 1951), pp. 691–9.

Erdmann, Karl Dietrich, 'Die Regierung Dönitz,' *Geschichte in Wissenschaft und Unterricht* 14(1963), pp. 359–75.

Erickson, George E., 'United States Navy War Crimes Trials (1945–1949),' *Washburn Law Journal* 5(1965–66), pp. 89–111.

Erickson, John, 'VE Day: The Soviet View,' *History Today* 35(1985), pp. 10–14.

Eriksen, Knut Einar, 'Great Britain and the Problem of Bases in the Nordic Area, 1945–1947,' *Scandinavian Journal of History* 7(1982), pp. 135–63.

Farquharson, John E., '"Emotional but Influential": Victor Gollancz, Richard Stokes, and the British Zone of Germany, 1945–49,' *Journal of Contemporary History* 22(1987), pp. 501–20.

Fenrick, William J., 'Legal Aspects of Targeting in the Law of Naval Warfare,' *Canadian Yearbook of International Law* 29(1991), pp. 238–82.

Foschepoth, Josef, 'Britische Deutschlandpolitik zwischen Jalta und Potsdam,' *Vierteljahrshefte für Zeitgeschichte* 30(1982), pp. 675–714.

—, 'British Interest in the Division of Germany after the Second World War,' *Journal of Contemporary History* 21(1986), pp. 391–411.

Garelow, M.A., 'Woher droht Gefahr?,' *Militärgeschichte* 28(1989), pp. 349–64.

Gibson, Charles Dana, 'Victim or Participant? Allied Fishing Fleets and U-Boat Attacks in World Wars I and II,' *The Northern Mariner* 1(1991), pp. 1–18.

Gilliland, Jane, 'Submarines and Targets: Suggestion for New Codified Rules of Submarine Warfare,' *Georgetown Law Journal* 73(1985), pp. 975–1005.

Glees, Anthony, 'War Crimes: The Security and Intelligence Dimension,' *Intelligence and National Security* 7(1992), pp. 242–67.

Glennon, A.N., 'The Weapon That Came Too Late,' *United States Naval Institute Proceedings* 87(May 1961), pp. 85–93.

Goldrick, James, 'Naval Publishing the British Way,' *Naval War College Review* 45(1992), pp. 85–99.

Gooch, John, 'The Chiefs of Staff and the Higher Organization for Defence in Britain, 1904–1984,' *Naval War College Review* 39(1986), pp. 53–65.

Gooderson, Ian, 'Allied Fighter Bombers versus German Armour in North-West Europe, 1944–1945: Myths and Realities,' *Journal of Strategic Studies* 14(1991), pp. 210–31.

Goulter, Christina, 'The Role of Intelligence in Coastal Command's Anti-Shipping Campaign, 1940–45,' *Intelligence and National Security* 5(1990), pp. 84–109.

Greenwood, David, 'Constraints and Choices in the Transformation of

Britain's Defence Effort since 1945,' *British Journal of International Studies* 2(1976), pp. 5–26.

Grove, Eric J., 'The Post War "Ten Year Rule" – Myth and Reality,' *Royal United Services Institution Journal* 129(Dec. 1984), pp. 48–53.

Harder, Hans Joachim, 'Militärische Operationen in der Endphase des Krieges: Die deutsche Sicht,' *Cahiers de l'Institut d'Histoire du Temps Présent* 13(1989), pp. 23–35.

Hasche, Walter, 'Britische Besatzungsgerichtsbarkeit in Hamburg, 1945–1948,' *Archiv des Völkerrechts* 26(1988), pp. 89–107.

Hattendorf, John B., 'The Anglo-American Way in Maritime Strategy,' *Naval War College Review* 43(1990), pp. 90–9.

Heinegg, Wolff Heintschel von, 'Visit, Search, Diversion, and Capture in Naval Warfare: Part I, The Traditional Law,' *Canadian Yearbook of International Law* 29(1991), pp. 283–329.

Hennicke, Otto, 'Über den Justizterror in der deutschen Wehrmacht am Ende des zweiten Weltkrieges,' *Zeitschrift für Militärgeschichte* 4(1965), pp. 715–20.

Hervieux, Pierre, 'The Heavy Cruiser Admiral Hipper at War,' *Warship* 36(1985), pp. 232–9.

Herwig, Holger H., 'The Failure of German Sea Power, 1914–1945: Mahan, Tirpitz, and Raeder Reconsidered,' *International History Review* 10(1988), pp. 68–103.

Herzog, Bodo, 'Der Kriegsverbrecher Karl Dönitz: Legende und Wirklichkeit,' *Jahrbuch des Instituts für deutsche Geschichte* 15(1986), pp. 477–89.

Holtsmark, Sven G., 'Atlantic Orientation or Regional Groupings: Elements of Norwegian Foreign Policy Discussions during the Second World War,' *Scandinavian Journal of History* 14(1989), pp. 311–24.

Jacobsen, Mark, 'Winston Churchill and the Third Front,' *Journal of Strategic Studies* 14(1991), pp. 337–62.

Jones, Jill, 'Eradicating Nazism From the British Zone of Germany: Early Policy and Practice,' *German History* 8(1990), pp. 145–62.

Jürgensen, Kurt, 'La fin de la Guerre (1945) en allemagne du nord et au danemark,' *Revue d'Allemagne* 25(1993), pp. 119–28.

Kettenacker, Lothar, 'The Anglo-Soviet Alliance and the Problem of Germany, 1941–1945,' *Journal of Contemporary History* 17(1982), pp. 435–58.

Kitchen, Martin, 'Winston Churchill and the Soviet Union During the Second World War,' *The Historical Journal* 30(1987), pp. 415–36.

Kitterman, David H., 'The Justice of the Wehrmacht Legal System: Servant or Opponent of National Socialism?,' *Central European History* 24(1991), pp. 450–62.

Knight, Wayne, 'Labourite Britain: America's "Sure Friend"? The Anglo-Soviet Treaty Issue, 1947,' *Diplomatic History* 7(1983), pp. 267–82.

Kochavi, Arieh J., 'Anglo-Soviet Differences over a Policy towards War Criminals, 1942–1943,' *Slavonic and East European Review* 69(1991), pp. 458–77.

—, 'Britain and the Establishment of the United Nations War Crimes Commission,' *English Historical Review* 107(1992), pp. 323–49.

—, 'Britain, the United States, and the Question of Asylum for War Criminals in the Neutral Countries during World War II,' *Canadian Journal of History* 38(1993), pp. 496–520.

—, 'The British Foreign Office versus the United Nations War Crimes Commission during the Second World War,' *Holocaust and Genocide Studies* 8(1994), pp. 28–49.

—, 'The Moscow Declaration, the Kharkov Trial, and the Question of a Policy on Major War Criminals in the Second World War,' *History* 76(1991), pp. 401–17.

Koester, C.B., 'The Liberation of Oslo and Copenhagen: A Midshipman's Memoir,' *The Northern Mariner* 4(1993), pp. 49–60.

Konvitz, Josef W., 'Bombs, Cities, and Submarines: Allied Bombing of the French Ports, 1942–1943,' *International History Review* 14(1992), pp. 23–44.

Krammer, Arnold, 'American Treatment of German Generals During World War II,' *Journal of Military History* 54(1990), pp. 27–46.

Kranzbühler, Otto, 'Nuremberg Eighteen Years Afterwards,' *De Paul Law Review* 14(1965), pp. 333–47.

Krüger, Peter, 'Die Verhandlungen über die deutsche Kriegs- und Handelsflotte auf der Konferenz von Potsdam 1945,' *Marine Rundschau* 63(1966), pp. 10–19, 81–94.

Kutznesov, N.G., 'Before the War,' *International Affairs* 12(1966), pp. 93–7.

—, 'The War Years,' *International Affairs* 12(1968), pp. 97–107.

Lacroix-Riz, Annie, 'L'entrée de la scandinavie dans le pacte Atlantique (1943–1949), un indispensable "révision déchirante" première partie,' *Guerres Mondiales et Conflits Contemporains* 38(1988), pp. 55–92.

Langdon, Robert M., 'Live Men Do Tell Tales,' *United States Naval Institute Proceedings* 78(Jan. 1952), pp. 16–21.

Laternser, Hans, 'Looking Back at the Nuremberg Trials with Special Consideration of the Processes against Military Leaders,' *Whittier Law Review* 8(1986), pp. 557–80.

Lautenschlager, Karl, 'The Submarine in Naval Warfare, 1901–2001,' *International Security* 11(1986–87), pp. 94–140.

Ledebur, Gerhard Freiherr von, 'Die Räumung von Seeminen in den Gewässern von Nord-, West- und Osteuropa nach 1945,' *Marine Rundschau* 67(1970), pp. 273–82, 341–8.

Lintz, Georg, 'Vom Schiffsdirector zum Admiralstabsrichter: Über die Entwicklung der Laufbahn der Marinerichter,' *Zeitschrift für Heereskunde* 46(1982), pp. 64–8.

Ludlow, Peter, 'Britain and Northern Europe, 1940–45,' *Scandinavian Journal of History* 5(1979), pp. 123–62.

MacKenzie, S.P., 'Essay and Reflection: On the Other Losses Debate,' *International History Review* 14(1992), pp. 661–880.

—, 'The Treatment of Prisoners of War in World War II,' *Journal of Modern History* 66(1994), pp. 487–520.

Madsen, Chris, 'Victims of Circumstance: The Execution of German Deserters by Surrendered German Troops under Canadian Control in Amsterdam, May 1945,' *Canadian Military History* 2(1993), pp. 93–113.

Marshall, Barbara, 'German Attitudes to British Military Government,' *Journal of Contemporary History* 15(1980), pp. 655–84.

Mawdsley, Evan, 'The Fate of Stalin's Naval Program,' *Warship International* 27(1990), pp. 400–5.

Mazower, Mark, 'Military Violence and National Socialist Values: The Wehrmacht in Greece 1941-1944,' *Past and Present* 134(1992), pp. 129–58.

Messerschmidt, Manfred, 'The Wehrmacht and Volksgemeinschaft,' *Journal of Contemporary History* 18(1983), pp. 719–44.

Milner, Marc, 'The Dawn of Modern Anti-Submarine Warfare: Allied Responses to the U-Boats, 1944–45,' *Royal United Services Institution Journal* 134(Spring 1989), pp. 61–8.

Montgomery, Bernard Law, 'The German Surrender at Lüneburg Heath,' *The Listener* (10 June 1954), p. 993.

—, 'Operations in North-West Europe from 6 June, 1944, to 5 May, 1945,' *Supplement to the London Gazette* (4 Sept. 1946), pp. 4431–51.

Moore, Bob, 'The Western Allies and Food Relief to the Occupied Netherlands, 1944–1945,' *War and Society* 10(1992), pp. 91–118.

Nevakivi, Jukka, 'Scandinavian Talks on Military Cooperation in 1946–47: Prelude to the Decisions of 1948–1949,' *Cooperation and Conflict: Nordic Journal of International Politics* 19(1984), pp. 165–75.

Nolte, Ernst, 'Zusammenbruch und Neubeginn: Die Bedeutung des 8 May 1945,' *Zeitschrift für Politik* 32(1985), pp. 296–303.

O'Connell, Jerome A., 'Radar and the U-Boat,' *United States Naval Institute Proceedings* 89(Sept. 1963), pp. 53–65.

Ovendale, Richard, 'Britain, the U.S.A. and the European Cold War, 1945–8,' *History* 67(1982), pp. 217–36.

Paradis, C.M., 'Canadian Army Occupation Force,' *Canadian Army Journal* 1(Oct. 1947), pp. 24–32.

Peillard, Léonce, 'Mes Rencontres avec le Grandadmiral Karl Dönitz,' *Historama* 24(1986), pp. 54–9.

Philipp, Joachim, 'Der Gerichtsherr in der deutschen Militärgerichtsbarkeit bis 1945,' *Militärgeschichte* 27(1988), pp. 533–47.

Picard, Ch., 'Une Crime de Guerre: Der Kommandobefehl,' *Guerres Mondiales et Conflits Contemporains* 42(1992), pp. 161–6.

Pingel, Falk, '"Die Russen am Rhein?": Zur Wende der britischen Besatzungspolitik im Frühjahr 1946,' *Vierteljahrhefte für Zeitgeschichte* 30(1982), pp. 99–116.

Pugh, Philip G., 'Maintenance of Post-War British Sea Power,' *Warship* 35(1986), pp. 56–62.

Quinault, Roland, 'Churchill and Russia,' *War and Society* 9(1991), pp. 99–120.

Raudzens, George, 'War-Winning Weapons: The Measurement of Technological Determinism in Military History,' *Journal of Military History* 54(1990), pp. 403–33.

Raumann, Helmut, 'Life as "Employed Enemy Personnel",' *Naval History* 3(1989), pp. 28–34.

Reynolds, David, 'Britain and the Cold War,' *Historical Journal* 35(1992), pp. 501–3.

Riste, Olav, 'Norway in Exile 1940–45: The Formation of an Alliance Relationship,' *Scandinavian Journal of History* 12(1987), pp. 317–29.

Robertson, Horace B., 'Submarine Warfare,' *The JAG Navy Journal* 10(Nov. 1956), pp. 3–9.

Rogers, A.P.V., 'War Crimes Trials under the Royal Warrant: British Practice 1945–1949,' *International and Comparative Law Quarterly* 39(1990), pp. 780–800.

Rohwer, Jürgen, 'Die Fahrzeuge des deutschen Minenräumdienstes,' *Marine Rundschau* 58(1961), pp. 31–49.

Rosenthal, Gabriel, 'May 8th 1945: The Biographical Meaning of a Historical Event,' *International Journal of Oral History* 10(1989), pp. 183–93.

Ross, Graham, 'Foreign Office Attitudes to the Soviet Union 1941–45,' *Journal of Contemporary History* 16(1981), pp. 521–40.

Rössler, Eberhard, 'Das Walter-Verfahren,' *Marine Rundschau* 78(1981), pp. 98–102.

Rowson, S.W.D., 'Prize Law during the Second World War,' *British Yearbook of International Law* 24(1947), pp. 160–215.

Rozkuszka, W. David, 'British Cabinet Office Records on the Second World War,' *Albion* 8(1976), pp. 296–9.

Sainsbury, Keith, 'British Policy and German Unity at the End of the Second World War,' *English Historical Review* 94(1979), pp. 786–804.

Salewski, Michael, 'Das Ende der deutschen Schlachtschiffe im Zweiten Weltkrieg,' *Militärgeschichtliche Mitteilungen* 12(1972), pp. 53–73.

Saunders, M.G., 'Hitler's Admirals: Reflections Inspired by Their Memoirs,' *Royal United Services Institution Journal* 104(Aug. 1959), pp. 320–30.

Schneider, Ullrich, 'Grundzüge Britischer Deutschland- und Besatzungspolitik,' *Zeitgeschichte* 9(1981), pp. 73–89.

—, 'Zur Deutschland- und Besatzungspolitik Grossbritanniens im Rahmen der Vier-Mächte-Kontrolle Deutschlands von Kriegsende bis Herbst 1945,' *Militärgeschichtliche Mitteilungen* 1(1982), pp. 77–112.

Schofield, Brian Betham, 'Britain's Postwar Naval Policy,' *United States Naval Institute Proceedings* 84(May 1958), pp. 75–83.

Schubert, Erwin, 'Die letzten Fahrten des U-Boot-Begleitschiffes *Otto Wünsche*,' *Marine Rundschau* 81(1984), pp. 76–8.

Schulte, Heinz, 'Die britische Militärpolitik im besetzten Deutschland, 1945–1949,' *Militärgeschichtliche Mitteilungen* 31(1982), pp. 51–75.

Seagren, Leonard W., 'The Last Führer,' *United States Naval Institute Proceedings* 80(May 1954), pp. 522–37.

Sebert, L.M., 'How the War Ended,' *Canadian Military History* 4(1995), pp. 89–90.

Seeber, Eva, 'Zur Nachkriegsregelung der Jahre 1944/45 und zu deren Bedeutung für den Frieden in Europa,' *Militärgeschichte* 22(1983), pp. 709–12.

Seidler, Franz W., 'Die Fahnenflucht in der deutschen Wehrmacht während des Zweiten Weltkrieges,' *Militärgeschichtliche Mitteilungen* 2(1977), pp. 23–42.

Senior, William, 'The History of Maritime Law,' *The Mariner's Mirror*

38(1952), pp. 260–74.

Shils, Edward A. and Morris Janowitz, 'Cohesion and Disintegration in the Wehrmacht in World War II,' *Public Opinion Quarterly* 12(1948), pp. 280–315.

Sieche, Erwin F., 'The German Heavy Cruiser Prinz Eugen: A Career under Two Flags,' Part I *Warship* (1988), pp. 44–8, Part II *Warship International* 27(1990), pp. 278–306.

—. 'The German Type XXIII Submarine,' *Warship* 19(1981), pp. 154–61.

—, 'The Type XXI Submarine,' *Warship* Part 1 17(1981), pp. 2–9; Part II 18(1981), pp. 112–21.

—, 'The Walter Submarine–1,' *Warship* 20(1981), pp. 235–46.

Skinner, G., 'Aerial Minelaying: Possibly the most Potent Sea Warfare Technique for the UK,' *Royal United Services Institution Journal* 126(Dec. 1981), pp. 57–61.

Smith, Adrian, 'Command and Control in Postwar Britain: Defence Decision Making in the United Kingdom, 1945–1984,' *Twentieth Century British History* 2(1991), pp. 291–327.

Smith, Arthur Lee Jr., 'Churchill et L'Armeé Allemande (1945),' *Revue d'Histoire de la deuxieme Guerre* 93(Jan. 1974), pp. 65–78.

Smith, C. Jay, 'The World War II Soviet Navy Revisited: A 1965 Evaluation and a Look at the Future,' *Naval War College Review* 18(1966), pp. 11–15.

Smith, Raymond, 'A Climate of Opinion: British Officials and the Development of British Soviet Policy, 1945–47,' *International Affairs* 64(1988), pp. 631–47.

Smith, Raymond and John Zametica, 'The Cold War Warrior: Clement Attlee Reconsidered 1945–47,' *International Affairs* 61(1985), pp. 237–52.

Spek, John D., 'The Dutch Naval Shipbuilding Program of 1939,' *Warship International* 25(1988), pp. 68–83.

Staff, W.I., 'Re: "The Fate of Stalin's Naval Program",' *Warship International* 29(1992), pp. 143–7.

Steinert, Marlis G., 'The Allied Decision to Arrest the Dönitz Government,' *The Historical Journal* 31(1988), pp. 651–63.

—, 'Die allierte Entscheidung zur Verhaftung der Regierung Dönitz,' *Militärgeschichtliche Mitteilungen* 40(1986), pp. 85–99.

Steininger, Rolf, 'Westdeutschland ein "Bollwerk gegen den Kommunismus"? Großbritannien und die deutsche Frage im Frühjahr 1946,' *Militärgeschichtliche Mitteilungen* 38(1985), pp. 163–207.

Stevenson, Gene C., 'Submarine Losses in the Eastern Baltic in World War II,' *Warship International* 23(1986), pp. 371–6.

Syrett, David, 'The Last Murmansk Convoys, 11 March–30 May 1945,' *The Northern Mariner* 4(1994), pp. 55–63.

Teitler, Gerke, 'Some Aspects of Dutch Naval Strategic Thinking 1945–1955,' *Militärhistorisk Tidskrift* 186(1982), pp. 97–109.

Thew, Robert W., 'The Type IX U-Boat,' *Warship International* 28(1991), pp. 14–29.

Thorne, Peter, 'Andrew Thorne and the Liberation of Norway,' *Intelligence and National Security* 7(1992), pp. 300–16.

Traynina, Mira, 'A.N. Traynin: A Legal Scholar under Tsar and Soviets,' *Soviet Jewish Affairs* 13(1983), pp. 45–54.

Trimble, E.G., 'Violations of Maritime Law by the Allied Powers during the World War,' *American Journal of International Law* 24(1930), pp. 79–99.

Vagts, Detlev F., 'International Law in the Third Reich,' *American Journal of International Law* 84(1990), pp. 661–704.

Vaisse, Maurice, 'La Capitulation de l'Allemagne,' *Histoire* 78(1985), pp. 14–23.

Wade, D.A.L., 'A Survey of the Trials of War Criminals,' *Royal United Services Institution Journal* 96(1951), pp. 66–70.

Wagner, Gerhard, 'Überlegungen der deutschen Marineführung zum Einsatz und Verlust der Schlachtschiffe während des Zweiten Weltkrieges,' *Militärgeschichtliche Mitteilungen* 15(1974), pp. 99–108.

Waldock, C.H.M., 'The Release of the *Altmark*'s Prisoners,' *British Yearbook of International Law* 24(1947), pp. 216–38.

Waller, Derek M., 'U-Boats That Survived,' *Warship International* 2(1970), pp. 110–21.

Watt, Donald Cameron, 'British Historians, the War Guilt Issue, and Post-War Germanphobia: A Documentary Note,' *The Historical Journal* 36(1993), pp. 179–85.

—, 'Every War Must End: War-time Planning for Post-War Security, in Britain and America in the Wars of 1914–18 and 1939–45. The Roles of Historical Example and of Professional Historians,' *Royal Historical Society Transactions* 28(1978), pp. 159–73.

—, 'Rethinking the Cold War: A Letter to a British Historian,' *Political Quarterly* 49(1978), pp. 446–56.

Weinberg, Gerhard L., 'German Plans for Victory, 1944–45,' *Central European History* 26(1993), pp. 215–28.

Weiss, Charles J., 'Problems of Submarine Warfare under International Law,' *Intramural Law Review of New York University* 22(1967), pp. 136–51.

Whitby, Michael, 'Instruments of Security: The Royal Canadian Navy's Procurement of the Tribal-Class Destroyers, 1938–1943,' *The Northern Mariner* 2(1992), pp. 1–15.

Whitley, Mike, 'The Kriegsfischkutter,' *Warship* 39(1986), pp. 166–73.

Wiebes, Cees and Zeeman, Bert, 'Baylis on Post-War Planning,' *Review of International Studies* 10(1985), pp. 923–37.

Wiggers, Richard D., 'The United States and the Denial of Prisoner of War (POW) Status at the End of the Second World War,' *Militärgeschichtliche Mitteilungen* 52(1993), pp. 91–104.

Wilson, Michael, 'The Walter Submarine–2,' *Warship* 20(1981), pp. 247–53.

Woods, John E., 'The Royal Navy since World War II,' *United States Naval Institute Proceedings* 108(March 1982), pp. 82–90.

Index

Aarhus, 54, 58, 90
Ackroyd, M.W., 167, 192, 196
Adams, Captain Bryan Fullerton, 7–8
Adieu, codeword, 57
Admiralty, xii–xv, 1, 2, 3–4, 6, 7, 8, 9, 10,
 11, 12, 13–14, 15, 16, 17–18, 19–20, 23,
 24, 27, 28, 29, 31, 32–3, 34, 35–6, 37,
 39, 41, 42, 43, 46, 52, 56–7, 59, 64, 66,
 70, 72, 77, 80–1, 89, 92, 94, 97, 100,
 102, 103, 106, 112–15, 116, 118, 120,
 123–6, 127, 132–4, 135, 138–9, 144,
 146–8, 150–1, 152, 154, 156–7, 161,
 165, 167, 168, 170, 192, 194, 197, 199,
 200–1, 205, 211–12, 214, 216, 217, 218,
 219, 223, 226; attitude towards death
 penalty, 97; black propaganda campaign,
 72; Civil Establishment Branch, 26;
 delays in formation of naval parties,
 35–6; demands for economy, 12, 15, 17,
 18, 35–6, 88, 223; Director of
 Dockyards, 217; Director of Electrical
 Engineering, 217; Director of
 Establishments, 26; Director of
 Manpower, 28, 45; Director of Naval
 Construction, 217; Director of Naval
 Equipment, 217; Director of Naval
 Intelligence, 2, 24, 38, 70, 121, 148, 156,
 157, 159, 167, 168, 169, 170, 188, 192,
 193, 195; Director of Naval Ordnance,
 214, 217; Director of Scientific Research,
 167; Director of Tactical and Staff Duties
 Division, 41, 43; Director of Torpedoes
 and Mining, 167; Hydrographer, 219;
 investigation and prosecution of war
 crimes, 173–82, 183–7, 191; and Italian
 fleet, 7; Military Branch, 3, 20, 22, 26,
 156, 169, 170, 194, 195, 196; Naval
 Historical Branch (Historical Section), 19,
 44; Naval Law Branch, 97; Operations
 Division, 42; Plans Division, 2; policy
 towards captured German records,
 156–7; policy towards retained German
 minesweeping forces, 131–4; publicity

surrounding Helgoland explosion, 206;
 representatives in Washington, 3, 5, 14,
 115–16; staff talks with the Americans,
 19
Admiralty House, 150, 221
Affanasiev, Gospodin A.A., 113
air attacks: on German warships and
 shipping, 29, 30–3, 42–3, 50–1
Air Ministry, 1, 43
Ainslie, Commander H.C.C., 79, 94
airborne troops: and proposed seizure of
 Kiel Canal, 40, 47; accompany SHAEF
 party to Denmark, 53; SAS troops at Kiel,
 154; seizure of airfields in Norway, 65
Alekseev, Engineer Rear-Admiral N.V., 113,
 114, 115
Alexander, Albert Victor, xv, 20, 56, 70, 72,
 126, 139, 148, 149, 183, 185, 193, 195;
 First Lord of Admiralty, 72, 106, 112,
 138–9, 148, 168, 173
Alexander, Captain Arthur Hoyer, 40, 47
Alleyne, Captain John Meynell, 80, 85
Allied Control Council, 78, 86, 96, 108,
 113, 117, 127, 130, 131, 132–4, 143,
 150, 160, 191, 224; Directive No. 22,
 204–5, 207, 216; Directive No. 39,
 210–11; Law No. 8, 130–2; Law No. 10,
 164; Law No. 34, 144; laws and
 restrictions, 144, 164–5, 170; Legal
 Directorate, 131; Naval Directorate, 212,
 219; Order No. 1, 130, 146
Allied Naval Commander Expeditionary
 Force, 27–8, 35–6, 38–9, 69, 70–2, 77,
 79–80, 85, 92, 93–100, 167, 168, 170,
 200, 214–15, 223; Deputy ANCXF, 17,
 27; opening of main headquarters at
 Minden, 92; and post-hostilities planning,
 10–14, 15, 16–19, 22, 23, 25, 26, 34, 37,
 42, 43, 45, 46, 170
American Zone, 156
amphibious landings: possibility of on
 German coast, 29, 33, 43–4
Amrum, 58

259

Titles of Related Interest

AUSTRO-HUNGARIAN NAVAL POLICY 1904–1914

Milan N Vego

A unique and comprehensive account which describes the interplay of internal and external factors in the emergence of the Austro-Hungarian Navy from a coastal defence force in 1904 to a respectable battle force capable of the joint operations with other Triple Alliance fleets in the Mediterranean by the eve of World War I. It is little known that by 1914 the Austro-Hungarian Navy was the sixth largest navy in the world and the quality of its officers and men was widely recognised by most European naval observers at the time.

240 pages   1996
0 7146 4678 4 cloth   0 7146 4209 6 paper
Naval Policy and History Series

SEAPOWER

Theory and Practice

Geoffrey Till (Ed)

> 'Geoffrey Till has edited a collection of eight articles written with the dual aim of exploring the relationship between landpower and seapower and the connections between naval theory and practice...These are worthwhile, well written and thoughtful articles.'
>
> **Paul Halpern,** Mariner's Mirror, 1995

210 pages table, fig   1994
0 7146 4604 0 cloth   0 7146 4122 7 paper

FAR FLUNG LINES

Studies in Imperial Defence in Honour of Donald Mackenzie Schurman

Keith Neilson (Ed) and **Greg Kennedy** (Ed)

This book shows how the British Empire used its maritime supremacy to construct and maintain a worldwide defence system that would protect its vital imperial interests. By combining a number of different historical threads – particularly imperial history, naval history and military history – Neilson and Kennedy rebut the idea that British defence policy in the late nineteenth and early twentieth centuries was primarily concerned with maintaining the balance of power in Europe.

228 pages 1996
0 7146 4683 0 cloth   0 7146 4216 9 paper
Naval Policy and History Series

MARITIME STRATEGY AND CONTINENTAL WARS

Rear Admiral K R Menon

This work contends that nations embroiled in Continental wars have historically had poor maritime strategies. After an analysis of existing literature on this subject and a discussion of case studies, Rear Admiral Menon develops the argument that those navies that have been involved in such wars have made poor contributions to the overall political objectives. Government neglect, inadequate funding and structures that are more appropriate to purely maritime wars are symptomatic of a universal strategic dilemma that arises from inadequate strategic theory.

232 pages   1998
0 7146 4793 4 cloth   0 7146 4348 3 paper
Naval Policy and History Series

THE WASHINGTON CONFERENCE, 1921–22

Naval Rivalry, East Asian Stability and the Road to Pearl Harbor

Erik Goldstein (Ed) and **John Maurer** (Ed)

With a foreword by **Ernest R May**

> 'An *excellent addition to the historiography not just of the Washington conference, but also of arms control in general.*'
>
> **Michael A Palmer**, The Northern Mariner

The Washington Conference regulated the inter-war naval race between the world powers. In the era when it was still believed that battleships were the epitome of naval power and a sign of a country's strength, this conference led to limitations on the building of such weapons by the naval powers of Britain, the USA and Japan. This collection of essays deals with many aspects of the conference; the factors that caused it, the interests of the participating nations both present and future, and the results.

319 pages   1994
0 7146 4559 1 cloth   0 7146 4136 7 paper